LEARNING UNDER THE LENS

Learning Under the Lens: Applying Findings from the Science of Learning to the Classroom highlights the innovative approach being undertaken by researchers from the disparate fields of neuroscience, education and psychology working together to gain a better understanding of how we learn, and its potential to impact student learning outcomes.

The book is structured in four parts: 'Science of learning: a policy perspective' sets the scene for this emerging field of research; 'Self-regulation of learning' and 'Technology and learning' feature findings by eminent international and national researchers in the field and provides an insight into some of the innovative research illustrating the depth, breadth and multi-disciplinarity of the research; and 'Research translation' focuses on the scaled-up implementation of research findings in authentic learning settings, and showcases research findings which are having impact in learning environments.

This fascinating book is intended as a reference tool to create awareness among researchers, policy makers, and education practitioners of the research being undertaken in the science of learning field and its potential to impact student learning outcomes.

Annemaree Carroll is Professor in Educational Psychology at The University of Queensland and Chief Investigator and Co-ordinator of Translational Outcomes within the Australian Research Council – Special Research Initiative, Science of Learning Research Centre.

Ross Cunnington is Professor in Cognitive Neuroscience at The University of Queensland and Deputy Director of the Science of Learning Research Centre. In 2016 Ross was appointed as an Honorary Senior Neuroscience Fellow by the International Bureau of Education, UNESCO.

Annita Nugent is the Manager of Research Translation with the Science of Learning Research Centre.

Local/Global Issues in Education
Greg Thompson *Murdoch University, Australia*
Peter Renshaw *The University of Queensland, Australia*

This series investigates the interplay between the local and the global in contemporary education policy and practice. While globalisation is transforming local education systems, the local cannot be conceived as homogeneous or passive. Local policy advocates, educators and researchers mediate globalisation by adapting, resisting and amplifying its effects and influences. In this book series, the local perspective taken is from Australia, whose geographical and cultural positioning provides a unique analytical lens through which processes of globalisation in education can be explored and understood. Published in association with the Australian Association for Research in Education, this series includes high-quality empirical, theoretical and conceptual work that uses a range of qualitative and quantitative methods to address contemporary challenges in education.

Advances in Cognitive Load Theory
Rethinking Teaching
Edited by John Sweller, Sharon Tindall-Ford and Shirley Agostinho

Learning Under the Lens
Applying Findings from the Science of Learning to the Classroom
Edited by Annemaree Carroll, Ross Cunnington and Annita Nugent

Challenges for Public Education
Reconceptualising Educational Leadership, Policy and Social Justice as Resources for Hope
Edited by Jane Wilkinson, Richard Niesche and Scott Eacott

The Relationality of Race in Education Research
Edited by Greg Vass, Jacinta Maxwell, Sophie Rudolph and Kalervo N. Gulson

Literacy, Leading and Learning
Beyond Pedagogies of Poverty
Debra Hayes, Robert Hattam, Barbara Comber, Lyn Kerkham, Ruth Lupton, Pat Thomson

National Testing in Schools
An Australian Assessment
Bob Lingard, Greg Thompson & Sam Sellar

LEARNING UNDER THE LENS

Applying Findings from the Science of Learning to the Classroom

*Edited by Annemaree Carroll,
Ross Cunnington and Annita Nugent*

LONDON AND NEW YORK

First published 2021
by Routledge
2 Park Square, Milton Park, Abingdon, Oxon OX14 4RN

and by Routledge
52 Vanderbilt Avenue, New York, NY 10017

Routledge is an imprint of the Taylor & Francis Group, an informa business

© 2021 selection and editorial matter, Annemaree Carroll, Ross Cunnington, Annita Nugent; individual chapters, the contributors

The right of Annemaree Carroll, Ross Cunnington, and Annita Nugent to be identified as the authors of the editorial material, and of the authors for their individual chapters, has been asserted in accordance with sections 77 and 78 of the Copyright, Designs and Patents Act 1988.

All rights reserved. No part of this book may be reprinted or reproduced or utilised in any form or by any electronic, mechanical, or other means, now known or hereafter invented, including photocopying and recording, or in any information storage or retrieval system, without permission in writing from the publishers.

Trademark notice: Product or corporate names may be trademarks or registered trademarks, and are used only for identification and explanation without intent to infringe.

British Library Cataloguing-in-Publication Data
A catalogue record for this book is available from the British Library

Library of Congress Cataloging-in-Publication Data
A catalog record has been requested for this book

Names: Carroll, Annemaree, editor. | Cunnington, Ross, editor. | Nugent, Annita, editor.
Title: Learning Under the Lens: Applying Findings from the Science of Learning to the Classroom/edited by Annemaree Carroll, Ross Cunnington and Annita Nugent.
Description: Abingdon, Oxon; New York, NY: Routledge, 2019. | Series: Local/global issues in education | Includes bibliographical references.
Identifiers: LCCN 2018044633 | ISBN 9780367135829 (hardback) | ISBN 9780367136635 (paperback) | ISBN 9780429027833 (ebook)
Subjects: LCSH: Learning, Psychology of. | Learning--Research.
Classification: LCC LB1060 .L44 2019 | DDC 370.15/23--dc23
LC record available at https://lccn.loc.gov/2018044633

ISBN: 978-0-367-13582-9 (hbk)
ISBN: 978-0-367-13663-5 (pbk)
ISBN: 978-0-429-02783-3 (ebk)

Typeset in Bembo
by KnowledgeWorks Global Ltd.

CONTENTS

Preface viii
Acknowledgements xii
List of contributors xiii

    Prologue: The science of learning: birth or renaissance   1
    John Hattie and Annita Nugent

PART I
Science of learning: a policy perspective   **7**

1 Science of learning: an international perspective   9
   Barry McGaw

2 National efforts in the science of learning: case reports from
   United States, Australia and Brazil   18
   Annita Nugent, Soo-Siang Lim and Roberto Lent

3 Creating an impact, leaving an impression – learnings from the
   Australian Science of Learning Research Centre   31
   Annita Nugent, Annemaree Carroll, John Hattie and Uwe Dulleck

PART II
Self regulation of learning   45

4 Neuroplasticity: from cells to circuits and brains towards the classroom   47
Roberto Lent, Sidarta Ribeiro and João Ricardo Sato

5 Foreign language anxiety: translating cognitive neuroscience to the classroom   63
Brendan S. Weekes

6 Addressing mathematics anxiety in primary teaching   78
Sarah Buckley, Kate Reid, Ottmar V. Lipp, Merrilyn Goos, Narelle Bethune and Sue Thomson

7 Innovative approaches to measure and promote emotion regulation in the classroom from a science of learning perspective   93
Annemaree Carroll and Julie Bower

8 Building a secure learning environment through social connectedness   112
Ross Cunnington, Stephanie MacMahon, Chase Sherwell and Robyn Gillies

9 The MASTER™ focus program: a theoretically informed meta-attention intervention for early adolescence   125
Deberea Sherlock and Aisling Mulvihill

PART III
Technology and learning   139

10 Design for learning in an age of rapidly evolving technology   141
Nancy Law

11 Digital learning environments, the science of learning, and the relationship between the teacher and the learner   154
Jason M. Lodge, Gregor Kennedy and Lori Lockyer

PART IV
Research translation — 169

12 Research to reality: feedback for learning: building capability to improve outcomes — 171
Cameron Brooks and Rochelle Burton

13 Translating the science of learning through co-design: working with teachers to prioritise executive functioning skills in mathematics education — 185
Simon N. Leonard and Martin S. Westwell

14 Developing a model for the translation of science of learning research to the classroom — 202
Stephanie MacMahon, Annita Nugent and Annemaree Carroll

Discussant: Charting new waters in the science of learning: Reflections on the emergence of the science of learning in Australia and its place on the international landscape by an outside insider — 220
Sean H. K. Kang

Index — 230

PREFACE

Learning Under the Lens – Applying Findings from the Science of Learning to the Classroom is intended as a reference tool to create awareness among researchers, policymakers, and education practitioners of the research being undertaken in the science of learning field and its potential to impact student learning outcomes. It reflects the activities of the Australian Research Council – Special Research Initiative, Science of Learning Research Centre (SLRC; 2014–2020) and the international and national colleagues who have become an integral part of the conversations and work of the Centre since its inception. Contributions to this edited book have been welcomed from our national and international colleagues and policymakers from Australia, Asia, Europe, South America, and the United States, together with Chief Investigators, Affiliate Members, Translation Manager, postdoctoral research fellows, and doctoral students within the SLRC. Awareness of research in the science of learning is steadily growing among educators and policymakers, which has converted into acceptance and adoption into practice of findings.

An introduction to the science of learning, what it is, its history and its potential to revolutionise the future of learning is provided by Professor John Hattie and Annita Nugent in the Prologue whilst in the Discussant, Dr Sean Kang reflects on common themes emerging throughout the book. He pays particular attention to the influence of social and emotional factors on learning and teaching, the impact of technology and education, and bridging the gap between research and practice in order to achieve lasting impact.

The book is divided into four parts, the first and final parts directed to policy and education practice, respectively. Commencing with an international policy perspective, Professor Barry McGaw, former Director for Education at the Organisation for Economic Co-operation and Development (OECD), and Chair of the SLRC Advisory Board, describes the role of international, intergovernmental organisations in taking up work on the science of learning and sponsoring its application in education policy and practice. In the second chapter, the development of the science of learning from three international perspectives is provided, highlighting the challenges, role of government and research institutions and the future of the science of learning as a discipline. This part concludes with Chapter 3 wherein a discussion by Ms. Annita Nugent and Professors John Hattie, Annemaree Carroll and Uwe Dulleck is provided of the journey of the SLRC in its goal to leave a lasting legacy on student learning and educational practice.

The middle parts of the book feature findings by eminent international and national researchers from the science of learning. With a focus on emotional regulation of learning, Part II illustrates the depth, breadth and multi-disciplinarity of the research and how insights from various disciplines, and levels of granularity, can serve not only to advance our understanding of the learning process, but inform practice and ultimately improve learning outcomes. Professor of Neuroscience, Roberto Lent and colleagues from the Federal University of Rio de Janeiro, Brazil, present examples from work by members of the Brazilian Network of Science for Education on knowledge about brain mechanisms and how these may illuminate novel practices translatable to the classroom, introducing the concept of transpersonal neuroplasticity. Research being conducted at the University of Hong Kong on language learning is presented by Professor Brendan Weekes, highlighting how learning and language shapes the brain in predictable ways through neuroplasticity, and the role anxiety can play in language acquisition. On a similar theme research on addressing maths anxiety in primary teaching is explored by Dr Sarah Buckley and colleagues.

Professor Annemaree Carroll and Dr Julie Bower focus on emotion regulation in the classroom and how insights from the science of learning have influenced their research on novel and neural data collection methods and well-being interventions for teachers and students. Professor Ross Cunnington and colleagues overview research on the biology and psychology of social connectedness and its importance for education, and discuss new biometric measures of social interaction during classroom learning. The role of metacognition in learning is discussed by Dr. Deberea Sherlock and Dr. Aisling Mulvihill, who also present the development of their learning to focus intervention.

In Part III, the role of technology in learning, and how insights from the science of learning can be applied to maximise the benefit from advancing technologies in the classroom, is explored. Professor Nancy Law discusses the role of technology in supporting learning and the implications on research in the science of learning. SLRC colleagues Associate Professor Jason Lodge and Professors Gregor Kennedy and Lori Lockyer continue the dialogue on educational technologies with a focus on higher education and self-regulation.

The final Part of the book focuses on the scaled-up implementation of research findings in authentic learning settings, and showcases research findings which are having impact in learning environments. This Part provides a number of exemplars for the implementation and scale up of interventions conducted by the SLRC. Dr. Cameron Brooks and Ms Rochelle Burton provide an overview of the implementation of coaching teachers in effective feedback practices. Leaving lasting change in mathematics education through co-design is the focus of the chapter by Associate Professor Simon Leonard and Professor Martin Westwell. In the final chapter of the book, Dr. Stephanie MacMahon, Ms Annita Nugent and Professor Annemareee Carroll provide an overview of a model of research translation and the development of the SLRC Partner Schools Program across a number of states of Australia.

There have been numerous challenges and highlights of being involved in the SLRC, with the editors of the book having each held important roles within the Centre. During the preparation of this book, the editors had the opportunity to reflect upon their respective journeys with the SLRC:

> The Science of Learning Research Centre has provided the opportunity for true interdisciplinary research, drawing on methodologies and research designs from other disciplines to answer problems of practice in classrooms and to make a real difference on the ground for teachers and students. Interdisciplinary research partnerships have provided major transformations to my program of research pertaining to attention and emotion regulation through: implementing new technologies to understand research problems; gaining a better understanding of underlying neural mechanisms provided insight into development of interventions; and focussing research questions that could be interrogated in an experimental setting and then applied and scaled in classroom environments.
> Professor Annemaree Carroll – Coordinator of Research Translation.

> The collaboration of my field of cognitive neuroscience with education, and the interactions and conversations with school leaders, teachers, and education departments that have been central to the Science of Learning Research Centre, have been both challenging and hugely rewarding. Research in the neurosciences typically ends with publication of our discoveries in 'high-impact' scientific journals. Working within the SLRC has constantly challenged me to step beyond that end, to listen to real-world problems in schools and gaps in research, and to consider how my research can address these issues from the perspectives of psychology and neuroscience to contribute to positive impact on student learning.
> Professor Ross Cunnington – Deputy Director – International Strategy.

> My fascination with the Centre, and what attracted me to the role, was to see if researchers from the three disparate disciplines of education, neuroscience and psychology could truly come together in a meaningful

collaboration to inform learning. Would the divide between the disciplines be too big, was it 'a bridge too far'? As the following chapters will attest, with dedication, goodwill and an open mind, researchers in the Centre were able to close the gap between their respective disciplines, and more importantly, close the gap between research and classroom practice.

Ms Annita Nugent – Executive Officer,
Research Translation and Stakeholder Engagement.

We hope that what has been captured within the pages of this book will convey the energy, passion and time that have been invested in the new field of the science of learning and in improving student outcomes, and that ultimately this work will lead to a lasting legacy across the many educational contexts that have been engaged. First and foremost, for the students – our next generation of leaders – that their places and ways of learning may be enhanced. For the teachers and educational leaders at the forefront of our education system, that their engagement and will to drive change and innovation in schools and classrooms will have the ripple effect of improving student outcomes and student and teacher well-being. For our doctoral and postdoctoral students who have brought so much enthusiasm and knowledge, that their futures guide the transformation of this new field of science of learning. For the scientific research endeavours, that they indeed may translate to impactful findings in educational practice. The future is bright in the field of the science of learning when true multidisciplinary research and authentic partnerships with the education departments, schools, teachers and students are at the forefront.

ACKNOWLEDGEMENTS

We acknowledge the support of the Australian Research Council Special Research Initiative for the Science of Learning. Without the support of the Australian Research Council, the Science of Learning Research Centre would not have come to fruition, the paths of the three editors would never have crossed, much of the multi-disciplinary research reported in this book by members of the Centre would not have been conducted, and this book would not have been written.

Graphic design – Dr. Nick Valmas,
Science Illustrator, Queensland Brain Institute,
The University of Queensland.

LIST OF CONTRIBUTORS

Narelle Bethune
Research Officer, Australian Council for Educational Research, Australia

Julie Bower*
Honorary Research Fellow, School of Education, The University of Queensland, Australia

Cameron Brooks*
Postdoctoral Research Fellow, School of Education, The University of Queensland, Australia

Sarah Buckley*
Senior Research Fellow, Australian Council for Educational Research, Australia

Rochelle Burton*
Adjunct Research Fellow and Teacher-in-Residence, Queensland Department of Education, and School of Education, The University of Queensland, Australia

Annemaree Carroll*
Associate Dean Research, Faculty of Humanities and Social Sciences, The University of Queensland, Australia

Ross Cunnington*
School of Psychology, The University of Queensland, Australia

Uwe Dulleck
Director, Centre for Behavioural Economics, Society and Technology, Queensland University of Technology, Australia

Robyn Gillies*
School of Education, The University of Queensland, Australia

Merrilyn Goos*
Director, National Centre for STEM Education, University of Limerick, Ireland

John Hattie*
Director, Melbourne Educational Research Institute, The University of Melbourne, Australia

Sean Kang
Director, Cognition and Education Laboratory, Dartmouth College, USA

Gregor Kennedy*
Pro Vice-Chancellor (Teaching and Learning), The University of Melbourne, Australia

Nancy Law
Deputy Director, Centre for Information Technology in Education, University of Hong Kong, Hong Kong

Roberto Lent
Professor Emeritus of Neuroscience, Institute of Biomedical Sciences, Federal University of Rio de Janeiro, Brazil

Simon Leonard
UniSA: Education Futures, The University of South Australia, Australia

Soo-Siang Lim
Director, US National Science Foundation Science of Learning Centers, USA

Ottmar V. Lipp*
School of Psychology, Curtin University, Australia

Lori Lockyer*
Dean, Graduate Research School, University of Technology Sydney, Australia

Jason Lodge*
School of Education and Institute for Teaching and Learning Innovation, The University of Queensland, Australia

Stephanie MacMahon*
Manager, Research Translation and Stakeholder Engagement, Australian Research Council Science of Learning Research Centre, The University of Queensland, Australia

Barry McGaw*
Vice-Chancellor's Fellow, Melbourne Graduate School of Education, The University of Melbourne, Australia

Aisling Mulvihill*
Postdoctoral Research Fellow, School of Psychology, The University of Queensland, Australia

Annita Nugent*
Executive Officer, Research Translation and Stakeholder Engagement, Australian Research Council Science of Learning Research Centre, The University of Queensland, Australia
PhD Candidate, Centre for Behavioural Economics, Society and Technology, Queensland University of Technology, Australia

Kate Reid*
Senior Research Fellow, Australian Council for Educational Research, Australia

Sidarta Ribeiro
Vice-Director, Brain Institute, Federal University of Rio Grande do Norte, Brazil

João Ricardo Sato,
Federal University of ABC, Santo André, Brazil

Deberea Sherlock*
Educational and Developmental Psychologist, MASTER Institute, Australia

Chase Sherwell*
Postdoctoral Research Fellow, Queensland Brain Institute, The University of Queensland, Australia

Sue Thomson*
Deputy CEO (Research), Australian Council for Educational Research, Australia

Brendan Weekes
Director of the Laboratory for Communication Science, University of Hong Kong, Hong Kong

Martin Westwell*
Chief Executive, South Australian Certificate of Education Board of South Australia, Australia
College of Science and Engineering, Flinders University, Australia

* Affiliated with the Science of Learning Research Centre, a Special Research Initiative of the Australian Research Council

PROLOGUE

The Science of Learning: birth or renaissance

John Hattie and Annita Nugent

Recent years have witnessed an unprecedented renaissance of *learning* and its growing recognition as the core business of education systems, with a move away from a teaching-focussed agenda to a learning agenda, supported by teaching. As Hattie and Yates lament in their book Visible Learning and the Science of How We Learn, learning is the common denominator in education, yet it is a term that is often absent from discussions in schools (Hattie & Yates, 2014). Note for example, the influential international rankings of countries' achievements (e.g., Programme for International Assessment (PISA), Progress in International Reading Literacy Skills (PIRLS), Trends in International Mathematics and Science Study (TiMSS)), that are so often used as indicators of health and progress of school systems. These rankings pay little to no attention to the notions of learning that must be enhanced to then demonstrate improved achievement. But this is changing as McGaw discusses in the opening chapter, and evidenced by the subtitle of the Organisation for Economic Cooperation and Development (OECD) 2018 education policy outlook – *Putting Student Learning at the Centre* (OECD, 2018). It is by understanding the processes of learning, the social, equity, and educational factors that relate to learning, that the achievement potential across our world will be unlocked. This becomes all the more important when it is noted that "quality education" is ranked fourth (behind only poverty, hunger, and health) of the 17 sustainable development goals in the 2030 Global Agenda "Transforming our World" of the United Nations General Assembly (United Nations, 2015).

For most young scholars studying in the science of learning, this is a new and exciting field, with the promise to revolutionise learning. One of its major contributions is the bringing together of neuroscience, cognitive psychology, and education. Such a multi-disciplinary venture brings together many and varied fields of research, methods, and philosophies all focussing on learning. This allows collaboration built around access to state-of-the-art research infrastructure ranging from functional magnetic resonance imaging (*f*MRI) to electroencephalogram (EEG), experimental classrooms fitted with high definition video-capture and eye-tracking technology, animal models of learning allowing for the interrogation of the learning process at a molecular and cellular level, and devices for monitoring physiological changes and social interactions in real-time in the classroom. Educational psychologists bring a rich history, their own methods, and models to help the neurosciences better understand and interpret their own findings.

The term *science of learning* to describe research into learning, leveraging knowledge from the disciplines of education, neuroscience, and psychology was only coined towards the end of the 20th century. However, neither research into the science of learning nor the connection between learning and the brain are in any way novel. Research into the science of learning dates back to ancient Greek epistemology, when teachers, in the broad sense, used systematic observation and experimentation to describe the general phenomena of learning (Seel, 2012). Plato was among the first to integrate learning into a systematic epistemology, developing the theory of reminiscence, equating learning to the recollection of already completed cognition (Seel, 2012).

Similarly, associations between the brain and learning are not new. Concerted efforts to link brain function and regions with learning came about in the mid-19th century as scientists began to delve into the inner workings of the brain. There was also the usual nonsense disguised as science. One such neuromyth was phrenology, where the bumps and contours on the head were linked to psychological dispositions (Parker Jones, Alfaro-Almagro, & Jbabdi, 2018), and the claim that the brain was like a muscle and the more you used it the more it would grow (hypertrophy). With fanciful claims still aplenty there is quite an industry dispelling their myths (see Tokuhama-Espinosa, 2018).

There were also many worthwhile claims. Paul Broca and Carl Wernike, for example, identified two major language areas in the frontal and temporal lobes responsible respectively for the production and comprehension of language (Grodzinsky & Amunts, 2006). At a cellular level Ramon y Cajal described the neuron as the basic functional and structural unit of the brain, laying the foundation for modern neuroscience (López-Muñoz, Boya & Alamo 2006). Jumping ahead to the middle of the 20th century, Donald Hebb made the observation that neurons that fire together wire together – describing how neural pathways through the brain can be strengthened or weakened by use and experience, and is the underpinning of neural plasticity (Munakata & Pfaffly, 2004). Not only has the brain's function been long associated with learning, so too has its development. The work of developmental psychologist Jean Piaget in the 20th century distinguished different processes of learning over progressive stages of childhood development (Tokuhama-Espinosa, 2011). Much of this research set the scene for linking the mind brain education field of research that took root at the end of the 20th century.

Advances in neuroscience laying the foundation for *mind brain education*

Although learning has always been a feature of humans, neuroscience as a discipline in its own right only came of age in the 1980s with the maturation of sophisticated neuroimaging tools such as computerised axial tomography (CAT) scans, magnetic resonance imaging (MRI), positron emission tomography (PET) scans, and transcranial magnetic stimulation (TMS). These methods allowed for the study of the brain in real-time during learning events. With access to new insights into brain activity and learning, around this time in psychology, there was also a shift in focus from behavioural studies to cognition, seeking to explain mental functions based on evidence of brain activity. The theory of the stages of cognitive development, as well as variations between students, formed one cornerstone for the research field coined *Mind Brain Education* (Tokuhama-Espinosa, 2011).

A new field of science requires a new generation of researchers to feed it, and the 1970s saw the birth of the *educational neuropsychologist*, followed shortly thereafter, and arguably superseded by, the *educational neuroscientist* in the 1990s. Educational neuroscience gives equal weight to each of the three contributing disciplines, whereas for educational neuropsychology, neuroscience was seen as a mere subfield of psychology. Undergraduate degrees in *educational neuroscience* emerged from the 1990s with Dartmouth University being a trail-blazer in the field, promoting principles of mind brain education. With the passage of time, educational neuroscience has evolved as a discipline, and whilst some still consider it a discipline relating to classroom teaching (Bowers, 2016), providing impact through the design of better learning environments (Mareschal, Butterworth, & Tolmie, 2013), others contend the *education* in educational neuroscience is broader than the classroom context (Howard-Jones et al., 2016).

Technology, learning, and the *learning sciences*

Also emerging from the late 1980s and early 1990s was the *learning sciences* born in response to the rapidly changing learning environment and a desire to maximise the benefit of new technology which was entering classrooms. As with mind brain education and the science of learning, this field of research also draws upon multiple disciplines for inspiration. As Hoadley (2018) described in his account of the history of the learning sciences, the field had a controversial beginning, with the International Society of the Learning Sciences (ISLS) stemming from an outshoot of the computer support for collaborative learning community (CSCL) of interdisciplinary researchers with an action-oriented, empirical, and contextualised view of learning. Perhaps this helps explain the field's bias towards studies of the incorporation of technology into the design of learning environments. Although the disciplines of neuroscience and psychology are included along with many other disciplines under the umbrella of learning sciences, neither are seen as essential components of the field. With a focus on learning-in-context and field-based studies of learning, design-based research methodology has been a major contribution of this field (Hoadley, 2018).

Re-enter the *science of learning*

Research into the science of learning has taken on new rigour, and with a revised set of guiding principles. As the title to this book suggests, the (re)birth of the science of learning places learning under an exciting new lens, viewed not through a monocle lens of education *or* neuroscience *or* psychology, or with a bifocal perspective, but through the multiple lenses of each discipline, developing a narrative on learning informed by evidence-focussed through the perspectives of all three disciplines. This is not to the exclusion of other disciplines, but it is the guiding principle of looking at learning through a tri-focal lens. In recommending the new Science of Learning initiative the Prime Minister's Science, Engineering, and Innovation Council (PMSEIC) report described the potential of embracing a multidisciplinary approach to address the science of learning in a more structured and sustained program (PMSEIC Expert Working Group, 2009). The merging of the three disciplines in a systematic fashion is what will expedite our advancement of knowledge around learning, and its implementation in the classroom.

Really, what does neuroscience have to offer the classroom?

Momentum in brain learning research grew rapidly at the end of the 20th century with the advances in neuro-imaging tools, computational neuroscience, and other technological advances. But what can this information truly offer that we didn't know already? We must keep in mind that although brain activity may correlate with learning, it is not the cause of learning. Similarly, seeing a region of the brain light up in an MRI does not necessarily correlate to a learning event. Some have argued that neuroscience is often used in a reductionist manner to make education sound more scientific, but it is likely that neuroscience can, and has, assisted to better explain some of the findings known in classrooms.

Around the time that educational neuroscience was gaining momentum, Bruer (1997) questioned whether the gap between education and neuroscience was a "bridge too far" for neuroscience to be of any use to education. Twenty plus years on, the place of neuroscience in education is still being debated with Bowers emphatically stating "neuroscientists cannot help educators" (Bowers, 2016) and Dougherty and Robey describing as a "bit far-fetched" the idea that neuroscience can have a direct impact in the classroom (Dougherty & Robey, 2018). However, Bruer is prepared to consider a time when neuroscience may have an application, contemplating a two-bridge approach with psychology being the middle pontoon (Howard-Jones et al., 2016). Naturally scholars toiling at the interface of neuroscience and education are defensive of their pursuit, highlighting that they are not looking to displace traditional methods of education research, but rather that these endeavours can complement each other

(Howard-Jones et al., 2016). Indirectly, neuroscience can contribute to education through its influence on psychology (Dougherty & Robey, 2018; Thomas, 2019). A greater understanding of brain function, and corresponding behavioural research, can inform our understanding of underlying learning processes, which in turn can inform teaching and learning (Howard-Jones et al., 2016).

It is difficult to find one new advance from neuroscience that has made noticeable differences in the classroom, but this does not mean that this may not be feasible, or that neuroscience cannot help explain classroom learning, or that educationalists have nothing to gain from using neuroscientific methods and ideas. One of the arguments is that the bridge may more likely come from neuroscience better explaining well-known phenomena in classrooms, with a greater understanding of underlying mechanisms being used to improve what is already known to work (Thomas, 2019). The Turing test in the science of learning may be when a combination of neuroscientists, cognitive psychologists, and educationalists (including teachers) discover some factor or feature that can be used to thence enhance students' learning in classrooms that they individually did not know already.

In order to pass this *science of learning Turing test* it is necessary for those in the various disciplines to work together, understand, and appreciate each other's strengths and methods, and collaborate to build the bridge. In Part II and Part III of this book researchers and practitioners from various disciplines demonstrate how they are working together to address shared problems. In Part IV we share case studies illustrating how the research–practitioner divide is being broken down in order to bring to life findings from the science of learning.

Conclusion

Throughout the history of academia there are moments when the origins of breakthrough can be located. Perhaps the recent marriage of education, neuroscience, and cognitive psychology is one of those moments; as already there is much evidence of a paradigm-shift in the methods, the questions, and the collaborations. It is hoped soon the findings, outcomes, implications, and enhanced learning in classrooms and other contexts can be realised and that this will justify the new cross-discipline. Given "uni"-versities are often formed around separate departments, separate traditions, separate buildings (and separate car parks), this co-joining may be a moment where the "uni"-fication of three groups may be realised. This book shows our own enjoyment, questioning, discovery, and journey – as we learn each other's ways of thinking and aim to bring these multiple perspectives to focus on the science of learning.

References

Bowers, J. S. (2016). The practical and principled problems with educational neuroscience. *Psychological Review*, *123*(5), 600–612.

Dougherty, D. R., & Robey, A. (2018). Neuroscience and education: A bridge astray? *Current Directions in Psychological Sciences, 27,* 401–406.

Bruer, J. (1997). Education and the brain: A bridge too far. *Educational Researcher, 26*(8), 4–16.

Grodzinsky, Y., & Amunts, K. (Eds.). (2006). *Broca's region.* New York: Oxford University Press.

Hattie, J., & Yates, G. (2014). *Visible learning and the science of how we learn.*: Milton Park, Abingdon, Oxon; New York, New York. Routledge.

Hoadley, C. (2018). A short history of the learning sciences. In Fischer, F., Hmelo-Silver, C., Goldman, S. & Reimann, P. (Ed.), *International handbook of the learning sciences* (pp. 11–23). Milton Park, Abingdon, Oxon; New York, New York Routledge.

Howard-Jones, P. A., Varma, S., Ansari, D., Butterworth, B., De Smedt, B., Goswami, U., ... Thomas, M. S. C. (2016). The principles and practices of educational neuroscience: Comment on Bowers (2016). *Psychological Review, 123*(5), 620–627.

López-Muñoz, F., Boya, J., & Alamo, C. (2006). Neuron theory, the cornerstone of neuroscience, on the centenary of the Nobel Prize award to Santiago Ramón y Cajal. *Brain Research Bulletin, 70,* 391–405.

Mareschal, D., Butterworth, B., & Tolmie, A. (2013). *Educational neuroscience.* West Sussex, UK: Wiley-Blackwell.

Munakata, Y., & Pfaffly, J. (2004). Hebbian learning and development. *Developmental Science, 7*(2), 141–148.

OECD. (2018). *Education policy outlook 2018: Putting student learning at the centre.* Retrieved from Paris: https://doi.org/10.1787/9789264301528-en

Parker Jones, O., Alfaro-Almagro, F., & Jbabdi, S. (2018). An empirical, 21st century evaluation of phrenology. *Cortex, 106,* 26–35.

PMSEIC Expert Working Group. (2009). *Transforming learning and the transmission of knowledge.* Retrieved July 1, 2018 from https://www.chiefscientist.gov.au/wp-content/uploads/Transforming-Learning-EWG-report-FINAL.pdf

Seel, N. M. (2012). History of the sciences of learning. In N. M. Seel (Ed.), *Encyclopedia of the sciences of learning* (pp. 1433–1442). Boston, MA: Springer US.

Thomas, M. (2019). Response to Dougherty and Robey (2018) on neuroscience and education: Enough bridge metaphors – Interdisciplinary research offers the best hope for progress. *Current Directions in Psychological Science, 28*(4), 337–340.

Tokuhama-Espinosa, T. (2011). *Mind, brain, and education science: A comprehensive guide to the new brain-based teaching* (1st ed.). New York: WW Norton.

Tokuhama-Espinosa, T. (2018). *Neuromyths: Debunking false ideas about the brain.* New York: WW Norton.

United Nations. (2015). Transforming our world: The 2030 agenda for sustainable development. Retrieved July 1, 2018 from https://sustainabledevelopment.un.org/post2015/transformingourworld/publication

PART I
Science of learning: a policy perspective

Created from a mix of disciplines including education, neuroscience, and psychology, science of learning has infiltrated education at all levels globally. For anyone associated with education, be it in policy, research, educator practitioners, or pre-service teachers, it is hard to remain oblivious to the hype around science of learning. This intrusion into our psyche is no mere alignment of the stars. Rather, it is the result of purposeful collusion by international, intergovernmental organisations, national and regional governments, research agencies, and academic networks alike. With later parts of this book illustrating outcomes and impact of research findings from the science of learning, Part 1 provides a discussion of why the science of learning has garnered so much attention in recent times, and how research in the field is being supported.

Discussion begins at a macro level with McGaw providing insights into the role international, intergovernmental organisations have played in promoting research in science of learning, and the application of findings into education policy and practice. Director for Education at the Organisation for Economic Co-operation and Development (OECD) from 1998 to 2005, McGaw describes why and how the OECD, United Nations Educational, Scientific and Cultural Organization International Bureau of Education (UNESCO-IBE), United Nations Children's Emergency Fund (UNICEF), and the World Bank have exerted their influence, and actively fostered research collaboration and dissemination of findings in the multi-disciplinary field. In particular he describes the critical role played by OECD as a broker of knowledge, and the follow-on efforts of UNESCO-IBE in translating key neuroscience research on learning and the brain to educators, policymakers, and government.

Keeping in step with international influences, at a meso level initiatives supporting research into the science of learning exist in many countries. Presenting the state of affairs in their own nations, Nugent, Lim, and Lent describe how the science of learning has been supported in their respective homelands – Australia, United States, and Brazil. Whereas in the United States and Australia government has played a critical role in directing research and innovation in the field, in Brazil a group of committed researchers has developed its own network as a means of driving research and collaboration.

International and national policy objectives discussed in the first two chapters were enacted in Australia through the establishment of the Australian Research Council funded Science of Learning Research Centre (SLRC). With many of the contributors to this book members of the SLRC, Nugent, Carroll, Hattie, and Dulleck take a moment to pause and critically reflect on the Centre, and its performance against policy objectives. The authors share the challenges associated with closing the gap, not only between science of learning research and the education context, but also between the disparate disciplines that underpin research in the field. Importantly, they use this opportunity to demonstrate that it is possible to close both gaps!

1
SCIENCE OF LEARNING: AN INTERNATIONAL PERSPECTIVE

Barry McGaw

Impact of international organisations' work on assessment

International organisations in education generally follow developments in the research and policy communities but, once they have embraced the development, they can exert a powerful influence, often shaping further developments. A good example is work in educational assessment and, more particularly, in monitoring levels of student learning (e.g., OECD, 2001).

When educational assessment was exclusively norm-referenced, individual student's performances were judged in comparison with the performances of others, most notably with the average (norm), and countries or systems were judged on the performances of their students in comparison with the performances of students in other countries or systems. In both cases, the judgements depended crucially on whom the others were. When educational assessment became standards or criterion-referenced, performances could be related to an achievement scale. Improvement no longer needed to be at the expense of others. Absolute change could be monitored as well as relative change (Lord & Novick, 1968; Rasch, 1960).

These developments in educational measurement can be seen in national assessment programs such as the US National Assessment of Educational Progress, commenced in 1969 (National Center for Education Statistics, 2020) and Australia's National Assessment Program: Literacy and Numeracy (NAPLAN) (Australian Curriculum, Assessment and Reporting Authority, 2020). They are also evident in the work of an international non-government organisation, the International Association for the Evaluation of Educational Achievement (IEA) which gathered international comparative data on student achievement for the first time in 1960 (International Association for the Evaluation of Educational Achievement, 2020).

The Organisation for Economic Co-operation and Development (OECD) has gathered statistics on a broad range of policy domains since its foundation in 1961. In education, its collections focused on inputs and outcomes such as educational attainment, measured as the number of years of education completed. It was only under pressure from the United States as one of its Members, that it extended the coverage to measures of student achievement, measured for the first time in 2000 for 15-year-olds in reading, mathematics, and science in its Program for International Student Assessment (PISA) (OECD, 2001).

OECD's PISA built on IEA's long tradition of international, comparative surveys of student achievement but, probably due to OECD's status as an inter-governmental body, the PISA surveys quickly attracted considerable interest and exerted considerable interest. One indicator is the extending nature of its coverage. The 1960 survey involved 28 of the then 29 OECD Member countries and four others. The most recent PISA survey in 2019 involved all 35 current OECD Member countries and 42 others (OECD, 2019b, pp. 57–58).

The international, inter-governmental work on educational measurement followed the academic research work and, by and large, national developments. The first PISA in 2000, for example, assessed only the traditional domains of reading, mathematics, and science. The second PISA in 2003 assessed these same domains but added an assessment of problem solving, though it was a limited view of problem solving since it was largely a test of analogical reasoning (OECD, 2003).

Problem solving in PISA 2003 was seen largely as a generic skill though, well before then, cognitive psychology research on the differences between experts and novices had distinguished generic and domain-specific problem solving. For example, Vos et al. (1983) had shown that high-level researchers in chemistry performed like novices not experts when seeking to solve a political science problem.

More recently, PISA has increasingly drawn on research on cognitive skills and learning to broaden the range of educational outcomes measured. PISA 2015 included an assessment of collaborative problem solving (OECD, 2017), PISA 2018 included an assessment of global competence (OECD, 2019a), and PISA 2021 will add an assessment of creative thinking that draws on the cognitive science research on the differences between domain-specific and general competences (OECD, 2019c, p. 8). PISA is now driving ahead of developments in many countries and stimulating further national developments.

OECD's work on brain research and learning science

In applications of brain research and learning science to education, OECD similarly built upon a substantial amount of work already underway in the scientific community. In this field, OECD could not play to its traditional strength as a source of powerful, comparative data. Rather it became essentially a knowledge broker through its Center for Educational Research and Innovation (CERI) within its Directorate for Education. The head of the Centre, Jarl Bengtsson, recognised the potential significance of this new field and obtained support for a new project, *Learning Sciences and Brain Research*, from OECD and external sources including the US National Science Foundation and the UK Lifelong Learning Foundation and the Japanese Ministry of Education, Culture, Sports, Science and Technology (OECD, 2002, pp. 3–4).

OECD's entry into this field capitalised on its convening power. It commenced with three High-Level Forums which it organised jointly with important research institutes and to which it attracted significant researchers in the field. The first, on *Brain Mechanisms and Early Learning*, was held in June 2000 at the Sackler Institute in New York City, the second, on *Brain Mechanisms and Youth Learning*, was held in February 2001 at the University of Granada in Spain and the third, on *Brain Mechanisms and Learning in Ageing*, was held at the RIKEN-Brain Science Institute in Tokyo, Japan. OECD's first publication in the field (OECD, 2002) derived from these forums. It reviewed the research field, speculated about how cognitive neuroscience could inform education policies and practices and charted a way ahead involving the establishment of three research areas, *Brain development and literacy*, *Brain development and numeracy*, and *Brain development and learning over the life cycle*. Each area was then addressed by an international research network.

Advancing its brokering role, OECD-CERI produced an online collection, *Brain and learning – Resources*, that included links to "Brain Primers," "Brain Maps," "Brain Glossary," and articles of interest that identified articles in research journals and popular magazines of potential interest to people in education following the project (OECD-CERI, 2020). OECD also published on its website a series outlining six neuromyths that were misrepresentations of the science that can generate misleading claims about implications of neuroscience for education. They can be found at https://www.oecd.org/education/ceri/neuromyth1.htm.

OECD's *Learning Sciences and Brain Research* project ran from 1999 to 2007. It culminated with the publication of a final report that synthesises progress on the brain-informed approach to learning, and uses this to address key issues for the education community. It offers no glib solutions nor does it claim that brain-based learning is a panacea (OECD, 2007, p. 13).

Reflecting on the work, key players in the project subsequently wrote;

> Education research is gradually accumulating a knowledge base linking educational policies and practices with learning outcomes. However, we often lack detailed explanations of how and why these outcomes arise. Studies are often based on correlations, making a policy or practice with a certain outcome while leaving the process in a "black box." Brain research allows us to look deeper into the underlying learning processes and shed more light on causal relationships (Hinton, Miyamoto, & della Chiesa, 2008, p. 87).

A year later, they were somewhat more sanguine, writing:

> This transdisciplinary project brought many challenges. Within the political community, participation in the project varied, with some countries

resisting approval of the project altogether, in the beginning. In the neuroscientific community, participants struggled to represent their knowledge in a way that would be meaningful and relevant to educators. Within the educational community, response to the project varied, with many educational researchers resisting it for fear that neuroscience research might make their work obsolete. Achieving dialogue among these communities was even more challenging. One clear obstacle was that participants had difficulty recognising tacit knowledge in their own field and making this knowledge explicit for partners in other fields (della Chiesa, Hinton, & Christoph, 2009, p. 17).

While OECD's *Learning Sciences and Brain Research* project ended and its active brokering role might have reduced in intensity, OECD has not disengaged from the area. This is evident in recent papers in the OECD Education Working Paper Series including papers on the neuroscience of mathematical cognition and learning (Looi et al., 2016), new technologies and 21st century children (Graafland, 2018), and impacts of technology use on children (Gottschalk, 2019). It is also clear in a significant further synthesising publication (Kuhl et al., 2019) which commences with an observation that "the science of learning is only in its infancy" and "a call for more research, and more communication and interaction between the world of science and the worlds of policy and practice" (p. 4).

UNESCO-IBE's work on brain research and learning science

Work within UNESCO on brain research and learning science and its application to education began later than in OECD but it is currently more active. It is being led by UNESCO's International Bureau of Education (IBE) which devoted a volume of its quarterly publication, *Prospects*, to brain science, education, and learning in which the Director, M. Marope, in the lead article noted:

From the press and the Internet's growing interest in the way the brain works, to commercial projects claiming that they are "brain based," fascination with the "learning brain" has recently exploded into the world's collective consciousness. The public excitement is matched by rigorous scientific efforts to bring biology and cognitive science into a closer relationship with education (Marope, 2016, p. 187).

That issue of *Prospects* included papers on the translation of research from neuroscience and psychology to the improvement of learning (Master, Meltzoff, & Lent, 2016), on forms of neuroplasticity and the biological bases of learning and teaching (Tovar-Moll & Lent, 2016), on the impact of childhood poverty on neural development (Lipina, 2016), and on the potential contribution of neuroendocrinology to early childhood education and care policy (D'Angiulli & Schibli, 2016).

What is most significant about UNESCO-IBE's work is that it goes beyond a brokering role in bringing together researchers in different disciplines in conferences or otherwise as contributing authors to develop publications that speak to general audiences in education. UNESCO-IBE is collaborating with the International Brain Research Organization (IBRO) in offering IBRO/UNESCO-IBE Science of Learning Fellowships for "Senior Scientists and Mid-Career Scientists with at least 10 years of experience practicing in the field of neuroscience, preferably in the science of learning." From the IBRO side, it is part of its "Science of Learning Initiative that aims to support and translate key neuroscience research on learning and the brain to educators, policymakers, and governments" (IBRO/IBE, 2019). From UNESCO-IBE's side, it is a creative contribution intended to have an impact on education policy and practice. The collaboration is seen as transdisciplinary rather than multidisciplinary because it emphasises the need for creative knowledge construction in the gap between the two areas, not a simple borrowing of concepts.

Three Fellows are recruited each year and are hosted at UNESCO-IBE Headquarters in Geneva for three months to provide an opportunity for intense collaboration. One outcome is provided by a collaborative article produced by one of the groups of Fellows (Howard-Jones et al., 2018).

IBE disseminates its work strategically in its own and others' publications and also in key events. In September 2019, it convened a "High-level Forum on Neuroscience and the Future of Education and Learning" within the *10th World Congress of the International Brain Research Organization*, co-organised in South Korea with the Korea Brain Research Institute and the Korean Society for Brain and Neuroscience, with support from the Korean Ministry of Science and Technology.

IBE' Science of Learning Portal is its most significant effort in "brokering cutting-edge neuroscience research to improve learning outcomes." The Portal features technical briefs on relevant neuroscience topics, with clear implications for education policy, teaching, and learning and a Blog, *IBE Speaks*, which "further supports and advocates for using credible research findings to improve teaching, learning, and assessment." The work in the Portal is structured around five themes: early childhood development, effective lifelong learning, effective teaching, emerging technologies and learning, and emotions and learning. The work also involves a growing list of strategic partners for which details are provided on the Portal website (IBE, 2020).

UNICEF's work on brain research and learning science

All international organisations that are involved in education are paying some attention to brain research and learning science. UNICEF is no exception though its level of engagement is much lower than those of OECD and UNESCO-IBE.

In 2014, UNICEF and the World Health Organization (WHO) contributed a comment to the UK medical journal, *The Lancet*, on building on gains in child survival and reductions in infant mortality worldwide, "by focusing new effort and attention not only on saving children's lives, but also on supporting the healthy development of their brains" (Lake & Chan, 2014, p. 1). In this article, the authors acknowledge the importance of education but argue that "to be most effective, interventions must be intersectoral, going beyond education to encompass health, nutrition, and protection" (p. 1).

Among the interesting resources from UNICEF, launched in 2017, is "#EarlyMomentsMatter, a new campaign supported by the LEGO Foundation to drive increased awareness about the importance of the first 1,000 days of a child's life and the impact of early experiences on the developing brain. The campaign kicks off with "#EatPlayLove – a digital and print initiative aimed at parents and caregivers that shares the neuroscience on how babies' brains develop. #EatPlayLove assets explain the science in a straightforward, visually interesting way to encourage parents and caregivers to continue to make the most of this unrivaled opportunity to provide their children with the best possible start in life" (UNICEF, 2019).

World Bank's work on brain research and learning science

The World Bank's strategy to 2020, published in 2011, said nothing about learning science but did note that "The emerging science of brain development shows that to develop properly, a child's growing brain needs nurturing long before formal schooling starts at age 6 or 7. Investments in prenatal health and early childhood development programs that include education and health are essential to realise this potential" (World Bank, 2011, p. 4). The World Bank had earlier published a book on insights from cognitive neuroscience for the "efficient learning of the poor" (Abadzi, 2006).

The World Bank's *World Development Report 2018* contains an extended discussion on the biology of learning which commences with the observation, "Research has dramatically expanded our understanding of how the brain works – and therefore how people learn" (World Bank, 2018, p. 68). The report goes on to make strong claims about how understanding brain development can influence choices about education. For example,

> The available insights on brain development have implications for investments in learning and skill formation. Because brain malleability is much greater earlier in life and brain development is sequential and cumulative, establishing sound foundations can lead to a virtuous cycle of skill acquisition. ... [but] the optimal periods for cultivating higher-order cognitive and socioemotional skills occur throughout childhood, adolescence, and early adulthood. ... Although foundational cognitive skills become less malleable after age 10, some areas associated with socioemotional development remain highly malleable through early adulthood. Accordingly, interventions that aim to improve the school-to-work transition, as well as

social inclusion for youth with weak foundational skills, may prove most effective when they emphasize socioemotional skills (p. 69).

Magnifying impact on policy and practice

There are some lessons from the international work on educational measurement that could inform strategies for magnifying the impact on educational policy and practice of current brain and learning science research. The work on educational measurement could hold up a mirror to countries in which they could see the quality of their students' learning in comparison with the quality in other countries. In the case of brain and learning science research, there might not be similar comparative measures that might particularly cause countries to pay attention, though cross-cultural brain imaging is creating a new field of cultural cognitive neuroscience (Howard-Jones, 2020). What would be influential would be powerful findings of impact of programs clearly informed by brain and learning science research.

If this research can deliver on its promise, it would be helpful to be clear on what the promise is to avoid unrealistic expectations being dashed. It could be expected to provide new teaching strategies well attuned to new understandings of student learning and to deliver improved student performances. Alternatively, it could lead to better understanding, selection, adaptation, and implementation of teaching strategies already known to be effective but not optimally used (Howard-Jones, 2020). Either way, there is every chance that the impact of the research will grow and broaden.

References

Abadzi, H. (2006). *Efficient learning for the poor: Insights from the frontier of cognitive neuroscience.* Washington, DC: World Bank.

Australian Curriculum, Assessment and Reporting Authority. (2020). National Assessment Program: Literacy and Numeracy (NAPLAN). Retrieved January 15, 2020 from https://nap.edu.au/naplan

D'Angiulli, A. & Schibli, K. (2016). How neuroendocrinology can contribute to early childhood education and care: Cortisol as a supplementary indicator of quality, *Prospects; Comparative Journal of Curriculum, Learning and Assessment*, 46, 281–299.

della Chiesa, B., Hinton, C., & Christoph, V. (2009). How many brains does it take to build a new light: Knowledge management challenges of a transdisciplinary project, *Mind, Brain and Education*, 3(1), 17–26.

Gottschalk, F. (2019). Impacts of technology use on children: Exploring literature on the brain, cognition and well-being. *OECD education working papers no. 195*. Paris: OECD.

Graafland, J. H. (2018). New technologies and 21st century children: Recent trends and outcomes. *OECD education working papers no. 179*. Paris: OECD.

Hinton, C., Miyamoto, K., & della Chiesa, B. (2008). Brain search, learning and emotions: Implications for education research policy and practice, *European Journal of Education*, 43, 87–103.

Howard-Jones, P. (2020). Personal communication.

Howard-Jones, P., Cunnington, R., D'Angiulli, A., Prado, J., & Reigosa, V. (2018). The neuroscience of and the global learning crisis. *IBE in focus, annual magazine*. Geneva: UNESCO International Bureau of Education.

IBE-UNESCO. (2020). IBE Science of Learning Portal. Retrieved February 12, 2020 from http://ibelearning.wpengine.com

IBRO/IBE-UNESCO.(2019).IBRO/IBE-UNESCO Science of Learning Fellowships.Retrieved September 25, 2019 from https://ibro.org/ibro-ibe-unesco-science-of-learning-fellowships/

International Association for the Evaluation of Educational Achievement. (2020). IEA History. Retrieved January 15, 2020 from https://www.iea.nl/about/org/history.

Kuhl, P. K., Lim, S., Guerriero, S., & van Damme, D. (2019). *Developing minds in the digital age: Towards a science of learning for 21st century education*. Paris: OECD.

Lake, A. & Chan, M. (2014). Comment: Putting science into practice for early child development, *The Lancet*, www.thelancet.com, Published online September 20, 2014 http://dx.doi.org/10.1016/S0140-6736(14)61680-9

Lipina, S. (2016). The biological side of social determinants: Neural costs of childhood poverty, *Prospects; Comparative Journal of Curriculum, Learning and Assessment*, 46, 265–280.

Looi, C. Y., Thompson, T., Krause, B., & Kadosh, R. C. (2016). The neuroscience of mathematical cognition and learning. *OECD education working papers no. 136*. Paris: OECD.

Lord, F. M. & Novick, M. R. (1968). *Statistical theories of mental test scores*. Reading, MA: Addison Wesley.

Marope, M. (2016). Brain science, education, and learning: Making connections, *Prospects; Comparative Journal of Curriculum, Learning and Assessment*, 46, 187–190.

Master, A., Meltzoff, A. N., & Lent, R. (2016). Neuroscience, psychology, and society: Translating research to improve learning, *Prospects; Comparative Journal of Curriculum, Learning and Assessment*, 46, 191–198.

National Center for Education Statistics. (2020). National *Assessment of Educational Progress: NAEP history and innovation*. Retrieved January 15, 2020 from https://nces.ed.gov/nationsreportcard/about/timeline.aspx.

OECD. (2001). *Knowledge and skills for life: First results from the OECD Programme for International Student Assessment (PISA)*. Paris: Author.

OECD. (2002). *Understanding the brain: Towards a new learning science*. Paris: Author.

OECD. (2003). *The PISA 2003 assessment framework – mathematics, reading, science, problem solving knowledge and skills*. Paris: Author.

OECD. (2007). *Understanding the brain: The birth of a new learning science*. Paris: Author.

OECD. (2017). *PISA 2015 assessment and analytical framework: Science, reading, mathematic, financial literacy and collaborative problem solving*, revised edition. Paris: Author, http://dx.doi.org/10.1787/9789264281820-en

OECD. (2019a). *PISA 2018 assessment and analytical framework*. Paris: Author, https://doi.org/10.1787/b25efab8-en

OECD. (2019b). *PISA 2018 results (volume I): what students know and can do*. Paris: Author, https://doi.org/10.1787/5f07c754-en

OECD. (2019c). *PISA 2021 creating thinking framework (third draft)*. Paris: Author.

OECD-CERI. (2020). *Brain and learning – resources*. Retrieved January 15, 2020 from https://www.oecd.org/education/ceri/brainandlearning-resources.htm.

Rasch, G. (1960). *Probabilistic models for some intelligence and attainment tests*. Copenhagen: Danmarks Paedogogiske Institut.

Tovar-Moll, F. & Lent, R. (2016). The various forms of neuroplasticity: Biological bases of learning and teaching, *Prospects; Comparative Journal of Curriculum, Learning and Assessment*, 46, 199–213.

UNICEF. (2019). "Early moments matter" for children's brain development. Retrieved September 25, 2019 from https://www.unicef.org/media/media_94379.html

Voss, J. F., Greene, T. R., Post, T. A., & Penner, B. C. (1983). Problem solving in the social sciences. In G. Bower (Ed.), *The psychology of learning and motivation* (Vol. 17, pp. 165–213). New York: Academic.

World Bank. (2011). *Learning for all: Investing in people's knowledge and skills to promote development – World bank group education strategy 2020.* Washington, DC: Author.

World Bank. (2018). *Learning to realize education's promise: world development report 2018.* Washington, DC: Author.

2

NATIONAL EFFORTS IN THE SCIENCE OF LEARNING: CASE REPORTS FROM UNITED STATES, AUSTRALIA AND BRAZIL

Annita Nugent, Soo-Siang Lim and Roberto Lent

US establishment of an interdisciplinary science of learning program[1]

Since 2003 the United States National Science Foundation (NSF) has strategically invested in the science of learning through a series of funding mechanisms starting from a Centers program, to a Collaborative Networks program, and now, Science of Learning and Augmented Intelligence is established as a core program in the Division of Behavioral and Cognitive Sciences, in the Social and Behavioral Science Directorate, accepting regular cycles of proposal submissions in science of learning for the foreseeable future.

NSF's vision of the new interdisciplinary science of learning was broadly inclusive of all learning – in humans, other animals, and in machines. The first phase of science of learning investments through establishment of large-scale research centers, illustrated in Figure 2.1, was purposeful; the center construct and the significant resources that were awarded (of up to $5 million/year) provided the intellectual, organisational, and physical infrastructure necessary for interdisciplinary teams to work together on important problems of learning that require multi-pronged and integrative research agendas beyond the capabilities afforded by regular grants to individuals or small groups. To this end, the Program emphasised generation of new discoveries and a deeper understanding of learning through knowledge integration and synthesis across disciplines, across levels of analysis, and encompassing the multitude of factors that impinge upon the learner (individuals and groups) to influence underlying learning processes/mechanisms, performance, and outcomes.

---

1 The views expressed in this article are those of the author. They do not necessarily represent the views of the National Science Foundation or the United States Government.

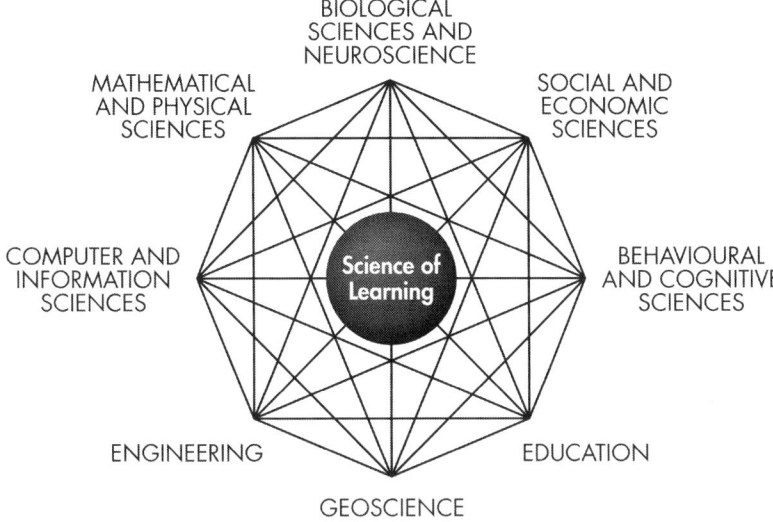

FIGURE 2.1 The intersection of disciplines in the science of learning

Phase 1 – NSF funded science of learning centers

The goals of the Science of Learning Centers Program are to: (1) advance fundamental knowledge about learning through integrative, interdisciplinary research; and (2) transfer knowledge so that it can be used to address societal challenges in education, technology innovation, and workforce preparation. Because learning is essential to and permeates every human endeavor, the totality of the scientific, translational, and education/training outputs from NSF investments in science of learning will enable our diverse research communities to flexibly capture new opportunities to address future challenges, many of which are yet unknown.

Six centres were successfully established through two centre competitions in 2003 and 2005. An overview of the centers is provided in Table 2.1

Research topics at the centers span a wide spectrum, ranging across cellular and molecular bases of learning, neural, cognitive processes, processes underlying learning in multiple domains (e.g., spatial learning in math, geosciences, and engineering, language learning), computational modelling of brain and behaviour, social/cultural influences on learning, artificial intelligence, machine learning, and social robotics. The centres were richly multidisciplinary environments where students were exposed to cutting-edge ideas and technologies.

Each of the centres were multi-institutional and funded as cooperative agreements involving a close working partnership between the centre leadership and NSF staff through strategic planning to achieve each centre's stated goals and monitoring of progress through annual site visit reviews. From knowledge exchange and building collaborations within a center's membership to facilitating the same across the six centres, the Program staff implemented a number of strategies,

TABLE 2.1 United States National Science Foundation funded science of learning centres

Centre	Host university	Overarching goal
Temporal Dynamics of Learning Center	University of California San Diego	The scientific goal of the center was to understand the dynamics of learning at multiple time-scales and how time and timing of event influences learning. This understanding was applied to inform innovations in educational practice and technology development.
The Learning in Informal and Formal Environments Center	University of Washington	Research of the LIFE Center focused on the social foundations of human learning in informal and formal environments, from infancy to adulthood. LIFE Center discoveries are finding broad applicability in guiding learning in homes, schools and teacher training, as well as development of learning technologies with improved socio-technical design.
Center of Excellence for Learning in Education, Science, and Technology	Boston University	By combining systems-level neuroscience and computational modelling, the focus of CELEST research was on autonomous, real-time learning; the ability of biological organisms to learn moment by moment in response to an ever-changing environment. CELEST research has advanced our understanding of how interacting brain regions work together to support learning, and this knowledge has inspired the development of technologies that support learning of artificial (man-made) systems.
Pittsburgh Science of Learning Center	Carnegie-Mellon University	The two main goals were to enhance scientific understanding of robust learning in educational settings and to create a research infrastructure/platform to support field-based experimentation, data collection, and data mining. Innovative integration of cognitive science and machine learning approaches have led to new data-driven learner models that include considerations of knowledge types, learning processes, and instructional principles.
Science of Learning Center, Visual Language, Visual Learning	Gallaudet University	The Center's focus is on the effects of visual processes, visual language, and social experience on the development of cognition, language, reading, and literacy. When auditory input is compromised as in deaf and hard-of-hearing individuals, VL2 research showed that early experience through the visual language can scaffold reading and comprehension of written language.
Spatial Intelligence and Learning Center	Temple University	SILC research made important advances in characterising spatial skills and demonstrated their importance to STEM learning. SILC research also demonstrated the malleability of spatial skills and developed effective interventions to improve spatial skills.

including: (1) formal strategic planning and development of strategic plans as blueprints guiding centre activities and decision-making; (2) annual attendance at an awardees' meeting to facilitate information exchange, sharing of resources and tools, joint student mentoring, and collaborative efforts; (3) encouragement of trainee (students and postdocs) governance and leadership through funding of an SLC trainee-organised annual meeting to foster cross-center peer-to-peer sharing of knowledge and skills, career development opportunities, and networking; and (4) workshops and symposia on topics of cross-cutting interest at the centers – taking these as opportunities to engage experts external to the centers to broaden perspectives and to assist in solving problems.

As researchers at the centers cohered as a community over the years, NSF investments in multiple centers targeted at understanding a specific topic of learning acquired new levels of added value and critical mass – increasingly synergistic and productive cross-center collaborations leveraged complementary expertise bases at other centers, building on relationships and awareness of each other's work facilitated through annual programmatic activities. Likewise, education and training opportunities were further enhanced by student exchanges and shared mentoring of students across centers.

Launching of the first phase of science of learning with up to ten years (maximum) of funding provided relatively stable environments conducive to committed, long-term planning, and interactions. These have been important for: (1) fostering trust and deep collaborations among researchers to reconceptualise and reorganise their thinking beyond the established paradigms of traditional disciplines; (2) fostering trust between the researchers and their stakeholder communities in education practice and industry; and (3) building the interdisciplinary science of learning community (including international partners) to advance scientific understanding of learning and to use the knowledge for societal benefit.

In recognition of the need to build capacity in the research communities for large-scale, interdisciplinary projects, the initial years of the Science of Learning Program sought to fill this need through funding of Catalyst awards (approximately 20 of about $200–$300K/2 years) to enable partnership-building and research activities in preparation for large center applications, which commanded a budget of up to $5 million/year for the first 5-year award, to be renewed for an additional 5 years if successful.

Phase 2 – Science of learning collaborative networks

The second phase of NSF investments in science of learning capitalised on momentum generated by the science of learning centres established in Phase 1 to continue the course of advancing interdisciplinary studies in learning through the creation of substantially smaller collaborative networks to broaden the range of topics in the science of learning portfolio. Consistent with earlier priorities of the science of learning centres, each network was required to identify an integrative research goal for which the convergence of evidence from the diverse disciplinary approaches used by the network would substantially advance understanding of a significant aspect of learning. Networks could focus on advancing basic research through experiments and theory, as well as translating findings from basic research on learning to applications in education, workforce training, or technology innovation (e.g., in health, national security, and space exploration).

As the science of learning investments entered this new phase, the science of learning goals were boosted by congruence with the Brain Research through Advancing Innovative Neurotechnologies (BRAIN) initiative, a major investment by the NSF, Defense Advanced Research Projects Agency, Intelligence Advanced Research Projects Activity, Food and Drug Administration, National Institutes of Health, and several non-government partners. As described in its fact sheet (September 30, 2014), the BRAIN Initiative "will accelerate the development and application of new technologies that will enable researchers to produce dynamic pictures of the brain that show how individual brain cells and complex neural circuits interact at the speed of thought. These technologies will open new doors to explore how the brain records, processes, uses, stores, and retrieves vast quantities of information, and shed light on the complex links between brain function and behavior." Additionally, science of learning goals also aligned with the National Robotics Initiative, an effort by the NSF, National Institutes of Health, US Department of Agriculture, National Aeronautics and Space Administration, Department of Defense, and Defense Advanced Research Projects Agency to support the development of robots that work with or beside people to extend or augment human capabilities. After two cycles of competition in the financial years of 2016 and 2017, 16 Collaborative Network awards were made of about $750,000 each including:

- SL-CN: Development of Neural Body Maps, Principal Investigator (PI) Andrew Meltzoff
- SL-CN: A Research-Practice Collaboration to Improve Math Learning in Young Children, PI Susan Levine
- SL-CN: Contributions of Executive Function Subdomains to Math and Reading Cognition in the Classroom, PI Adam Gazzaley
- SL-CN: Project LENS: Leveraging Expertise in Neuro-technologies to Study Individual Differences in Multimedia Learning, PI Pasha Antonenko
- SL-CN: Cortical Architectures for Robust Adaptive Perception and Action, PI Cornelia Fermuller
- SL-CN: Science of Nature-based Learning Collaborative Research Network, PI Catherine Jordan
- SL-CN: Engaging Learning Network, PI Barbara Shinn-Cunningham
- SL-CN: Group Brain Dynamics in Learning Network, PI John Iversen
- SL-CN: Mapping, Measuring, and Modelling Perceptual Expertise, PI Isabel Gauthier
- SL-CN: Understanding and Promoting Spatial Learning Processes in the Geosciences, PI Thomas Shipley
- SL-CN: Guiding Guided Learning: Developmental, Educational, and Computational Perspectives, PI Patrick Shafto

- SL-CN: Science of Learning in Adolescence: Integrating Developmental Studies in Animals and Humans, PI Ronald Dahl
- SL-CN: Inter-generational Transfer of Beliefs about Math, PI Dario Cvencek
- SL-CN: The Role of Gesture in Mathematics Learning: From Research to Practice, PI Susan Goldin-Meadow
- SL-CN: Learning to Move and Moving to Learn, PI Leanne Chukoskie
- SL-CN: Harnessing the Power of Drawing for the Enhancement of Learning across Levels of Vision Function, PI Lora Likova

Phase 3 – Establishment of science of learning as a standing research program

To ensure that the "engine" of new scientific discoveries in science of learning continues to produce applications in education, technology innovation, and workforce preparation, 2017 saw science of learning established as a new core program in the Division of Behavioral and Cognitive Sciences in the Directorate for Social, Behavioral and Economic Sciences. This means that for the foreseeable future, there would be a "home" at the NSF for the continued support of science of learning research by the Science of Learning and Augmented Intelligence (SL) Program. The SL Program supports potentially transformative research that develops basic theoretical insights and fundamental knowledge about principles, processes, and mechanisms of learning, and about augmented intelligence – how human cognitive function can be augmented through interactions with others, contextual variations, and technological advances.

Emergence of the science of learning in Australia

Momentum for the science of learning in Australia began in the early years of the 21st century, with prominent researchers such as Queensland Brain Institute Director Professor Perry Bartlett and Australian Council for Education Research Chief Executive Officer Professor Geoff Masters strategising to draw together education researchers, neuroscientists, and cognitive psychologists at the interface of learning. Setting the foundation for collaboration, in 2009 the Queensland Brain Institute and the Australian Council for Education Research partnered to form the Science of Learning Centre at The University of Queensland. However, despite the best of intentions, and support from both home institutions, research activities in the Centre were fettered due to a lack of funding.

The science of learning as a field of research first came on to the radar of the Australian government in 2009 in a report to the Prime Minister's Science, Engineering and Innovation Council (PMSEIC) entitled *Transforming Learning and the Transmission of Knowledge* (PMSEIC Expert Working Group, 2009). The report expounded "new knowledge about the brain, cognitive processing and human motivation applied to the subject of how we learn has the potential to drive transformational changes in teaching and learning" (p. 2). Recommendation 1 of the report was the establishment of a "Science of Learning Program, delivered through a number of interdisciplinary, inter-professional Science of Learning Centres" (p. 38). The report also recommended focus areas for centres: Science of Learning Practice, Science of Learning Environment, and Science of Learning Process. Although the rationale for having multiple centres is not articulated in the report, it may well be that this was based on the NSF Science of Learning Centers program.

Following changes in leadership at a federal level, implementation of the PMSEIC report was put on hold until 2012 when the Australian Research Council (ARC) released a call for applications to establish a Science of Learning Research Centre as a Special Research Initiative (Australian Research Council, 2012). However, rather than adopting the PMSEIC recommendation of establishing multiple centres, a single centre incorporating the three focus areas was the aim. The government investment was significant, AU$16 million, but over the relatively short period of four years[2] compared to the duration of other ARC research centres funded under comparable schemes, which usually have a duration of seven years, and the NSF science of learning centres that received funding for up to ten years. However, this gave Australian researchers the opportunity to establish themselves as key players on the international stage, and to demonstrate the value of the Centre, and the science of learning as a field of research, to education in Australia.

The ARC received applications from 2 consortia to establish a science of learning research centre, with the University of Queensland led bid ultimately being successful (Australian Research Council, 2013). Headed by Professor Ottmar Lipp (replaced by Professor Pankaj Sah on Lipp's departure from UQ in 2015) the Centre comprised eight collaborating organisations across Australia, including two regional universities, and eight partner organisations. Usually only Australian universities are eligible to receive ARC funding, but recognising the significant position that the Australian Council for Education Research (a not for profit research organisation) held in the Australian education and learning landscape, it was permitted to be a collaborating organisation. Three of the eight partner organisations were state education departments. Starting with 25 chief investigators comprising 4 neuroscientists, 5 cognitive neuroscientists, and 16 education researchers, the virtual Centre grew to over 100 members. The Centre was fortunate to benefit from the involvement of teachers-in-residence based at two of its nodes, funded by state education departments. The overarching goal of the Centre was to have an impact on learners, and in order to achieve this the Centre developed a research translation group which was tasked not only with outreach and translation activities, but the study of research translation in education as a science.

Funding of only one centre, compared to six in the United States for example, had associated challenges and benefits, and sometimes these were one and the same. One challenge is that it forced players from the divergent disciplines into

---

2 An additional $1 million was awarded, supporting research and translation activities to 2019.

the one arena, hence the necessity to develop a common language uniting all of the disciplines. No one was excluded. The objectives set by the ARC for the Science of Learning Centre incorporated the focus areas of all three suggested Centres in the PMSEIC report, as well as: to build a critical mass of research through cross-disciplinary collaboration; provide a high-quality postgraduate and postdoctoral training environment for the next generation of researchers; and engage with stakeholders and live educational settings to identify and explore opportunities for research translation and knowledge transfer. In some jurisdictions, such as the United States, machine learning falls within the ambit of the science of learning but this is currently not the situation in Australia.

Such a broad range of objectives required the recruitment of a diverse group of researchers. In attempting to meet the objectives of the Centre (Australian Research Council, 2012), ranging from addressing "issues relating to Indigenous learners, learners in regional and remote locations, and learners from underprivileged backgrounds" (p. 8) to the "role and integration of digital technology as a learning tool" (p. 8), and undertaking research "with a strategic focus on the learning processes" (p. 9), meant that sometimes the Centre could be accused of lacking scientific direction. The leadership group of the Centre invested a great deal of effort into ensuring the Centre's research program was coherent and focused. The Centre invested in research infrastructure such as the educational neuroscience classroom at The University of Queensland fitted with EEG, eye-tracking and physiological monitoring capabilities, the social interaction classroom at the University of Melbourne able to record the interactions of an entire class to a fine level of granularity, and portable equipment for in situ use in classrooms to monitor physiological and emotional events. This served to facilitate collaboration as a shared language evolved around the application of new technologies to answer shared questions.

Federal funding for the SLRC as a Special Research Initiative was extended to 2019. The course of time will tell whether a strong enough foundation has been set for the science of learning to continue to grow and transform into a stand-alone field in the Australian research landscape. During the seven years of ARC funding, the Centre built many bridges, across the constituent disciplines of research and with educators and policy makers, as it endeavoured to translate the research findings of Centre investigators to have a true impact on Australian learners. Researchers must now bid for mainstream competitive funding in order to support their collaborative efforts in the science of learning.

The Brazilian network of science for education: An attempt of confluence and synergy to translate research to the classroom

Science of learning has emerged in Brazil as an important foundation for translational research focusing on educational matters, after the seminal review by Meltzoff and collaborators (2009), all of whom were members of the then established US Science of Learning Centers. The main idea behind the term was to employ neuroscience concepts in conjunction with other disciplines and technology advances to investigate learning processes that could result in useful interventions to solve educational problems.

Inspired by the new concept, some initiatives started to flourish in a few countries, designed to foster this new field. In Brazil, the move started some years later, with a similarly broad scope of conceiving basic research into how people learn as a stepping stone/foundation to translational research in education. The inspiration is to draw from all scientific disciplines that could generate basic knowledge, technologies, and/or solutions to educational problems. The principles of the Pasteur's quadrant (Stokes, 1997) were proposed as a unifying framework towards multi-disciplinary, confluent approaches translatable to education, from neuroscience and cognitive psychology to economy and the social sciences, including pedagogy, computer science, mathematics and statistics, linguistics, and medicine. With this broad scope, the Brazilian Network of Science for Education (Rede CpE[3]) was founded in November 2014, as a non-profit association of researchers.

One of the most important advances in the world during the last few decades was the consolidation of this confluent concept of translational research inspired by social use, implemented with great success in health and engineering in practically all countries of middle and high gross domestic product (GDP). In the biomedical sciences, for instance, translational research ("from bench to bedside") acquired a consistent set of players – from scientists in universities and research institutions, on one side, to hospitals and clinics on the other side, with business and governmental players in between. This model has capillarised in many countries, and produced great advances in health during the last decades worldwide, despite inequalities and internal difficulties of each country (World Health Organization, 2018). This evolution can be assessed by general health indicators such as child mortality, life expectancy, and the growing therapeutic possibilities developed for many diseases. A similar rationale can be extended to the "hard" sciences and their technological applications.

The same process, however, has not occurred in education. There is still no clear perception by social agents, even in developed countries, that scientific research is already able to understand how students learn, how teachers communicate with students, what are some of the mechanisms that accelerates learning and teaching, and how this would impact on the economy and social progress of nations. It is also not perceived that technological innovations can be validated with population studies to rationalise in great scale education within the classroom, nor which competencies future citizens should have in order to become inserted in companies more and more automatised and informatised. The players who act in health and engineering have not been connected in education ("from bench to the

---

3 CpE is the acronym of Ciência para Educação, the Portuguese equivalent of Science for Education. http://cienciaparaeducacao.org/eng

classroom"). Therefore, educational policies are either intuitive or ideological but seldom based on scientific evidence, both for the proposal of new interventions in the school system and for the evaluation of those effectively implemented.

Perhaps because of this conceptual shortcoming, at least partially, progress of the Brazilian educational indicators has been so modest (Programme for International Student Assessment, 2012), with maintenance of the gap relative to countries with a more aggressive stance in this issue. In the case of health, public policies not only invest in material improvements (sanitation, hospital attendance, nutritional balance), but also in science and innovation to create new options. Differently, in the case of education, investment is exclusively focused on material improvements (more schools, better salaries for teachers), necessary but insufficient to increase Brazilian indicators at rates faster and more competitive, and allow the country at least to reach the educational levels of top countries in less time.

The potential contribution of the different scientific disciplines to education, nonetheless, is becoming undisputable. Gradually, more and more, neuroscience manages to unravel brain connectivity and the dynamics of functional interaction between the brain, behaviour, and the environment (Misic, 2016), as well as the pathways of nervous system development and plasticity (Tovar-Moll, 2017) that make the brain capable of moulding, adapting, and modulating its development in response to external stimuli. Mathematics develops algorithms and models capable of describing and reproducing cognitive processing, a knowledge that transfers to computer science with an aim at creating machines that change their performance by learning from the inputs (Ghahramani, 2015). Moreover, molecular and cell biology advance in understanding the interactions between molecules and cells of different organic systems, during learning and social interchange (Kandel, 2012; Liu, 2014) and social sciences and economy develop tools to assess and predict success or failure of educational policies in different countries (Duckworth & Yeager, 2015; Hai & Heckman, 2017). This multidisciplinary development has created processes and tools that accelerate learning (especially regarding educational applications and software of extensive social diffusion), with a high scaling potential. Besides, it has stimulated the work of policymakers in the effort to unravel macro- and microeconomic determinants that may underpin public policies (Doyle, 2009).

The aforementioned scenario has opened to Brazil a window of opportunity, aiming to create alternatives with this profile, with laboratories conceived to perform research translatable to education. To give concreteness to this possibility, the proposal offered for discussion among Brazilian policymakers is that new initiatives of funding by public and private agencies should adopt Science for Education as a structuring axis.

Due to the lack of tradition in translational research for education, there was no structured information available about who did – or could do – such kind of work in Brazilian universities and research institutions. A survey was planned to identify research groups with this profile in the whole country (Lent, 2019) and a data mining tool was used with this purpose (Mena-Chalco, 2009). It was possible to search the bank of PhD theses and MSc dissertations of the Brazilian Ministry of Education, and also the Lattes CV Platform[4] of the Ministry of Science and Technology, using keywords and filters to identify those scientists by their research lines, their connection to graduate programs, and their degree of seniority and productivity. The result was an extensive list of mature researchers whose work in different disciplines was found potentially or already important for education.

By May 2020, almost 150 research group leaders had agreed to comprise part of the network, working in different disciplines, namely biochemistry, biology, computer science, genetics, economy, epidemiology, information technology, linguistics, neuroscience, pedagogy, psychology, and sociology. Some examples of research topics investigated by CpE members are: synaptic plasticity and sleep (Blanco, 2015); number transcoding and phonemic awareness (Lopes-Silva, 2016); computational modelling of synaptic plasticity (Antunes, 2016); reading comprehension in dyslexics (Kida Ade, 2016); brain representation of bilingualism (Buchweitz, 2012); relation between school performance and future wages (Curi, 2014); machine learning (Garcia, 2014); and biochemistry of memory (Furini, 2015).

Besides the censitary data mining just mentioned, different initiatives were conducted in the last seven years, including national and international meetings; work documents and books written by groups of members about topics as literacy, learning disorders, socioemotional competences, physiological factors that influence learning, and others (Ciência para Educação, n.d.); as well as proposals for policymakers, creation of communication channels with the public at large, and fundraising for research.

To conclude, the mission of the CpE Network can be summarised by four main objectives: (1) to perform and foster scientific research in any discipline having a potential to impact educational policies and practices; (2) to establish a bridge between scientists and society at large, especially the educational actors (policymakers, educators, teachers), through a strong presence in communication and diffusion by the media, mainly among young people; (3) to maintain links and partnerships with universities and research institutions, on the one hand, and the public and private sectors, on the other hand, with an aim to facilitate knowledge production translatable to educational products and processes; and (4) to form human resources of high level (scientists and educators) through university graduate programs.

A bridge too far?

Making the link between education and neuroscience has been described as a "bridge too far" (Bruer, 1997). Yet policy makers, research institutions, and researchers worldwide have invested significantly in trying to meet this challenge

---

4 The Lattes CV Platform is a database run by the Brazilian federal government, that includes about 4.5 million curricula encompassing researchers, graduate students and undergraduates involved in research. It is considered an example of successful experience and of high quality academic dataset.

by corralling not just neuroscience, but all disciplines in pursuit of understanding brain function in relation to behavioural and cognitive aspects of human learning, in order to improve educational practice. As the science of learning has evolved within various international contexts, its form has been moulded by the needs and relative policy influences of the region. Like many other new and emerging fields of research, the science of learning has had to grow a new workforce of interdisciplinary researchers. While many students and young researchers recognised the significance of the growing field and have been excited to be part of it, working at the confluence of basic research and educational practice has presented challenges.

Fortunately, the governments, universities, and/or other research organisations of many countries including the United States of America, Australia, and Brazil have supported the growth of the science of learning, facilitating cross-disciplinary collaboration and providing funding to support collaborative research efforts, and harvesting the rewards of this investment as demonstrated in later chapters. Most recently, US-led private sector efforts involving many of SLC investigators and their national and international collaborators have led to the formation of the Global Science of Learning Education Network (GSoLEN) with the mission "to achieve maximum worldwide benefit from science-based strategies designed to meet the learning needs of our global future and to overcome poverty's impact on learning. A key next focus will be to deeply understand the science of learning and the extent to which it can be generalised, thereby developing best practices for learning, education, and policy resources that take into account for whom, at what developmental stage, under what conditions, and in what context science of learning can be implemented in the world's distinctive cultures and conditions."

References

Antunes, G., Roque, A. C., & Simoes-de-Souza, F. M. (2016). Stochastic induction of long-term potentiation and long-term depression. *Scientific Reports*, 6, 30899.

Australian Research Council. (2012). *ARC Special Research Initiative for a Science of Learning Research Centre for funding commencing* 2012. Retrieved from http://www.arc.gov.au/arc-special-research-initiative-science-learning-research-centre-funding-commencing-2012

Australian Research Council. (2013). *SR12 Science of Learning Research Centre Selection Report*. Retrieved from https://www.arc.gov.au/grants-and-funding/funding-outcomes/selection-outcome-reports/SR12-science-learning-research-centre-selection-report

Blanco, W. P. (2015). Synaptic homeostasis and restructuring across the sleep-wake cycle. *PLoS Computational Biology*, 11(5), e1004241.

Bruer, J. T. (1997). Education and the brain: A bridge too far. *Educational Researcher*, 26(8), 4–16.

Buchweitz, A. S. (2012). Identifying bilingual neural representations across languages. *Brain and Language*, 120, 282–289.

Ciência para Educação. (n.d.). Retrieved from http://cienciaparaeducacao.org/publicacoes-da-rede-cpe/

Curi, A. Z. & Menezes-Filho, N. (2014). The relationship between school performance and future wages in Brazil. *Economia*, *15*, 261–274.

Doyle, O., Harmon, C., Heckman, J., & Tremblay, R. (2009). Investing in early human development: Timing and economic efficiency. *Economics and Human Biology*, 7(1), 1–6.

Duckworth, A. & Yeager, D. (2015). Measurement matters: Assessing personal qualities other than cognitive ability for educational purposes. *Educational Researcher*, *44*(4), 237–251.

Furini, C. M. (2015). The relationship between protein synthesis and protein degradation in object recognition memory. *Behavioral Brain Research*, *294*, 17–24.

Garcia, L. P. F., de Carvalho A. C. P. L. F., & Lorena, A. C. (2014). Noise detection in the meta-learning level. *Neurocomputing*, *176*, 14–25.

Ghahramani, Z. (2015). Probabilistic machine learning and artificial intelligence. *Nature*, *28*, 452–459.

Hai, R. & Heckman, J. (2017). Inequality in human capital and endogenous credit constraints. *Review of Economic Dynamics*, *25*, 4–36.

Kandel, E. (2012). The molecular biology of memory: cAMP, PKA, CRE, CREB-1, CREB-2, and CPEB. *Molecular Brain*, *5*, 14.

Kida A. de S. B., Ávila, C. R. B. de., & Capellini, S. A. (2016). Reading comprehension assessment through retelling: Performance profiles of children with dyslexia and language-based learning disability. *Frontiers in Psychology*, 7, 787.

Lent, R., Foguel, D., Guimarães, M.Z., Botaro, D., & Mena-Chalco, J. (2019) Science for Education network: The Brazilian proposal. In *Developing Minds in the Digital Age: Towards a Science of Learning for 21st Century* (Kuhl P. et al., eds.). OECD Publishing, Paris. https://doi.org/10.1787/562a8659-en

Liu, X. R., Ramirez, S., Redondo, R., & Tonegawa, S. (2014). Identification and manipulation of memory engram cells. *Cold Spring Harbor Symposia on Quantitative Biology*, *79*, 59–65.

Lopes-Silva, J. B., Moura, R., Júlio-Costa, A., Wood, G., Salles, J. F., & Haase V. G. (2016). What is specific and what is shared between numbers and words? *Frontiers in Psychology*, 7, 22.

Meltzoff, A. K. (2009). Foundations for a new Science of Learning. *Science*, *325*, 284–288.

Mena-Chalco, J. P., Cesar Junior, R. M. (2009). ScriptLattes: An open-source knowledge extraction system from the Lattes platform. *Journal of the Brazilian Computer Society*, *15*(4), 31–39.

Misic, B. S. (2016). From regions to connections and networks: New bridges between brain and behavior. *Current Opinion in Neurobiology*, *40*, 1–7.

PMSEIC Expert Working Group. (2009). *Transforming learning and the transmission of knowledge*. Canberra: Commonwealth of Australia.

Programme for International Student Assessment, PISA. (2012). *What students know and can do: Students performance in mathematics, reading and Science*. Retrieved from http://www.oecd.org/pisa/keyfindings/PISA-2012-results-snapshot-Volume-I-ENG.pdf.

Stokes, D. (1997). *Pasteur's Quadrant – Basic science and technological innovation*. Washington, D.C.: Brookings Institution Press.

Tovar-Moll, F. & Lent, R. (2017). The various forms of neuroplasticity: biological bases of teaching and learning. *Prospects (UNESCO)*, *46*, 199–213.

World Health Organization. (2018). Retrieved from http://www.who.int/healthinfo/indicators/2018/metadata/en/

3

CREATING AN IMPACT, LEAVING AN IMPRESSION – LEARNINGS FROM THE AUSTRALIAN SCIENCE OF LEARNING RESEARCH CENTRE

Annita Nugent, Annemaree Carroll, John Hattie and Uwe Dulleck

Setting the scene

The Australian Research Council (ARC) released a call for applications for a Special Research Initiative for a Science of Learning Research Centre (SLRC) in June 2012 (Australian Research Council, 2012). The ARC set as the primary objective of the Centre "to develop a scientific evidence base that can be used to inform teaching practices" (Australian Research Council, 2012). Initially funded for four years from 2013, funding was extended to 2019 to support research translation activities. The emphasis on impact was conveyed throughout the ARC Funding Rules, with *transfer* and *translation* of research findings mentioned several times in the document:

> Collaboration with live educational settings, families and educational groups will be integral to the centre's program to test the *transfer* of new insights in the learning process into practice
> Engage with stakeholders and live educational settings to identify and explore opportunities for *translation* and development of research in learning processes that will deliver benefits to Australia
> Facilitate the *transfer* of knowledge through public education of the outcomes of learning processes research and provide support for policy development

Aligning with the objectives of the Special Research Initiative, post-award the ARC set key performance indicators for the centre around *community engagement, translation,* and *outreach*. Many of these key performance indicators speak to transfer of information or knowledge; see, for example, the SLRC 2013 Annual

32 Annita Nugent et al.

Report (Science of Learning Research Centre, 2014). Key performance indicators include the following:

- Number of strategic partnerships with community, national, and international organisations with a view to providing access to the Program's research;
- Number of government, industry, business, and community briefings to inform policy;
- Number and nature of industry awareness/outreach programs;
- Number and nature of public awareness/outreach programs;
- Currency of information on the Program's website;
- Number of website hits; and
- Number of talks given by Program staff open to the public.

The successful funding application promised to create a collaborative environment for experts from the disparate fields of education, neuroscience, and psychology to tackle the grand questions around learning. Most importantly, the proposal outlined a plan for disseminating research findings and transferring knowledge through a range of avenues including publication in journals, conference presentations, and engagement with policymakers, which the Centre delivered on, consistently achieving above the milestones set by the ARC.

Establishment of the Science of Learning Research Centre

The successful bid for the ARC SLRC was The University of Queensland led consortium, with the University of Melbourne and the Australian Council for Educational Research as major partners, and comprising 25 chief investigators from six Australian universities and the Australian Council for Educational Research (Curtin University joined in 2014). The Centre was partnered by three state departments of education (South Australia, Queensland, and Victoria) and four international universities (Carnegie Mellon University (USA), North Carolina State University (USA), University College London (UK), and Institute of Education, London (UK)). Each of Australia's mainland states was represented in the Centre. Mindful of the challenge to effective collaboration presented by the tyranny of distance (Katz, 1994; Luo, Xia, Haddow, Willson, & Yang, 2018), combined with the lack of a common language between researchers from disparate disciplines of education, neuroscience, and cognitive psychology (Institute of Medicine (US) Committee on Building Bridges in the Brain Behavioral and Clinical Sciences, 2000), from the outset the SLRC put in place strategies to circumvent the barriers. Specialised research infrastructure, including the Learning Interaction Classroom at the University of Melbourne and the Educational Neuroscience Classroom at The University of Queensland, was established to provide a focal point for researchers to collaborate on common questions and develop a shared language (see Figure 3.1). Funding was set aside in

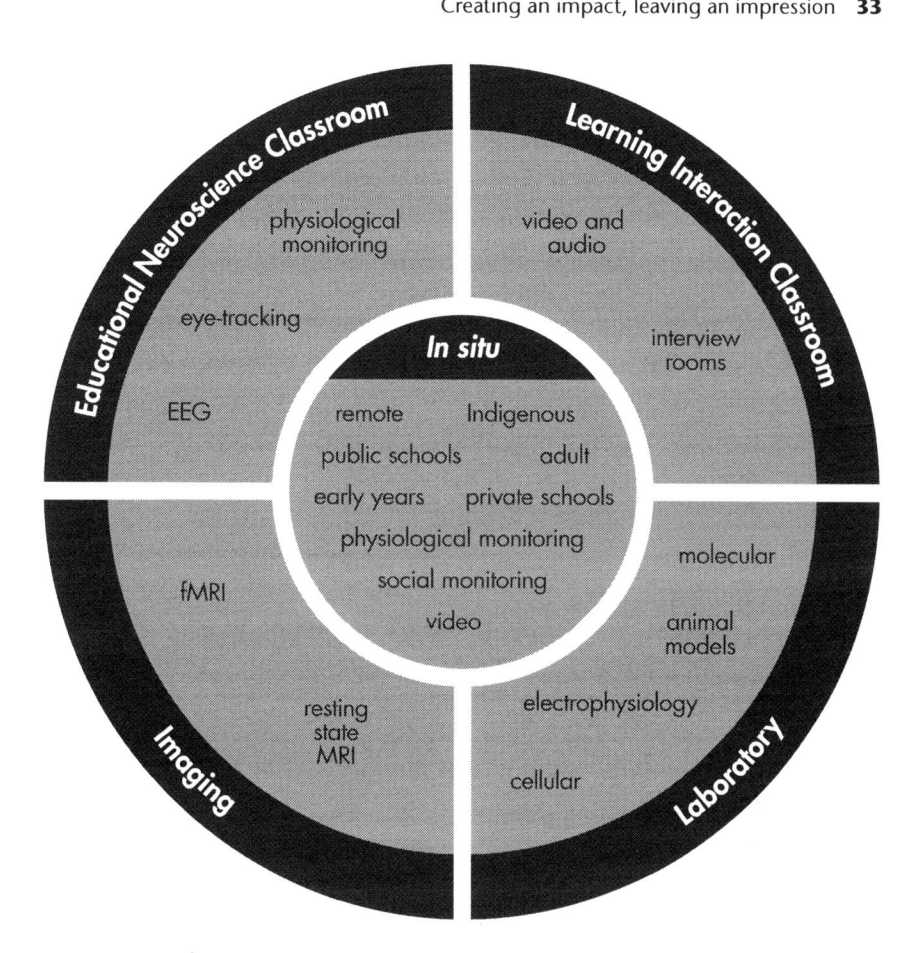

FIGURE 3.1 Infrastructure providing a foundation for translation

the Centre's budget to support travel costs for researchers to utilise the facilities. The sharing of common research infrastructure has been described as a powerful tool to create a shared language, and indeed it was the foundation upon which a common vocabulary was created within the SLRC.

Indeed, one of the most powerful aspects of the Centre has been the research infrastructure that it draws together, allowing for the study of learning at multiple levels of granularity ranging from in situ in the classroom to the Educational Neuroscience Classroom equipped with EEG, eye-tracking, and physiological monitoring; the Learning Interaction Classroom capable of accommodating an entire class equipped with video and audio recording; magnetic resonance imaging to monitor changes in brain activity; and the molecular laboratory. This allowed for the interrogation of common research questions through a multi-layered lens, and the transition of research knowledge funnelling from fundamental laboratory-based understandings to near-classroom applicability.

34 Annita Nugent et al.

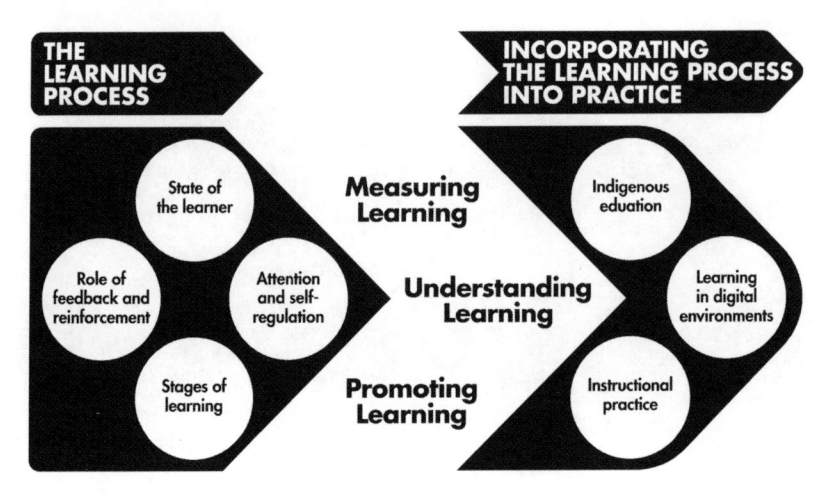

FIGURE 3.2 SLRC programs of research

In keeping with the ARC's intention for the Centre of transferring and translating new research knowledge, programs of research designed to transverse from understanding the learning process to incorporation of the learning process into practice were put in place. The Centre commenced life with three broad themes: understanding learning, measuring learning, and promoting learning. As the research direction took shape, seven programs of research emerged spanning the three themes, with four programs focussed at understanding the learning process and three programs directed to incorporating the learning process into practice. Figure 3.2 illustrates the SLRC programs of research.

A shared vision to improve learning outcomes – early challenges

With the overarching goal of the SLRC being to improve learning outcomes, the leadership team set the vision for the Centre: "an organisation that makes a positive impact on learning outcomes through the promotion and implementation of scientifically-validated learning strategies and tools, both novel and existing."

In order to achieve any sort of impact on learning it was necessary to form connections with policymakers, education practitioners, and the general community. However, only one of the four foundation members of the Centre Executive had significant connection with schools or policy, with the neuro and psychological scientists of the Centre having not previously engaged with the education sector. This initially made inroads into schools and policy somewhat challenging. Fortunately, the leadership team quickly identified and addressed this deficit, expanding the team to include a second member with strong connections with partner education departments and schools.

Our very first engagement with schools came shortly after the commencement of the Centre. The Centre hosted a breakfast round-table, inviting school leaders from progressive schools in the local area. The Centre wanted to know: (i) what the science of learning meant to educators, (ii) the best way to communicate research outcomes, and (iii) how to involve schools with Centre research. On reflection, this was a rather awkward meeting, with neither side quite understanding what the other was wanting. That said, many of the educators who attended this first ice-breaker meeting now form part of the successful and growing SLRC Partner Schools Program, which is described in detail in Chapter 14 (MacMahon, Nugent, and Carroll).

In a similar vein to our interaction with schools, we set about talking to partner state education departments, with regular meetings scheduled to update on Centre activities. In the initial stages, there was uncertainty within the departments of their role in the partnership and the Centre lacked understanding of departmental function. Therefore, delineating clear roles was challenging, with both groups searching for meaning from their ambitions and needs. All groups saw there was a way – but what way? Clearly, both the Centre and its partner departments of education persisted and post the original funding period, the Centre has maintained strong connections with all three state education departments – the cultivation of these relationships is discussed later in the chapter.

Developing avenues for research translation

In the beginning, the Centre's approach to research translation was very much influenced by the key performance indicators set by the ARC. The approach was ad hoc; easily deliverable activities were undertaken initially. For example, a website was established, there was a grand launch of the Centre at The University of Queensland, followed by the official opening of the Learning Interaction Classroom at the University of Melbourne, both events attracting media attention.

A seminar series was established at the Queensland and Victorian nodes for researchers to share their knowledge with educators, and with an after-school time slot chosen to be convenient for teachers, attendee numbers gradually increased. Over time, the Centre's database for seminar attendees has grown to over 1,000 people, and continues to grow. In the second year, the Centre formed a Translation Team. The team was tasked with developing a two-day professional learning workshop for teachers to be delivered at the Queensland and Victorian nodes, with the intention of expanding to other nodes in following years. The format of these workshops, which are still delivered annually, has evolved over time as we reflected on the purpose of the activity to the point that we are now confident to expand to other nodes applying the Partner Schools Program model. Importantly, the model has transformed to be far more purposeful. No longer does the program consist of researchers delivering all that they know about learning to dedicated expert practitioners in a linear manner with little emphasis on translation to classroom practice. Rather, professional learning is now a two-way exchange, with researchers and practitioners alike benefitting from the collaboration.

As the Translation Team began to consolidate, its brief also expanded. The team drew on the enthusiasm of research higher degree students and early career researchers working under the guidance of the Translation Team Coordinators, Professors Annemaree Carroll and John Hattie, Chief Investigators from the universities of Queensland and Melbourne, respectively. The Translation Team developed course content for pre-service and post-graduate teacher training, as well as teacher resources such as the Psychology, Education and Neuroscience (PEN) Principles – a set of learning principles developed through the lens of psychology, education, and neuroscience which are accessible on the SLRC website. One of the major features of the development of the PEN principles was research about how to translate this science of learning into the classroom. We insisted that every part of the PEN principles be subjected to evaluation, trial, and listening to how the readers were interpreting and intending to use them. If they misinterpreted or commented that they were "interesting" but could not see how to use the information, the team returned to the developmental stage for further refinement. It took many school conferences and visits to schools to determine the optimal format – which included a one-page overview, a video, and a podcast.

Engaging with policy was another of the Centre's KPIs, designed to gauge its impact through the transfer of knowledge. Many of the Centre's 25 Chief Investigators engaged with education at a policy level, sitting on boards of state and national curriculum authorities, education departments, teaching and school leadership authorities, as well as international organisations such as the UNESCO. Relationship managers for the relevant nodes engaged with their respective state education departments. The building of relationships with education department partners required considerable time and investment. It was necessary to develop an understanding of each department, its unique drivers and priorities, in order to establish how the respective departments could benefit from the partnership, and how the Centre could benefit from its engagement with the departments in addition to the financial support provided. As the Centre was administered through The University of Queensland, there were more resources available in the form of senior administrative staff dedicated to stakeholder engagement to invest in developing the relationship with the Queensland Department of Education. Passionate and committed Chief Investigators in the respective nodes ensured departmental relationships grew in both strength and breadth.

The effective translation of research outcomes to the classroom has always been core to the Centre. Through critical reflection and evaluation we continuously sought to improve the impact of our research, with the Centre outcomes during the initial four-year period far outstripping its aims both in terms of quantity, and more importantly, quality, as shown in Table 3.1.

TABLE 3.1 SLRC research translation activities – a report card for the first four years[1]

Aim	Outcome
Create industry and public awareness of the research	*Lectures, visits, and events* During its four-year term the Centre consistently exceeded key performance indicators for lectures, visits, and events with respect to industry and public outreach. *npj Science of Learning* Dedicated to the science of learning, the *Nature Partner Journal* provides open-access to the latest scientific research in the field. Providing information accessible to practitioners and the general public, in 2019 the associated *Community* site recorded over 96,400 visits. *Deep Learning through Transformative Pedagogy MOOC* Developed by SLRC chief investigators targeting in-service teachers over 8,000 participants enrolled in the initial offering. *Science of Learning – research to reality conference* Hosted by the SLRC the conference attracted over 280 delegates including national and international researchers, educators, and education department representatives. What became apparent during the conference was how advanced the SLRC was in terms of its engagement with end-user stakeholders compared to other international science of learning initiatives.
Form new strategic partnerships in order to provide access to Centre research	*Creating new and growing existing partnerships* The Centre made many new connections locally and internationally. Importantly, it grew the partnerships with key stakeholders, for example, engaging with education departments at multiple entry points from research services to school improvements and human resource divisions. As with universities, education departments are large organisations and being connected with one section of the organisation does not transfer to connection to the whole organisation. We purposefully set about to embrace the entire organisation.
Inform policy through briefings to government, industry, business, and community groups	*Informing policy* Centre researchers informed policy on an international, national, state, and school level through the engagement of researchers on boards, committees, working parties, and various advisory capacities, including the Australian Institute for Teaching and School Leadership. Notably, the SLRC was represented in UNESCO-IBE's effort to translate research from the science of learning into policy, with the Deputy Director of the Centre the recipient of a Senior Fellowship in 2016. *Informed by policy* Briefings with end-user stakeholders played a critical role in informing the research activities of the SLRC, particularly with respect to implementation. It was during these briefings that we learnt, for example, that our stakeholders did not only want to hear about research findings, but also research questions, and wanted to be able to contribute to the development of the questions.

(*Continued*)

1 The SLRC was initially awarded ARC funding of $16 million over four years commencing in 2013. An additional $1 million was awarded, supporting research and translation activities to 2019.

TABLE 3.1 SLRC research translation activities – a report card for the first four years[1] (*Continued*)

Aim	Outcome
Develop a website for sharing current research findings	*Social media* One of the first activities of the SLRC was to develop a website. With a repository for resources, including teacher resources and past presentations, as well as events and latest research findings. Coupled to the website, the Centre also has a presence on Facebook and Twitter, further increasing its reach. *Incorporation of science of learning into pre-service and post graduate courses* SLRC-designed curricula have been integrated into ten undergraduate and post-graduate teacher education programs. These courses are designed to provide practicing and future teachers with the necessary skill set to engage with research. This is particularly timely as the education profession is being called upon to engage with evidence-informed practice. This course material is available to be shared with other universities.
Additional outcomes	*Implementation* With an emphasis on moving beyond dissemination of research findings to classroom implementation, the Centre developed its SLRC Partner Schools Program, which is continuing to grow with the support of state education departments and independent school bodies. This is a legacy that was not envisioned at the commencement of the Centre, and was only made possible through rich collaboration with industry stakeholders across all levels. *Resources to support implementation* PEN Principle – Developed through the lens of Psychology, Education and Neuroscience, this freely available series of videos, podcasts, and factsheets has been employed by educators across Australia and internationally. HELF – A higher education learning framework providing seven guiding principles for tertiary learning, including implications for teachers, students, and assessment, the framework was downloaded over 1,000 times in the first three months of its release.

A chance to reflect

Being a Special Research Initiative, the ARC reviewed the Centre after its first two years of operation. Although at the time this seemed like an onerous task, it provided an opportunity to reflect on the various outreach and translation activities that the Centre had undertaken, the purpose of the activities, and to ask the question – *how do these activities impact on the learning outcomes of students?*

As part of the process, the outreach and translation activities undertaken by the Centre were reviewed, and links between each activity and its impact on learners were mapped. For many activities, the link was long and tenuous and there was no clear line of sight between the activity and impact in the classroom. For example, we regularly gave briefings on Centre research to representatives of various state education departments. This is a crucial activity and one of the Centre's key performance indicators, but a briefing to a member of the education department, regardless of the level, does not result in a change to student learning, at least not directly or in the short term. Similarly, the Centre conducted seminar series for educators across several of its nodes. Over time the regular following of attendees at the seminars increased and educators found the topics interesting and insightful. However, research tells us that one-off seminars do not make a difference to student learning (Hattie, 2009).

Seeking to make sense of the Centre's translation activities, we adopted an alternative approach. Starting with the desired objective, improving learning outcomes, we reverse mapped activities to the desired outcome. As part of this process we collaborated with partner education departments to develop a communication and translation framework, as illustrated in Figure 3.3. This framework has been extremely beneficial in providing a basis for how we engage with the education system, and how the education system engages with the Centre and its research.

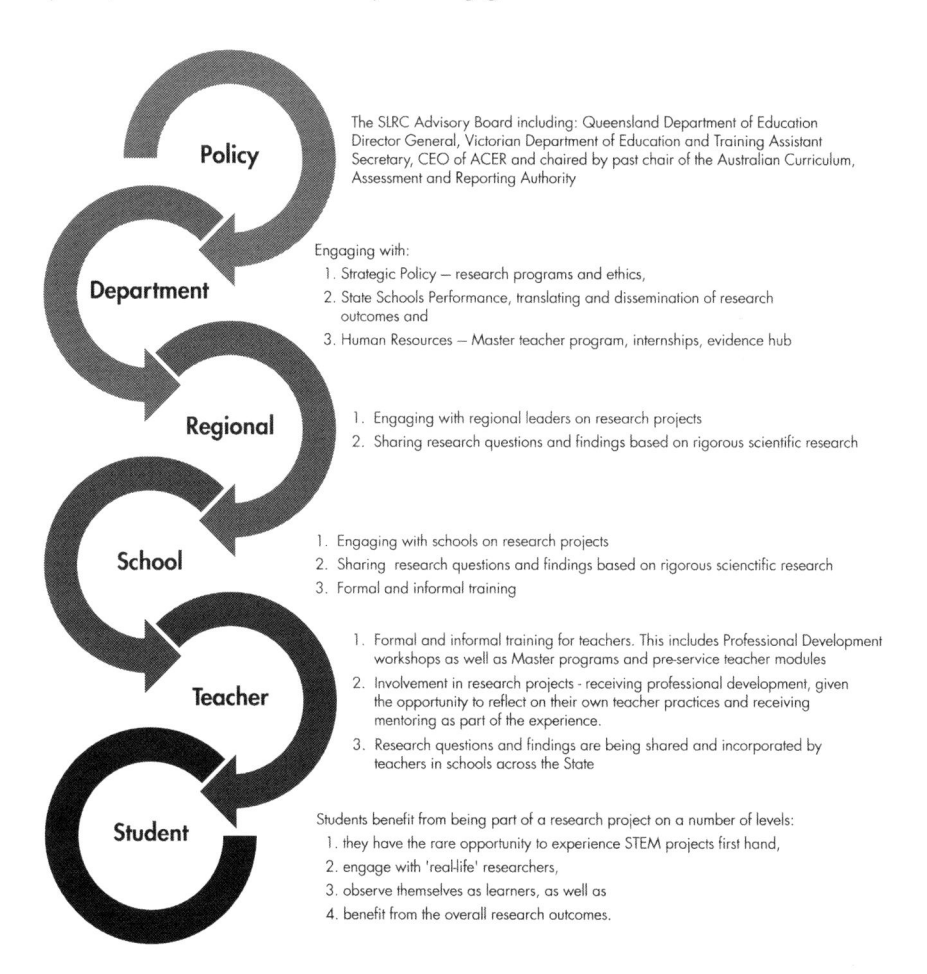

Policy — The SLRC Advisory Board including: Queensland Department of Education Director General, Victorian Department of Education and Training Assistant Secretary, CEO of ACER and chaired by past chair of the Australian Curriculum, Assessment and Reporting Authority

Department — Engaging with:
1. Strategic Policy – research programs and ethics,
2. State Schools Performance, translating and dissemination of research outcomes and
3. Human Resources – Master teacher program, internships, evidence hub

Regional
1. Engaging with regional leaders on research projects
2. Sharing research questions and findings based on rigorous scientific research

School
1. Engaging with schools on research projects
2. Sharing research questions and findings based on rigorous scienctific research
3. Formal and informal training

Teacher
1. Formal and informal training for teachers. This includes Professional Development workshops as well as Master programs and pre-service teacher modules
2. Involvement in research projects - receiving professional development, given the opportunity to reflect on their own teacher practices and receiving mentoring as part of the experience.
3. Research questions and findings are being shared and incorporated by teachers in schools across the State

Student — Students benefit from being part of a research project on a number of levels:
1. they have the rare opportunity to experience STEM projects first hand,
2. engage with 'real-life' researchers,
3. observe themselves as learners, as well as
4. benefit from the overall research outcomes.

FIGURE 3.3 Communication and translation framework of engaging with state departments of education

The communication and translation framework was developed with a focus on engaging with end-user stakeholders across various levels of influence. Although not all stakeholders are directly involved with the translation process, the support of these groups hastens the incorporation of research findings into learning practice. Key actors influencing translation of research findings into classroom practice are discussed next.

Researchers

As the SLRC's ethos is grounded in developing an evidence-based narrative around learning, it only seeks to translate research findings that are supported by scientific evidence and that have been fully validated. However, there is often a difference of opinion between academics as to when the science is ready for translation, when the evidence is sufficiently robust to support the claims of effectiveness (Green & Seifert, 2005). Several research programs within the Centre have yielded implementable outcomes that have been shown to have a large effect. The validation and scale-up of two of these outcomes is described in Chapters 12 (Brooks & Burton) and 13 (Leonard & Westwell).

Somewhat surprisingly at the time, through engagement with educators and policymakers alike, we learnt that the adopters of the research did not only want to be presented with a finished product. End-users of our research wanted to learn about the research as it was occurring, have the opportunity to influence its direction, and assist researchers to understand the implications of research findings in the classroom. Collaboration between researchers and practitioners as part of the translation process is not uncommon in other fields such as health (Greenhalgh & Fahy, 2015). The co-creation of new knowledge as part of the translation process can be pivotal in ensuring the effective uptake of research outcomes (Greenhalgh, Jackson, Shaw, & Janamian, 2016). In response to the demand to be involved earlier in the research stage, the SLRC developed its Partner Schools program.

Educators

Teachers are at the learning interface. According to Hattie (Hattie, 2009), teacher efficacy has the largest single effect on student learning outcomes. In order to improve knowledge in the science of learning of the next generation of teachers, the Translation Team developed new courses and material for pre-service teachers, as well as post-graduate students at the University of Melbourne and The University of Queensland. A number of Chief Investigators contributed to a MOOC on the science of learning which attracted over 8,000 participants in its first delivery and in excess of 1,000 educators engaged with the SLRC's professional learning activities, attending seminars and partaking in workshops. However, as discussed previously, the benefit of one-off professional learning sessions in bringing about adoption, particularly if the events are not supported at a whole-of-school level, is questionable. Notwithstanding these limitations, the activities clearly served to raise the awareness and acceptance of science of learning research.

School leaders

The support of school leadership is essential in bringing about sustainable and scalable change. It is the school leadership that identifies the school priorities and sets the strategic direction and pedagogical framework within which teachers operate. Although many participants willingly paid their own way to attend the Centre's professional learning activities, leaving feeling empowered by their new knowledge, they subsequently reported being frustrated by their inability to bring about change once back in the school setting. It is for this reason that the SLRC Partner School Program, an evidence informed model for the effective translation of research findings into actionable, scalable, and sustainable outcomes developed by the SLRC, requires the participation of both school leaders and classroom teachers.

Policy advocacy groups

Organisations such as UNESCO and OECD influence government agendas on a global scale. Although these groups do not have any direct control over policy at a national level, their ability to highlight non-conforming behaviour and under-performance on an international stage can nudge policy reform at a national level (Lingard, Martino, & Rezai-Rashti, 2015; Volante, Fazio, & Maastricht, 2017). Indeed, the UNESCO International Bureau of Education has been an extremely influential advocate for bringing scientific rigour into learning research, and several members of the SLRC have contributed to its charge.

Government and policymakers

Government provides funding for schools to operate, and sets the overall policy for education. Policy design is usually based on fictitious characters – homoeconomicus in economics, the reasonable person in law (Dulleck, 2018), and the "average" student, teacher, and school. However, in reality, the average actor is rarely to be found in the messy and diverse setting of education, and how policy is interpreted differs significantly in the natural school setting. For example, Australia has a national curriculum, however what that looks like in practice varies greatly between classes, schools, regions, and states, with the 2014 Review of the Australian Curriculum describing its implementation as "patchy" (Department of Education and Training, 2014). In the same way that policy advocacy groups can only influence reforms, the ability of government to control events at the level of the individual learner in a single classroom is limited. In order to remain competitive, governments invest in learning innovation, such as the science of learning. It is essential for the SLRC to engage with policymakers, ensuring they have access to robust evidence for the design of education policy, and realise the benefits of investing in research in order to retain an internationally competitive education system.

Community groups, media, social media

The importance of engaging with the community cannot be underestimated. Society can influence governments' decision to invest in research and encourage schools to engage with the research. Much is written about the correlation between education and well-being and future employment (Michalos, 2008), and how Australia is lagging behind. People are demanding an innovative and progressive education system, where policymakers and educators are making evidence-informed decisions.

Education departments

As education falls within the remit of the state departments of education, with all state school teachers being employed by state departments, these have a significant influence on what transpires at the classroom level. The departments set local policy agenda and provide support to schools in identifying priority areas for improvement and developing strategies to implement said improvements. State departments are also able to provide additional resources to ensure all students are provided with equal opportunity to excel.

A different way of thinking about translation

Post the ARC mid-term review, the remit of the Translation Team expanded to take on arguably its most important role. No longer tasked with simply "doing" research translation, the team was challenged with improving the effectiveness of research translation, developing efficient models to facilitate research findings to the classroom that could be trialled and validated. We drew upon the model of Green et al. (2005), describing translation as a non-linear process involving at least three stages: (a) awareness, (b) acceptance, and (c) adoption. Using this model, we were able to categorise the translation activities of the Centre, look to where our strengths were, and identify areas for improvement.

As we reflected on our approach to research translation, it became apparent that our focus had been on creating awareness and acceptance, but we were now ready to concentrate efforts on the adoption stage, as well as continuing to create awareness and acceptance. Further, conversation with policymakers and educators had informed us that it was not just adoption that was required. In order to have a lasting impact on student learning research findings need to be transformed into an outcome that is actionable, scalable, and sustainable.

Recognising that there is no "one-size-fits all" solution to research translation in the complex environment that is education, the team drew upon research around implementation science, knowledge transfer, and technology transfer from other fields such as healthcare, agriculture, and business, as well as education, to develop both "bespoke" (school-directed) and "off-the-shelf" (researcher-directed) models for translation. The SLRC Partner Schools Program is an example of a bespoke model. The school group identifies a priority to focus on, research brokers match the relevant research, and researchers from within the SLRC provide mentorship to the school in the development of an action research program addressing its priority. In contrast to this, the off-the-shelf model is based on a professional learning program that has been developed by a researcher in their area of expertise.

Evaluating the merit of various models, the Translation Team is now investigating influences such as (a) the role of the researcher in translation, (b) the dose effect of professional learning (i.e., two hours versus two days versus two years), and (c) the role of the school leadership team. Being a national Centre, the challenge of implementing interventions in every classroom across the country persists. Requiring support of effective policy at a state and federal level, we are now beginning to explore the potential for behavioural economics to assist in this regard, applying experimental approaches to the design and evaluation of government policy and providing a protocol for learning what works in education policy (Dulleck, 2018).

A final word

As we said at the outset, the purpose of this reflection was to share our efforts in translating research findings from the science of learning so that others can learn from our experience. Overall, we are extremely proud of what we achieved in four short years (2013–2016). Our initial endeavours have laid the foundation for translation of research findings in the years since, collaborating with educators, schools, and education departments, we have now co-designed a self-sustaining model for research translation. If we were given our time again are there things that we would do differently? Perhaps not differently but more efficiently, we would invest more resources into the translation arm of the Centre, and research into translation as a science in its own right. To arrive at where we are today, we have created awareness of the science of learning research, and acceptance of its relevance across key stakeholder groups, and now concentrate on adoption of research outcomes. Arguably our greatest achievement, at least from the perspective of the SLRC Translation Team, has been to place research translation on the table as a shared problem across research, policy, and education, and to develop the translation of research findings as a research priority in its own right. In Australia, we have some of the world's best researchers in the field of the science of learning and equally brilliant educators – the grand challenge remains to produce research outcomes that are actionable, sustainable, and scalable in the learning context.

References

Australian Research Council. (2012). *Special research initiative for a Science of Learning Research Centre funding rules for funding commencing in 2012*. Canberra. Retrieved from https://webarchive.nla.gov.au/awa/20171113123104/http://www.arc.gov.au/sites/default/files/filedepot/Public/NCGP/SRIs/PDF/SLRC_Funding_Rules.pdf accessed 30 June 2018

Department of Education and Training. (2014). *Review of the Australian curriculum – final report*. Canberra. Retrieved 30 June 2018, from https://docs.education.gov.au/documents/review-australian-curriculum-final-report

Dulleck, U. (2018). Behavioural theories and public policy. In M. Fabian & R. Bruenig (Eds.), *Hybrid public policy innovations*. New York: Routledge.

Green, L., & Seifert, C. (2005). Translation of research into practice: Why we can't "just do it." *Journal of the American Board of Family Practice, 18*(6), 541–545.

Greenhalgh, T., & Fahy, N. (2015). Research impact in the community-based health sciences: An analysis of 162 case studies from the 2014 UK research excellence framework. *BMC Medicine, 13* (2). https://doi.org/10.1186/s12916-015-0467-4

Greenhalgh, T., Jackson, C., Shaw, S., & Janamian, T. (2016). Achieving research impact through co-creation in community-based health services: Literature review and case study. *The Milbank Quarterly, 94*(2), 392–429.

Hattie, J. (2009). *Visible learning: A synthesis of 800+ meta-analyses on achievement*. Abingdon: Routledge.

Institute of Medicine (US) Committee on Building Bridges in the Brain Behavioral and Clinical Sciences. (2000). Barriers to interdisciplinary research and training. In E. Pellmar. T. & L. Eisenberg (Eds.), *Bridging disciplines in the brain, behavioral, and clinical sciences*. Washington, DC: National Academies Press.

Katz, J. (1994). Geographical proximity and scientific collaboration. *Scientometrics, 31*, 31–43.

Lingard, B., Martino, W., & Rezai-Rashti, G. (2015). *Globalizing educational accountabilities*. New York: Routledge.

Luo, Q., Xia, J. C., Haddow, G., Willson, M., & Yang, J. (2018). Does distance hinder the collaboration between Australian universities in the humanities, arts and social sciences? *Scientometrics, 115*(2), 695–715.

Michalos, A. (2008). Education, happiness and wellbeing. *Social Indicators Research, 87*(3), 347–366.

Science of Learning Research Centre. (2014). *Science of learning research centre annual report 2013*. Brisbane. Retrieved 30 June 2018, from https://www.slrc.org.au/wp-content/uploads/2014/05/2013-Annual-Report1.pdf

Volante, L., Fazio, X., & Maastricht, J. (2017). The OECD and educational policy reform: International surveys, governance, and policy evidence. *Canadian Journal of Educational Administration and Policy, 184*, 34–48.

PART II
Self regulation of learning

Education systems today are under increasing pressure to move beyond a focus on specific content knowledge, towards developing capabilities in individuals that prepare them to acquire new expertise efficiently – in essence, "learn how to learn," as McGaw discussed in the opening chapter. This shift is critically needed in contemporary education to develop people who are self-regulated learners, who have explicit knowledge of the internal and external factors required to manage cognitive, social, and emotional demands and are able to regulate them.

Abilities for self-regulation of learning are multi-faceted and associated with brain development and plasticity. Self-regulation includes key processes linked to the control of attention and high-level planning (also known as executive functioning), social and emotional functioning, and anxiety through challenge and failure. In Part Two, we consider the broad term "self-regulation" as encompassing the range of psychological processes that are critical for one's ability to optimally regulate cognitive, social, and emotional processes tied to learning. These abilities are strongly associated with functional and structural maturational change and plasticity in the brain from childhood through to adolescence.

Lent, Ribeiro, and Sato's chapter highlights three areas of neuroscience research within the Brazilian Network of Science for Education, laying the foundation of neuroplasticity as the basis of learning within the brain. They show applications of research on sleep in children and adolescents, known to be a critical time for neuroplastic changes in the brain associated with memory consolidation, neurodevelopment of long-range connections between different brain regions and between the two hemispheres of the brain in children, and measurement of shared brain activity between people during social interaction.

In relation to anxiety, chapters by Weekes and Buckley et al. highlight the challenges to learning associated with foreign language anxiety in second-language learners and mathematics anxiety particularly in pre-service primary teachers.

Highly anxious foreign language learners are found to recruit brain networks associated with motivation to a greater extent than low anxious learners, while interventions that separately consider the long-term (trait) and short-term (state) components of anxiety are found to be effective in reducing mathematics anxiety in pre-service teachers.

Chapters by Carroll and Bower and by Cunnington et al. address both emotional and social factors in classroom learning. Carroll and Bower review the importance of emotional regulation for learning and academic performance, methods to track both teacher and student perceptions of their emotional states and associated physiological responses, and interventions to improve emotion awareness and management. Cunnington et al. further review the importance of the classroom as a social environment and methods to track brain and physiological responses associated with collaborative engagement in learning tasks.

Finally, Sherlock and Mulvihill highlight the importance of higher-order attentional and metacognitive skills for learning at different stages of development. Their chapter presents an intervention program aimed at building adolescent capacity for focused attention and cognitive control, developing critical skills for self-regulated learning.

In sum, these chapters overview the core research in the science of learning that contributes to understanding the cognitive, emotional, social, and metacognitive processes critical for the learner's self-regulation of their learning. Strategies for developing self-regulated learners in a classroom setting, informed by evidence from the science of learning, are described by Brooks and Burton (Chapter 12) and Leonard and Westwell (Chapter 13) in Part Four.

4

NEUROPLASTICITY: FROM CELLS TO CIRCUITS AND BRAINS TOWARDS THE CLASSROOM

Roberto Lent, Sidarta Ribeiro and João Ricardo Sato

Introduction: the multiple levels of neuroplasticity

It has become nearly consensual that natural objects can be approached at different heuristic levels, as suggested at least 50 years ago (Rose, 1969). A good example is that of the Earth. For an astrophysicist, our planet is no more than a minuscule grain of dust moving together with thousands, millions, billions of other similar (or different) grains. For a geologist, on the other hand, the Earth is a gigantic sphere formed by concentric layers between the surface and the center, of diverse thickness, composition, temperature, and physical state. For a particle physicist, the Earth is perhaps of a disconcerting simplicity, composed of about 20 elementary particles, and nothing else. Botanists and zoologists, on the other hand, focus their interest specifically on the surface, that is, on the plant and animal species that inhabit it. Finally, anthropologists and social scientists have eyes only to the human species and their networks of collective interactions.

All of them, however, tackle the same natural object – the Earth – which exists and is studied at the same time at different heuristic planes or levels, each one requiring a particular scientific approach. Each level is accessible to scientists by use of appropriate methodologies, oftentimes exclusive of each of them. That is, it is not effective to use a telescope to study the chemical composition of the sea, or a structured scale to study the behaviour of quarks.

This conception, as applied to the brain, was well described by Steven Rose in his cited book, as analysing the nervous system from the molecular pathways of neuronal metabolism and synaptic transmission, which are the object of study of neurochemists, to the most complex multipersonal phenomena, which are focused by psychologists. Rose's great contribution was to call attention to the simultaneous existence of these various heuristic levels and to analyse critically the excluding alternatives proposed by the so-called reductionists, on one side, and the so-called holists, on the opposite side. To the former, for example, mental phenomena could be explained entirely by reducing them to their cell and molecular mechanisms. To the latter, mind would be at most an emergent property of the brain and would acquire an existence independent from it. Mind, therefore, would be explainable by specific laws and principles unrelated to functioning of the brain. According to Rose, on the other hand, mind and brain would simply be different heuristic levels of the same object, which perhaps could be called conscience, for the lack of a better, unifying term. The great challenge would be to establish bridges between the levels, since they would not exist as independent territories, but would overlap and mix at the borders (Cooper & Shallice, 2010).

Neuroplasticity can be approached along these lines of reasoning. It can be defined as the ability of the brain to undergo temporary or permanent changes, whenever it becomes influenced by its own function, by other brains, or by the external environment. Neuroplasticity exists at multiple levels in all living beings that have neural systems (Tovar-Moll & Lent, 2016). The following levels could be proposed in the context of this chapter: molecular/cellular, within neurons and glial cells (the micro-scale level); systemic, concerning circuits or chains of neurons that form networks (the meso-scale level); and interpersonal or social, involving human pairs, groups or even populations of human beings connected by an organised social structure (macro-scale level).

In this short review, we aim to show three experimental examples of these heuristic levels, as concerns different neuroplastic phenomena related to education. Educational practice relates mainly to learning, although this is not its only aspect. Learning, on the other hand, is the ability that animals possess to acquire, store, and retrieve memories, employing different neural mechanisms. One important issue, thus, is to investigate which factors can facilitate these plastic phenomena in synapses and neurons. We will show that sleep is one of these factors, which, therefore, can be used in educational settings to improve learning. Since much of the result of learning and memory implies a long-term, often lifelong change in the brain, it is reasonable to suppose that its structural connectivity changes after environmental influences derived from teaching and learning. This is to say that the brain connectome is not genetically hardwired, but that its circuits can be changed and become differently sculpted in each individual. We will provide an example that this is so, by using a model derived from a developmental "mistake" to form long-distance circuits in the brain. Finally, although it is possible to learn alone, education is a social enterprise and benefits from organised interactions between human beings – teachers and learners, as well as learners together. Neuroplasticity reaches, in this case, a macro-scale level by which brains interact and change themselves. It becomes a transpersonal, multibrain set of phenomena than can be approached by modern hyperscanning experiments.

The micro-scale level: sleep-dependent mechanisms of memory

Memories are acquired and processed throughout life by way of an intricate web of molecular mechanisms that transform new patterns of neuronal activation, in the timescale of milliseconds, into new patterns of neuronal connectivity, in the timescale of minutes, hours, days, and well beyond. Initiation of this chain of events requires the synchronous firing of pre- and post-synaptic neurons, which produces sustained depolarisation able to open calcium channels, one of the complex proteins that allow neurons to communicate electrochemically across synapses. The elevated influx of calcium triggers various biochemical phenomena inside neurons, such as phosphorylation cascades provided by enzymes (protein kinases) that quickly transduce the cytoplasmic signals into a genomic response, by way of transcription factors such as cAMP response element-binding protein (CREB), which directly control DNA function. Consequently, a few minutes after the initial calcium influx, the transcriptional activation of multiple immediate-early genes (IEGs) leads to the nuclear and then cytoplasmic accumulation of mRNA coded by those genes. While some of these IEGs encode effector proteins that act directly in synaptic remodelling within minutes, other IEGs encode regulatory proteins that act indirectly in synaptic remodelling as transcription factors, which take hours to provoke gene regulatory changes in the nucleus (Bliss & Collingridge, 1993).

During waking (Figure 4.1A), encoding is represented by presynaptic stimulation of glutamatergic synapses, following rapid calcium influx in the post-synaptic terminal via receptors of N-methyl-D-aspartate (NMDA), one of the most important excitatory neurotransmitters. These receptors promote activation of multiple kinases and signaling cascades (e.g., PKA, CaMKII, ERK[1]) that can modulate the transcription factor CREB, and trigger IEG expression (e.g., Arc, Zif-268[2]). Memory formation requires transcription- and translation-dependent mechanisms to modify synaptic connectivity.

By recording brain activity during sleep using the electroencephalogram (EEG), it is shown that slow wave sleep (SWS, Figure 4.1B) promotes synaptic downscaling and restorative biosynthesis. Some EEG markers such as hippocampal sharp wave–ripples (SWRs) and thalamocortical sleep spindles are involved with memory consolidation. During rapid-eye movements (REM) sleep (Figure 4.1C), on the other hand, the transcription of plasticity-related IEGs is reinduced. CREB is a target of microRNA modulation, which interferes with hippocampus-dependent memory storage. CREB regulates gene transcription

---

1 Abbreviations of the enzymes *protein kinase A*, *calcium/calmodulin-dependent kinase II*, and *extracellular signal-regulated kinases*, respectively.
2 Abbreviations of the genes that encode the proteins *activity-regulated cytoskeleton-associated protein*, and *zinc-finger protein-268*, respectively.

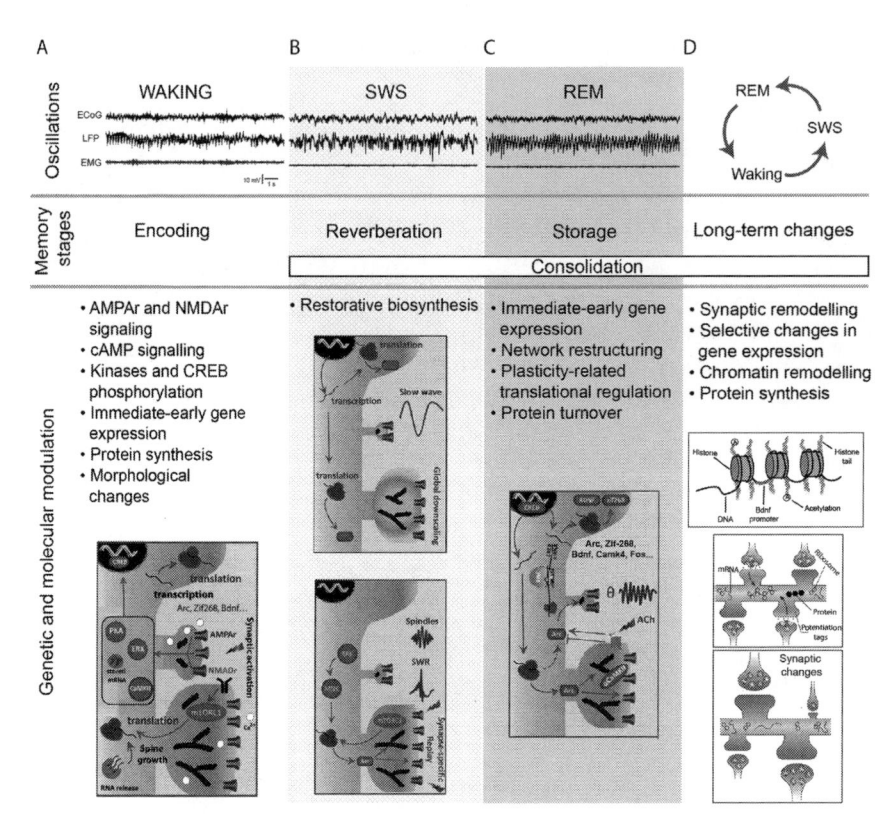

FIGURE 4.1 Molecular cascades putatively involved with sleep-dependent learning, and evidence that post-training sleep boosts learning in the school setting. (A) Waking. (B) Slow-wave sleep (SWS). (C) Rapid-eye-movement sleep (REM), and (D) Long-term changes. Abbreviations: CaMKII, *calcium/calmodulin-dependent protein kinase II*; cAMP, *cyclic adenosine monophosphate*; CREB, *cAMP response element–binding protein*; ERK, *extracellular signal–regulated protein kinase*; LTP, *long-term potentiation*; NMDA, *N-methyl-D-aspartate*; PKA, *protein kinase A*; REM, *rapid eye movement*; SWS, *slow-wave sleep*. Adapted from, Duan et al. (2016); Golbert et al. (2017); and Govindarajan et al. (2006).

by promoting binding of the transcriptional molecules to target genes and by making the latter more accessible by altering chromatin structure. Chromatin remodelling is linked to long-term changes (Figure 4.1D) which are necessary for learning and memory.

Several of the plasticity mechanisms mentioned above are reactivated during sleep, including firing rate increases, neuronal synchronisation, kinase phosphorylation, and IEG expression (Ribeiro, 2012). Specific oscillations that appear in EEG brain recordings, such as cortical spindles, ripples, and slow waves, are augmented during post-learning sleep (Diekelmann & Born, 2010). In the past three decades, a large body of laboratory-based evidence has accumulated showing that sleep promotes learning. While pre-training sleep facilitates memory acquisition (Yoo et al., 2007), post-training sleep has been shown to facilitate the selective strengthening, forgetting, and restructuring of memory traces (Saletin et al., 2011; Wilhelm et al., 2011).

Although much remains to be learned about the role of different sleep states in this phenomenon, current evidence indicates that the two main sleep states are both beneficial for learning. SWS and REM seem to play complementary roles in memory processing, with SWS being more important for declarative memory consolidation and REM more important for emotional and procedural memories. This set of evidence from neuroscience provides a biological basis for establishing a bridge with cognitive and educational psychology, and therefore proposes the implementation of changes concerning sleep in school.

In fact, the use of post-training naps in the school setting is an incipient field with great promise as a low-cost enhancer of school learning. To date, only two classroom studies have been published. The first study (Kurdziel et al., 2013) investigated the effect of post-training naps on the learning of spatial locations in 40 preschoolers (ages 36–67 months). The results (Figure 4.2A) showed that children already used to napping at home could benefit from post-training naps, obtaining ~15% increase in task performance, measured as accuracy of spatial location. A subgroup of the children ($N = 14$) was taken to the laboratory for polysomnographic recordings and the results showed a significant correlation between cortical spindles and memory gains.

The second study (Lemos et al., 2014) investigated 371 adolescents (ages 10–15 years) exposed to novel information during an experimental lecture, and then randomised into nap and no-nap groups. When tested 1 day after the experimental lecture, both groups showed ~10% increase in retention. However, when

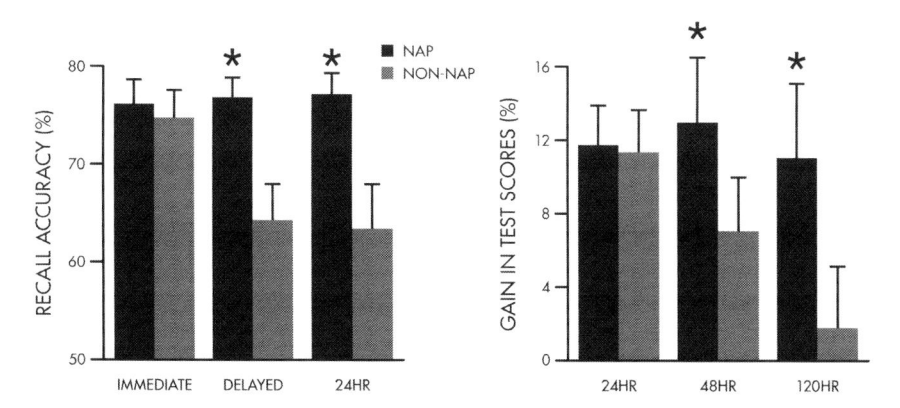

FIGURE 4.2 (A) Recall accuracy of spatial locations was tested in preschoolers immediately after encoding ("Immediate"), soon after a nap ("Delayed"), and one day later ("24 h"). Error bars represent ±1 SE, ★ for $p < 0.05$. Adapted from ref. 13. (B) Gains in test scores applied to adolescents 1, 2, or 5 days after learning. Error bars represent ±1 SEM, ★ for $p < 0.05$. Adapted from Lemos et al. (2014).

tested 5 days post-training, the no-nap group lost the gains entirely, while the nap group kept them (Figure 4.2B). This study suggests that post-training sleep increases memory duration.

Although school curricula usually lean heavily on declarative content, the importance of procedural and emotional learning is becoming increasingly recognised (Tyng et al., 2017). For this reason, in principle, a full cycle of post-training sleep, lasting about 90 minutes and comprising both SWS and REM, should be the most advantageous in the school setting. However, the reality of schools, with compressed schedules and little time to spare, often precludes such long naps. In the laboratory, sleep-related benefits in memory retention have been observed with naps as short as 6 minutes, during which the brain barely has the chance to enter SWS. The optimisation of post-training naps will require extensive research regarding (1) the best duration and frequency of classes and naps, (2) which brain oscillations are most relevant, (3) when do they occur, and (4) the role of self-regulation to make the most of school sleep (Kurdziel et al., 2013; Sigman et al., 2014). Pre-training sleep should also be considered as a powerful and yet simple way to balance physiological deficits originating at home (Ribeiro et al., 2016).

The meso-scale level: the connectome is plastic

If you close your eyes, let someone put a wooden cube in your left hand for some minutes, and then have it taken out and hidden from your view, you will be able to recognise it with your right hand among a series of pictures of different objects. Not only that, you will be able to say the word "cube" when asked what you have seen. The anatomy of brain circuits explains this behavior: somatic sensations driven by your left hand are directed to the right hemisphere, to be processed in the cerebral cortex. Therein, the brain processes the information to make it possible for you to recognise the cube by palpation, even in the absence of visual input. Now, the problem is that you ought to transfer this perceptual information to the opposite (left) hemisphere, in order to allow your right hand to point to the cube picture. Also, it is the left hemisphere that produces speech, and for this reason linguistic regions therein must receive the corresponding information from the right hemisphere. Normally, the circuit that provides this interhemispheric communication is contained in the corpus callosum, a robust fiber tract of 200 million fibers connecting cortical regions at the right and the left side.

Now, what happens if an adult person needs a surgery to control epilepsy, and have the corpus callosum transected? These patients were studied by Roger Sperry and colleagues (Sperry, 1982) in a seminal series of papers (Gazzaniga, 1962, 1965, 1967) that rendered him the Nobel prize in medicine or physiology in 1981. Sperry and colleagues showed that callosally-transected people failed to succeed in the simple task we described above. They became unable to recognise an object with the opposite hand/hemisphere and could not speak its name. The phenomenon became known as the disconnection, or split-brain, syndrome.

However, what if developmental disorders interfere with the formation of these long circuits from the start? When, for instance, a blockage of midline crossing of callosal fibers takes place during early development? This happens, in some cases, and the baby is born without part or all of the corpus callosum. Our tendency is to think that all communication between the hemispheres would be absent in these people when they grow up. Wrong. A paradoxical situation was revealed by Sperry himself, in one such case with callosal dysgenesis (Saul & Sperry, 1968; Sperry, 1968). Besides being cognitively normal, this person did not show the interhemispheric disconnection syndrome. Among the different hypotheses proposed by different investigators after Sperry, one turned out to be more relevant recently: the possibility that anomalous fiber tracts would form in these brains, some of them crossing through alternative commissures situated in the ventral forebrain or in the midbrain.

Callosal dysgenesis, therefore, represents an interesting model to evaluate the capacity of white matter tracts to undergo radical alterations in their trajectory and generate new networks, entirely different from typically developing subjects. Some of these cases were studied by neuroimaging tools and revealed a set of anomalous circuits involving redirected callosal fibers (Tovar-Moll et al., 2007, 2014).

Two different sets of anomalous tracts were shown in the brain of dyscallosal subjects (Figure 4.3). The first set is formed by two longitudinal bundles, one entirely ipsilateral (the long-known Probst bundle; Probst, 1901), and the other coursing longitudinally but crossing through a remnant of the corpus callosum that is present in some of the subjects (named the sigmoid bundle). Although these two anomalous bundles have been reported functional by an EEG coherence study (Lazarev et al., 2016), the very nature of their function is unknown. That is: we know that the connected regions are talking to each other, but we do not know the subject of the conversation. The second set of anomalous connections (Figures 4.3A and 4.3B) is formed by two homotopically crossed bundles, connecting posterior parietal regions of the cerebral cortex through the posterior and the anterior commissure (two other interhemispheric tracts smaller but similar to the corpus callosum). In this case, as we will see, the subject of the conversation could be revealed.

Since these latter circuits connected a cortical area (BA39) of known function related to crossed transfer of tactile perception of objects, it was hypothesised that these alternative tracts acquired a compensatory role in substitution to the lacking corpus callosum. The ability of these subjects to identify objects placed in their left hands was tested exactly as described above, and the hypothesis was confirmed: they could do it as efficiently as the control group of normal people (Figures 4.3C and 4.3D). So, the alternative interhemispheric tracts compensated for the lack of the corpus callosum, assuming the function of crossed tactile transfer between the hemispheres.

The main conclusion of these experiments is that, during development, the human connectome can be largely altered (Figures 4.3E and 4.3F), not only

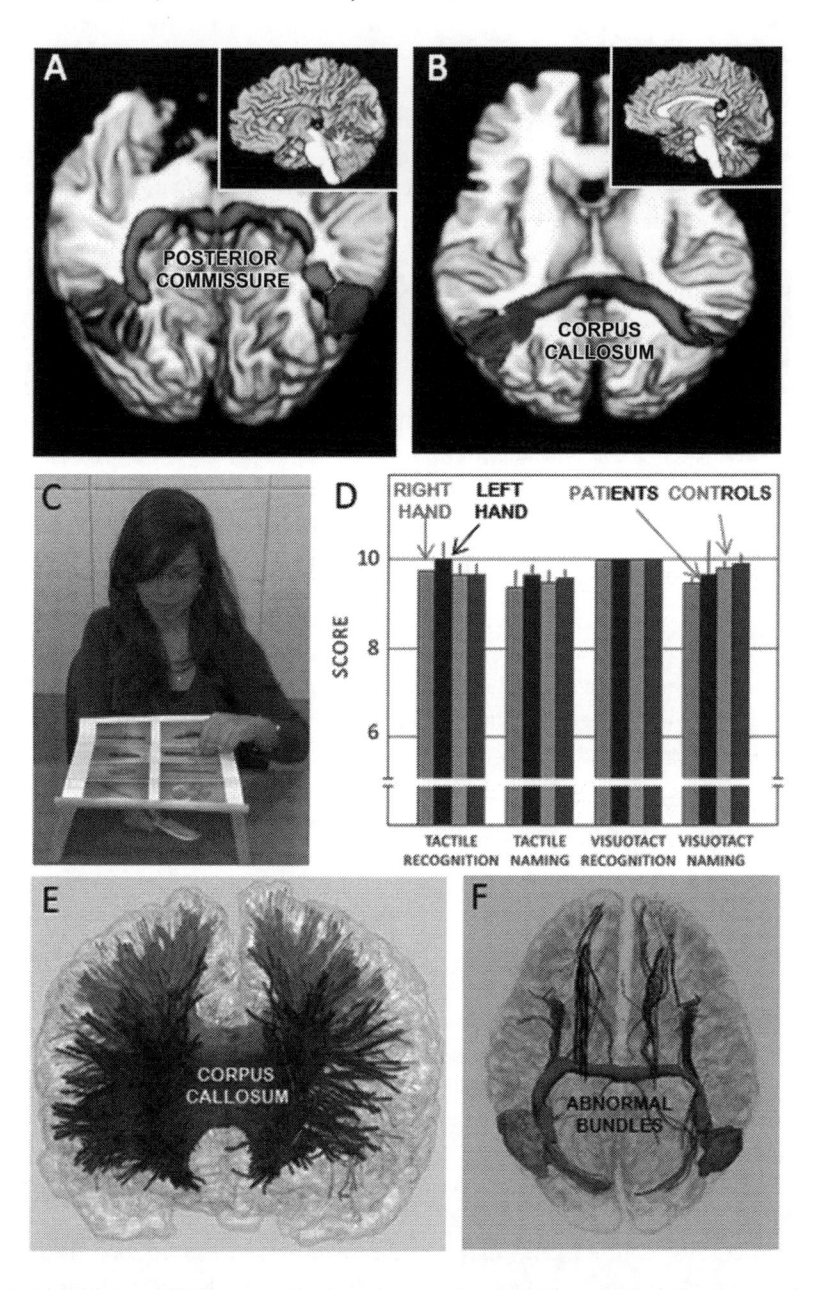

FIGURE 4.3 A and B show magnetic resonance images of an abnormal tract crossing through the posterior commissure at the midbrain (A) of subjects lacking the corpus callosum (inset in A), as compared with the corpus callosum of typical subjects (inset in B). C illustrates the tactile transfer test, demonstrating the normal performance of patients as compared with controls (D), both with the right and with the left hands. E shows the structural connectivity of a typical subject, while F shows that of a dyscallosal individual. A–D were modified from Tovar-Moll et al. (2007).

by the external environment, but also by the internal environment and by the genome itself, that control embryogenesis – this is the phenomenon named long-distance plasticity. The connectome, therefore, taken as the complete map of human brain circuits, may be in fact greatly plastic, not only in subjects under intensive training, certainly children and youngsters, but also adults. Even more so during development, from early embryonic phases to the first months after birth. It is conceivable, therefore, that not only the developmental disorders that impact on learning may display an abnormal connectome, but also that different educational interventions in children may have similar meso-scale effects. This issue deserves further investigation.

The macro-scale level: brain and body hyperscanning during learning

If education consists of interactions between people and therefore between their brains, how could this process be approached dynamically, comparing brain functions of the teacher with those of the learners? Would it be possible to record this "transpersonal neuroplasticity"?

In fact, a number of attempts have started to emerge in some laboratories, based on the synchronicity of brain waves that reflect directly or indirectly the activity of brain regions involved in the different cognitive and affective processing related to learning.

Electroencephalography (EEG) is probably the most used technique to record brain activity. Briefly, it requires the placement of some electrodes on the scalp of the subject and a powerful amplifier to record brain electrical waves. The system quantifies the temporal variations of voltage between two electrodes. Current evidence suggests that EEG is capable of detecting changes in the sum of synchronous activity of a large population of neurons (in the order of thousands to millions) organised in similar spatial orientation. Despite presenting a low spatial resolution (i.e., definition), the EEG provides a high temporal resolution, with sampling rates in the order of hundreds to thousands of observations per second. In neuroscience, EEG is used to enhance our understanding of the neural substrates of cognitive processes, such as perception, attention, memory, consciousness, and decision making.

Functional near-infrared spectroscopy (*f*NIRS) is a more recent technique based on hemodynamic coupling mechanisms, that is, changes in local tissue oxygenation that take place as a consequence of neuronal activity. Thus, when the metabolic activity of a brain region increases, a chain of processes (named hemodynamic coupling) is triggered, resulting in the local increase of blood flow, decreasing the concentration of deoxyhemoglobin and increasing oxyhemoglobin. Similar to EEG, sensors (optodes) are placed on the scalp, connected to a control device. An optode is either an emitter or a detector of near-infrared light. Interestingly, near-infrared light penetrates biological tissues such as the cranium and the brain, being partially attenuated by molecules within these tissues. However, the attenuation properties of oxy and of deoxyhemoglobin across the near-infrared spectrum are different. Thus, it is possible to quantify temporal changes in the local concentration of oxy/deoxyhemoglobin along the path traveled by the light between a source and detector pair. Therefore, *f*NIRS provides an indirect measurement of local brain activity, by estimating the oxy/deoxyhemoglobin concentration changes over time, with the advantage of being more robust to motion and eye-movements/muscular artifacts than EEG. These advantages are desired in naturalistic experimentation, such as protocols involving educational setups. However, it is important to mention that *f*NIRS presents a lower temporal resolution than EEG (in the order of tens of observations per second) and has some limitations due to indirect measurement of neural activity (e.g., systemic vascular artifacts, drug effects on neurovascular coupling, etc.).

The gold standard to achieve the goal of recording two or more brains simultaneously and correlate their activity along time during psychological interactions is called *hyperscanning*. This is a promising technique in neuroscience, in which brain activity of many subjects can be simultaneously recorded. In most cases, the experimental protocol involves the interaction between subjects while doing a predetermined task. Basically, a shift is necessary "from a single-brain to a multi-brain frame of reference" (Hasson et al., 2012) to enhance our understanding of the neural correlates of interpersonal interactions and dynamics. Illustrative examples of these cognitive functions are verbal communication, cooperation or competition activities and imitation.

One of the pioneering studies using multiple subjects' simultaneous recording was conducted by Duane and Behrendt in 1965 (Duane & Behrendt, 1965) using EEG. Almost 40 years later, another study (Montague et al., 2002) employed functional magnetic resonance imaging (*f*MRI) with simultaneous acquisition of two subjects performing a task of social interaction, and in 2011 the first hyperscanning report with *f*NIRS was published (Funane, 2011).

Most hyperscanning studies aim to investigate inter-subject brain activity synchronisation and information flow (Bilek et al., 2015) (Figure 4.4). In other words, these experiments focus on characterising a many-in-one system, allowing discoveries in social neuroscience, game theory and learning. Usually, hyperscanning protocols involve the execution of a joint task with interaction between participants and one device (or more) for simultaneous brain activity measurement. In neuroscience, functional connectivity in a single subject is defined as the correlated activity among different brain regions. So, functional hyperconnectivity can be defined as an extension of this concept, when brain activities of multiple subjects are correlated as a consequence of the interaction between them. Although the analyses of synchronous activity among different subjects can be useful to investigate brain processes in more naturalistic conditions, this interpersonal correlation could be achieved without an actual simultaneous acquisition by exposing them to the same stimuli (e.g., the excerpt of a movie). However, this interpersonal brain activity correlation does not reveal an authentic hyperconnectivity, since the local activity of one subject is not influencing

From cells to circuits and brains   57

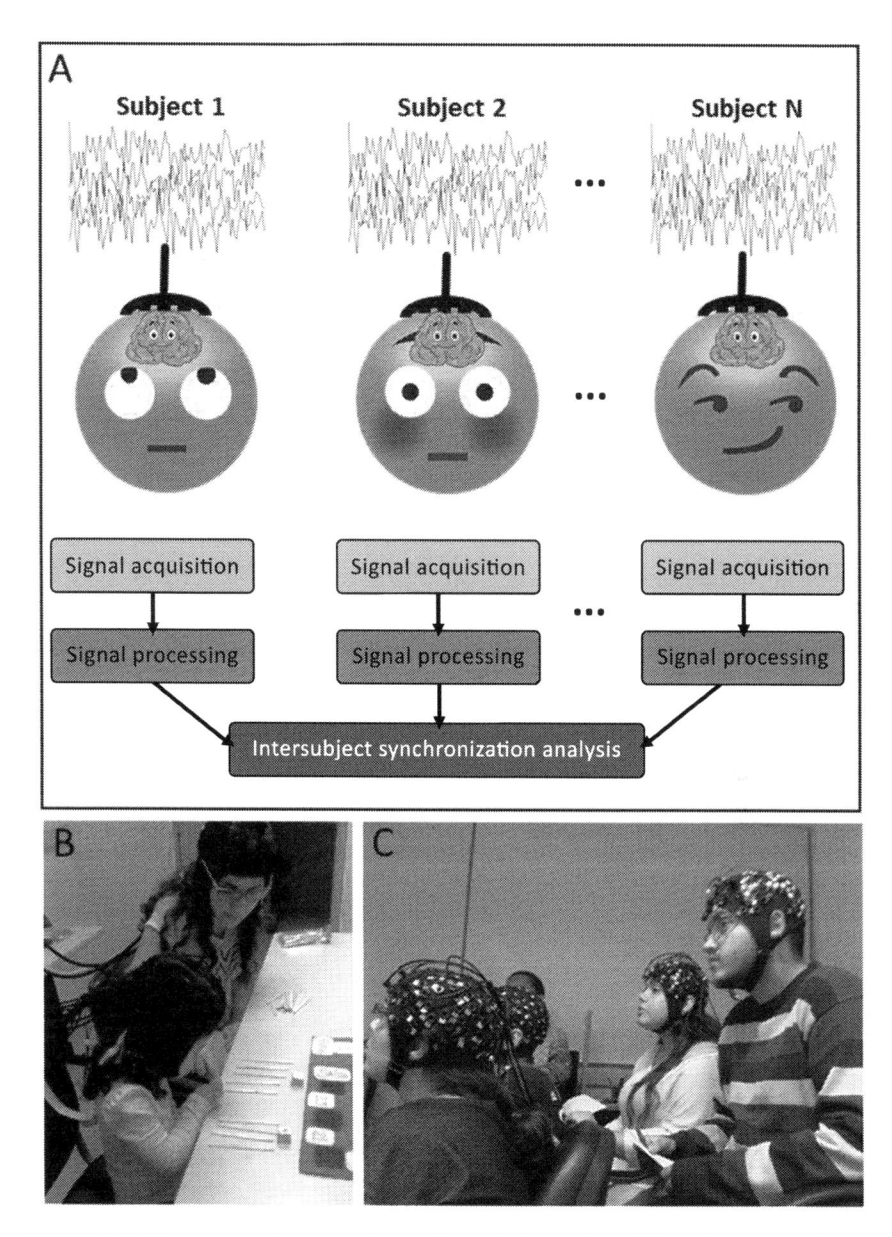

FIGURE 4.4 Hyperscanning experiments in realistic settings. The scheme in A shows the basic protocol of fNIRS recording in multiple brains, followed by processing and intersubject synchronisation analysis. B and C show respectively the experiment with a teacher and a girl learning how to add integer numbers, and university students listening to a lecture.

the activity of other subjects and there is also no feedback. This is why hyperscanning protocols involving the interaction among multiple subjects caused an impact in the field of social neuroscience. In this case, interacting brains can be studied as a big network (all subjects) comprised of subnetworks (each subject), which are constituted by even smaller sub-subnetworks (neural modules and systems of each subject), which are finally built of neurons. Note that this provides a scenario of multiple interacting agents at different scales, from individual cells to different subjects.

Despite the fact that hyperscanning is an established method in social neuroscience, there are few hyperscanning studies in educational research. A pioneering study described an experiment of teacher–student interactions using the Socratic dialogue and arithmetic problems (Holper et al., 2013). It was performed on 17 teacher–student pairs using prefrontal cortex fNIRS hyperscanning. Remarkably, the findings demonstrated that successful educational dialogues were associated with brain activity of teacher and student "dancing at the same pace." The authors suggested that fNIRS hyperscanning could provide a physiological marker of promising educational interactions. More recently, by using simultaneous EEG recording in multiple subjects (from 9 to 12 participants), synchronisation of neural activity during video presentations was investigated in a classroom (Poulsen et al., 2017). The authors concluded that some stimuli modulated by attention could produce interpersonal correlations of brain activity. Another study (Dikker et al., 2017) used EEG hyperscanning in 12 subjects during a typical class activity in a real school. Interestingly, the authors reported that interpersonal synchrony in brain activity could predict both social dynamics and classroom engagement.

A proof of concept of the use of hyperscanning experiments together with other recording techniques was recently performed by our group (Brockington et al., 2018). In this work, single cases were studied highlighting how fNIRS could be applied in realistic educational interactions. As an illustrative example, an experiment is presented in which a teacher and a three year old child interact by using two dice and a track-board (Figure 4.4B). Basically, the adult explained how to sum the outcomes of the dice toss (using sticks) and the child should count the number of steps on the board. Interestingly, a brain activity coupling was found between the two participants, reinforcing the framework that educational activities should involve social interactions. Moreover, it was found that the temporo-parietal junction activity of the teacher was synchronous to the child's prefrontal cortex. The temporo-parietal junction is a region involved in mentalising and social cognition, in agreement with the initial hypotheses. In a second case study (Figure 4.4C), the brain activities of four students were simultaneously recorded while they were attending a lecture. In this case, it was demonstrated that the activity of prefrontal cortex was synchronous among the students only during the first 8 minutes of the class, becoming gradually desynchronised during the next 8 minutes until turning totally asynchronous. This finding was interpreted as an expression of attentional focus and/or arousal in the beginning of the class, with a decrease of both along the experiment.

Some examples of relevant questions that could be explored in future hyperscanning studies are: which environmental and genetic factors could influence the synchronisation of brain activity between teacher and students? How do previous knowledge and life experiences modulate interpersonal information flow? How are the synchronisation levels correlated with effectiveness in learning? Which pedagogical strategies provide stronger hyperconnectivity? How are socioemotional skills related to the multiple students' synchronisation? Could hyperscanning in educational contexts provide information to elaborate public policies?

Coda: building bridges between cells and persons

In this chapter, we described experimental examples of neuroplasticity phenomena related to education, at three different levels of analysis: the micro-scale level, corresponding to molecular/cellular phenomena that characterise memory; the meso-scale level, illustrating the changes of long-range circuitry that may take place in the brain during development; and finally, the macro-scale level or transpersonal plasticity, involving the interactions between individuals and their brains. Of course, these levels are very distinct, so, in order to understand comprehensively the complex matters of education, bridges have to be built between these approaches.

How to build these bridges is the key issue, as it is for all attempts of translating science into practical applications. This difficult task is well accepted and faced by researchers in biomedical and hard science disciplines related, respectively, to medicine and to engineering. No one doubts the importance of knowing as much as possible about the molecular mechanisms within cancer cells to be able to arrive at therapeutic alternatives. Similarly, there are few doubts that investing in astrophysical research will eventually benefit the manufacture of satellites and, as a consequence, create better ways of dealing with environmental problems of the earth. Although less explored, the same rationale can be applied to education: not only neuroscience but many other disciplines can be useful to arrive at good evidence-based practices and policies for education. This chapter was an attempt to illustrate this possibility with some examples.

Despite the skepticism of some authors (Bowers, 2016; Bruer, 1997), a growing effort is being conducted in different countries to foster an interdisciplinary approach that would allow us to face education from an evidence-based point of view (Meltzoff et al., 2009; Sigman et al., 2014). This convergent movement is still beginning in a few countries, sometimes under the name of *educational neuroscience* or *science of learning*, some other times under the broader term of *science for education* (Lent et al., 2019). It is expected that this may lead to innovation of practices, processes, and products related to education, therefore contributing to improved and accelerated development of educational policies all over the world.

References

Bilek, E., Ruf, M., Schäfer, A., Akdeniz, C., Calhoun, V. D., Schmahl, C., Demanuele, C., Tost, H., Kirsch, P., & Meyer-Lindenberg, A. (2015). Information flow between interacting human brains: Identification, validation, and relationship to social expertise. *Proceedings of the National Academy of Sciences of the U.S.A., 112*, 5207–5212.

Bliss, T. V. & Collingridge, G. L. (1993). A synaptic model of memory: Long-term potentiation in the hippocampus. *Nature, 361*, 31–39.

Bowers, J. S. (2016). The practical and principled problems with educational neuroscience. *Psychological Review, 123*, 600–612.

Brockington, G., Balardin, J. B., Morais, G. A. Z., Malheiros, A., Lent, R., Moura, L. M., & Sato, J. R. (2018). Towards the classroom: The potential of fNIRS and physiological multirecordings in educational neuroscience. *Frontiers in Psychology, 9*, 1840.

Bruer, J. T. (1997). Education and the brain: A bridge too far. *Education Research, 26*, 4–16.

Cooper, R. P. & Shallice, T. (2010). Cognitive neuroscience: The troubled marriage of cognitive science and neuroscience. *Topics in Cognitive Science, 2*, 398–406.

Diekelmann, S. & Born, J. (2010). The memory function of sleep. *Nature Reviews Neuroscience, 11*, 114–126.

Dikker, S., Wan, L., Davidesco, I., Kaggen, L., Oostrik, M., McClintock, J., Rowland, J., Michalareas, G., Van Bavel, J. J., Ding, M., & Poeppel, D. (2017). Brain-to-brain synchrony tracks real-world dynamic group interactions in the classroom. *Current Biology, 27*, 1375–1380.

Duan, R., Liu X., Wang, T., Wu, L., Gao, X., & Zhang, Z. (2016). Histone acetylation regulation in sleep deprivation-induced spatial memory impairment. *Neurochemical Research, 41*, 2223–2232.

Duane, T. D. & Behrendt, T. (1965). Extrasensory electroencephalographic induction between identical twins. *Science, 150*, 367.

Funane, T., Kiguchi, M., Atsumori, H., Sato, H., Kubota, K., & Koizumi, H. (2011). Synchronous activity of two people's prefrontal cortices during a cooperative task measured by simultaneous near-infrared spectroscopy. *Journal of Biomedical Optics, 16*, 077011.

Gazzaniga, M. S., Bogen, J. E., & Sperry, R. W. (1962). Some functional effects of sectioning the cerebral commissures in man. *Proceedings of the National Academy of Sciences of the U.S.A., 48*, 1765–1769.

Gazzaniga, M. S., Bogen, J. E., & Sperry, R. W. (1965). Observations on visual perception after disconnexion of the cerebral hemispheres in man. *Brain, 88*, 221–236.

Gazzaniga, M. S. & Sperry, R. W. (1967). Language after section of the cerebral commissures. *Brain, 90*, 131–148.

Golbert D. C. F., Souza, A. C., Almeida-Filho, D. G., & Ribeiro, S. (2017). Sleep, Synaptic Plasticity, and Memory. In *Mechanisms of Memory* (Sara, S. J., ed.), Vol. 4 of *Learning and Memory: A Comprehensive Reference*, (Byrne, J. H., ed.), 2nd ed., pp. 539–562. Academic Press, Oxford.

Govindarajan, A., Kelleher, R. J., & Tonegawa, S. (2006). A clustered plasticity model of long-term memory engrams. *Nature Reviews Neuroscience, 7*, 575–583.

Hasson, U., Ghazanfar, A. A., Galantucci, B., Garrod, S., & Keysers, C. (2012). Brain-to-brain coupling: A mechanism for creating and sharing a social world. *Trends in Cognitive Sciences, 16*, 114–121.

Holper, L., Goldin, A. P., Shalóm, D. E., Battro, A. M., Wolf, M., & Sigman, M. (2013). The teaching and the learning brain: A cortical hemodynamic marker of teacher-student interactions in the Socratic dialog. *International Journal of Educational Research*, *59*, 1–10.

Kurdziel, L., Duclos, K., & Spencer, R. M. (2013). Sleep spindles in midday naps enhance learning in preschool children. *Proceedings of the National Academy of Sciences of the U.S.A.*, *110*, 17267–17272.

Lazarev, V., Monteiro, M., Vianna-Barbosa, R., Azevedo, L. C., Lent, R., & Tovar-Moll, F. (2016). Electrophysiological correlates of morphological neuroplasticity in human callosal dysgenesis. *PLOS ONE*, *11*(4), e052668.

Lemos, N., Weissheimer, J., & Ribeiro, S. (2014). Naps in school can enhance the duration of declarative memories learned by adolescents. *Frontiers in Systems Neuroscience*, *8*, 103.

Lent, R., Foguel, D., & Guimarães, M. Z., Botaro, D., Mena-Chalco, J. (2019). Science for Education Network: The Brazilian Proposal. In: *Developing Minds in the Digital Age* (Kuhl, P. K. et al., eds.), Chapter 20, pp. 221–230. OECD Publishing, Paris.

Meltzoff, A. N., Kuhl, P. K., Movellan, J., & Sejnowsky, T. J. (2009). Foundations for a new science of learning. *Science*, *325*, 284–288.

Montague, P. R., Berns, G. S., Cohen, J. D., McClure, S. M., Pagnoni, G., Dhamala, M., Wiest, M. C., Karpov, I., King, R. D., Apple, N., & Fisher, R. E. (2002). Hyperscanning: Simultaneous fMRI during linked social interactions. *Neuroimage*, *16*, 1159–1164.

Poulsen, A. T., Kamronn, S., Dmochowski, J., Parra, L. C., & Hansen, L. K. (2017). EEG in the classroom: Synchronized neural recordings during video presentation. *Scientific Reports*, *7*, 43916.

Probst, M. (1901). Ueber den Blau des balkenlosen Grosshirns, sowie uber Mikrogirie un Heteropie der grauen substanz. *Archiv für Psychiatrie und Nervenkrankheiten*, *34*, 709–786.

Ribeiro, S. (2012). Sleep and plasticity. *Pflugers Archives*, *463*, 111–120.

Ribeiro, S., Mota, N. B., Fernandes, V. R., Deslandes, A. C., Brockington, G., & Copelli, M. (2016). Physiology and assessment as low-hanging fruit for education overhaul. *Prospects UNESCO*, *46*, 249–264.

Rose, S. (1969). *The conscious brain*. Penguin Books, New York.

Saletin, J. M., Goldstein, A. N., & Walker, M. P. (2011). The role of sleep in directed forgetting and remembering of human memories. *Cerebral Cortex*, *21*, 2534–2541.

Saul, R. E., & Sperry, R. W. (1968). Absence of commissurotomy symptoms with agenesis of the corpus callosum. *Neurology*, *18*, 307.

Sigman, M., Peña, M., Goldin, A. P., & Ribeiro, S. (2014). Neuroscience and education: Prime time to build the bridge. *Nature Neuroscience*, *17*, 497–502.

Sperry, R. W. (1968). Plasticity of neural maturation. *Developmental Biology*, (suppl. 2), 306–327.

Sperry, R. W. (1982). Some effects of disconnecting the cerebral hemispheres. Nobel Lecture. *Bioscience Reports*, *2*, 265–276.

Tovar-Moll, F., & Lent, R. (2016). The various forms of neuroplasticity: Biological bases of learning and teaching. *Prospects UNESCO*, *46*, 199–213.

Tovar-Moll, F., Moll, J., Oliveira-Souza, R., Bramati, I. E., Andreiuolo, P. A., & Lent, R. (2007). Neuroplasticity in human callosal dysgenesis: A diffusion tensor imaging study. *Cerebral Cortex*, *17*, 531–541.

Tovar-Moll, F., Monteiro, M., Andrade, J., Bramati, I. E., Vianna-Barbosa, R., Marins, T., Rodrigues, E., Dantas, N., Behrens, T. E. J., Oliveira-Souza, R., Moll, J., & Lent, R. (2014). Structural and functional brain rewiring clarifies preserved interhemispheric transfer in humans born without the corpus callosum. *Proceedings of the National Academy of Sciences of the U.S.A., 111*, 7843–7848.

Tyng, C. M., Amin, H. U, Saad, M. N. M., & Malik, A. S. (2017). The influences of emotion on learning and memory. *Frontiers in Psychology, 8*, 1454.

Wilhelm, I., Diekelmann, S., Molzow, I., Ayoub, A., Mölle, M., & Born, J. (2011). Sleep selectively enhances memory expected to be of future relevance. *Journal of Neuroscience, 31*, 1563–1569.

Yoo, S. S., Hu, P. T., Gujar, N., Jolesz, F. A., & Walker, M. P. (2007). A deficit in the ability to form new human memories without sleep. *Nature Neuroscience, 10*, 385–392.

5
FOREIGN LANGUAGE ANXIETY: TRANSLATING COGNITIVE NEUROSCIENCE TO THE CLASSROOM

Brendan S. Weekes

Introduction

We know that language experience shapes the human brain in fundamental ways. Since ancient times (e.g., Valerius Maximus 14 AD to 37 AD), philosophers have marvelled at the link between damage to the brain and language processing (Benton, 1964. However, advances in brain technology have changed how we view the neurobiology of language processing resulting in a vast range of research studies and theories (Hagoort & Indefrey, 2014), and the emergence of learned societies, and scholarly works (Hickok & Small, 2015). A majority of this research has been concerned with the neurobiological constraints on learning a second language and the neurobiological consequences of bilingualism.

Bilingual and monolingual speakers differ in gray matter volume (GMV) (Abutalebi et al., 2012; Bialystok et al., 2012; Mechelli et al., 2004) and white matter microstructure as measured by diffusion tensor imaging (DTI) reflecting neuroplasticity due to lifelong bilingual language experience (Luk et al., 2011; Singh et al., 2018. Turning to language learning, numerous studies show that GMV can be altered by learning a foreign language. For example, there is an increase in cortical thickness for simultaneous interpretation trainees after completion of a post-graduate degree in conference interpreting (Elmer et al., 2011; Hervais-Adelman et al., 2017; Martensson et al., 2012). Similarly, white-matter tracts change after language training including in the direct pathway connecting the posterior superior temporal gyrus to the anterior part of the inferior frontal gyrus (Hickok & Poeppel, 2004, 2007) as well as an indirect pathway connecting the inferior parietal cortex to the anterior language cortices (Catani, Jones & Ffytche, 2005). Moreover, Hosoda et al. (2013) report that language training produces an increase in structural connectivity between the inferior frontal gyrus and the caudate nucleus and Qi et al. (2015) report that foreign language training (native English speakers learning Mandarin) and increased language proficiency after new learning is associated with changes to white matter structures in studies of native English speakers (see also Schlegel et al., 2012; Zatorre, Fields & Johansen-Berg, 2012). See also *Neuropsychologia* special issue on Language Learning, doi: 10.1016/j.neuropsychologia.2017.01.008.

Scientific knowledge about the cognitive neuroscience of foreign language learning is founded on themes uncovered by studies of the neural representation of language, language acquisition, and language use. Such themes draw on scientific disciplines that reflect the history of cognitive neuroscience including artificial intelligence (AI), computational modelling, information processing, linguistics, neuropsychology, and neuropathology. Much has been learned and many debates have been largely settled in the field over the past 20 years mostly due to integration of advanced methods in brain imaging. The next frontier is to reconcile the neuroscience of language with microstructures in the brain at biochemical and cellular levels.

To date, there is little known about the interaction between neurochemistry and language learning. The purpose of this chapter is to initiate a discussion about how neurobiology constrains second language learning. The initiative owes much to the pioneers of studies of native and second language acquisition (Patricia Kuhl, Janet Werker) that revealed an interplay between neurobiology and language experience focusing first on changes in auditory, visual, and multimodal perception in the first months of life to the developmental trajectory of speech comprehension and production that are constrained by the timing of neuroplasticity, including cortical microcircuits and effective connectivity that is linked to critical periods and epigenesis. For example, work by Werker and Hensch (2015) translates findings from animal models of cortical plasticity using a neurotransmitter called Gamma-aminobutyric acid (GABA: an inhibitory neurotransmitter) by linking GABA to known critical periods for perceptual plasticity of speech sounds and subsequent language development. This is the first attempt to articulate how neurobiology constrains native and non-native language acquisition at a molecular level (see also Woo et al., 2017). The proposal here is that acquisition of a non-native language can be linked to these neurobiological constraints albeit via a little known link connecting anxiety to language acquisition. The conceptual link is founded upon an effect called *foreign language anxiety* (FLA) a well described impediment to learning in environments where the medium of instruction (MoI) is the not native language i.e., English. The new conceptualisation of links between FLA, neurobiology, and science of learning a language seems *prima facie* to be of value.

Foreign language anxiety

Anxiety is generated by arousal of the autonomic nervous system (ANS). It is accompanied by subjective feelings of tension, apprehension, nervousness, and worry. Anxiety can be regarded as both a state and a trait reflecting the long debate around the causal factors of behaviour in clinical psychology (Spielberger, 1972).

FLA and – by extension – second language anxiety (SLA) are defined as the fear or apprehension experienced when a language learner or language user is required to perform in a non-native language situation (state) (Dewaele, Petrides & Furnham, 2008). FLA can also be considered a type of linguistic insecurity that is linked to any situation where the goal of the speaker is to rise within the social scale of the dominant language environment (Labov, 2006; Sevinç, 2017). Models of trait FLA are less developed and most likely depend on a range of (state) factors including exposure to second language use, demands given the sociocultural context (age, gender, status) and predisposition due to life experiences (poverty). It is not known whether FLA when conceptualised as a trait can be distinguished from these state variables.

Models of FLA do however locate effects on behaviour and learning at an individual (psychological) level. For example, cognitive appraisal is assumed to play the function of orienting the self to a potential threat. Communicating in a non-native language in the classroom can induce a threat to self-esteem within power structures triggering physiological effects which have been verified with subjective (self-report) and objective (skin conductance) recordings. In most "state" accounts, FLA is determined by cross-linguistic contact in power structures that are determined socially by variability in age, dialect, gender, student–teacher status, and socioeconomic class (Sevinç, 2017). However, we do know that situation specific FLA is mediated by neurobiological states and these have measurable physiological correlates (Levenson, 2014). For example, FLA is manifest as physical changes via the ANS tremors, rapid heart palpitations, sweaty palms, gastrointestinal discomfort, and blushing that are coordinated by certain parts of the CNS (Croft et al., 2004; Sevinç, 2017).

Studies show that just as monolingual speakers show CNS changes via electrodermal biomarkers such as skin conductance level (SCL) while public speaking (Croft et al., 2004), second language users demonstrate FLA in similar situations but, critically, show more widespread FLA in a range of situations e.g., when examined in a second language (Gregersen, Macintyre & Meza, 2014). Indeed, FLA is reported in classrooms around the world (for Spanish see Arabic, Elmahjoubi, 2011; Chinese, Xiao & Wong, 2014; Coryell & Clark, 2009; Korean, Jee, 2016; Levine, 2003; Odeh, 2014; Tallon, 2009, 2011). Some studies report a negative relationship between FLA and second language achievement although this relationship is definitely not linear (Dewaele, 2007). Reflecting the Yerkes-Dodson (1908) law there is a positive relationship between arousal and performance, but only up to a plateau upon which the relationship becomes negative i.e., there appears to be an inverted U shaped relationship between FLA and performance. Studies with tertiary Hong Kong pupils who are learning in English as the MoI support this conjecture (Weekes, 2018 although this can vary according to pupil gender (see Figures 5.1A and 5.1B).

MacIntyre (2017) systematically reviewed the literature on FLA and proposed classification of the causes and effects of FLA as deriving from academic, cognitive, and social variables. However, causes of FLA are not independent from

66 Brendan S. Weekes

Female Students

R² linear = 0.058

Male Students

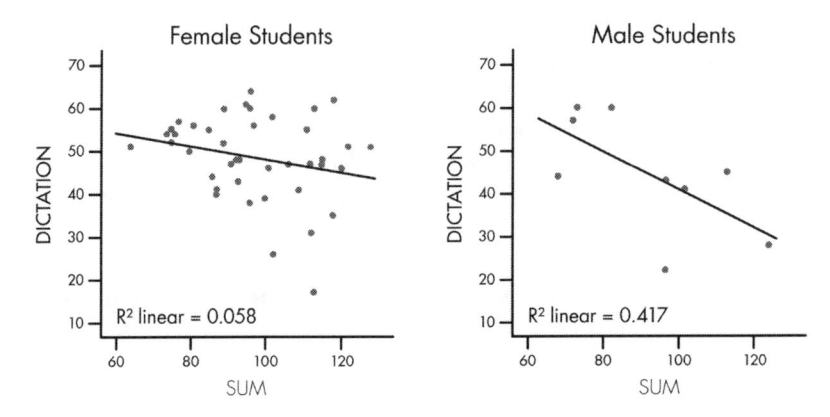

R² linear = 0.417

FIGURE 5.1 Correlation between dictation and FLA in female and male students

one another and similarly the observed responses (anatomical, behavioural, and psychological are not different). For instance, one possible cognitive cause of FLA (e.g., fear of losing a sense of identity) could be linked to social causes that are determined by power structures in the testing environment such as the status of the language in use and the proficiency of the interlocutor (teacher). Such related academic and cognitive causes are also intertwined with socially embedded factors such as gender and status which are in turn linked to embarrassment during social interaction, in classrooms and examinations (Sevinç, 2017). Perhaps unsurprisingly therefore, studies report associations between FLA, age (Dewaele, 2007), gender, education, second language use (Onwuegbuzie et al., 1999), and proficiency (Santos, Cenoz & Gorter, 2015). Although these random variables could be considered "traits," this is not meaningful.

There is substantial evidence to support the hypothesis that FLA has a wide impact on learning using a non-native MoI. Gregerson et al. (2014) reported that students who are not anxious when using a second language nevertheless experience greater FLA in evaluative situations specifically in classroom settings. Classroom settings may raise FLA for a variety of reasons. Lower proficiency could increase frustration in the communication of known concepts and vocabulary (in the native language). Perceived confidence in the use of a second language in scholastic contexts may diminish when the vocabulary is specific to a domain of learning e.g., neuroanatomy (see Weekes, 2018). If errors/negative feedback has consequences for assessment, progression, and qualification (as when learning exclusively via English at the University of Hong Kong), this can have escalating effects on FLA leading to a vicious downward cycle. It is notable that throughout East Asia, English is used as the MoI by *teachers who are not native English speakers*. These endogenous, psychological or "trait" factors need to be positioned within the sociocultural context. MacIntyre and Serroul (2015) call attention to the power relationships in such situations particularly if the interlocutor (teacher) is a native speaker in the MoI (English) but the student is not although this extends to situations within which the interlocutor is a non-native speaker in the MoI. Perceived status in these situations is a critical determinant of FLA regardless of other random variables. Furthermore, when the MoI is the language of achievement within the sociocultural context (as it nearly always is), there is even greater potential for FLA to circumvent new learning across all school subjects. The secondary effects of FLA post-instruction include lower self-confidence, self-esteem, and social participation causing further avoidance of the anxiety-provoking language (Gregersen, 2003). FLA might then diminish proficiency in the second language and contribute to effects on performance, leading to a negative feedback loop linking behavioural avoidance, "competence," mobility and opportunity (see E. Horwitz, Horwitz & Cope, 1986).

Theoretical models of FLA increasingly recognise the multiplicity of variables that can lead to FLA. For example, MacIntyre's Dynamic Approach (2017) argues that FLA should be studied as a complex of the language and socioemotional experiences that link a learner to specific situational circumstances, as well as individual differences in *physiological reaction*, linguistic ability, self-related appraisals, interpersonal relationships, and sociocultural context surrounding the learner and interlocutor (MacIntyre & Serroul, 2015). In this account, FLA is viewed as a self-reflection on language experience including the learner perceptions, situational circumstances, and other intra-individual (random) factors. To test this account, it is useful to use an objective method to separate the subjective experience of FLA from the physiological effects of FLA to achieve a fully explanatory account. Figure 5.2 summarises the factors that potentially

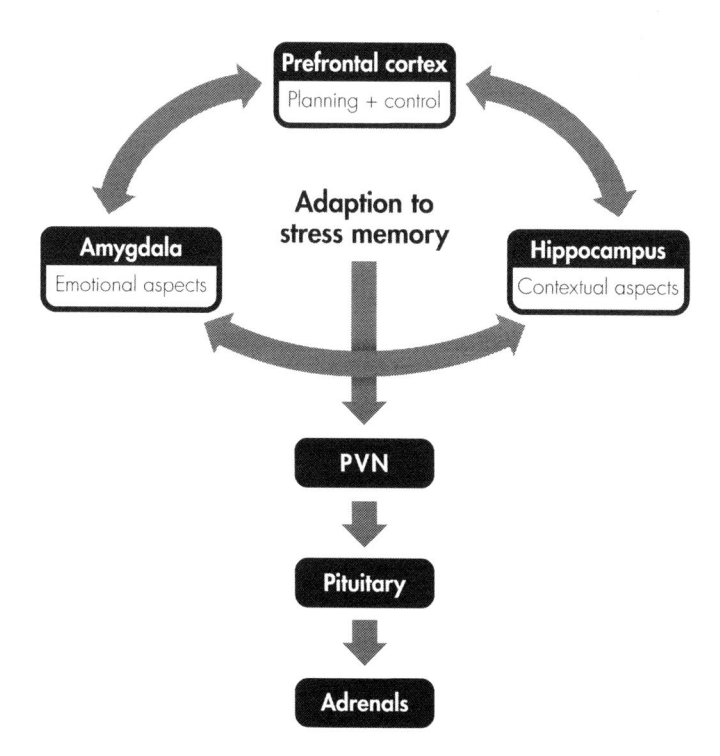

FIGURE 5.2 Model of FLA and new word learning

contribute to FLA when learning new (domain) words acquired in a non-native language. This model has been tested in Hong Kong where students learn vocabulary in a curriculum using a MoI that is non-native.

FLA and the science of learning

An enduring problem in studies of FLA is lack of methodological rigour. The complexity of FLA is reflected in the multiple forms of measurement of emotional states and stress. There are at least three valid methods to measure anxiety: behavioural observation or ratings; physiological assessment such as heart rate or blood pressure; and self-report i.e., feelings and impressions are recorded. FLA is typically measured via self-report in second language classrooms e.g., records in diaries, observed in focus groups and group interviews, recorded in surveys, or third-party observations. However, objective data to validate FLA in these studies has been lacking (de Bot, Lowie & Verspoor, 2007). Dewaele et al. (2008) argue that self-rated perceptions of FLA are too subjective and thus cannot reveal cause and effect of the processes underlying FLA across varying situations. The reasons include circularity of logic when testing models of FLA e.g., if a speaker is anxious about using a second language in a classroom, they may underestimate a number of self-rated factors such as age of acquisition (AoA), frequency of use or proficiency simply due to poorer self-evaluations whereas a less anxious student may overestimate the same variables. Little progress can be made using self-report measures alone.

Early studies of FLA (in the second language classroom) in Hong Kong were all based on self-report and little work had been done on objective markers of FLA in second language classrooms or in classrooms where English is the MoI. Recent work (Weekes, 2018) has pushed the outstanding questions in the field further by introducing science of learning to the study of FLA in the typical classroom at the University of Hong Kong. Furthermore, including reliable biomarkers of FLA has enhanced interpretation of cognitive variables previously known to contribute to learning domain word vocabularies in a non-native language (see Weekes, 2018) and by extension to the effects of FLA (see Figure 5.2). Methodology designed to measure the physiological changes associated with FLA (electrodermal activity, electroencephalogy, salivary cortisol, skin conductance), has been able to validate the experience of FLA with more precision than self-report measures.

Current studies using a physiological measurement of FLA with a wearable device that measures the extent of electrodermal activity are used in Hong Kong classrooms during the learning of written words. Electrodermal activity is widely used in psychophysiology to estimate levels of state anxiety (Dawson, Schell & Filion, 2007). Electrodermal activity is an ideal index of variation in electrical characteristics of the skin (Boucsein, 2012) and wearable devices record skin conductance response (SCR), and SCL. Skin conductance is an indication of psychological and physiological arousal. Skin conductance increases with sweating. The sympathetic branch of ANS controls sweating activity. Skin conductance is therefore a measure of sympathetic nervous system (SNS) responses. Woodrow (2006) reported that SNS activity such as increased heart and perspiration rates, dry mouth, muscle contractions, and sweaty palms increase during observations taken in a second language classroom and also noted behavioural phenomena such as class avoidance, preoccupation on performance of others, not completing assignments on time, and general lack of motivation for learning (Sevinç, 2017). It is apparent from interviews with (non-native speaking) instructors from the University of Hong Kong (Vice-President of Teaching and Learning Amy Tsui, 2016 and focus groups at other institutions that FLA is evident in many classrooms.

According to Gilissen et al. (2007), SCL reflects changes in autonomic arousal associated with emotional reactivity, fear, and stress whereas SCR refers to the specific and faster changing elements of the signal in relation to presented stimuli at a phasic level (Braithwaite et al., 2015). SCR occurs within 1–1.5 seconds following appearance of the stimulus, and may last for 2–6 seconds. In contrast, SCL the phasic component of the electrodermal activity, refers to the specific and faster changing elements of the signal in relation to stimuli presented (Braithwaite et al., 2015). Knight and Borden (1979) report that the anticipation of public speaking led to increased SCL and Bradford, Moore and Baron (1983) suggest SCR reflects a motivational process associated with stress in monolingual speakers, whereas SCL reflects cognitive processing. Geen (1984) also reports more spontaneous SCRs in the presence of an observer than when the participant was alone suggesting a social effect.

Croft et al. (2004) found that SCL correlates with increases in arousal during the anticipation of public speaking for monolingual speakers with a significant decrease upon completion. Conversely, the speech act itself is related to cardiac activity. Such results highlight distinctions between cardiac and measures of electrodermal activity and suggest that they can be measured independently in research on FLA. Sevinç (2017) evaluated FLA using measures of FLA for the first time in bilingual speakers during a video-retelling task. A language background questionnaire recorded information on AoA, proficiency, frequency of language use, and other variables such as level of education. She found that SCLs and SCRs were correlated with FLA self-report. Higher levels of SCL/SCRs were also negatively correlated with proficiency and frequency of use of the heritage language (Turkish). These results confirmed the feasibility of recording physiological biomarkers with self-reports of FLA and were the first evidence of relationships between FLA and autonomic arousal.

Liu et al. (2018) report on the brain mechanism and the neural bases of FLA modulating the process of language production in behavioural experiments and two *f*MRI experiments. Two groups of subjects were selected from 280 undergraduates using the Foreign Language Classroom Anxiety Scale (FLCAS): a high anxious and a low anxious group. Their results show that the high anxious group had a higher heart rate when reading English nouns and verbs. In addition, the ƒMRI activity of the left superior temporal gyrus and left precentral gyrus was greater in the high anxious group than low anxious group. Furthermore, the high anxious group had greater deactivation in the ventral anterior cingulate cortex compared to the low anxious group. There was a linear correlation between FLA scores and deactivation in the ventral anterior cingulate cortex when reading in English but not in reading Chinese and a linear correlation between ƒMRI activation in ventral anterior cingulate cortex, left superior temporal gyrus, and left precentral gyrus when generating an action from a visually presented object in English but not in Chinese. The results also show that the high anxious group has less activity in the ventral striatum than the low anxious group in English verb generation. We suggest that greater activity for high anxious participants in left superior temporal gyrus, right superior frontal gyrus, right middle frontal gyrus, and right cuneus suggests greater demands on the language and attentional networks. A negative correlation between activity in the ventral striatum and this network suggest an interaction between brain areas related with language processing and brain regions related to emotional functions; which indicates FLA is specific type of endogenous anxiety.

Cortisol (CORT) and FLA

Research in neuroscience reveals a negative impact of anxiety in brain circuitry that is related to learning, memory, and executive functions (Vogel & Schwabe, 2016). Animal models show a correlation between new learning (inhibition, navigation, spatial skills) with measures of stress such as cortisol and other biological indices (Tang et al., 2014). Anxiety is also a modifying variable in models of learning and memory at the neurochemical level. Less is known about the contribution of cortisol to language learning and more specifically learning vocabulary when the MoI is a second language. We know anxiety affects memory for new learning (Vogel & Schwabe, 2016) and that the formation of new memories – long-term potentiation (LTP) – is optimal when glucocorticoid levels are elevated (Lupien et al., 2007). Lupien et al. (2007) reported significant decreases in LTP after exogenous glucocorticoid administration (high GC state) and also after adrenalectomy (low GC state). Lupien et al. (2007) also showed that a novel, unpredictable and uncontrollable learning context causes a stress response if it is perceived as self-threatening i.e., given a negative evaluation by a learner. Crucially, relationships are time-dependent, impairing memory retrieval, and the acquisition of information encoded after a stressful event while enhancing new memory formation around the time of a stressful encounter.

We found evidence that the learning of expert words in a neuroanatomy curriculum at the University of Hong Kong (Weekes, 2018) is related to electrodermal activity and self-ratings of FLA. The results show that differences in cognitive (memory) components of executive function and memory for serial order predict acquisition of vocabulary in English. Specifically, inhibition measured with a verbal Stroop task explains a significant amount of variation in new word learning. In this paradigm, Hong Kong students learn new words during the first year of study. All stimuli are late acquired low frequency words so that possible effects of extant vocabulary knowledge on new learning are minimised. Domain words are taken from curricula and form a corpus of 300 words that are unfamiliar to native Cantonese speakers. Knowledge of the words before learning is assessed via a lexical decision task and writing to dictation task. Results show that inhibition, number of hours of study, and individual differences in non-verbal IQ predict new word learning. Female students reported more hours of study than male students consistent with findings from PISA (2003 and 2012) and girls report more anxiety than boys despite better new learning of domain words overall. Using the Horowitz (1986) scale modified for Hong Kong students (Walker, 1997 the results also show female students report higher FLA than male students despite outperforming boys on a test of word knowledge. Such data suggest that (1) late acquisition of domain words is more successful for females than males in Hong Kong and (2) FLA predicts domain word learning in female Hong Kong students when the MoI is English. To validate results, electrodermal activity is measured in the same group and variability across learning trials via electrodermal activity is recorded with a wearable device. Pilot results show that electrodermal activity levels drop towards the end of each trial but electrodermal activity is higher when more words needed to be written. In addition, males are far more variable in electrodermal activity than females. One limitation of the results is that if the participants are aware of the goals of the study, it is possible that demand characteristics influence FLA measurement. Furthermore, status of the teacher (age, gender, native language) has not been manipulated experimentally. Although electrodermal activity has been validated with objective measures of circulating cortisol using mouth swab, there are difficulties recording cortisol reliably in baseline and experimental conditions. This is a limitation as the long-term goal is to link electrodermal activity, FLA and other measures of stress to the neurochemistry of anxiety and learning. Although reasonably successful in animal models, such studies have proven hard to implement in human participants particularly with underage subjects such as secondary school students. Therefore, an additional measure is under development using a more reliable measure of cortisol based on the methodology developed by Tang et al. (2014). This methodology relies on establishing a baseline during the early waking hours, measurements at rest and then also in experimentally controlled situations such as in an examination room, learning environment, or in classrooms with confederates and in vivo instruction.

Next steps in neurobiological modelling of FLA

Animal studies show that new learning and LTP is associated with the hypothalamic-pituitary-adrenal (HPA) axis (Tang et al. 2012, 2014), which is reflected in both the basal and stress-evoked corticosterone (CORT-E) responses. For example, the context of a novelty-induced facilitation (disinhibition) is reflected in a low-basal CORT-E and a high-evoked CORT-E profile (see further discussion below Tang et al. 2011, 2014). In terms of the model in Figure 5.2, the hypotheses are: that FLA as measured by CORT-E, electrodermal activity, and stress report will influence learning of expert words; FLA effects will interact with status in learning. To test these hypotheses, electrodermal activity and CORT-E measures will be used as an objective biomarker of FAS that is validated with subjective ratings. Although we know FLA is associated with learning words in Hong Kong students, the neurobiological mechanisms are unknown. Therefore we plan to identify biomarkers underlying the relationship between FLA, cognition, gender and word learning by adding effects of electrodermal activity and CORT-E into a multivariate model. We expect cortisol measures of FLA to explain additional variance in learning performance that is independent of FLA, language background variables (AoA, proficiency, frequency of use), cognition (IQ, attention, working memory) and electrodermal activity. We also expect these effects will interact with student gender and native language of the instructor. It is expected that electrodermal activity levels will be higher (1) in females than males; (2) if the examiner is male; and (3) if the examiner is a native speaker of English; and (4) highest if the examiner is a male native speaker of English. Students from the University of Hong Kong are recruited at the beginning of first year of study. Measures of electrodermal activity, circulating cortisol, self-reported FLA, language background, cognitive and verbal abilities of students are assessed. Groups of students are then randomly assigned to an oral exam condition to be given at the end of Year 1. Group 1 is tested on the definition of new words with a native English speaking male instructor; Group 2 is tested by a native Cantonese speaker (male instructor); Group 3 is tested by a native English speaking female instructor; and Group 4 by a Cantonese female instructor. Samples of saliva cortisol are taken prior to, during, and after a learning task. We will therefore collect saliva samples independently of the oral exam at two times, at the trough of the cortisol circadian cycle and again shortly after awakening to estimate parameters characterising HPA functions. This innovative approach translates insights from animal research to humans (Tang et al., 2014).

Specifically, we will be obtaining a measure of cortisol regulation at a time separated from tasks wherein situational CORT-E will be sampled. To validate results to spoken language performance, students are asked to complete an oral dictation task. A pretest cortisol measure is collected before sleep and within 5 minutes after the participant wakes by obtaining repeated saliva samples (Tang et al., 2014). Change in cortisol levels are computed by [(post-sleep minus pre-sleep)/pre-sleep]. Electrodermal activity measures are taken during tasks. In Phase 2, done after 12 months, participants are presented with an examination requiring a definition of expert words in English. All other procedures are identical to Phase 1. Task-related changes in cortisol levels are measured before oral exam and 5 minutes after oral exam. Change of task-related cortisol levels are computed using the formula [(during-task minus pre-task)/pre-task]. Electrodermal activity measures are taken during the examination. A Biopac system with a module for skin conductance and cardiovascular activity (PPG100C) is also used (Sevinç, 2017). During all phases, self-report levels of FLA are tested with a 5-point Likert scale (Sevinç, 2017).

Following Sevinç (2017), the analysis of electrodermal activity data is performed with AcqKnowledge 4.1 software. First, data is cleaned, as movements can alter electrodermal activity signals. For the SCL, the background tonic electrodermal activity can differ between individuals. Therefore a relative value is derived to test for changes in SCL during experimental manipulations. The SCL signal contains SCRs, which elevate the measure (Boucsein, 2012). Therefore, the amplitudes of SCRs will be subtracted from the tonic signal (SCL) to establish a reliable measure of background SCL. A change in mean SCL scores is calculated relative to the mean baseline for each phase for each individual. To test the predictions, comparisons are made between gender and the native language of the instructor. The mean amplitude and frequency of SCL and SCR in native and non-native modes is subtracted from each first and then from the male and female interlocutors. After subtractions, higher SCL and SCR values are considered to signify tonic and phasic levels of secretion (Dawson et al., 2007). In addition to Biopac, a wearable device is used to record electrodermal activity (Figure 5.2). The Empatica E4 wristband records and uploads electrodermal activity, GSR, Blood Volume Pulse, Acceleration, Heart Rate and Temperature on a secure platform and shows real-time physiological data acquisition and software for later analysis and visualisation https://www.empatica.com/en-eu/research/e4/. A measure of basal CORT (CORTB) (Tang et al., 2012) is also used. Tang et al., (2012) defines CORTB as a sample obtained in an undisturbed state. Participants are awakened at a predetermined time with a reminder to collect a sample from the bed without rising. Participants carry out their normal daily routine. CORTS is a stress-evoked measure that captures the rising phase of the CORT response to measure one's ability to mount a rise in response to the start of the daily activity. CORTS is defined as the percentage of CORT increase relative to CORTB within 5 and 15 min of waking and rising from the bed. An evoked CORT response, CORT-E, is defined as the difference between CORTS and CORTB normalised by CORTB CORT-E = (CORTS minus CORTB)/CORTB × 100. Both samples will be brought to the lab for further processing on the morning of the testing session. CORT-E is a measure of trait as opposed to a state cortisol as it reflects the ability of a participant to regulate the level of circulating stress hormone.

Towards a neurobiological model of FLA

A connection between hippocampal activity and language learning has been long established. Opitz and Friederici (2003) proposed the hippocampal system and the prefrontal cortex as the neural mechanism underlying grammar learning. Mårtensson et al. (2012) showed that adult foreign-language acquisition drives increases in cortical thickness and hippocampal volume of novice interpreters

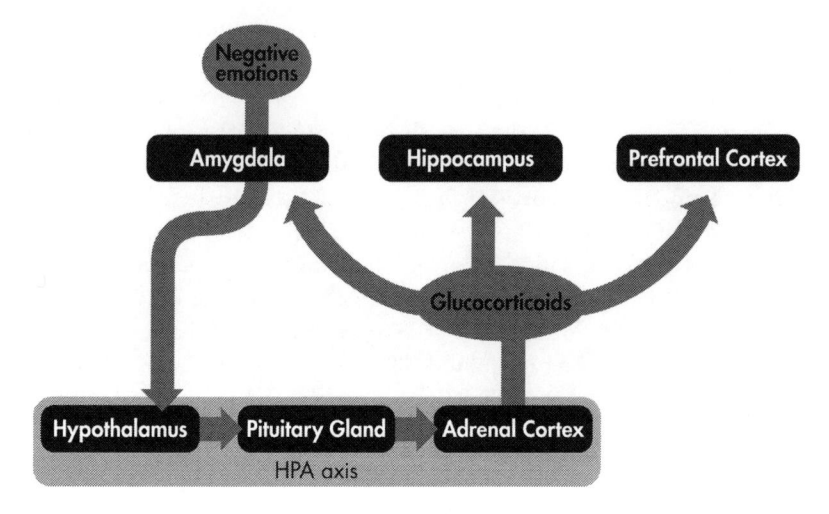

FIGURE 5.3 The hypothalamic pituitary adrenal (HPA) axis and FLA

before and after three months of intense language studies. Results revealed an increase in hippocampus volume and in cortical thickness of the left middle frontal gyrus, inferior frontal gyrus, and superior temporal gyrus for interpreters relative to multilingual controls. Such findings show that changes to the hippocampus reflect foreign-language acquisition. It is not clear however what neurochemical changes explain these changes. One hypothesis is that the HPA axis mediates language learning which is reflected in the basal and stress-evoked corticosterone (CORT-E) responses (Tang et al., 2014). Testing this hypothesis offers a novel way to bridge education, gender, learning, mental health, neurobiology, and wellbeing. A short-term goal is to extend models of expert word learning (Figure 5.3) to the neurobiological level when MoI is a non-native language thus creating considerable anxiety and stress in the classroom. In the long term, this neurobiological model could be translated into anxiety reduction techniques to enhance learning in second language classrooms particularly not exclusively when MoI is a non-native language.

References

Abutalebi, J., Della Rosa, P., Green, D., Hernandez, M., Scifo, P., Keim, R., Cappa, S., & Costa, A. (2012). Bilingualism Tunes the Anterior Cingulate Cortex for Conflict Monitoring. *Cerebral Cortex*, 22(9), 2076–2086.
Benton, A. L. (1964). Contributions to aphasia before Broca. *Cortex*, 1, 314–327.
Boucsein, W. (2012). *Electrodermal activity* (2nd ed.). New York, NY: Springer, Nature.
Bialystok, E., Craik, F., & Luk, G. (2012). Bilingualism: Consequences for Mind and Brain. *Trends in Cognitive Sciences*, 16(4) 240–250.
Braithwaite, J., Watson, D. G., Jones, R., & Rowe, M. (2015). *A guide for analyzing electrodermal activity (eda) and skin conductance responses (scrs) for psychological experiments*. Technical Report: Behavioural Brain Centre, UK: University of Birmingham.

Catani, M., Jones, D. K., & Ffytche, D. H. (2005). Perisylvian language networks of the human brain. *Annals of Neurology*, *57*(1), 8–16.

Croft, R. J., Gonsalvez, C. J., Gander, J., Lechem, L., & Barry, R. J. (2004). Differential relations between heart rate and skin conductance, and public speaking anxiety. *Journal of Behavior Therapy and Experimental Psychiatry*, *35*, 259–271.

Coryell, J. E., & Clark, M. C. (2009). One right way, intercultural participation, and language learning anxiety: A qualitative analysis of adult online heritage and non-heritage language learners. *Foreign Language Annals*, *42*, 483–504.

Dawson, M. E., Schell, A. M., & Filion, D. L. (2007). The electrodermal system. In J. T. Cacioppo, L. G. Tassinary, & G. G. Berntson (Eds.), *Handbook of psychophysiology* (3rd ed., pp. 159–181). New York, NY: Cambridge University Press.

De Bot, K., Lowie, W., & Verspoor, M. (2007). A dynamic systems theory approach to second language acquisition. *Bilingualism: Language and Cognition*, *10*(1), 7–21.

Dewaele, J-M. (2007). The effect of multilingualism and socio-situational factors on communicative anxiety and foreign language anxiety of mature language learners. *International Journal of Bilingualism*, *11*(4), 391–410.

Dewaele, J-M., Petrides, K. V., & Furnham, A. (2008). Effects of trait emotional intelligence and socio-biographical variables on FLA among adult multilinguals: A review and empirical investigation. *Language Learning*, *58*, 911–960.

Elmahjoubi, M. A. (2011). *The effect of mixing heritage and non-heritage students of Arabic on anxiety and attitude*. (Unpublished thesis). William Paterson University of New Jersey.

Elmer, S., Hanggi, J., Meyer, M., & Jancke, L. (2011). Differential language expertise related to white matter in regions subserving sensory-motor coupling, articulation, and interhemispheric transfer. *Human Brain Mapping*, *32*(12), 2064–2074. https://doi.org/10.1002/hbm.21169.

Geen, R. (1984). Preferred stimulation levels in introverts and extroverts: Effects on arousal and performance. *Journal of Personality and Social Psychology*, *46*(6), 1303–1312.

Gilissen R., Koolstra C. M., van Ijzendoorn M. H., Bakermans-Kranenburg M. J., & van der Veer R. (2007). Physiological reactions of preschoolers to fear-inducing film clips: Effects of temperamental fearfulness and quality of the parent-child relationship. *Developmental Psychobiology*, *49*(2), 187–195.

Gregersen, T., Macintyre, P. D., & Meza, M. D. (2014). The motion of emotion: Idiodynamic studies of learners' foreign language anxiety. *The Modern Language Journal*, *98*, 574–588.

Gregersen, T. (2003). To err is human: A reminder to teachers of language-anxious students. *Foreign Language Annals*, *36*(1), 25–32.

Groff, B. D., Baron, R. S., & Moore, D. L. (1983). Distraction, attentional conflict, and drive-like behavior. *Journal of Experimental Social Psychology*, *19*(4), 359–380.

Hagoort, P. & Indefrey. P. (2014). The neurobiology of language beyond single words. *Annual Review of Neuroscience*, *37*(1), 347–362.

Hervais-Adelman, A., Moser-Mercer, B., Murray, Micah, & Golestani, N. (2017). Cortical thickness increases after simultaneous interpretation training. *Neuropsychologia*, *98*, 212–219.

Hickok, G., & Poeppel, D. (2004). Dorsal and ventral streams: a framework for understanding aspects of the functional anatomy of language. *Cognition*, *92*(1-2), 67–99.

Hickok, G., & Poeppel, D. (2007). The cortical organization of speech processing. *Nature Review of Neuroscience*, *8*, 393–402.

Hickok, G. & Small, S. (Eds.). (2015). Neurobiology of Language. *Academic press*.

Horwitz, E., Horwitz, M., & Cope, J. (1986). Foreign language classroom anxiety. *The Modern Language Journal*, *70*, 125–132.

Hosoda, C., Tanaka, K., Nariai, T., Honda, M., & Hanakawa, T. (2013). Dynamic neural network reorganization associated with second language vocabulary acquisition: A multimodal imaging study. *Journal of Neuroscience, 33*(34), 13663–13672.

Jee, M. J. (2016). Exploring Korean heritage language learners' anxiety: "We are not afraid of Korean!." *Journal of Multilingual and Multicultural Development, 37*, 56–74.

Knight, M. L., & Borden, R. J. (1979). Autonomic and affective reactions of high and low socially-anxious individuals awaiting public performance. *Psychophysiology*, 16(3), 209–21.

Labov, W. (2006). *The social stratification of English in New York* (2nd ed.). Cambridge: University of Cambridge Press.

Levenson, R. W. (2014). The Autonomic Nervous System and Emotion. *Emotion Review*, 6(2), 100–112.

Levine, G. S. (2003). Student and instructor beliefs and attitudes about target language use, first language use, and anxiety: Report of a questionnaire study. *The Modern Language Journal, 87*(3), 343–364.

Liu, C-H., Peng, D-L., Yang, Y-H., & Weekes, B. (2018). English learning anxiety: An EDA and functional MRI study. *Proceedings of the 1st cognitive neuroscience of second and artificial language learning conference*. Bangor, UK: Bangor University.

Luk, G., Bialystok, E., Craik, F. I. M., & Grady, C. L. (2011). Lifelong bilingualism maintains white matter integrity. *Journal of Neuroscience, 31*(46), 16808–16813.

Lupien, S. J., Maheu, F., Tu, M., Fiocco, A., & Schramek, T. E. (2007). The effects of stress and stress hormones on human cognition: Implications for the field of brain and cognition. *Brain and Cognition, 65*(3), 209–237.

MacIntyre, P. D. (2017). An overview of language anxiety research and trends in its development. In C. Gkonou, M. Daubney, & J.-M. Dewaele (Eds.), *New insights into language anxiety: Theory, research and educational implications* (pp. 11–30). Bristol: Multilingual Matters.

MacIntyre, P. D., & Serroul, A. (2015). Motivation per-second timescale: Examining approach-avoidance motivation during L2 task performance. In Z. Dörnyei, P. D. MacIntyre, & A. Henry (Eds.), *Motivational dynamics in language learning* (pp. 109–138). Bristol: Multilingual Matters.

Mårtensson, J., Eriksson, J., Bodammer, N. C., Lindgren, M., Johansson, M., Nyberg, L., & Lovden, M. (2012). Growth of language-related brain areas after foreign language learning. *NeuroImage, 63*(1), 240–244. http://dx.doi.org/10.1016/j.neuroimage.2012.06.043.

Mechelli, A., Crinion, J. T., Noppeney, U., Doherty, J. O., Ashburner, J., Frackowiak, R. S., & Price, C. J. (2004). Structural plasticity in the bilingual brain. *Nature, 431*, 757.

Odeh, W. (2014). *Foreign Language Anxiety and foreign language enjoyment: A study of Arabic Heritage and non-heritage language learners*. (Unpublished MA Thesis). Birkbeck, London.

Onwuegbuzie, A. J., Bailey, P., & Daley, C. E. (1999). Relationships between Anxiety and Achievement at Three Stages of Learning a Foreign Language. *Perceptual and Motor Skills, 88*(3_suppl), 1085–1093.

Opitz, B. & Friederici, A. (2003). Interactions of the hippocampal system and the prefrontal cortex in learning language-like rules. *NeuroImage, 19*(4), 1730–1737.

Qi, Z., Han, M., Garel, K., San, E., & Gabrieli, J. D. E. (2015). White-matter structure in the right hemisphere predicts mandarin Chinese learning success. *Journal of Neurolinguistics, 33*, 14–28. https://doi.org/10.1016/j.jneuroling.2014.08.004.

Santos, A., Cenoz, J., & Gorter, D. (2015). Communicative anxiety in English as a third language. *International Journal of Bilingual Education and Bilingualism, 20*(7), 823–836.

Schlegel, A. A., Rudelson, J. J., & Tse, P. U. (2012). White matter structure changes as adults learn a second language. *Journal of Cognitive Neuroscience, 24*(8), 1664–1670.

Sevinç, Y. (2017). Language anxiety in the immigrant context: Sweaty palms? *International Journal of Bilingualism*. https://doi.org/10.1177/1367006917690914.

Singh, N. C., Rajan, A., Malagi, A., Ramanujan, K., Canini, M., Della Rosa, P. A., Raghunathan, P., Weekes, B. S., & Abutalebi J. A. (2018). Microstructural anatomical differences between bilinguals and monolinguals. *Bilingualism: Language and Cognition, 21*(5), 995–1008.

Spielberger, C. D. (1972). Anxiety as an emotional state. In C. D. Spielberger (Ed.), *Anxiety: Current trends in theory and research* (pp. 23–49). New York, NY: Academic Press.

Strauss, A., & Corbin, J. (1990). *Basics of qualitative research*. Newbury Park, CA: Sage.

Tallon, M. (2009). Foreign language anxiety and heritage students of Spanish: A quantitative study. *Foreign Language Annals, 42,* 112–137.

Tallon, M. (2011). Heritage speakers of Spanish and foreign language anxiety: A pilot study. *Texas Papers in Foreign Language Education, 15,* 70–87.

Tang, A. C., Reeb-Sutherland, B., Romeo, R. D., & McEwen, B. S. (2012). Reducing behavioral inhibition via systematic novelty exposure: The influence of maternal hypothalamic-pituitary-adrenal regulation. *Biological Psychiatry, 72*(2), 150–156.

Tang, A. C., Reeb-Sutherland, B. C., Romeo, R. D., & McEwen, B. S. (2014). On the causes of early life experience effects: Evaluating the role of mom. *Frontiers of Neuroendocrinology, 35*(2), 245–251. doi: 10.1016/j.yfrne.2013.11.002.

Tang, A. C., Reeb-Sutherland, B. C., Yang, Z., Romeo, R. D., & McEwen, B. S. (2011). Neonatal novelty-induced persistent enhancement in offspring spatial memory and modulatory role of maternal self-stress regulation. *Journal of Neuroscience, 31*(14), 5348–5352.

Tsui, A. M. B. (2016). *Personal communication with vice president*. Pokfulam, Hong Kong. University of Hong Kong.

Vogel, S., & Schwabe, L. (2016). Learning and memory under stress: Implications for the classroom. *Npj Science of Learning, 1.* doi:10.1038/npjscilearn.2016.11.

Walker, E. A. (1997). *FLA in Hong Kong Secondary Schools: Relationship with age-related Factors, school form and self-perception*. PhD thesis, University of Hong Kong.

Weekes, B. S. (2018). Learning written word vocabulary in a second language: Theoretical and practical implications. *Bilingualism: Language and cognition, 21*(3), 585–597.

Werker, J., & Hensch, T. (2015). Critical periods in speech perception: new directions. *Annual Review of Psychology, 66,* 173–196.

Woo, J., Kim, J. E., Im, J. J., Lee, J., Jeong, H. S., Park, S., ... & Lee, S. (2017). Astrocytic water channel aquaporin-4 modulates brain plasticity in both mice and humans: A potential gliogenetic mechanism underlying language-associated learning. *Molecular Psychiatry*. doi:10.1038/mp.2017.113.

Woodrow, L. (2006). Anxiety and speaking English as a second language. *RELC Journal, 37,* 308–328.

Xiao, Y., & Wong, K. F. (2014). Exploring heritage language anxiety: A study of Chinese heritage language learners. *The Modern Language Journal, 98*(2), 589–611.

Yerkes, R. M. & Dodson, J. D. (1908). The relation of strength stimulus to rapidity of habit-formation. *Journal of Comparative Neurology and Psychology. 18*(5), 459-482.

Zatorre, R. J., Fields, R. D., & Johansen-Berg, H. (2012). Plasticity in gray and white matter: Changes in brain structure in learning. *Nature, 15*(4), 528–536. https://doi.org/10.1038/nn.3045.

6
ADDRESSING MATHEMATICS ANXIETY IN PRIMARY TEACHING

Sarah Buckley, Kate Reid, Ottmar V. Lipp, Merrilyn Goos, Narelle Bethune and Sue Thomson

Introduction

Student learning in mathematics can be compromised by mathematics anxiety (MA). MA also impedes teachers' learning and may in turn impact on the effectiveness of their mathematics teaching. Primary teachers, in particular, report high levels of MA (Hembree, 1990; Philipp, 2007), which is concerning as research shows higher MA in teachers is associated with a reliance on traditional teaching methods, a focus on teaching basic skills and lower mathematics teaching confidence (Gresham, 2018). Research has also found that female primary teachers who are more mathematically anxious are more likely to have female students who learn less over a school year (Beilock, Gunderson, Ramirez, & Levine, 2010). Many researchers emphasise that MA should not be considered as simply the consequence of having poor skills in mathematics (Beilock & Willingham, 2014; Buckley, Reid, Goos, Lipp, & Thomson, 2016). Multiple factors can cause MA to develop and reducing MA will improve an individual's capacity to learn and/or teach in mathematics.

Research from education, psychology, and neuroscience can be used to identify how MA develops, the mechanisms that lead MA to negatively influence teaching and learning, and strategies for reducing these negative effects. In this chapter, we will discuss the following:

1. Our psychological approach to addressing MA and how it can complement educational approaches;
2. Our multidisciplinary research framework for MA that underpins our approach, including a summary of relevant findings from psychology, education, and neuroscience; and,

3. Our previous research and how it has informed our current work developing a professional learning program designed to address MA in primary teachers and to provide them with the skills to alleviate MA among students.

We aim to demonstrate to educators and policymakers the value of our research framework and approach to understanding MA, and how they can be used in educational practice to benefit teaching and learning in mathematics. Furthermore, we propose that our approach can complement others, particularly those designed to build primary teachers' mathematics content and pedagogical content knowledge.

A psychological approach to addressing mathematics anxiety

Many educational interventions designed to alleviate MA focus on improving teachers' mathematics content knowledge, particularly during pre-service teacher education. The rationale for this approach is that improved mathematics content knowledge will increase confidence and thereby decrease MA (Raynor, Pitsolantis, & Osana, 2009). There is evidence that, on average, levels of MA decrease among pre-service teachers after they take a mathematics methods course (Harper & Daane, 1998; Sloan, 2010). The increase in conceptual understanding of mathematics, often taught through the use of manipulatives, appears to be beneficial in reducing MA (Sloan, 2010). As a result, pre-service teachers report that they are more confident in their ability to teach mathematics and have more positive attitudes towards mathematics (Bursal & Paznokas, 2006; Sloan, 2010). However, these effects may not persist given that practising teachers can report high levels of MA (Beilock et al., 2010). Undertaking mathematics content knowledge training also may not address all teachers' MA. Some pre-service teachers show an increase in MA after undertaking education training courses (Harper & Daane, 1998).

Fundamental to our approach is the proposal that MA must be addressed directly, concurrent with or prior to content knowledge interventions, to manage the causes and effects of MA. Dealing with MA directly is also necessary because one of the most significant consequences of MA is avoidance (Devine, Fawcett, Szűcs, & Dowker, 2012). Primary teachers with MA who also need content knowledge support may avoid experiences that could improve their mathematics skills, such as professional learning, investigating mathematics resources or by seeking assistance from colleagues. After addressing MA directly and removing it as a barrier, the effects of professional learning designed to build mathematics content and pedagogical content knowledge can be maximised. Teachers who experience MA but have good content knowledge are also likely to benefit from direct support to address MA.

Recent reviews (Beilock, Schaeffer, & Rozek, 2017; Buckley et al., 2016; Maloney, Schaeffer, & Beilock, 2013; Ramirez, Shaw, & Maloney, 2018) have emphasised a psychological approach to dealing with MA. These reviews highlight research showing that psychological strategies can reduce the negative effects of MA. Research in this area has typically used small-scale studies with participants who are not teachers (e.g., Brunyé et al., 2013) and assessed only one or two strategies (e.g., Zettle, 2003). However, the insights from this work are compelling and suggest that a psychological approach with teachers and students could be effective.

Our approach to addressing MA is based on recognising the existence of two different types – state and trait MA (Buckley et al., 2016). This allows for (a) a better understanding of how MA impacts on teaching and learning and (b) clearer identification of multiple psychological strategies for reducing MA. State MA is the type of anxiety that is felt "in the moment," when mathematical information is in the individual's immediate environment. For instance, state MA may be experienced by a student completing a mathematics test or doing mathematics homework, or by a teacher preparing or presenting a mathematics lesson, or by someone calculating how much they need to contribute to a split bill at a restaurant. In comparison, trait MA represents an enduring tendency to become anxious and worry about mathematics that an individual is subject to every day. It relates to how threatening an individual perceives mathematics to be. As an example, imagine there are two students in a class, Student A and Student B. While Student A experiences high levels of state MA when she completes a mathematics test or when she has to answer mathematics questions in front of her classmates, she doesn't experience state MA in any other context. On the other hand, Student B experiences high levels of state MA when he completes a mathematics test or answers mathematics questions in front of classmates and state MA when he has to learn something new in mathematics or while he is completing his mathematics homework. So while Student A and B both experience state MA, Student B has a greater tendency to feel it in situations that involve mathematics and therefore has higher levels of trait MA. Someone with very high levels of trait MA could even experience anxiety when mathematics is not part of their immediate environment. We differentiate state and trait MA because each type impacts learning differently, and each should be addressed separately. For instance, Student A and Student B could learn and practice similar strategies to help reduce their state MA; however, Student B would also learn and practice additional strategies to target his trait MA and to assist him to perceive mathematics as less threatening.

A multidisciplinary research framework for mathematics anxiety

We propose that addressing MA should include strategies designed to increase individuals' capacities to control their thoughts and actions during teaching or when performing mathematics tasks (to reduce state MA), as well as challenging and changing their self-beliefs that they have low control in mathematics (to reduce trait MA). This proposal is based on an understanding of MA that follows the control-value theory of achievement emotions (Pekrun, 2006). According to this theory, emotions experienced during learning are the product of value and control appraisals. Value appraisals relate to how enjoyable, how useful or how important something is perceived to be whereas control appraisals relate to judgements about competence and confidence and how much control individuals feel they can exert in a situation (Frenzel, Pekrun, & Goetz 2007). MA is a product of a particular pattern of these two learning appraisals – higher levels of perceived value (most likely valuing the usefulness and/or importance of mathematics for career or job opportunities) combined with lower levels of perceived control (feeling that mathematics skills or ability are fixed, determined by factors such as genetics and gender, and thereby not feeling confident). Research has demonstrated that the combination of high value and low control appraisals is evident in individuals who experience MA (Frenzel, Pekrun, & Goetz, 2007; Lauermann, Eccles, & Pekrun, 2017).

Our framework for understanding MA is supported by research from psychology, education and neuroscience that highlights how control issues underlie the experience of state and trait MA in teaching and learning (Buckley et al., 2016). A summary of research across the three research areas will be presented along with examples of psychological strategies for reducing MA.

How does state mathematics anxiety impact on teaching and learning?

State MA is characterised by both physiological responses (emotionality) and cognitive or mental processes (worry). Emotionality involves physiological reactions such as increased heart and breathing rates, while worry involves intrusive negative thoughts (e.g., I am never going to understand algebra), which have the potential to disrupt task focus (Hembree, 1990; Ho et al., 2000; Lauermann, Eccles, & Pekrun, 2017). Together these aspects of state MA can impact task performance and undermine a teachers' or students' capacities to access and control their mathematics knowledge and skills effectively (Buckley et al., 2016; Maloney, Sattizahn, & Beilock, 2014).

Research in neuroscience and cognitive psychology has illustrated how MA impacts on performance, in particular, by interfering with executive functions. Executive functions are used to monitor and control thinking, emotions and actions, and include three core domains: inhibition control, working memory, and cognitive flexibility (Clements, Sarama, & Germeroth, 2016). Inhibition control involves paying specific attention to one thing and ignoring something else as well as the ability to control or regulate thoughts and emotions (Diamond, 2013). Research has demonstrated that individuals who experience high levels of MA show poorer performance on mathematics tasks and have trouble inhibiting or ignoring task irrelevant information (Beilock, Kulp, Holt, & Carr, 2004; Suárez-Pellicioni, Núñez-Peña, & Colomé, 2013; Suárez-Pellicioni,

Núñez-Peña, & Colomé, 2014). A study also found that 7-to 9-year-old children with higher MA were more likely to exhibit patterns of brain activation associated with a reduced capacity to regulate emotion (e.g., worry), suggesting that these children may have had access to fewer cognitive or mental resources to control their anxiety (Young, Wu, & Menon, 2012).

Researchers believe that difficulties regulating or controlling the worry component of state MA relate to the negative influence of anxiety on working memory (e.g., Ashcraft & Kirk, 2001; Hopko, McNeil, Gleason, & Rabalais, 2002). Working memory is an executive function that allows us to retain and manipulate information; however, these processes can become monopolised by the negative thoughts characteristic of worry (Beilock, Schaeffer, & Rozek, 2017; Dowker, Sarkar, & Looi, 2016). In other words, in an individual with MA, working memory resources are consumed by ruminating on anxiety rather than by performing the mathematics task, which can result in poorer mathematics performance (Ashcraft & Ridley, 2005). Working memory overload may occur when trying to undertake a mathematics task while experiencing intense worry, and could explain the experience of "blanking" or "freezing" that is often reported in test situations by those with MA. This phenomenon could also underlie findings that teachers with high MA can be less effective at teaching mathematics (Gresham, 2018). It may be that intense worry experienced in the act of teaching mathematics results in less capacity to draw on existing knowledge or to flexibly respond to student queries.

Part of our approach to addressing MA involves raising awareness of how state MA impacts executive functioning thereby reducing an individual's control over their mathematics performance. We believe that increasing understanding of these processes is important for those who are mathematically anxious as the first step towards addressing the negative effects of MA in the classroom for teachers and students.

What strategies can target state mathematics anxiety?

Distinguishing between the emotionality and worry components of state MA allows us to suggest specific strategies for addressing the physiological effects of anxiety (emotionality) and the negative thoughts that arise when undertaking a mathematics task (worry). We will describe several strategies that research has shown are effective in dealing with anxiety generally and with MA specifically. These strategies are easy to learn, practise, and integrate into everyday activities. The strategies are suitable for teachers and could be easily adapted for students. Introducing teachers to a range of strategies is important for two reasons. First, individuals may prefer one strategy over another, or elect to engage with particular strategies under different circumstances. Second, it is possible that individuals may gain the most benefit from practising a range of strategies.

The physiological component of state MA automatically prepares the individual to deal with a perceived threat by, for instance, increasing heart and breathing rate to prepare the body to either stand and fight, or run away from danger. Physiological responses characteristic of high state MA produce negative emotions and may decrease task performance (Jamieson, Mendes, Blackstock, & Schmader, 2010; Mattarella-Micke, Mateo, Kozak, Foster, & Beilock, 2011). A simple strategy to counteract the effects of high physiological arousal is deep breathing relaxation, also known as diaphragmatic breathing. Under stress, breathing may become shallow and more rapid, which increases physiological arousal and anxious feelings (Hazlett-Stevens, 2008). Breathing from the diaphragm is slower, deeper and does not rely on the chest muscles. Breathing in this way promotes muscle relaxation, slows the heartbeat, and counters the physiological arousal components of state MA. Deep breathing could also be combined with a muscle relaxation strategy, which has been used extensively to address the physiological effects of anxiety (Manzoni, Pagnini, Castelnuovo, & Molinari, 2008). These techniques rely on slowly and systematically tensing and relaxing different muscle groups and are based on the idea that muscle tension is associated with anxious feelings. Learning to identify feelings of muscle tension and to deliberately relax allows the individual to exert more control in anxiety-provoking situations (Hazlett-Stevens, 2008). Muscle relaxation combined with progressive desensitisation has also shown benefits in addressing MA (Wadlington, Austin, & Bitner, 1992). The desensitisation component of this strategy involves visualising mathematics situations that elicit anxiety while practising muscle relaxation. Because it is not possible to be both relaxed and fearful, the individual learns through practising this strategy to relax in situations that would normally elicit MA.

The worry component of state MA can be addressed through positive reframing and mindfulness. Positive reframing involves making deliberate efforts to reinterpret a negative situation or emotion by taking a positive perspective. One study found that university students with high MA could be separated into those that did and did not perform well on a mathematics task, and that these two groups of students differed in their pattern of brain activation before the mathematics task began. High MA students that performed better on the mathematics task had greater activation in an area of the brain associated with mentally coordinating thoughts and actions (cognitive control) and controlling the impact of negative emotions (Lyons & Beilock, 2012). These researchers suggested that high MA individuals with better performance could access cognitive control resources before the task that allowed them to positively reframe how they would approach the task. Reframing anxiety as a performance facilitator can also be beneficial. Another study found that when students were reminded that some anxiety could increase performance outcomes, they had higher achievement on a mathematics test compared with a control group who were not given this instruction (Jamieson et al., 2010).

A further strategy to address state MA involves simple mindfulness exercises that encourage mathematically anxious individuals to maintain focussed attention on their breathing, to recognise and acknowledge distractions (such as worries) without judgement and to shift attention back to mindful breathing. The practice of mindfulness has been associated with increased attention, faster responses, elevated mood, and decreased stress (Tang et al., 2007; Zeidan, Johnson, Diamond, David, & Goolkasian, 2010). Mindfulness practise among individuals with high MA has been shown to decrease anxiety and increase performance (Brunyé et al., 2013). Mindfulness addresses the worries that are part of state MA through increasing cognitive control and increasing cognitive resources to focus on mathematics tasks.

How does trait mathematics anxiety develop and impact on learning and teaching?

In contrast to the on-task fear associated with state MA in the moment, trait MA is an enduring characteristic associated with negative attitudes towards mathematics and a tendency to be fearful of mathematics. Individuals with trait MA often avoid situations involving mathematics that could elicit state MA. Trait and state MA are thus closely related. It is possible for trait MA to increase for some individuals if they experience repeated state MA and their general fear of mathematics becomes greater.

State and trait MA either lead to or originate from control issues related to mathematics. Our framework proposes that trait MA evolves from an individual's core beliefs about mathematics (Buckley et al., 2016), specifically beliefs about control over mathematics performance and learning. According to the control-value theory, several factors may influence the development of mathematics control beliefs including judgements about competence or confidence and how much control an individual feels they can exert over their mathematics performance (Frenzel, Pekrun, & Goetz, 2007). Experiences of struggling with mathematics may lead to the development of trait MA by impacting on control beliefs. For example, repeated mathematics difficulties may lead individuals to believe that they cannot improve their mathematics skills, which in turn could be a predisposition for MA (Beilock, Schaeffer, & Rozek, 2017; Dowker, Sarkar, & Looi, 2016; Gunderson, Park, Maloney, Beilock, & Levine, 2018). Several researchers have proposed that individuals who have difficulties with mathematics from an early age are also more prone to negative perceptions of mathematics and may be more influenced by the negative attitudes of others (e.g., peers or teachers) (Maloney & Beilock, 2012).

Other factors that contribute to control beliefs about mathematics include the attitudes of parents and teachers and more pervasive societal gender stereotypes. Children's mathematics competence beliefs and their career choices are shaped by parents' perceptions, particularly those of their mothers (Bleeker & Jacobs, 2004; Jacobs, 1991; Tomasetto, Alparone, & Cadinu, 2011). One study found that children in first and second grade whose parents were more mathematically anxious, tended to record lower mathematics achievement than their peers throughout the school year, but only if their mathematically anxious parents often helped them with their mathematics homework (Maloney, Ramirez, Gunderson, Levine, & Beilock, 2015). In other words, parents may transmit their MA, or their low control beliefs about mathematics that form the basis of MA, when doing homework with their children, which in turn may impact their children's mathematics achievement at school. Another study focusing on the impact of teachers found that first and second grade girls demonstrated less mathematical growth over a year of schooling and were more likely to support negative mathematics gender stereotypes (e.g., girls aren't good at mathematics) if their female teacher had higher levels of MA (Beilock et al., 2010). This study illustrates that teachers' behaviour can significantly influence the development of negative beliefs about mathematics among students. Findings such as these support the importance of addressing MA in primary teachers.

There are many pervasive negative stereotypes about girls and mathematics (e.g., girls do not do as well at mathematics as boys). Research has shown that girls report higher levels of MA than boys (Devine et al., 2012; Hill et al., 2016; Thomson, DeBortoli, & Buckley, 2014). Some researchers propose that gender stereotypes about mathematics may make girls more susceptible to experiencing MA and more likely to develop low control beliefs about mathematics (Maloney, Schaeffer, & Beilock, 2013). Gender stereotypes instil ideas that being female places limits on mathematical capabilities and that factors outside an individual's control determine their mathematics performance. These stereotypes are particularly damaging because they are evident among young children. Researchers have found that girls as young as six identify less strongly with mathematics than boys and were aware of gender stereotypes about mathematics (Cvenvek, Meltzoff, & Greenwald, 2011). They propose that gender stereotypes about mathematics form after children have developed their gender identity. Children then observe a presence (for boys) or absence (for girls) of people of the same gender taking on mathematical roles. For instance, a lack of female role models in mathematics leads girls to infer that if they are a girl and girls do not do mathematics or are not good at mathematics, then they too must also lack mathematics ability (Cvenvek, Meltzoff, & Greenwald, 2011). This tendency to perceive mathematics negatively in young girls can extend through to later education. Research has shown that female college students with low control beliefs, who endorsed negative gender stereotypes (i.e., who believed that their mathematics ability was fixed and that women had lower levels of mathematical ability), tended to feel that they didn't belong when it came to mathematics (i.e., feel part of the mathematics community or valued by others who were enrolled in or had completed mathematics courses) (Good, Rattan, & Dweck, 2012).

A recent investigation of data from the Programme for International Student Assessment (PISA), which is a study of 15-year-old students in 68 countries around the world, highlighted the complex relationship between MA and gender. In this study, students in less economically developed countries had higher MA; however, there were larger differences in levels of MA between boys and girls, with girls reporting higher levels of MA, in more economically developed countries like Australia (Stoet, Bailey, Moore, & Geary, 2016). Across most countries, boys rated their parents valuing of mathematics higher than girls; however, the discrepancy between boys' and girls' ratings was also larger in more economically developed countries. These findings emphasise that the relationship between gender and trait MA is complex and influenced by multiple factors including those related to society and culture (Buckley et al., 2016). Low control beliefs about mathematics, influenced by factors such as struggling with mathematics, and the influence of teachers, parents, and gender stereotypes, underlie the development of trait MA. Low control beliefs increase vulnerability to the experience of state MA and result in behaviours designed to avoid mathematics wherever possible.

What strategies can target trait mathematics anxiety?

Addressing trait MA involves understanding that core beliefs can generate negative feelings about mathematics and encourage unhelpful mathematics behaviours (such as procrastination and avoidance). In situations perceived as stressful, such as completing mathematics homework, individuals with MA use task-oriented or problem-focussed strategies less often and are more likely to use avoidance to manage their anxiety (Kariv & Heiman, 2005). Avoidance, as a coping strategy, is more likely to be used when a situation is perceived as beyond the individual's control (Anshel & Kaissidis, 1997), whereas situations perceived to be controllable generate more positive coping behaviours (Karasek & Theorell, 1990). This suggests that targeting the low control beliefs of individuals with high trait MA will not only help them engage with rather than avoid mathematics opportunities, but will also help them to see the benefit of positive coping strategies (e.g., positive reframing) for addressing their state MA.

Identifying negative attitudes and stereotypes, which can often be implicit, is a first step towards challenging and changing negative core beliefs. Several interventions show promise in improving teachers' and students' beliefs about their mathematics potential and in challenging negative stereotypes. Strategies drawn from cognitive-behavioural approaches are effective in decreasing MA and enhancing achievement, particularly if used in conjunction with strategies to address state MA, such as relaxation (Gregor, 2005; Zettle, 2003).

Core beliefs that imply that mathematics ability is fixed are fundamental to trait MA. Short growth mind-set interventions based on the work of Dweck and colleagues focus on challenging and changing beliefs that academic ability cannot be changed (Paunesku, Walton, Romero, Smith, Yeager, & Dweck, 2015). In some cases, the interventions introduce the idea of neural plasticity to demonstrate the impact of learning on neural connections (see Blackwell, Trzesniewski, & Dweck, 2007; Good, Aronson, & Inzlicht, 2003; Yeager et al., 2016). Research evidence suggests that these interventions show positive effects such as improving students' academic achievement (Paunesku et al., 2015), reducing gender differences in performance (Good, Aronson, & Inzlicht, 2003) and improving the type of feedback that teachers give on mathematics tasks (Good, Rattan, & Dweck, 2012).

Viewing learning as something that is consciously controlled is key to the notions of metacognition and self-regulation, which revolve around students and teachers being active participants in their own learning (Cleary & Zimmerman, 2012; Kramarski & Gutman, 2006). This includes the use of strategies like goal setting, behaviour evaluation, and organisation. Research suggests that these types of strategies are important for helping to reduce the negative effects of MA on performance via an initial effect on competence beliefs (Jain & Dowson, 2009; Legg & Locker, 2009). In other words, self-regulation strategies help to develop more positive judgements about mathematics competence and a greater sense of control over mathematical learning.

Our research

We have proposed that a multidisciplinary research framework and psychological approach to MA have the potential to benefit teaching and learning in mathematics. Our framework for MA developed from research conducted in the Australian Research Council-Special Research Initiative Science of Learning Research Centre (SLRC). Our initial research involved using this framework to design an informative, interactive workshop designed to assist pre-service primary teachers understand and address MA. We chose to trial the workshop with pre-service primary teachers because of the typically high levels of MA reported among prospective teachers (Gresham, 2009, 2018). The workshop adopted our approach to addressing MA and introduced participants to the idea that MA can be separated into MA in the moment (state MA) and long-term MA (trait MA). The workshop was designed to increase pre-service teachers' understanding of MA, to demonstrate how MA disrupts learning, and how MA influences long-term behaviour in relation to mathematics. After providing participants with a thorough understanding of the origins of state and trait MA and their effects on learning, participants practised a range of strategies to alleviate MA in the moment and to address long-term MA. Preliminary findings showed that participating pre-service teachers were very positive about the usefulness of the workshop content for understanding and addressing MA. As we anticipated, participants with MA described how the workshop helped them understand MA from a different perspective and equipped them with new strategies to deal with their MA. Participants without MA, who already had confidence in their mathematics ability, also found the workshop useful. These pre-service teachers noted that the workshop provided insight into the perspectives of those with MA, thus helping them to understand the experience of students, colleagues, or parents with MA.

This small-scale intervention was instrumental in refining our approach to dealing with MA in teachers. Although encompassing just a few hours of time in the context of pre-service teacher education, the immediate post-workshop evaluation confirmed the usefulness of addressing MA among participants. Preliminary data from a delayed follow-up of workshop attendees confirmed that many were continuing to employ the strategies that they learned in the workshop, and were investigating approaches to using these strategies with students with MA. Ideally, a longer intervention would allow more time for teachers to discuss and reflect on the research and their experiences, and to practise strategies. Though we initially trialled the workshop content with pre-service primary teachers, it is also the case that many practising primary teachers experience MA (Beilock et al., 2010). Using the initial trial of the workshop as a basis, we directed our efforts to developing an extended professional learning program for practising primary teachers. The agenda of this program is to Reduce-Prevent-Protect. This involves the following:

1. Reducing the negative effects of MA on teaching and learning by recognising the symptoms of MA (state MA) and learning to apply appropriate coping strategies;
2. Preventing the further development of MA in teachers and students by addressing its causes (trait MA); and,
3. Protecting mathematics teaching and learning and maintaining opportunities for mathematics growth by developing a positive approach to mathematics in individual teachers, students and entire school communities.

Conclusion

In this chapter we have provided a rationale for our multidisciplinary framework and approach to understanding and addressing MA. We believe that it has the potential to improve mathematics teaching and learning and that it is likely to have the greatest impact when it is run prior to, or is augmenting, approaches designed to build content knowledge in teachers and students. We differentiate state and trait MA and focussed on how issues of control in mathematics learning underlie the experience of each of these anxieties. Our approach to addressing state MA involves identifying strategies that allow the individual to regain control over their thoughts and actions during teaching and/or learning and regulate the symptoms of MA, while for trait MA we focussed on modifying low control beliefs about mathematics to address the causes of MA. We believe this type of integrated intervention targeting state and trait MA is more likely to have a sustained positive impact in reducing the negative effects of MA in the classroom on teaching and learning and can encourage more positive engagement with mathematics.

References

Anshel, M. H. & Kaissidis, A. N. (1997). Coping style and situational appraisals as predictors of coping strategies following stressful events in sport as a function of gender and skill level. *British Journal of Psychology, 88*(2), 263–276.

Ashcraft, M. H. & Kirk, E. P. (2001). The relationships among working memory, math anxiety, and performance. *Journal of Experimental Psychology: General, 130*(2), 224–237.

Ashcraft, M. H. & Ridley, K. S. (2005). Math anxiety and its cognitive consequences: A tutorial review. In J. I. D. Campbell (Ed.), *Handbook of mathematical cognition* (pp. 315–327). New York: Psychology Press.

Beilock, S. L., Gunderson, E. A., Ramirez, G., & Levine, S. C. (2010). Female teachers' math anxiety affects girls' math achievement. *Proceedings of the National Academy of Sciences, 107*(5), 1860–1863.

Beilock, S. L., Kulp, C. A., Holt, L. E., & Carr, T. H. (2004). More on the fragility of performance: Choking under pressure in mathematical problem solving. *Journal of Experimental Psychology: General, 133*(4), 584–600.

Beilock, S. L., Schaeffer, M. W., & Rozek, C. S. (2017). Understanding and addressing performance anxiety. In A. J. Elliot, C. S. Dweck, & D. S. Yeager (Eds.), *Handbook of competence and motivation: Theory and application* (pp. 155–172). New York: The Guilford Press.

Beilock, S. L. & Willingham, D. T. (2014). Math anxiety: Can teachers help students reduce it. *American Educator, 38*(2), 28–43.

Blackwell, L. S., Trzesniewski, K. H., & Dweck, C. S. (2007). Implicit theories of intelligence predict achievement across an adolescent transition: A longitudinal study and an intervention. *Child Development, 78*(1), 246–263.

Bleeker, M. M. & Jacobs, J. E. (2004). Achievement in math and science: Do mothers' beliefs matter 12 years later? *Journal of Educational Psychology, 96*(1), 97–109.

Brunyé, T. T., Mahoney, C. R., Giles, G. E., Rapp, D. N., Taylor, H. A., & Kanarek, R. B. (2013). Learning to relax: Evaluating four brief interventions for overcoming the negative emotions accompanying math anxiety. *Learning and Individual Differences, 27*, 1–7.

Buckley, S., Reid, K., Goos, M., Lipp, O. V., & Thomson, S. (2016). Understanding and addressing mathematics anxiety using perspectives from education, psychology and neuroscience. *Australian Journal of Education, 60*(2), 157–170.

Bursal, M. & Paznokas, L. (2006). Mathematics anxiety and preservice elementary teachers' confidence to teach mathematics and science. *School Science and Mathematics, 106*(4), 173–180.

Cleary, T. J. & Zimmerman, B. J. (2012). A cyclical self-regulatory account of student engagement: Theoretical foundations and applications. In S. L. Christenson, A. L. Reschly, & C. Wylie (Eds.), *Handbook of research on student engagement* (pp. 237–257). Boston, MA: Springer.

Clements, D. H., Sarama, J., & Germeroth, C. (2016). Learning executive function and early mathematics: Directions of causal relations. *Early Childhood Research Quarterly, 36*, 79–90.

Cvencek, D., Meltzoff, A. N., & Greenwald, A. G. (2011). Math–gender stereotypes in elementary school children. *Child Development, 82*(3), 766–779.

Devine, A., Fawcett, K., Szücs, D., & Dowker, A. (2012). Gender differences in mathematics anxiety and the relation to mathematics performance while controlling for test anxiety. *Behavioral and Brain Functions, 8*(33), 1–9.

Diamond, A. (2013). Executive functions. *Annual Review of Psychology, 64*, 135–168.

Dowker, A., Sarkar, A., & Looi, C. Y. (2016). Mathematics anxiety: What have we learned in 60 years? *Frontiers in Psychology, 7*, 508.

Frenzel, A. C., Pekrun, R., & Goetz, T. (2007). Girls and mathematics – A "hopeless" issue? A control-value approach to gender differences in emotions towards mathematics. *European Journal of Psychology of Education, 22*(4), 497–514.

Good, C., Aronson, J., & Inzlicht, M. (2003). Improving adolescents' standardized test performance: An intervention to reduce the effects of stereotype threat. *Journal of Applied Developmental Psychology, 24*(6), 645–662.

Good, C., Rattan, A., & Dweck, C. S. (2012). Why do women opt out? Sense of belonging and women's representation in mathematics. *Journal of Personality and Social Psychology*, *102*(4), 700–717.

Gregor, A. (2005). Examination anxiety. Live with it, control it or make it work for you? *School Psychology International*, *26*(5), 617–635.

Gresham, G. (2009). An examination of mathematics teacher efficacy and mathematics anxiety in elementary pre-service teachers. *The Journal of Classroom Interaction*, *44*(2), 22–38.

Gresham, G. (2018). Preservice to inservice: Does mathematics anxiety change with teaching experience? *Journal of Teacher Education*, *69*(1), 90–107.

Gunderson, E. A., Park, D., Maloney, E. A., Beilock, S. L., & Levine, S. C. (2018). Reciprocal relations among motivational frameworks, math anxiety, and math achievement in early elementary school. *Journal of Cognition and Development*, *19*(1), 21–46.

Harper, N. W. & Daane, C. J. (1998). Causes and reduction of math anxiety in preservice elementary teachers. *Action in Teacher Education*, *19*(4), 29–38.

Hazlett-Stevens, H. (2008). *Psychological approaches to generalized anxiety disorder: A clinician's guide to assessment and treatment*. New York: Springer Science & Business Media.

Hembree, R. (1990). The nature, effects, and relief of mathematics anxiety. *Journal for Research in Mathematics Education*, *21*(1), 33–46.

Hill, F., Mammarella, I. C., Devine, A., Caviola, S., Passolunghi, M. C., & Szűcs, D. (2016). Maths anxiety in primary and secondary school students: Gender differences, developmental changes and anxiety specificity. *Learning and Individual Differences*, *48*, 45–53.

Ho, H.-Z., Senturk, D., Lam, A. G., Zimmer, J. M., Hong, S., Okamoto, Y., Chiu, S-Y., Nakazawa, Y., & Wang, C.-P. (2000). The affective and cognitive dimensions of math anxiety: A cross-national study. *Journal for Research in Mathematics Education*, *31*(3), 362–379.

Hopko, D. R., McNeil, D. W., Gleason, P. J., & Rabalais, A. E. (2002). The emotional Stroop paradigm: Performance as a function of stimulus properties and self-reported mathematics anxiety. *Cognitive Therapy and Research*, *26*(2), 157–166.

Jacobs, J. E. (1991). Influence of gender stereotypes on parent and child mathematics attitudes. *Journal of Educational Psychology*, *83*(4), 518–527.

Jain, S. & Dowson, M. (2009). Mathematics anxiety as a function of multidimensional self-regulation and self-efficacy. *Contemporary Educational Psychology*, *34*(3), 240–249.

Jamieson, J. P., Mendes, W. B., Blackstock, E., & Schmader, T. (2010). Turning the knots in your stomach into bows: Reappraising arousal improves performance on the GRE. *Journal of Experimental Social Psychology*, *46*(1), 208–212.

Karasek, R. & Theorell, T. (1990). *Healthy work: Stress, productivity and the reconstruction of working life*. New York: Basic books.

Kariv, D. & Heiman, T. (2005). Task-oriented versus emotion-oriented coping strategies: The case of college students. *College Student Journal*, *39*(1), 72–85.

Kramarski, B. & Gutman, M. (2006). How can self-regulated learning be supported in mathematical E-learning environments? *Journal of Computer Assisted Learning*, *22*(1), 24–33.

Lauermann, F., Eccles, J. S., & Pekrun, R. (2017). Why do children worry about their academic achievement? An expectancy-value perspective on elementary students' worries about their mathematics and reading performance. *ZDM*, *49*(3), 339–354.

Legg, A. M. & Locker, L., Jr. (2009). Math performance and its relationship to math anxiety and metacognition. *North American Journal of Psychology*, *11*(3), 471–486.

Lyons, I. M. & Beilock, S. L. (2012). Mathematics anxiety: Separating the math from the anxiety. *Cerebral Cortex*, *22*(9), 2102–2110.

Maloney, E. A. & Beilock, S. L. (2012). Math anxiety: Who has it, why it develops, and how to guard against it. *Trends in Cognitive Sciences*, *16*(8), 404–406.

Maloney, E. A., Ramirez, G., Gunderson, E. A., Levine, S. C., & Beilock, S. L. (2015). Intergenerational effects of parents' math anxiety on children's math achievement and anxiety. *Psychological Science*, *26*(9), 1480–1488.

Maloney, E. A., Sattizahn, J. R., & Beilock, S. L. (2014). Anxiety and cognition. *WIREs: Cognitive Science*, *5*(4), 403–411.

Maloney, E. A., Schaeffer, M. W., & Beilock, S. L. (2013). Mathematics anxiety and stereotype threat: Shared mechanisms, negative consequences and promising interventions. *Research in Mathematics Education*, *15*(2), 115–128.

Manzoni, G. M., Pagnini, F., Castelnuovo, G., & Molinari, E. (2008). Relaxation training for anxiety: A ten-years systematic review with meta-analysis. *BMC Psychiatry*, *8*(1), 41.

Mattarella-Micke, A., Mateo, J., Kozak, M. N., Foster, K., & Beilock, S. L. (2011). Choke or thrive? The relation between salivary cortisol and math performance depends on individual differences in working memory and math-anxiety. *Emotion*, *11*(4), 1000.

Paunesku, D., Walton, G. M., Romero, C., Smith, E. N., Yeager, D. S., & Dweck, C. S. (2015). Mind-set interventions are a scalable treatment for academic underachievement. *Psychological Science*, *26*(6), 784–793.

Pekrun, R. (2006). The control-value theory of achievement emotions: Assumptions, corollaries, and implications for educational research and practice. *Educational Psychology Review*, *18*(4), 315–341.

Philipp, R. (2007). Mathematics teachers' beliefs and affect. In F. K. Lester Jr. (Ed.), *Second handbook of research on mathematics teaching and learning* (pp. 257–315). Reston, VA: National Council of Teachers of Mathematics.

Ramirez, G., Shaw, S. T., & Maloney, E. A. (2018). Math anxiety: Past research, promising interventions, and a new interpretation framework. *Educational Psychologist*, *53*(3), 145–164.

Rayner, V., Pitsolantis, N., & Osana, H. (2009). Mathematics anxiety in preservice teachers: Its relationship to their conceptual and procedural knowledge of fractions. *Mathematics Education Research Journal*, *21*(3), 60–85.

Sloan, T. R. (2010). A quantitative and qualitative study of math anxiety among preservice teachers. *The Educational Forum*, *74*(3), 242–256.

Stoet, G., Bailey, D. H., Moore, A. M., & Geary, D. C. (2016). Countries with higher levels of gender equality show larger national sex differences in mathematics anxiety and relatively lower parental mathematics valuation for girls. *PLoS One*, *11*(4), e0153857.

Suárez-Pellicioni, M., Núñez-Peña, M. I., & Colomé, À. (2013). Mathematical anxiety effects on simple arithmetic processing efficiency: An event-related potential study. *Biological Psychology*, *94*(3), 517–526.

Suárez-Pellicioni, M., Núñez-Peña, M. I., & Colomé, À. (2014). Reactive recruitment of attentional control in math anxiety: An ERP study of numeric conflict monitoring and adaptation. *PloS one*, *9*(6), e99579.

Tang, Y.-Y., Ma, Y., Wang, J., Fan, Y., Feng, S., Lu, Q., Yu, Q., Sui, D., Rothbart, M. K., Fan, M., & Posner, M. I. (2007). Short-term meditation training improves attention and self-regulation. *Proceedings of the National Academy of Sciences*, *104*(43), 17152–17156.

Thomson, S., De Bortoli, L. J., & Buckley, S. (2014). *PISA 2012: How Australia measures up*. Melbourne: Australian Council for Educational Research.

Tomasetto, C., Alparone, F. R., & Cadinu, M. (2011). Girls' math performance under stereotype threat: The moderating role of mothers' gender stereotypes. *Developmental Psychology*, *47*(4), 943–949.

Wadlington, E., Austin, S., & Bitner, J. (1992). The treatment of math anxiety and negative math self-concept in college students. *College Student Journal*, *26*(1), 61–65.

Yeager, D. S., Romero, C., Paunesku, D., Hulleman, C. S., Schneider, B., Hinojosa, C., Lee, H.Y., O'Brien, J., Flint, K., Roberts, A., & Trott, J. (2016). Using design thinking to improve psychological interventions: The case of the growth mindset during the transition to high school. *Journal of Educational Psychology, 108*(3), 374.

Young, C. B., Wu, S. S., & Menon, V. (2012). The neurodevelopmental basis of math anxiety. *Psychological Science, 23*(5), 492–501.

Zeidan, F., Johnson, S. K., Diamond, B. J., David, Z., & Goolkasian, P. (2010). Mindfulness meditation improves cognition: Evidence of brief mental training. *Consciousness and Cognition, 19*(2), 597–605.

Zettle, R. D. (2003). Acceptance and commitment therapy (ACT) vs. systematic desensitization in treatment of mathematics anxiety. *The Psychological Record, 53*(2), 197–215.

7

INNOVATIVE APPROACHES TO MEASURE AND PROMOTE EMOTION REGULATION IN THE CLASSROOM FROM A SCIENCE OF LEARNING PERSPECTIVE

Annemaree Carroll and Julie Bower

Introduction

How do teachers know the emotional states of their learners when the learners arrive in their classrooms? How do they know if their learners' most basic needs have been met on arrival at school to start their day? It is widely known that emotions are inherent and crucial to survival and social functioning (Le Doux, 2012). Traditionally, in "basic approaches" to understanding emotions, it was believed that the face was the only indicator of emotions (Ekman & Friesen, 1971), but it is now widely known that emotions are much more complex and involve an important component of appraisal which can differ from person to person. Appraisal approaches to understanding emotions introduced an evaluative element that was absent from basic approaches. A cognitive appraisal creates understanding about the stimulus and this then produces the emotion (Scherer, 2005). The resulting emotion triggers a set of physiological changes, facial muscle movements, behaviour, and feelings (Lindquist, 2013). For example, when a person evaluates their situation as dangerous, they may start to feel very anxious, which increases their heart rate, causes them to perspire, and invokes a desire to run away. Different people will evaluate the same situation in different ways and therefore they experience different emotions. We make meaning of our emotional responses based on how they have been experienced in the past in similar social contexts. Emotions, then, are highly dependent on social contexts in which they operate (Stallen & Sanfey, 2013).

Recently, researchers such as Immordino-Yang have found that there is a complex dynamic feedback loop between the brain, mind, and body known as the "embodied experience of emotion" (Immordino-Yang, 2016). Emotions are constructed when sensations and feelings from the body are interpreted in light of prior experience and knowledge which have been formulated in the social contexts of homes and classrooms. These interpretations bring to light how we perceive, manage, and regulate these emotions. Immordino-Yang confirmed that emotions are integral to and intertwined with all aspects of learning and teaching at all stages of development. Problem-solving, attention, memory, curiosity, decision-making, social interaction, information processing, and motivation are key aspects of cognition and are regulated, influenced, and informed by emotion (Immordino-Yang, 2016). In her model, the neurological relationship between cognition and emotion is depicted as a large overlap called emotional thought. This encompasses the processes of learning, memory, and decision making, and is where creativity, rational thought, and higher reasoning play out (Immordino-Yang & Damasico, 2007).

What does all this mean in the social context of the classroom environment for learning? If we look at what is happening within the context of the classroom, there are layers of emotions associated with many influences. Consider a group of students working to solve certain mathematical problems. Why do some persist to solve the math problem while others don't? Is it intrinsic rewards to find the solution, to get a good grade, to understand the math problem at a deep level, or to avoid punishment, or please the teacher? Perhaps it is because they do not understand the question, there is no feedback, or they do not like the teacher or classmates, or do not feel competent at maths. There are emotions around the topic being taught and these influence the level of interest in the subject. Epistemic emotions are those that are related to generating new knowledge. Achievement emotions are those emotions "tied directly to achievement activities or outcomes" (Pekrun, 2006, p. 317). According to Pekrun et al. (2007), achievement emotions can be either outcome- or activity-related. Outcome-related achievement emotions include things such as joy and pride when academic goals are met, or frustration and shame when efforts fail. Activity-related achievement emotions are things like excitement from learning, boredom in classroom instruction, or anger about task demands. Importantly there are also incidental emotions: those not connected to the learning context (e.g., family issues) but that may influence the context, both for teachers and for students.

Incidental emotions are of particular interest in our research. Learning generally occurs in a social context, and emotions are almost always triggered through social interaction. These social emotions may or may not influence achievement, but they strongly influence engagement, motivation, and interest as well as the quality of the students' and the teachers' classroom interactions that occur within the learning environment. Crucial to this social context is the teacher–student relationship. Modelling genuine passion and enthusiasm for learning and for their subject can illicit similar emotional responses in students through the process of emotional contagion. The opposite can also be true. Not only are the emotional and social contexts for students important, but the regulation and monitoring of teachers' own emotional responses and states is also vital. This can be a challenge as the expectations on teachers increase. Emotions, in conjunction with the triggers for those emotions, can inform us about the emotional state of the learner and how attentive they are to the learning process.

Social emotions make a fundamental contribution to how neural pathways are laid down when we learn something we enjoy (Forbes & Dahl, 2005; Immordino-Yang, 2016). It is through interaction with others that we learn to think. Interestingly, there appears to be greater activation in brain regions associated with reward-based learning through cooperative behaviours (Stallen & Sanfey, 2013). Therefore, when students have the ability to work together on a common group goal and learn positive social and emotional skills to do so, positive outcomes can be anticipated.

In summary, within the social context of the classroom, the emotions that students experience will vary depending on whether the environment is safe and supportive, their interactions with peers or teachers, and their internal or perceived belief or confidence in their ability to execute a task. Equally, how they regulate those emotions will be crucial to successful learning. In fact, students' self-regulatory abilities are better predictors of their academic and personal success than general intelligence (Kitsantas et al., 2008).

Emotion regulation, academic performance, and well-being

Emotion regulation is integral to social competence and general well-being, with life-long impacts. Though linked to executive functioning in the brain, a full consensus on the definition of emotion regulation has been difficult to establish (Bridges et al., 2004; Cole et al., 2004; Eisenberg & Spinrad, 2004). According to Gross (1998), emotion regulation is "the processes by which individuals influence which emotions they have, when they have them and how they experience and express these emotions" (p. 275). These processes allow individuals to cope with difficult emotions and achieve their goals in situations that are emotionally arousing (Cicchetti et al., 1991; Denham, 1998). As such, emotion regulation involves both the control of attention and action in both unemotional and affectively heightened contexts. It includes the prevention of an impulsive response and undertaking an opposite act (Carlson & Wang, 2007).

According to Denham (1998), the process of emotion regulation consists of three components: an emotional component, a cognitive/perceptual component, and a behavioural component. In the emotional component, individuals experience and monitor their emotions. In the cognitive/perceptual component, individuals evaluate and interpret the experienced emotion and either focus their attention on it or direct it elsewhere. In the behavioural component, individuals employ strategies to cope with the interpreted emotion or to alter the situation.

As emotion regulation consists of emotional, cognitive/perceptual, and behavioural components, the emotion regulation abilities and strategies of children differ as a function of their age due to the development of other abilities. For infants and toddlers, the regulation of their emotions is largely facilitated by their caregivers, although they do regulate their own emotions using basic strategies such as physical self-soothing (e.g., thumb sucking) (Bridges & Grolnick, 1995; Denham, 1998; Kopp, 1989). During the pre-school period (3–5 years), developments in cognitive abilities, theory of mind, self-awareness, and increased socialisation allow children to become more effective at regulating their own emotions (Denham, 1998; Johnson & Maratsos, 1977; Perner et al., 1987).

Emotion regulation develops rapidly in early childhood and continues to evolve through to mid-adolescence, although not fully developed until early adulthood, an important factor for those who work with adolescents to understand. Adolescence is a time of great change and growth, physically, neurologically, mentally, and emotionally. It is characterised by the selecting and enacting of behaviours that may achieve goals that are pertinent to the individual (Brandtstädter, 1999). Self-regulation, including emotion regulation, when developed becomes a significant moderator of the person's actions (Gestsdóttir & Lerner, 2007).

During adolescence, young people learn to better understand emotions, process them appropriately, and inhibit negative responses where necessary. Such skills, including emotion awareness (Rieffe et al., 2008) are vital in interacting and negotiating with peers. Successful independent interaction with same age peers is a key predictor of later academic success, mental health, and well-being (Denham et al., 2003). Explicitly teaching skills for emotion regulation assists in shaping the positive trajectory of many children who are struggling. It is imperative to support students in school to better understand themselves, to understand their values, and grasp what their intuition tells them when it comes to making the right decision.

In summary, it is well established that positive emotion regulation capacities contribute to better educational attainment, a reduction in future mental health issues, and greater peer socialisation, with early school performance being predictive of outcomes later in a child's schooling life (Cybele & Knitze, 2002). The ability of a child to regulate his or her emotions, impulses, and attention have been found to significantly impact predictions of kindergarten retention, even when controlling for memory, language, and motor skills (Agostin & Bain, 1997). Young children who struggle to appropriately regulate their emotions and, in turn, their behaviour, are less likely to participate in classroom activities and to be socially accepted by peers and teachers (Cybele & Knitze, 2002). As such, these children have unfavourable views of school and often do not want to attend. Thus, if there is a way to provide support to young children around positive social competence and emotion regulation, it may place them on the right trajectory, before negative attitudes and behaviours escalate. Investment in the early years is likely to have far-reaching, long-term effects.

Current research methodologies meeting the challenges of measuring emotions

There are challenges when measuring emotional states and the regulation of emotions, especially in a classroom setting where a variety of triggers can affect emotions from moment-to-moment. Traditional self-report measures, interviews, and affect grids are useful if we want to tap into mood or affective states, but less useful if we want a snap-shot of what is happening in real-time. Innovative approaches are required to measure emotional states in the classroom in real-time rather than retrospectively and in ways that can complement established self-report measures of emotions with objectivity.

There are limited studies to date using portable technology to observe social networking, however some promising examples indicate that these devices may be useful in a classroom setting as an alternative to self-report measures that for some populations can be problematic. For example, one study by Bieg, Goetz, and Lipnevich (2014) used a personal device assistant (PDA) with a cohort of secondary school students. These researchers demonstrated that students' reporting of their own emotions varied significantly between what the students thought they felt and what they actually felt, possibly due to self-concept. This seems to indicate that self-report measures can encourage intensity bias when recalling and evaluating emotions.

Wearable devices such as wristbands that measure electrodermal activity and sociometric badges that can provide interactive between-person data have opened opportunities to collect emotion data in automated, more rapid, and non-biased ways. This is particularly relevant in classroom observations relating to student engagement, social interactions, and emotional climate (Sung et al., 2016). Empatica E4 wristbands measure electrodermal activity on the skin and are used to measure sympathetic nervous system arousal and to understand the features related to stress, engagement, and excitement. Elevated activity can correspond to increased affect. Sociometric badges are portable devices, approximately the size of a large business card, worn around the neck in front of the chest area. Through built-in Bluetooth, infrared, and accelerometer capabilities, these can measure turn-taking, proximity, and mirroring of group behaviour. While the badges were originally designed by Pentland and colleagues at MIT Media Laboratory in 2008 (see Pentland, 2010) for use with larger organisations such as banks and hospitals (e.g., Waber et al., 2008), research by Carroll, Gillies, and colleagues demonstrate that these technologies also show promise in school settings for students undertaking group work (Carroll et al., 2019; Gillies et al., 2016). In a classroom where students work collaboratively, these data can provide rich insights into cooperative behaviour.

Our research team have been exploring new technologies to tap into teacher and student perceptions of their emotional states in classrooms in real-time. The teacher emotions app t★ was developed from a review of literature and interviews with teachers and allows momentary time sampling to gather real-time data about the subjective appraisal of teacher emotional states and triggers associated with the teaching and learning process (see Bower & Carroll, 2017). The t★ is a web-based application accessed on a smart phone or tablet to collect data directly prior to and post lessons. It has a simple yet engaging interface and is intended to collect sampling data within approximately three minutes. Eleven opposing pairs of common emotions or emotional states are presented to teachers in a quick and easy format to capture common emotional states that are relevant to teachers in high school settings (e.g., Flustered–Calm, Angry–Content, and Upset–Happy). A slider connects the paired words on a semantic differential scale. Teachers drag the slider to indicate where they assess themselves along the continuum. Five triggers for emotional states are presented at the bottom of the screen for each pair of emotions. These are student, workload, staffroom, other, and nothing in particular.

Student includes conduct behaviour in the classroom, personal issues of students, and learning behaviours. *Staffroom* includes relationships and interaction with other teachers, feelings of belonging and connectedness with other teachers, opportunities to work collaboratively with other teachers, and support from other teachers. *Workload* includes teaching time, preparation time (spares), other duties (e.g., lunchtime duty, staff meetings, roles other than teaching, camps, excursions, extra tuition). *Other* includes all that did not fit into the other three categories such as technology (e.g., internet crashes, computers not working), personal, or other issues or crisis situations. *Nothing in particular* is included for instances where emotions were experienced with no apparent trigger.

Based on the t★, the student app S★³ has been developed and, as the name suggests, has undergone three iterations: S★, S★² and S★³. The S★ was the original version of the student emotion app. It differed to the t★ in 3 ways: (a) three additional questions were included to gather data about the context of the situation; (b) the anchors captured intensity of emotion (e.g., *happy/not happy*) rather than opposing emotional states (e.g., *happy/sad*); and (c) a native function format was used so that the app was contained offline and positioned on the tablet itself rather than being web-based. This allowed for data to be downloaded after collection.

The S★² was a modification of the S★ and was designed to be a quick check-in of emotions for students. Common emotions as reported by 415 young people in Australian high schools (see Bourgeois et al., 2020) were included so that students could choose from 20 discreet emotions rather than a sliding scale with opposing anchors of emotions. The S★² was piloted with students to learn more about what emotions young people were experiencing and the triggers to those emotions. The possible triggers for each emotion were: Teacher, Friends, Schoolwork, Home, or Other. While students could choose up to three emotions and three triggers, in this version, it was unclear which of the triggers were associated with each of the emotions. The three opening contextual questions were omitted for this version which focussed on speed.

The S★³ therefore brought together the strengths of each of the first two student apps, the S★ and the S★². It collected data about the context of the emotions by keeping the first three questions from the S★. It allowed multiple selection of 20 discreet emotions as in the S★², but then each emotion was displayed individually so that the student could indicate the trigger for that particular emotion (e.g., *You said you were feeling happy, what was the cause?*). The possible triggers for each emotion were: Teacher, Friends, Schoolwork, Home, or Other. The trial of the S★³ in conjunction with the t★, Empatica E4 wristbands, and classroom observations has been conducted in a Year 8 classroom to explore the effect of mindfulness on the emotional states of teachers and students (see Sherwell et al., 2020). Future research will continue to refine the teacher and student emotion apps and use these alongside retrospective self-report pencil and paper measures, classroom observations, physiological data, and wearable devices to enhance our understanding of classroom emotions.

Student and teacher interventions promoting emotion regulation

The explicit teaching of social and emotional skills is an important component of fostering emotion regulation. Research at the Collaborative of Academic, Social and Emotional Learning (CASEL) has demonstrated the importance of social and emotional competence to learning. Through a meta-analysis of 213 studies and more than 270,000 students, Durlak and colleagues have demonstrated that students who took part in an evidence-based social and emotional learning program, had an 11% increase in standardised test scores in maths and reading compared to those who had not (Durlak et al., 2011). This research supports the notion that emotional states are increasingly recognised as integral for learning. Research by Carroll, Bower et al. (2020) confirmed that all levels of stakeholders in the education process recognise the importance of social and emotional learning. An excerpt from an interview with a senior education executive member stated: *"Social and emotional learning is the most prominent thing that happens in a school. It is the most prominent way to improving outcomes, to improving lives, to improving economic development … The social and emotional needs of teachers and students are the foundation for social and emotional well-being. You can't teach kids until you have kids that have got their basic needs met."*

Student interventions

A vital component of social emotional learning programs is teaching children emotion regulation. Regulating emotions comprises a necessary set of skills that are important to master to successfully negotiate daily lives and get along well with others (Macklem, 2008). A range of interacting skills are involved in regulating emotions, including: (a) reading the facial and bodily expressions of emotion in self and others (information processing); (b) being aware of body sensations and thoughts associated with emotions (emotional awareness); (c) being able to identify and label emotions (emotional literacy); (d) being able to express emotions in culturally appropriate ways (emotional expression); (e) understanding emotional triggers and the consequences of expressing various emotions; and (f) the ability to manage and modulate the intensity to which an emotion is felt and expressed (Macklem, 2008; Shipman et al., 2004; Zeidner et al., 2006).

There is a range of school-based social and emotional learning programs available for children. Research has identified some features of programs that increase the likelihood of effectiveness of these programs, which have been carefully incorporated into the design of the *KooLKIDS* and *Mindfields* suite of programs (developed by the present authors and described below). Park and Peterson (2006) found that the degree to which interventions demonstrated lasting effects was due to the ability and ease with which people could integrate them into their regular behavioural routines. Many interventions in the past have been devised on a deficit model, focussing on ameliorating problem behaviours and "fixing" issues (Seligman et al., 2009). *KooLKIDS* and *Mindfields* have followed a strengths-based approach, focussing on building resilience, enhancing positive growth, and change, rather than viewing students as having a "problem to fix." This approach is likely to decrease stigma and increase student engagement in the program.

In their large meta-analysis of SEL programs, Durlak et al. (2011) identified some operational program features that were associated with better results. Having teachers as facilitators of SEL programs allows for specific tailoring of program content to the specific needs of students. They are also able to use relevant and real-life examples to explain concepts and there is greater opportunity for follow-up and practice of skills because teachers are likely to know their students well. Where facilitators utilised evidence-based practices in delivering the program content, the programs were more likely to be effective, and potentially more engaging and interactive in nature (e.g., through the use of coaching, role playing, and structured activities to guide young people towards specific goals) (DuBois et al., 2002; Tobler et al., 2000). The quality of the implementation of programs was also important, with positive outcomes more likely when programs were well conducted according to plan. Common challenges encountered when delivering school-based programs include: insufficient time due to busy schedules; teacher workload; student absence; low teacher buy-in; limited follow-up of content or practice of skills; insufficient support from administration or families; and teacher discomfort teaching social–emotional content (e.g., Carroll et al., 2017; Petermann & Natzke, 2008; Smith et al., 2009). As such, it is important for programs to allow for flexibility in delivery, be tailored to fit within a naturalistic school environment, and provide teachers with appropriate support and training.

In summary, well-designed, well-implemented, teacher-taught social emotional learning programs with a focus on building emotion regulation capacities and the development of skills and strengths, as opposed to "fixing a deficit," have great potential to enhance students' social, emotional, and academic development and bolster their resilience in the face of life's inevitable challenges. As noted by Durlak and Weisberg (2011), "fostering young people's personal and social development should be a fundamental focus of our educational institutions" (p. 3). *KooLKIDS* and *Mindfields* suite of programs aim to make a meaningful contribution to such a cause.

KooLKIDS

KooLKIDS has been developed on the basis of a solid theoretical and empirically driven background. Drawing primarily from an emotion regulation framework and the social emotional learning and resilience literature, *KooLKIDS* is a 13-week positive, skills-based multi-media emotion regulation program which aims to assist children aged 8 to 11 years to learn social, emotional, and behavioural regulation skills. The program aims to empower children to live well with themselves and others by learning social, emotional, and cognitive skills that promote self-regulation, resilience and well-being.

The *KooLKIDS* program is divided into four key modules. Through completion of the KOOL modules, children learn how to: Know their strengths and develop self-esteem (K); Understand and manage their emotions (O); Recognise that everyone has feelings and develop empathy (O); and Improve their social and friendship skills (L). Originally the *KooLKIDS* program was targeted to children at high risk of suspension from school, and following promising results and positive feedback from teachers, the program was developed as a Whole of Class program. As such the *KooLKIDS* program is delivered in two modes: Intensive and Whole of Class.

The *KooLKIDS Intensive* program is designed to assist children aged 8 to 11 years who present with challenging behaviours and are at risk of disengagement from their educational setting. It is delivered using a combination of whole-of-class and individual sessions and is organised around the four KOOL modules. Each module consists of one whole-of-class session to build peer cohesion and two separate individual sessions with the at-risk child. The individual sessions assist the at-risk child to consolidate learning of the four key modules and focus on issues of self-esteem, anger management, emotion recognition, empathy building, and social skills. This intensive session provides the child with opportunities to develop greater insight and practise these skills.

The *KooLKIDs Whole of Class* program is a 13-session, school-based program organised around the four KOOL modules. Each of the four modules comprises three class sessions, with the final session being a class review and celebration. The intervention teaches children a range of emotion regulation strategies, supports children to develop a better sense of self-worth and self-awareness, and helps them to understand how to manage their emotional well-being and develop prosocial behaviours. The format of the sessions includes a variety of tasks, utilising a combination of group collaboration and individual self-reflection, games, written tasks, artistic activities, role plays, story-telling, and behavioural challenges. It provides weekly opportunities to revise strategies through homework tasks. A range of tip sheets developed around the "KIDS" acronym (K = Keep it simple; I = It's about accommodation; D = Describe what you like; S = Set clear boundaries) are available for parents and teachers. The program has been designed to be delivered either using paper-based or online materials. The online component provides an interactive facility for students to engage with the materials (see http://www.kool-kids.com.au). See Carroll, McCarthy et al. (2020) and Carroll, Houghton et al. (2020) for recent evaluations of the program.

Mindfields Intensive

The *Mindfields Intensive* program was based on extensive research on at-risk youth in Australia and involved consultation with young people in high schools and detention centres, Aboriginal and Torres Strait Islander (ATSI) groups (including rural community workers, professional groups, urban community groups, and Elders), and professionals associated with detention centres and the juvenile justice system, such as Children's Court Magistrates, caseworkers, social workers, psychologists, and mental health workers. The *Mindfields Intensive* program was developed as a self-regulatory intervention for young people with offending histories to empower them to challenge their own actions, make informed choices about their behaviours, and create positive changes to their lives. It was the first evidence-based program to take such a comprehensive approach to the problems of young people to change their behaviour, it clearly demonstrates theory-practice links, and it provides highly engaging materials to young people with low literacy and poor motivation.

Using a web-based interface, educational and therapeutic strategies are delivered to young offenders over a six-week program via cartoon characters and video role-models. The *Mindfields* six-week program is designed to help young people to achieve a short-term goal, while at the same time helping them to consider their actions and choices and make better-informed decisions when faced with problems. The young people learn life skills such as self-identity, goal-setting, social problem-solving, asking for help, and dealing with peer pressure. See Figure 7.1 for the *Mindfields Intensive* model.

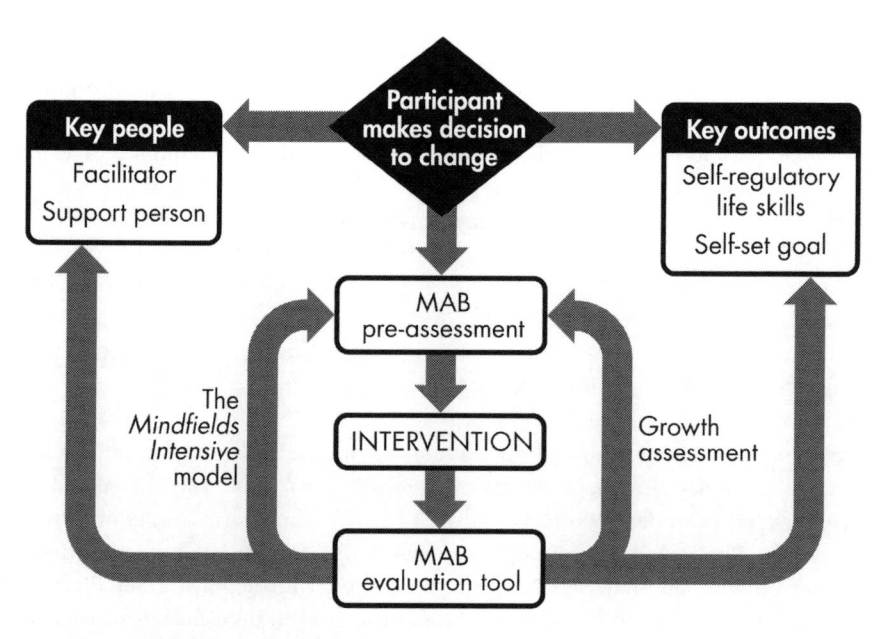

FIGURE 7.1 The *Mindfields Intensive* model

Mindfields High School – Junior

Interest by school professionals in the emotional resilience components within *Mindfields Intensive* led to further development of universal programs for whole of class usage. *Mindfields High School Junior (MHSJ)* was developed in close collaboration and extensive consultation with high school teachers and students. The purpose of *MHSJ* is to assist students at the transition from primary to secondary school with social and emotional skills for well-being. A social emotional learning program aimed at middle school or early secondary school students (aged 12 to 14 years), *MHSJ* has been developed from a robust theoretical evidence base, with CASEL's five core SEL principles of self-awareness, social awareness, responsible decision-making, self-management, and relationship skills woven throughout each session. *MHSJ* maps onto the Australian National Curriculum General and Personal Social Capability Standards, and can be embedded into select curriculum classes (English, Health and Physical Education, Social and Personal Development classes). It is a strengths-based intervention, sharing similarities with the principles of positive psychology and the concept of "flourishing" (Seligman & Csikszentmihalyi, 2000, 2014), supporting students to further develop positive emotions, character, and engagement by understanding and regulating their emotions. Three central components of the program include: social and emotional skill development; mindfulness exercises; and group-based cooperative goal-setting and achievement (Carroll et al., 2017).

MHSJ is an eight-session, classroom-based intervention designed to be flexibly delivered within a school term, with teachers as facilitators. Taking a universal preventative approach, it is aimed at building resilience in students by building a toolkit for social and emotional well-being. Each hour-long session provides a range of group, individual, and experiential activities for teachers to utilise. *MHSJ* explicitly teaches self-regulatory strategies for social and emotional competence. The program incorporates understanding how emotions work, brain body connection, and brain development during adolescence. It introduces students to mindfulness as a strategy to calm the body and mind in times of stress. The class works together to achieve a group goal to be of service to others. *MHSJ* is linked to the national curriculum assisting teachers in time and resource management and offers resources for both online and offline delivery.

Mindfields High School – Junior Gamified

The initial development of *MHSJ* was as a "standard" social emotional learning program, with information delivered by the teacher to the class, and students then completing activities to reinforce the information taught. With an awareness of the burgeoning area of gamification within education, a second format was devised, *MHSJ Gamified*. In the gamified format, the principles and information are the same as the "standard" format, however gamified elements have been incorporated into the program, to enhance engagement and motivation within students. A narrative context has been devised, along with new "your choice adventure" storylines. There are characters and avatars that can be selected at the start of the program, so students can feel a sense of personalisation, with novel and engaging challenges set within each session. Students can earn badges for the completion of set tasks, with badges to be traded in for rewards at the finalisation of the program. There are also elements of cooperation, healthy competition, and some digital enhancements, with students "competing" against other participating schools to enact a group goal. Information is delivered via audio clips with accompanying basic animations and illustrated characters. *MHSJ Gamified* is delivered over the same timeline as the standard version, and the activities are matched on core tasks and themes, so they can be reliably compared.

Mindfields High School – Senior

The *Mindfields High School Senior* (*MHSS*) program is aimed at students in Years 10 and 11 transitioning from school to the workplace (aged 15 to 17 years) to live positive and meaningful lives. Utilising the same format as *MHSJ*, *MHSS* encompasses eight modules, which focus on concepts such as setting life goals, preparing for life after school, understanding self and others, acceptance and resilience, and giving back. The major goal of the program is to provide a strengths-based approach to assist high school students to develop positive emotions, character, and engagement that will assist them in life beyond school and to feel confident in being able to handle situations as they arise in young adulthood. Importantly the program aims to help high school students develop self- and social awareness, understand their emotions and how they influence decision-making, develop social problem-solving skills, manage day-to-day conflict, make informed choices about their behaviours, and work together to set achievable goals and remain focussed on them.

Adding to the key outcomes within each session, there is an overarching group goal that weaves throughout the entire program. This is also a feature of the Junior Program. The key outcome anticipated from such a task is to enhance social connectedness between the students and to experience a sense of self-worth and achievement from working together to collectively achieve a goal. In *MHSS*, the group goal focusses more on giving back, providing independence, and responsibility as high school students head into young adulthood. This is beneficial to developing a sense of gratitude and to encourage students to see that they can be the positive change they want to see in the wider community, particularly as they leave school.

Teacher interventions

Student interventions can only be successful with the support of the dedicated teachers facilitating the program. They are at the "coalface," working with students as they journey through the intervention sessions. Teachers are integral to the delivery of the materials and are a prime source of support for students. However, what happens when a teacher does not have the capacity to teach and model social and emotional learning to their students? There is little doubt that teaching is an extremely important and meaningful profession. Teachers matter – they play an incredibly important role in society. And most teachers find their work extremely satisfying, however it can also be tough. Not only do teachers need content, pedagogical, and developmental knowledge, but they also need assets to deal with all of the other roles that are played by teachers. That is, teaching involves immense amounts of emotional labour. Naturally, this impacts teacher well-being. In fact, research shows that teaching is rated as one of the most stressful professions. Up to 50% of teachers will leave in the first 5 years (Pillay et al., 2005). Many experienced teachers are retiring early, or going part-time to manage workload. Mental health concerns are frequently reported amongst educators (Kyriacou, 2001). In a recent study with 886 participants through an online survey, 77% of Australian teachers rated their job as moderately, very, or extremely stressful, and 50% of respondents reported considering leaving their role in the past month due to stress or dissatisfaction. Of those who considered leaving, 75% reported that these thoughts were moderately to extremely serious (see Carroll, Forrest et al., 2020; Carroll, Flynn et al., 2020). With this in mind, we have trialled the effects of a number of interventions to reduce teacher stress and increase their emotion regulation.

MBSR and HEP study with science of learning

The first study involved 75 teachers and used *f*MRI, cognitive tasks, and questionnaire measures to investigate the impact and benefits of teacher stress-reduction programs, both for teachers themselves, and to see whether there were any "downstream" effects on their students (see Carroll, Sanders O'Connor et al., 2020). In this study, participants were allocated into one of two programs: Mindfulness Based Stress Reduction (MBSR) or Health Enhancement Program (HEP). Each program was of eight weeks duration with 2.5 hours per class-time per week. There was daily home practice and a full day retreat at the end of Week 5 of the program. Fully qualified practitioners facilitated both programs based on scientific practices and provided individual support.

The MBSR Program developed by Kabat-Zinn (2003) is designed to assist individuals to develop mental, physical, and psychological well-being and resilience by teaching them how to cultivate an observant, accepting, and compassionate stance towards their thoughts, emotions, body sensations, and impulses. The program involves: training in mindfulness meditation, gentle yoga and body awareness; exploration of patterns of thinking, feeling, and action; brief lectures and discussions about stress physiology, emotion regulation, cognitive-behavioural strategies, interpersonal communication, and self-care; feedback and support; and a scientific rationale for the practice.

The HEP, originally developed by MacCoon and colleagues (2012) is designed to help participants develop and reinforce habits that are known to increase well-being, focussing on physical activity, functional movement, music therapy, and nutrition. The program is facilitated by an exercise physiologist, music therapist, and nutritionist. The program consists of: music therapy sessions involving listening to and creating music, relaxation, imagery, and drawing; education about healthy eating and meal planning; physical activity and practice involving walking/jogging and stretching; posture, balance, and core strength; brief lectures and group discussions and exercises; individual feedback and support; and a scientific rationale for the practice (see Carroll, Sanders O'Connor et al., 2020).

Overall, the intervention effects were comparable between the MBSR and HEP groups suggesting that either intervention is suitable to improve subjective well-being in teachers. Small yet important changes in students were also noted following the teacher-based interventions, suggesting a connection between improved teacher well-being and student outcomes. When looking at interactions between teacher outcomes and student outcomes, reduced teacher anxiety predicted fewer student difficulties, while greater teacher engagement was a predictor of students' perceptions that their classroom environment was more ordered and organised. Finally, reduced levels of burnout in teachers was found to predict positive changes to students' academic self-perceptions. Such results reiterate the importance of addressing teacher stress and burnout by demonstrating that stress intervention programs can have a positive downstream effect on students and the classroom.

Mindful practice for teachers

In a second much smaller study we also found a successful intervention for teachers. This study involved 18 teachers. What was different about this intervention was that this 8-week program was developed in collaboration with teachers for teachers. It incorporated various aspects of MBSR but was much shorter to fit with the timetable of most teachers. The key components of the *Mindful practice for teachers (MPT)* included: reflection of the week and sharing with colleagues; theory about the science of well-being; mindful movement; and brief non-compulsory homework. Positive changes were also found in the teachers in this study. For example, there were changes in perceived stress which significantly reduced from Time 1 to Time 2. The *MPT* provided regular, meaningful time with colleagues.

Conclusions

Insights into the science of how we learn have provided researchers and educators a platform to better understand the key role of social emotional learning in classrooms. Social and emotional learning skills are a vital and integral component of learning and, without these skills, students face immense challenges with their academic outcomes. Similarly, the ability of teachers to manage their emotions in a prosocial and positive way can provide an immense bonus to learning. By using novel and neural data collection methods such as the t★ teacher and s★ student emotion apps and wearable devices, ways to measure real-time emotions in the classroom can be enhanced. These can be used alongside established self-report measures of emotions to provide objective recordings.

Moreover, the importance of emotion regulation interventions in the everyday lives of students and teachers has been shown to be critical to improve emotion awareness and management, subjective well-being, and learning outcomes. Student interventions such as the *KooLKIDS* and *Mindfields* suite of programs, when implemented with integrity and fidelity (see Carroll et al., 2017), have been found to build emotion regulation capacities and develop social emotional learning skills which ultimately strengthen resilience to cope with daily challenges. Teacher interventions centred on the practice of mindfulness and health enhancement through a focus on nutrition, physical activity, and healthy use of music (see Carroll, Sanders O'Connor et al., 2020) benefit teachers in allowing them time to connect with colleagues, learn about the science of well-being, feel supported, and develop skills and practice for self-management and self-awareness. These interventions have also been found to have downstream benefits for the students in terms of their well-being and learning.

Future research aims to identify ways to develop scalable solutions for implementation of these student and teacher interventions in order to embed critical evidence-based social and emotional learning strategies in the everyday lives of students and teachers to improve their emotional states, increase learning outcomes, and develop positive relationships and connectedness that sustain and permeate the many social contexts of each individual.

References

Agostin, T. M. & Bain, S. (1997). Retention in kindergarten. *Psychology in the Schools, 34*(3), 219–228.

Australian Curriculum, Assessment and Reporting Authority (2013, January). *The Australian curriculum. General capabilities*. Retrieved (April 14, 2017) from http://www.acara.edu.au/default.asp

Bieg, M., Goetz, T., & Lipnevich, A. A. (2014). What students think they feel differs from what they really feel – Academic self-concept moderates the discrepancy between students' trait and state emotional self-reports. *PloS One, 9*(3), e92563.

Bourgeois, A., Carroll, A., & Bower, J. (2020). Exploring adolescent emotions in the classroom: Development of the S★2 emotion application. Submitted to *Teaching and Teacher Education*.

Bower, J. & Carroll, A. (2017). Capturing real-time emotional states and triggers for teachers through the teacher wellbeing web-based application t★: A pilot study. *Teaching and Teacher Education, 65*, 183–191. DOI: 10.1016/j.tate.2017.03.015

Brandtstädter, J. (1999). The self in action and development: Cultural, biosocial, and ontogenetic bases of intentional self-development. In J. Brandtstädter & R. Lerner (Eds.), *Action and self-development: Theory and research through the life span* (pp. 37–65). Thousand Oaks, CA: Sage Publications, Inc.

Bridges, L. J., Denham, S. A., & Ganiban, S. A. (2004). Definitional issues in emotion regulation research. *Child Development*, 75, 340–345. https://doi.org/10.1111/j.1467-8624.2004.00675.x

Bridges, L. J. & Grolnick, W. S. (1995). The development of emotional self-regulation in infancy and early childhood. *Social Development*, 15, 185–211.

Carlson, S. M. & Wang, T. S. (2007). Inhibitory control and emotion regulation in preschool children. *Cognitive Development*, 22, 498–510. https://doi.org/10.1016/j.cogdev.2007.08.002

Carroll, A., Bower, J., Ashman, A., & Lynn, S. (2017). Early secondary high school – A Mindfield® for social and emotional learning. In E. Frydenberg, A. J. Martin, & R. J. Collie (Eds.), *Social and emotional learning in Australia and the Asia Pacific* (pp. 335–352). New York: Springer.

Carroll, A., Bower, J., Chen, H., Watterston, J., & Ferguson, A. (2020). Towards a new pedagogical framework for social and emotional well-being: Focus group interviews with system and school stakeholders in Australia. Submitted to *Educational Policy*.

Carroll, A., Flynn, L., Sanders O'Connor, E., Forrest, K., Bower, J., Fynes-Clinton, S., York, A., & Ziaei, M. (2020). In their words: Listening to teachers' perceptions about stress in the workplace and how to address it. *Asia Pacific Journal of Teacher Education*, DOI: 10.1080/1359866X.2020.178991.

Carroll, A., Forrest, K., Sanders O'Connor, E., Flynn, L., Bower, J., Fynes-Clinton, S., York, A., & Ziaei, M. (2020). Teacher stress and burnout in Australia: Examining the role of intrapersonal factors. Submitted to *Australian Journal of Education*.

Carroll, A., Gillies, R., Cunnington, R., McCarthy, M., Sherwell, C., Palghat, K., Goh, F., Baffour, B., Bourgeois, A., Rafter, M., & Seary, T. (2019). Changes in science attitudes, beliefs, knowledge and physiological arousal after implementation of a multimodal, cooperative intervention in primary school science classes. *Information and Learning Science*. 120, 409–425.

Carroll, A., Houghton, S., Forrest, K., McCarthy, M., & Sanders-O'Connor, E. (2020). Who benefits most? Predicting the effectiveness of a social and emotional learning intervention according to children's emotional and behavioural difficulties. *School Psychology International*, 41(3), 197–217.

Carroll, A., McCarthy, M., Houghton, S., & Sanders O'Connor, E. (2020). Evaluating the effectiveness of KooLKIDS: An interactive social emotional learning program for Australian primary school children. *Psychology in the Schools*, 57(6), 851–867.

Carroll, A., Sanders O'Connor, E., Forrest, K., Fynes-Clinton, S., York, A., Ziaei, M., Flynn, L., Bower, J., & Reutens, D. (2020). Improving emotion regulation, well-being and neuro-cognitive functioning in teachers: A matched controlled study comparing the mindfulness-based stress reduction and health enhancement programs. Submitted to *Mindfulness*.

Cicchetti, D., Ganiban, J., & Barnett, D. (1991). Contributions from the study of high-risk populations to understanding the development of emotion regulation. In J. Garber & K. A. Dodge (Eds.), *The development of emotion regulation and dysregulation* (pp. 15–48). Cambridge: Cambridge University Press.

Cole, P. M., Martin, S. E., & Dennis, T. A. (2004). Emotion regulation as a scientific construct: Methodological challenges and directions for child development research. *Child Development*, 75, 317–333. https://doi.org/10.1111/j.1467-8624.2004.00673.x

Collaborative for Academic, Social, and Emotional Learning. (2015). What is social and emotional learning? Retrieved (September 28, 2017) from http://www.casel.org/social-and-emotional-learning/

Cybele Raver, C. & Knitze, J. (2002). Ready to enter: What research tells policymakers about strategies to promote social and emotional school readiness among three and four year old children. *Promoting the emotional well-being of children and families*. Policy Paper No. 3. New York: National Council on Children in Poverty.

Denham, S. A. (1998). *Emotional development in young children*. New York: Guilford Press.

Denham, S. A., Blair, K. A., DeMulder, E., Levitas, J., Sawyer, K., Auerbach-Major, S., & Queenan, P. (2003). Preschool emotional competence: Pathway to social competence? *Child Development*, 74(1), 238–256. https://doi.org/10.1111/1467-8624.00533

DuBois, D. L., Holloway, B. E., Valentine, J. C., & Cooper, H. (2002). Effectiveness of mentoring programs for youth: A meta-analytic review. *American Journal of Community Psychology*, 30, 157–198. https://doi.org/10.1023/A:1014628810714

Durlak, J. A. & Weissberg, R. P. (2011). Promoting social and emotional development is an essential part of students' education. *Human Development*, 54, 1–3. https://doi.org/10.1159/000324337

Durlak, J. A., Weissberg, R. P., Dymnicki, A. B., Taylor, R. D., & Schellinger, K. B. (2011). The impact of enhancing students' social and emotional learning: A meta-analysis of school-based universal interventions. *Child Development*, 82(1), 405–432. https://doi.org/10.1111/j.1467-8624.2010.01564.x

Eisenberg, N. & Spinrad, T. L. (2004). Emotion-related regulation: Sharpening the definition. *Child Development*, 75, 334–339. https://doi.org/10.1111/j.1467-8624.2004.00674.x

Ekman, P. & Friesen, W. V. (1971). Constants across cultures in the face and emotion. *Journal of Personality and Social Psychology*, 17(2), 124.

Forbes, E. E. & Dahl, R. E. (2005). Neural systems of positive affect: Relevance to understanding child and adolescent depression? *Development and Psychopathology*, 17(3), 827–850. https://doi.org/10.1017/S095457940505039X

Gestsdóttir, S. & Lerner, R. M. (2007). Intentional self-regulation and positive youth development in early adolescence: Findings from the 4-h study of positive youth development. *Developmental Psychology*, 43(2), 508.

Gillies, R., Carroll, A., Cunnington, R., Rafter, M. Palghat, K., Bednark, J., & Bourgeois, A. (2016). Multimodal representations during inquiry problem-solving activities in a Year 6 science class: A case study investigating students' engagement in science, physiological arousal and belief states. *Australian Journal of Education*, 60(2), 111–127. DOI: 10.1177/0004944116650701.

Gross, J. J. (1998). The emerging field of emotion regulation: An integrative review. *Review of General Psychology*, 2(3), 271–299. DOI: 10.1037/1089-2680.2.3.271

Immordino-Yang, M. H. (2016). Embodied brains, social minds: Toward a cultural neuroscience of social emotion. *Oxford Handbook of Cultural Neuroscience, Part II: Cultural Neuroscience of Emotion*, 129–142.

Immordino-Yang, M. H. & Damasio, A. (2007). We feel, therefore we learn: The relevance of affective and social neuroscience to education. *Mind, Brain, and Education*, 1(1), 3–10.

Johnson, C. & Maratsos, M. (1977). Early comprehension of mental verbs: Think and know. *Child Development*, 48(4), 1743–1747. DOI: 10.2307/1128549

Kabat-Zinn, J. (2003). Mindfulness-based interventions in context: Past, present, and future. *Clinical Psychology: Science and Practice*, 10(2), 144–156.

Kitsantas, A., Winsler, A., & Huie, F. (2008). Self-regulation and ability predictors of academic success during college: A predictive validity study. *Journal of Advanced Academics*, 20(1), 42–68. https://doi.org/10.4219/jaa-2008-867

Kopp, C. (1989). Regulation of distress and negative emotions: A developmental view. *Developmental Psychology*, 25(3), 343–354.

Kyriacou, C. (2001). Teacher stress: Directions for future research. *Educational Review, 53*(1), 27–35.

Le Doux, J. (2012). Rethinking the emotional brain. *Neuron, 73*(4), 653–676. https://doi.org/10.1016/j.neuron.2012.02.004

Lindquist, K. A. (2013). Emotions emerge from more basic psychological ingredients: A modern psychological constructionist model. *Emotion Review, 5*(4), 356–368.

MacCoon, D. G., Imel, Z. E., Rosenkranz, M. A., Sheftel, J. G., Weng, H. Y., Sullivan, J. C., Bonus, K. A., Stoney, C. M., Salomons, T. V., Davidson, R. J., & Lutz, A. (2012). The validation of an active control intervention for Mindfulness Based Stress Reduction (MBSR). *Behaviour Research and Therapy, 50*(1), 3–12.

Macklem, G. L. (2008). *Practitioner's guide to emotion regulation in school-aged children.* New York: Springer.

Park, N. & Peterson, C. (2006). Moral competence and character strengths among adolescents. The development and validation of the values in action inventory of strengths for youth. *Journal of Adolescence, 29*(6), 891–909. https://doi.org/10.1016/j.adolescence.2006.04.011

Pekrun, R. (2006). The control-value theory of achievement emotions: Assumptions, corollaries, and implications for educational research and practice. *Educational Psychology Review, 18*, 315–341. https://doi.org/10.1007/s10648-006-9029-9

Pekrun, R., Frenzel, A. C., Goetz, T., & Perry, R. P. (2007). The control-value theory of achievement emotions: An integrative approach to emotions in education. In P. A. Schutz & R. Pekrun (Eds.), *Educational psychology series. Emotion in education* (pp. 13–36). San Diego, CA: Elsevier Academic Press.

Pentland, A. (2010). *Honest signals: How they shape our world.* Boston, MA. MIT press.

Perner, J., Leekam, S. R., & Wimmer, H. (1987). Three-year-olds difficulty with false belief: The case for a conceptual deficit. *British Journal of Developmental Psychology, 5*(2), 125–137. DOI: 10.1111/j.2044-835X.1987.tb01048.x

Petermann, F. & Natzke, H. (2008). Preliminary results of a comprehensive approach to prevent antisocial behaviour in preschool and primary schools in Luxembourg. *School Psychology International, 29*(5), 606–626. https://doi.org/10.1177/0143034308099204

Pillay, H., Goddard, R., & Wilss, L. (2005). Well-being, burnout and competence: Implications for teachers. *Australian Journal of Teacher Education, 30*(2), 21–31.

Rieffe, C., Oosterveld, P., Miers, A. C., Terwogt, M. M., & Ly, V. (2008). Emotion awareness and internalising symptoms in children and adolescents: The emotion awareness questionnaire revised. *Personality and Individual Differences, 45*(8), 756–761.

Scherer, K. R. (2005). What are emotions? And how can they be measured? *Social Science Information, 44*(4), 695–729. https://doi.org/10.1177/0539018405058216

Seligman, M. E. & Csikszentmihalyi, M. (2000). Positive psychology: An Introduction. *American Psychologist, 55*(1), 5–14.

Seligman, M. E. & Csikszentmihalyi, M. (2014). Positive psychology: An Introduction. In M. Csikszentmihalyi (Ed.), *Flow and the foundations of positive psychology.* (pp. 279–298). Dordrecht: Springer Netherlands.

Seligman, M. E. P., Ernst, R. M., Gillham, J., Reivich, K., & Linkins, M. (2009). Positive education: Positive psychology and classroom interventions. *Oxford Review of Education, 35*(3), 293–311. https://doi.org/10.1080/03054980902934563

Sherwell, C., Bower, J., Carroll, A., & Cunnington, R. (2020). Effects of mindfulness on emotional states in the classroom. Submitted to *Frontiers in Education.*

Shipman, K., Schneider, R., & Brown, A. (2004). Emotion dysregulation and psychopathology. In M. Beauregard (Ed.), *Consciousness, emotional self-regulation and the brain* (pp. 61–86). Philadelphia, PA: John Benjamins Publishing Company.

Smith, S. W., Graber, J. A., & Daunic, A. P. (2009). Review of research and research-to-practice issues. In M. J. Mayer, R. Van Acker, J. E. Lochman, & F. M. Gresham (Eds.), *Cognitive-behavioral interventions for emotional and behavioral disorders: School-based practice* (pp. 111–142). New York: Guilford.

Stallen, M. & Sanfey, A. G. (2013). The cooperative brain. *The Neuroscientist, 19*(3), 292–303. https://doi.org/10.1177/1073858412469728

Sung, Y. T., Chang, K. E., & Liu, T. C. (2016). The effects of integrating mobile devices with teaching and learning on students' learning performance: A meta-analysis and research synthesis. *Computers & Education, 94,* 252–275.

Tobler, N. S., Roona, M. R., Ochshorn, P., Marshall, D. G., Streke, A. V., & Stackpole, K. M. (2000). School-based adolescent drug prevention programs: 1998 meta-analysis. *Journal of Primary Prevention, 30,* 275–336. https://doi.org/10.1023/A:1021314704811

Waber, B. N., Olguin Olguin, D., Kim, T., & Pentland, A. (2008). *Understanding organizational behavior with wearable sensing technology.* Cambridge, MA: MIT Media Laboratory.

Zeidner, M., Matthews, G., & Roberts, R. D. (2006). Emotional intelligence, coping with stress, and adaptation. In J. Ciarrochi & J. D. Meyer (Eds.), *Emotional intelligence in everyday life* (pp. 100–125). New York: Psychology Press.

8
BUILDING A SECURE LEARNING ENVIRONMENT THROUGH SOCIAL CONNECTEDNESS

Ross Cunnington, Stephanie MacMahon, Chase Sherwell and Robyn Gillies

The classroom is a dynamic and highly social environment that features interpersonal interactions between students, as well as between teachers and students. The quality of this learning environment directly impacts learner achievement and engagement (Shernoff, 2013). Learner engagement, defined as a sense of connection to what is being learnt, how it is being learnt, and who it is being learnt with (Suarez-Orozco, Sattin-Bajaj, & Suarez-Orozco, 2010), is fundamental to attention, motivation, and achievement. Effective teachers achieve connectedness in the classroom through being aware of, deliberately managing, and equally valuing the behavioural, cognitive, affective, and social aspects of engagement (Hatano & Oura, 2003; Hattie, 2003; Mainhard, Brekelmans, den Brok, Wubbels, 2010; Rodriguez, 2013). Therefore, an understanding of the conscious and unconscious processes underpinning social connectedness can provide teachers with insight into ways to enhance, not just the quality of the learning environment, but also learner outcomes.

Imitation, mirroring, and social connectedness

We are, by nature, highly social beings. We develop a need and drive for social interaction from birth that continues throughout the lifespan. Social behaviour is crucial for learning and early development across several cognitive domains. For example, infants are believed to learn how to imitate by interacting with adults, who typically mimic the infant's actions or expressions (Heyes, 2016). Such reciprocal behaviours teach the infant to "mirror" the behaviour of others, a mental ability that leads to the development of further pro-social behaviours (Baaren, Janssen, & Chartrand, 2009), the ability to understand the goals of others (Rizzolatti, Fogassi, & Gallese, 2001), acquiring motor skills (Calvo-Merino, Glaser, Grèzes, Passingham, & Haggard, 2005), the ability to empathise with others' emotional states (de Waal & Preston, 2017), and cooperative behaviour (Newman-Norlund, Van Schie, Van Zuijlen, & Bekkering, 2007). Indeed, social learning is a foundation upon which further learning takes place. Social behaviour is a seed planted early in life that continues to support more advanced cognitive and social development throughout the lifespan.

Nearly 20 years ago, the discovery of *mirror neurons* in the brains of macaque monkeys was cause for great excitement in psychology and neuroscience (Gallese, Fadiga, Fogassi, & Rizzolatti, 1996). Mirror neurons are brain cells that have the property of firing both when a monkey performs a particular action and when the monkey observes the same action being performed. These brain cells therefore represent a particular action whether it is performed by the monkey itself or performed by another. These cells are therefore said to mirror the brain state of the actor in the observer's own brain. Although neurons with mirror properties have only been conclusively identified in the brains of monkeys, we presume that as close genetic relatives (and both with highly developed and intricate social behaviours), such mirror neurons would also exist in the human brain. As we cannot measure neurons directly in the human brain through invasive recording, we consider instead *mirror processes* in the human brain that we presume are undertaken by neurons with mirroring properties. The fundamental property by which we identify a mirror process is that similar functioning of a brain area can be observed when we perform an action *or* observe another performing the same action. Evidence supports the existence of such mirror processes in human brain areas that support action observation and execution, as well as areas involved in non-motor functions such as sensory and affective processing (Molenberghs, Cunnington, & Mattingley, 2012). Perhaps most interestingly, mirror processes are *automatic* (Heyes, 2011), in the sense that visuo-motor mapping of observed actions (and similar mappings of observed sensory states) appear to occur without conscious effort or intention (although the outcome of such mappings can be altered by intention, see Campbell, Mehrkanoon, & Cunnington, 2018).

The functional role of mirror processes, and mirror neurons more generally, has often been ascribed to imitating and understanding the actions of others (Kilner, Friston, & Frith, 2007; Rizzolatti & Craighero, 2004). An interesting corollary of this automatic representation of others actions is the role of the human mirror system in social interaction. Social communication and learning relies on imitation from infancy (Meltzoff & Decety, 2003), and social imitation can directly affect how we perceive others. Known as the *chameleon effect*, people typically report higher likeability and positive emotions about social interactions when the conversant subtly mimics their body language (Chartrand & Bargh, 1999). People also tend to unconsciously mimic those they feel more socially connected to or feel greater rapport for (Bernieri, 1988; Lakin, Jefferis, Cheng, & Chartrand, 2003). This form of unconscious mirroring, called *social coordination* (Marsh, Richardson, & Schmidt, 2009), appears to play a role in social cohesion. Indeed, manipulation of the degree to which participants are synchronised in their actions has been shown to increase interpersonal affiliation and cooperation

(Good, Choma, & Russo, 2017; Hove & Risen, 2009; Jackson, Jong, Bilkey, & Whitehouse, 2018; Lakens & Stel, 2011).

In the social classroom environment, students and teachers are continuously receiving, processing, and responding to various conscious and unconscious social cues. The teacher has the capacity to powerfully influence the nature of these interactions and the classroom environment through modelling and promoting positive social behaviours and emotions. Classroom norms and values can thus be consciously and unconsciously communicated to students who, through the observation of teachers and peers, can vicariously experience the emotions and behaviours of others, and establish a shared understanding and sense of connection. Through social interaction, individual students consciously and unconsciously "tune in" to the actions, thoughts, and feelings of others in the classroom, sharing their emotional, cognitive, and physiological states, and this leads to a wider sense of connection, understanding, and communication (Farmer, Dawes, Alexander, & Brooks, 2016; Rodriguez, 2012; Wheatley, Kang, Parkinson, & Looser, 2012). Groups that connect in this way will typically be more agreeable, experience more positive emotions, and will be more likely to achieve success. Ultimately, students who connect well will be more motivated to actively engage in the learning experience due to the alignment of their goals and beliefs. These processes of neural and behavioural synchrony appear to support human connectedness, allowing connection with a group on a broader scale (Wheatley et al., 2012), essential for positive, engaged classroom learning environments.

Group behaviour and bias

Given our natural propensity to engage in meaningful social relationships, it is no surprise that there exists a long history in psychology of studying the influence that social groups can exert and its effect on human behaviour. People are very quick to take on group attitudes and start behaving in ways that are consistent with their perceived expectations of the groups of which they are a part, typically in an unconscious manner. Understanding these unconscious drives on our behaviour is crucially important for understanding how we might promote positive social behaviours and actions between students.

A prominent theory as to why we can so readily form group associations and act in ways appropriate to those groups is *social identity theory* (Hogg, 2016). According to this theory, one of our primary goals in our behaviour, thoughts, and actions is to maintain a positive self-identity. We do this by forming associations with people who share particular characteristics with us that we view positively, thereby maintaining a positive self-identity as a member of that group. According to social-identity theory, we form *in-group* associations with people that we consider similar to us and view positively, and we form *out-group* associations with people that we consider different from us (Hewstone, Rubin, & Willis, 2002). We will then act in ways that are consistent with the norms, expectations, and roles of the in-group, and differently from those of the out-group. It is important to stress that this is often not a conscious decision, but rather an unconscious influence on our behaviour in order to maintain our own positive image of ourselves. Nonetheless, this can be a powerful drive that can exert considerable influence on how we think and how we act towards others. Group associations can be formed on the basis of explicit distinctions such as gender, age, religion, and race. They can also be relatively arbitrary divisions such as school house teams, classes, or year level cohorts. Indeed, a popular experimental paradigm for investigating implicit attitudes towards in-group and out-group members (*group bias*) is known as the *minimal group paradigm* – whereby participants are assigned to trivial groups in order to examine group bias attitudes (Tajfel, 1970), where often meaningless group divisions can induce intergroup attitudes including negative bias and prejudice (Ashburn-Nardo, Voils, & Monteith, 2001; Lemyre & Smith, 1985; Otten & Wentura, 1999).

In educational settings, management of group bias can provide a grounding framework which can assist in building a safe and positive learning environment. As discussed, a connection to another is often intuitive, resulting in a sense of belonging as part of the "in-group" or a sense of exclusion as part of an "out-group." Such distinctions can begin to unconsciously drive anti-social feelings and behaviours towards people who are not perceived as part of the in-group. In a classroom context, when there are strong small group affiliations these are referred to as "social cliques." The social awareness of the hierarchy and influence of these cliques can promote negative learner behaviours such as an unwillingness to voluntarily answer questions or engage in discussion, academic, and social rivalry, and even exclusion. These behaviours, attitudes, and associated emotions disrupt the sense of connectedness across the class, and therefore the experience of social, emotional, cognitive, and relational engagement. Teachers can design the learning environment to promote a wider sense of connection to the in-group and minimise out-group divisions in the classroom. Some pro-social pedagogical practices include:

- Frequent, structured opportunities for social interaction and learning across the whole class;
- Minimising classroom practices that promote competition between students;
- Providing safe avenues for all students to contribute;
- Establishing and modelling class norms around positive social interaction; and
- Limiting the attribution of group status such as deliberately seating boys and girls separately or grouping students according to ability.

Imagine this scenario: a group of students relatively unfamiliar to each other are working together on a problem or task. At the start of the task, the students may be somewhat isolated, but through careful teacher scaffolding, as they bring themselves and their thoughts to the goal, they start to experience a shared understanding of the goal of the group and their roles as members of the group. If the group is functioning well socially, the students may start to demonstrate a shared behavioural state: similar body language, vocal tone and volume, and shared emotional states. This behavioural and emotional contagion further strengthens group cohesiveness.

The teacher can play an important role in constructing this positive social interaction that leads the group towards their goal. The teacher can:

- Draw the students' interest towards the task;
- Direct questions and discussion to each member of the group;
- Model a range of positive pro-social behaviours such as eye-contact, warmth, and shared interest in the learners and the topic;
- Use close physical proximity; and
- Provide guidelines to support students to work cooperatively to complete the task.

These often intuitive teacher practices are evident in the practice of expert teachers, frequently developed through explicit reflection on and adaptation of practice over time. The pedagogical skills and understanding involved in monitoring and engineering the somewhat intangible conscious and unconscious processes underpinning positive social synchrony in the classroom have been articulated in a teacher self-regulatory matrix designed to support teachers of all levels of experience and expertise to enhance connectedness in the classroom (MacMahon, 2018).

Promoting cohesion in the classroom

An important way that teachers can promote social engagement and connectedness in the classroom is through cooperative group work. Cooperative group work involves students working together to accomplish shared goals. When this happens, students learn that they must not only complete their share of the work but assist others to do likewise if the group is to achieve its goals. The name for this dual responsibility is positive interdependence, where group members realise that they cannot succeed unless all group members succeed and they must learn to coordinate their efforts to ensure this occurs.

A key component of successful small-group cooperation is to establish tasks that are open and discovery-based, where there is no correct answer and students learn that they must coordinate their activities, such as discussing how they will proceed, allocating tasks, sharing ideas and information, and working productively together if they are to solve the problem at hand. With this type of task, productivity depends on students coordinating their behaviours and interactions so that they learn to listen to what others have to say, use language to explain their ideas and experiences, and negotiate meaning around a task. In so doing, students develop new ways of thinking and behaving that they may not previously have considered.

Therefore being aware of both the conscious and unconscious factors that drive group behaviour and using pedagogical practices that can facilitate group connectedness and cooperation provides teachers with powerful resources to promote student engagement and learning. Fostering a positive social culture within the classroom brings many benefits to learning. Learners report feeling safer working with people that they know and who they know understand them. Within these safe groups, learners are more likely to take academic risks, contribute ideas, and engage in discussions. Cooperation within small groups can also extend to broader cooperative group behaviour across the class. As students become more comfortable working in small groups, and as they innately take on the pro-social behaviours and attitudes of the teacher, students can start to expand this influence to broader groups. Modelling pro-social behaviours and deliberately constructing social learning environments in this way motivates students to support one another to achieve a shared sense of understanding and experience. In turn, these positive social interactions further enhance group connectedness.

Measuring connections in the classroom

Education researchers are increasingly interested in measuring interpersonal synchrony in school classrooms as a means of identifying potential factors and interventions that aim to increase social cohesiveness. However, conducting research in the dynamic and somewhat unpredictable environment of school classrooms can pose significant problems when translating research from the laboratory undertaken under tightly controlled experimental conditions.

A potential means of overcoming this hurdle is wireless, wearable technology that allows relatively naturalistic measurement of students' social, biological, or physiological states during regular learning activities in the classroom. Wearable technology devices are easily removable items such as watches, jewelry, caps or headbands, fabrics, and textiles that can measure data on the wearer's activity level, social interactions, or physiological states. Consumer-level devices usually provide information back to the wearer through the device, via mobile phone or tablet applications, or via cloud internet services. There has been an incredible growth in the general use of wearable devices such as activity and fitness bands, and the utility of commercial and consumer devices has allowed researchers to record information from entire classrooms simultaneously without significant disruption to normal classroom activity.

In education, these devices can provide automated and naturalistic measurement of data that can be used to make inferences about the state of the learner. Heart rate and skin conductance, for example, are physiological measures that change in response to multiple psychological and social processes including arousal, emotional states, and attention (Critchley, 2002; Farrow et al., 2013; Hugdahl, 1996; Öhman, Hamm, & Hugdahl, 2000). Wearable sociometric badges allow measurement of social interaction through proximity and vocal detection

(Kim, McFee, Olguin, Waber, & Pentland, 2012; Olguin & Pentland, 2008). Portable electroencephalogram (EEG) systems have even enabled the collection of real-time brain activity from multiple students concurrently (Bevilacqua et al., 2018; Dikker et al., 2017). These measurements can be used in conjunction with qualitative measures as usually employed in education research, but can give unique insights not readily available with observation. For example, they can be used to measure the states of non-communicative students such as those with autism spectrum disorders, or provide information from a large number of students simultaneously. A particular challenge for this area of research is the development of computational methods that can translate the biometric data into metrics that are meaningful and useful for educators in relation to teaching and learning practices. At present such wearable technology and the development of computational methods to deal with the data are at the forefront of research in education neuroscience (Ahonen, Cowley, Hellas, & Puolamäki, 2018; Poulsen, Kamronn, Dmochowski, Parra, & Hansen, 2016). As research tools, wearable devices have enormous potential to provide further understanding of how classroom and pedagogical practices influence the physiological and brain states of students as learners. These methods also provide a bridge between education and the enormous body of knowledge that exists in psychology and neuroscience on brain processes for attention, cognition, memory, and learning.

But as computational methods and real-time metrics are developed, this opens possibilities for wearable technology to be used to facilitate pedagogical practice rather than only as research tools. In this area, there are still many social and ethical issues to address. Imagine a simple biometric wristband that can provide the teacher with a real-time measure of "engagement level" for every student in the class via a mobile tablet. Or imagine a wireless headset that could detect real-time anxiety experienced by students during cognitively challenging tasks, and feed back to an artificial intelligence digital learning computer program to alter the content being delivered to the student. These technologies are certainly possible in the near future, and with the enormous global value of wearable technology, these devices are likely to be marketed very heavily towards schools and educational organisations. The challenge for educators is to consider how best these devices and analysis methods could be adapted for use in classrooms if they are to positively impact teaching and learning.

Perhaps the best example of an unobtrusive recording device is the biometric wristband. These lightweight wristbands are worn on the wrist similar to a watch or fitness band, and provide measures of physical activity and physiological responses. They will usually contain sensors to detect movement of the band, representing the student's physical activity, while physiological sensors detect the student's heart rate and skin sweating response (also known as electrodermal activity). A person's physiological arousal level is measurable by physical changes in their body as they transition between arousal states on a spectrum of disengaged, bored, or fatigued, through to states of over-arousal such as anxious or stressed. As psychological arousal level increases there are concomitant increases in heart rate and perspiration. This is the result of the actions of the *autonomic* nervous system that is primarily driven by activity of the brainstem in the lower parts of the brain (Rybak, Molkov, Paton, Abdala, & Zoccal, 2012). By measuring changes in heart rate and electrodermal activity, these biometric wristbands can provide a measure of changes in the student's physiological arousal level throughout different learning activities in the classroom. As physiological differences between individuals may lead to great differences in the rate of change or baseline level of activity, such devices are limited in their ability to quantify states of high or low arousal. Rather, their utility lies in measuring *changes* in arousal. Dynamic changes in student states, as they increase or decrease in physiological arousal in response to events or activities in the classroom, may represent changes in cognitive engagement (Nagai, Critchley, Featherstone, Trimble, & Dolan, 2004; Pecchinenda, 1996) or emotional state (Kreibig, 2010; Lang, Bradley, & Cuthbert, 1998). Such shifts can be assessed within particular types of pedagogical practice, or with particular student–student or student–teacher interactions. However, it is important to note that the valence (i.e., positive or negative) of emotional states or outcomes of social interaction cannot be readily evaluated from these indicators alone – current analyses of dynamic changes require further contextual information. Physiological measures require qualitative assessments of student behaviour in order to interpret their relevance.

A major challenge with biometric measurement is devising computational methods that are suitable to answer research questions of interest to educators, or to provide simple metrics that are meaningful and useful in relation to classroom learning or pedagogical practice. Of course, physiological measures can be simply correlated with educational research measures. For example, we can examine the relationship between electrodermal activity and coded student behaviours, with questionnaire and survey measures of students' beliefs and attitudes, or with academic abilities or learning outcomes. Perhaps of more pertinence to the present discussion, we can also examine "connectivity" or synchrony between students through their physiological arousal levels (Ahonen et al., 2018; Ahonen, Cowley, Torniainen, Ukkonen, & Vihavainen, 2016; Gillies et al., 2016; Palumbo et al., 2017). These analysis methods aim to examine the level of mutual changes in physiological states between students during classroom learning. In psychological research, this is defined by a phenomenon known as *social physiological compliance*, where the physiological arousal levels (as measured by biometrics such as heart rate or electrodermal activity) appear to simultaneously change between people involved in cooperative work or positive social interaction (Timmons, Margolin, & Saxbe, 2015). Synchronous fluctuations in physiology between students is typically greater when engaged in a common task or by a shared stimulus such as the teacher during teacher-led instruction (Gillies et al., 2016). Similarly, students working in pairs will display shifts in their physiological state that are more similar to each other when compared to shifts in the physiological state of others in the same classroom, completing the same activity (Ahonen et al., 2018). Similar analyses investigating synchrony in brain activity as measured by EEG shows that greater interpersonal coherence in brain activity predicts student engagement, peer relations between students, and student–teacher relationships (Bevilacqua et al., 2018; Dikker et al., 2017). This is a potentially powerful technique to quantify how "connected" students are with each other and their teacher, or with the ongoing events in the classroom environment. Already this is providing good evidence to inform effective pedagogical practices and student-centred learning experiences that promote engagement (Bevilacqua et al., 2018; Gillies et al., 2016).

As research tools, such wearable technologies provide an objective and unobtrusive means of recording large amounts of valuable data from real-life classroom settings that can tell us much about the states of learners. As the hardware and computational analytic techniques in this field develop, it opens the possibilities for wearable technology to be used as additional tools for teachers or for schools to track various aspects of student engagement and performance during classroom learning. Considering the increasing growth in the general use of wearable devices in the global market as consumer technology, it is likely that they will be increasingly marketed for use in schools. While educational neuroscientists are developing increasingly sophisticated methods for measuring the social synchrony between students in real classrooms, the challenge for educators is to consider how such tools and metrics can be adapted and used most effectively if they are to really benefit teaching and learning.

Conclusions

Physiological and neural synchrony between members of a group is associated with shared behavioural, emotional, and arousal states. These shared states both result from and further reinforce positive social interactions between group members that lead to positive group attitudes and behaviours. As humans, we have an underlying biological drive to associate positively with people who form part of our in-group, but conversely can unconsciously develop negative feelings and behaviours towards others we might associate with an out-group. Although we have these unconscious drives, we can also consciously reflect on and control our choices and behaviours, to act in more positive pro-social ways. Being aware of these conscious and unconscious factors that drive social interactions and group behaviours can provide valuable pedagogical insight for teachers seeking to enhance classroom engagement. Fostering a positive social culture within the classroom, modelling positive pro-social behaviours, and being aware of and avoiding divisions that can lead to in-group versus out-group biases, will create a sense of group belonging and safeness amongst learners that will enhance the teaching and learning experience. The future for assessment of interpersonal dynamics and social and emotional states in the classroom is very like to involve the integration of psychophysiology and biometric measures. Wearable technologies allow us to unobtrusively measure the state of the learner, and it remains an open question for educators how and if such knowledge can be used in pedagogical practice to positively impact student learning.

References

Ahonen, L., Cowley, B., Hellas, A., & Puolamäki, K. (2018). Biosignals reflect pair-dynamics in collaborative work: EDA and ECG study of pair-programming in a classroom environment. *Scientific Reports, 8*(February), 1–16. https://doi.org/10.1038/s41598-018-21518-3

Ahonen, L., Cowley, B., Torniainen, J., Ukkonen, A., & Vihavainen, A. (2016). Cognitive collaboration found in cardiac physiology: Study in classroom environment. *PLoS One, 11*(7), 1–16. https://doi.org/10.1371/journal.pone.0159178

Ashburn-Nardo, L., Voils, C. I., & Monteith, M. J. (2001). Implicit associations as the seeds of intergroup bias: How easily do they take root? *Journal of Personality and Social Psychology, 81*(5), 789–799. https://doi.org/10.1037/0022-3514.81.5.789

Baaren, R. van, Janssen, L., Chartrand, T. L., & Dijksterhuis, Ap. (2009). Where is the love? The social aspects of mimicry. *Philosophical Transactions of the Royal Society of London. Series B Biological Science. 364*(1528), 2381–2389. https://doi.org/10.1098/rstb.2009.0057

Bernieri, F. J. (1988). Coordinated movement and rapport in teacher–student interactions. *Journal of Nonverbal Behavior, 12*(2), 120–138. https://doi.org/10.1007/BF00986930

Bevilacqua, D., Davidesco, I., Wan, L., Oostrik, M., Chaloner, K., Rowland, J., ... Dikker, S. (2018). Brain-to-brain synchrony and learning outcomes vary by student–teacher dynamics: Evidence from a real-world classroom electroencephalography study. *Journal of Cognitive Neuroscience, 26*(3), 1–11. https://doi.org/10.1162/jocn_a_01274

Calvo-Merino, B., Glaser, D. E., Grèzes, J., Passingham, R. E., & Haggard, P. (2005). Action observation and acquired motor skills: An fMRI study with expert dancers. *Cerebral Cortex, 15*(8), 1243–1249. https://doi.org/10.1093/cercor/bhi007

Campbell, M. E. J., Mehrkanoon, S., & Cunnington, R. (2018). Intentionally not imitating: Insula cortex engaged for top-down control of action mirroring. *Neuropsychologia, 111*(January), 241–251. https://doi.org/10.1016/j.neuropsychologia.2018.01.037

Chartrand, T. L., & Bargh, J. A. (1999). The chameleon effect: The perception-behavior link and social interaction. *Journal of Personality and Social Psychology, 76*(6), 893–910. https://doi.org/10.1037/0022-3514.76.6.893

Critchley, H. D. (2002). Electrodermal responses: What happens in the brain. *The Neuroscientist, 8*(2), 132–142. https://doi.org/10.1177/107385840200800209

de Waal, F. B. M., & Preston, S. D. (2017). Mammalian empathy: Behavioural manifestations and neural basis. *Nature Reviews Neuroscience, 18*(8), 498–509. https://doi.org/10.1038/nrn.2017.72

Dikker, S., Wan, L., Davidesco, I., Kaggen, L., Oostrik, M., McClintock, J., ... Poeppel, D. (2017). Brain-to-brain synchrony tracks real-world dynamic group interactions in the classroom. *Current Biology, 27*(9), 1375–1380. https://doi.org/10.1016/j.cub.2017.04.002

Farmer, T. W., Dawes, M., Alexander, Q., & Brooks, D. S. (2016). Challenges associated with applications and interventions: Correlated constraints, shadows of synchrony, and teacher/institutional factors that impact social change. In K. R. Wentzel & G. B. Ramani (Eds.), *Handbook of social influences in school contexts: Social-emotional, motivation, and cognitive outcomes* (pp. 423–437). New York, NY: Routledge.

Farrow, T. F. D., Johnson, N. K., Hunter, M. D., Barker, A. T., Wilkinson, I. D., & Woodruff, P. W. R. (2013). Neural correlates of the behavioral-autonomic interaction response to potentially threatening stimuli. *Frontiers in Human Neuroscience, 6*(January), 1–17. https://doi.org/10.3389/fnhum.2012.00349

Gallese, V., Fadiga, L., Fogassi, L., & Rizzolatti, G. (1996). Action recognition in the premotor cortex. *Brain : A Journal of Neurology, 5*(2), 593–609. https://doi.org/10.1093/brain/119.2.593

Gillies, R. M., Carroll, A., Cunnington, R., Rafter, M., Palghat, K., Bednark, J., & Bourgeois, A. (2016). Multimodal representations during an inquiry problem-solving activity in a Year 6 science class: A case study investigating cooperation, physiological arousal and belief states. *Australian Journal of Education, 60*(2), 111–127. https://doi.org/10.1177/0004944116650701

Good, A., Choma, B., & Russo, F. A. (2017). Movement synchrony influences intergroup relations in a minimal groups paradigm. *Basic and Applied Social Psychology, 39*(4), 231–238. https://doi.org/10.1080/01973533.2017.1337015

Hatano, G., & Oura, Y. (2003). Commentary: Reconceptualizing school learning using insight from expertise research. *Educational Researcher, 32*(8), 26–29.

Hattie, J. (2003, October). *Teachers make a difference: What is the research evidence?* Paper presented at the Building Teacher Quality: What does the research tell us ACER Research Conference, Melbourne, Australia. Retrieved June 26, 2014 from http://research.acer.edu.au/research_conference_2003/4/

Hewstone, M., Rubin, M., & Willis, H. (2002). Intergroup bias. *Annual Review of Psychology, 53*(1), 575–604. https://doi.org/10.1146/annurev.psych.53.100901.135109

Heyes, C. (2011). Automatic imitation, *Psychological Bulletin, 137*(3), 463–483. https://doi.org/10.1037/a0022288

Heyes, C. (2016). Imitation: Not in our genes. *Current Biology, 26*(10), R412–R414. https://doi.org/10.1016/j.cub.2016.03.060

Hogg, M. A. (2016). Social identity theory. In S. McKeown, R. Haji, & N. Ferguson (Eds.), *Understanding peace and conflict through social identity theory: Contemporary global perspectives* (pp. 3–17). Cham, Switzerland: Springer International Publishing. https://doi.org/10.1007/978-3-319-29869-6_1

Hove, M. J., & Risen, J. L. (2009). It's all in the timing: Interpersonal synchrony increases affiliation. *Social Cognition, 27*(6), 949–960. https://doi.org/10.1521/soco.2009.27.6.949

Hugdahl, K. (1996). Cognitive influences on human autonomic nervous system function. *Current Opinion in Neurobiology, 6*(2), 252–258. https://doi.org/10.1016/S0959-4388(96)80080-8

Jackson, J. C., Jong, J., Bilkey, D., & Whitehouse, H. (2018). Synchrony and physiological arousal increase cohesion and cooperation in large naturalistic groups. *Scientific Reports*, (November 2017), 1–8. https://doi.org/10.1038/s41598-017-18023-4

Kilner, J. M., Friston, K. J., & Frith, C. D. (2007). Predictive coding: An account of the mirror neuron system. *Cognitive Processing, 8*(3), 159–166. https://doi.org/10.1007/s10339-007-0170-2

Kim, T., McFee, E., Olguin, D., Waber, B., & Pentland, A. (2012). Sociometric badges: Using sensor technology to capture new forms of collaboration. *Journal of Organizational Behaviour, 33*, 412–427. https://doi.org/10.1002/job.1776

Kreibig, S. D. (2010). Autonomic nervous system activity in emotion: A review. *Biological Psychology, 84*(3), 394–421. https://doi.org/10.1016/j.biopsycho.2010.03.010

Lakens, D., & Stel, M. (2011). If they move in sync, they must feel in sync: Movement synchrony leads to attributions of rapport and entitativity. *Social Cognition, 29*(1), 1–14. Retrieved 30 June 2018, from http://guilfordjournals.com/doi/abs/10.1521/soco.2011.29.1.1

Lakin, J. L., Jefferis, V. E., Cheng, C. M., & Chartrand, T. L. (2003). The Chameleon effect as social glue: Evidence for the evolutionary significance of nonconscious mimicry. *Journal of Nonverbal Behavior, 27*(3), 145–161. https://doi.org/10.1023/A:1025389814290

Lang, P. J., Bradley, M. M., & Cuthbert, B. N. (1998). Emotion, motivation, and anxiety: Brain mechanisms and psychophysiology. *Biological Psychiatry, 44*(12), 1248–1263. https://doi.org/10.1016/S0006-3223(98)00275-3

Lemyre, L., & Smith, P. M. (1985). Intergroup discrimination and self-esteem in the minimal group paradigm. *Journal of Personality and Social Psychology, 49*(3), 660–670. https://doi.org/10.1111/j.2044-8309.1991.tb00922.x

MacMahon, S. (2018). Capturing the "vibe": The role of social synchrony in developing connectedness. Unpublished thesis. Brisbane: The University of Queensland.

Mainhard, M. T., Brekelmans, M., den Brok, P., & Wubbels, T. (2010). The development of the classroom climate during the first months of the school year. *Contemporary Educational Psychology, 36*(3), 190–200.

Marsh, K. L., Richardson, M. J., & Schmidt, R. C. (2009). Social connection through joint action and interpersonal coordination, *Topics in Cognitive Science, 1*, 320–339. https://doi.org/10.1111/j.1756-8765.2009.01022.x

Meltzoff, A. N., & Decety, J. (2003). What imitation tells us about social cognition: A rapprochement between developmental psychology and cognitive neuroscience. *Philosophical Transactions of the Royal Society of London. Series B Biological Science* (February), 491–500. https://doi.org/10.1098/rstb.2002.1261

Molenberghs, P., Cunnington, R., & Mattingley, J. B. (2012). Brain regions with mirror properties: A meta-analysis of 125 human fMRI studies. *Neuroscience and Biobehavioral Reviews, 36*(1), 341–349. https://doi.org/10.1016/j.neubiorev.2011.07.004

Nagai, Y., Critchley, H. D., Featherstone, E., Trimble, M. R., & Dolan, R. J. (2004). Activity in ventromedial prefrontal cortex covaries with sympathetic skin conductance level: A physiological account of a "default mode" of brain function. *NeuroImage, 22*(1), 243–251. https://doi.org/10.1016/j.neuroimage.2004.01.019

Newman-Norlund, R. D., Van Schie, H. T., Van Zuijlen, A. M. J., & Bekkering, H. (2007). The mirror neuron system is more active during complementary compared with imitative action. *Nature Neuroscience, 10*(7), 817–818. https://doi.org/10.1038/nn1911

Öhman, A., Hamm, A., & Hugdahl, K. (2000). Cognition and the autonomic nervous system: Orienting, anticipation, and conditioning. In J. Cacioppo & G. Bernston. (Eds.), *Handbook of psychophysiology* (2nd ed., pp. 533–575). New York, NY: Cambridge University Press.

Olguin, D., & Pentland, A. (2008). Social sensors for automatic data collection. *Americas Conference on Information Systems 2008 Proceedings, 171*. Retrieved 30 June 2018, from http://aisel.aisnet.org/amcis2008/171

Otten, S., & Wentura, D. (1999). About the impact of automaticity in the minimal group paradigm: Evidence from affective priming tasks. *European Journal of Social Psychology, 29*(8), 1049–1071. https://doi.org/10.1002/(SICI)1099-0992(199912)29:8<1049::AID-EJSP985>3.0.CO;2-Q

Palumbo, R. V., Marraccini, M. E., Weyandt, L. L., Wilder-Smith, O., McGee, H. A., Liu, S., & Goodwin, M. S. (2017). Interpersonal autonomic physiology: A systematic review of the literature. *Personality and Social Psychology Review, 21*(2), 99–141. https://doi.org/10.1177/1088868316628405

Pecchinenda, A. (1996). The affective significance of skin conductance activity during a difficult problem-solving task. *Cognition & Emotion, 10*(5), 481–504. https://doi.org/10.1080/026999396380123

Poulsen, A. T., Kamronn, S., Dmochowski, J., Parra, L. C., & Hansen, L. K. (2016). EEG in the classroom: Synchronised neural recordings during video presentation. *Scientific Reports, 7.* https://doi.org/10.1038/srep43916

Rizzolatti, G., & Craighero, L. (2004). The mirror-neuron system. *Annual Review of Neuroscience, 27*(1), 169–192. https://doi.org/10.1146/annurev.neuro.27.070203.144230

Rizzolatti, G., Fogassi, L., & Gallese, V. (2001). Neurophysiological mechanisms underlying the understanding and imitation of action. *Nature Reviews Neuroscience, 2*(9), 661–670. https://doi.org/10.1038/35090060

Rodriguez, V. (2012). The teaching brain and the end of the empty vessel. *Mind, Brain and Education, 6*(4), 177–185.

Rodriguez, V. (2013). The potential of systems thinking in teacher reform as theorized for the teaching brain framework. *Mind, Brain and Education, 7*(2), 77–85.

Rybak, I. A., Molkov, Y. I., Paton, J. F. R., Abdala, A. P. L., & Zoccal, D. B. (2012). Modeling the autonomic nervous system. In D. Robertson, I. Biaggioni, G. Burnstock, P. Low & J. Paton (Eds.), *Primer on the autonomic nervous system* (pp. 681–687). Oxford: Academic Press. https://doi.org/10.1016/B978-0-12-386525-0.00143-8

Shernoff, D. J. (2013). *Optimal learning environments to promote student engagement*. New York, NY: Springer. DOI: 10.1007/978-1-4614-7089-2

Suarez-Orozco, M. M., Sattin-Bajaj, C., & Suarez-Orozco, S. (2010). *Educating the whole child for the whole world*. New York, NY: NYU Press.

Tajfel, H. (1970). Experiments in intergroup discrimination. *Scientific American, 223*(5), 96–102. https://doi.org/10.1038/scientificamerican1170-96

Timmons, A. C., Margolin, G., & Saxbe, D. E. (2015). Physiological linkage in couples and its implications for individual and interpersonal functioning: A literature review. *Journal of Family Psychology, 29*(5), 720–731. https://doi.org/10.1037/fam0000115.Physiological

Wheatley, T., Kang, O., Parkinson, C., & Looser, C. E. (2012). From mind perception to mental connection: Synchrony as a mechanism for social understanding. *Social and Personality Psychology Compass, 6*(8), 589–606.

9

THE MASTER™ FOCUS PROGRAM: A THEORETICALLY INFORMED META-ATTENTION INTERVENTION FOR EARLY ADOLESCENCE

Deberea Sherlock and Aisling Mulvihill

Introduction

Advances in neuroscience and the science of learning substantiate a gap between what we know about neuroscience from research and what we do in practice (Ansari & Coch, 2006; Shonkoff, 2000). Extraordinary insights can be drawn from neuroscience that explicate dynamic interactions in which environmental influences and personal experiences impact upon the expression of genetic predispositions, developing neural circuits, and the unfolding of a child's development (Fox, Levitt, & Nelson, 2010; Grossman et al., 2003). Indeed, environmental and experiential influences are particularly potent when the neural circuit is maturing. Proactive intervention and skill building mediation therefore can have significant influence on neural development.

Developmental research tells us that children are developmentally primed to acquire and master different skills at different stages (Whitebread & Basilio, 2012). Recent advances in developmental science document early adolescence as a neurologically sensitive period, providing a "second window of opportunity" for learning experiences that shape and develop neural structures (Fuhrmann, Knoll, & Blakemore, 2015; Steinberg, 2014; UNICEF Office of Research – Innocenti, 2017). For example, a body of research has documented structural neural changes in white and grey matter volume in adolescence (Gogtay et al., 2004; Tamnes et al., 2010) that are accompanied by functional changes in higher order cognition relating to cognitive control (Luna, Marek, Larsen, Tervo-Clemmens, & Chahal, 2015) and mentalising abilities (Dumontheil, Apperly, & Blakemore, 2010). The idea that cognitive control is critically important for the conscious control of impulses, self-management of attention, and engagement in goal-directed behaviour has enjoyed wide currency in the literature (e.g., Diamond, 2013; Posner, 2012). While it is understood that the foundations of cognitive control are developed by late childhood (Ordaz, Foran, Velanova, & Luna, 2013; Posner, 2012; Posner & Rothbart, 2007b), increased neural connectivity throughout adolescence allows for increasingly proactive and sophisticated control (Diamond, 2013; Hwang, Velanova, & Luna, 2010).

Adolescence marks a neurologically sensitive period that is accompanied by significant environmental demands on self-regulatory capacities. With transition to high school, students are required to be increasingly self-directed in learning. Large workloads and a competing need for peer connection place considerable demand on self-regulated learning capacities. Students are expected to work towards set goals, plan and prioritise their time and academic demands, organise materials and information, self-manage distraction, and self-monitor their progress, often without explicit instruction in how to carry out these management skills. Despite clear and consistent findings that self-regulatory skills are critical for academic, economic, and social success (Ayduk et al., 2000; Best, Miller, & Naglieri, 2011; Heckman & Kautz, 2012; Nota, Soresi, & Zimmerman, 2004), support for self-regulatory skills in the educational context remains very much the "hidden curriculum" (Kistner et al., 2010; Pintrich, 2002). Furthermore, despite acknowledgement of the protracted developmental period, there remains a paucity of research-based interventions that target self-regulation in later childhood and adolescence (Benzing et al., 2018; Otero, Barker, & Naglieri, 2014).

In recent years, commercially available computerised cognitive training programs have attracted attention in educational settings for their accessibility, implementation integrity, and provision of direct skills training (Otero et al., 2014). While some of these programs publicise gains in attention, problem solving, and academic achievement, a direct computerised training approach has been criticised for lack of functional transfer beyond the task or training context (Diamond & Ling, 2016; Redick et al., 2013; Redick, Shipstead, Wiemers, Melby-Lervåg, & Hulme, 2015). Reviews of working memory training in particular highlight short-term gains that are specific to working memory but evidence of improvement in attention or self-control is limited (Diamond & Ling, 2016; Melby-Lervag & Hulme, 2013). In contrast, research reviews of self-regulatory interventions highlight metacognitive strategy instruction as a preferred approach over neurocognitive behavioural interventions (Meltzer, Pollica, & Barzillai, 2007; Otero et al., 2014). Although this research notes that specific skill gains are not as strong as those reported by computerised neurocognitive interventions, strategy-based interventions provide more cognitive and context-based transfer and can be integrated into educational instruction to a greater degree (Benzing et al., 2018; Otero et al., 2014). While research highlights the importance of strategy instruction for performance gains in high school students (Dignath & Büttner, 2008), it is rarely utilised in educational contexts (Kistner et al., 2010; Leutwyler, 2009; Pintrich, 2002). The "second window of developmental opportunity" evidenced in early adolescence therefore inspires invigorated efforts to optimise self-regulatory skill building during this developmental period.

The MASTER™ Focus Program

Rationale

In recognition of the neurological sensitivity and heightened social and educational demands of early adolescence, the authors of this chapter developed the MASTER™ Focus Program.

Description of the program

The MASTER™ Focus Program is a meta-attention training program for early adolescence (see Figure 9.1 for an overview of the MASTER™ Focus Program). It exemplifies a science of learning approach to intervention in combining an educationally established metacognitive instructional framework with skill building in focused attention and cognitive control that is informed by Posner and colleagues' (2008; 2007a, 2007b) neurocognitive attention network model.

The MASTER™ Focus Program comprises of a parent information session followed by eight weekly sessions that are delivered in a group format for one hour and thirty minutes. Sessions facilitate self-discovery of personal strengths and weaknesses, and provide both age appropriate psychoeducation and instruction in a range of skills to self-manage attention and cognitive control. Each session is structured with clearly defined learning objectives and accompanying activities, and students receive sessional workbooks that step-out key learning content. Following each session, students are encouraged to complete five short

Psycho-education on Neural Network Model

Neural Network Model	Metacognitive Instructional Outline	Skills
Alerting An alert state for focussed and productive work	(1) Knowledge of one's ability to sustain alertness for focussed and productive work (2) Knowledge of skills to sustain an alert state (3) Knowledge of when to use skills to sustain an alert state	✓ Self-Talk ✓ Tune into Your Energy ✓ Supercharged Thinking ✓ Brain and Body Breaks
Orienting Selectively attending to relevant information	(1) Knowledge of one's ability to recognise and inhibit internal and/or external distraction (2) Knowledge of skills to inhibit internal and external distraction (3) Knowledge of when to selectively narrow one's attention	✓ Self-Talk ✓ Focussed Listening ✓ Focussed Breathing
Executive Attention Proactive control of thought, behaviour and emotion for goal-directed learning	(1) Knowledge of one's ability to self-manage thoughts, behaviour and emotion (2) Knowledge of skills for the self-management of behaviour (3) Knowledge of when to engage voluntary control	✓ Self-Talk ✓ Take a Moment in Time ✓ Tune into Thinking ✓ Planning ✓ Goal Setting

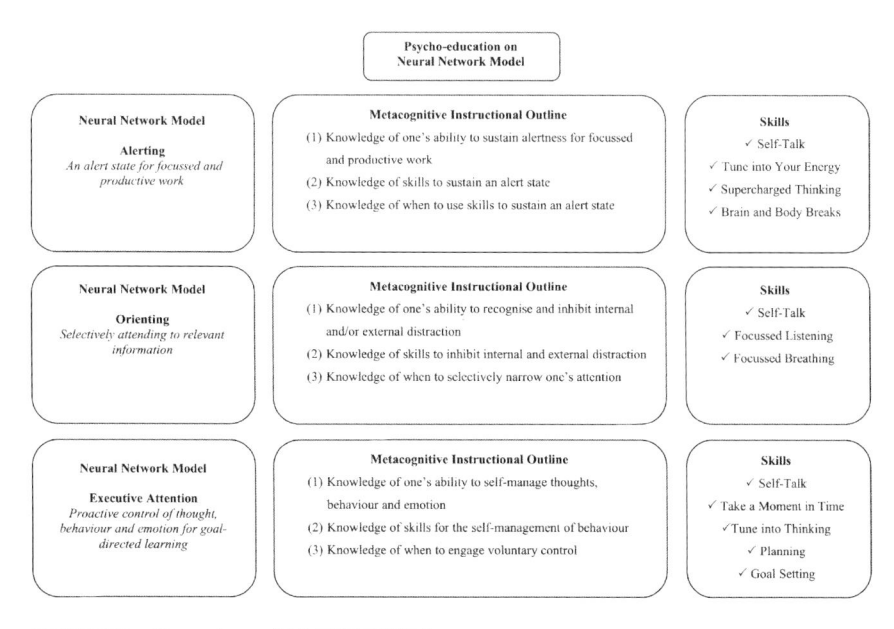

FIGURE 9.1 Overview of MASTER™ focus program

guided reflections. These reflections serve to prime students' strategic application of skills and provide opportunity to self-monitor the frequency and effectiveness of application of learning in functional daily contexts.

Theoretical foundations of the program

The scientist–practitioner ideal holds high value in educational practice. In upholding this ideal, the MASTER™ Focus Program appeals to Posner and colleagues' (2008; 2007a, 2007b) neural network model of attention that is grounded upon a widely published body of functional neuroimaging and experimental studies (e.g., Fan, McCandliss, Fossella, Flombaum, & Posner, 2005; Rueda et al., 2004), as the empirical basis for the development of integrated skill sets that support focused attention and regulated learning behaviours.

In accordance with this theoretical model and body of research, Posner and colleagues (2008; 2007a, 2007b) postulate a fundamental role for attention that operates to moderate the activity of sensory, cognitive, and emotional systems. Attention is understood to lie at the heart of the psychological enterprise in enabling self-, other-, and context-awareness, and voluntary regulation of thoughts, feelings, and actions. Posner and colleagues' (2008; 2007a, 2007b) model of attention explicates the operations of three neural networks that carry out separate attentional functions within an integrated functional system. Each network relates to different mechanisms or functions of attention and are associated with both well-defined and detailed areas of brain anatomy and chemical modulators. The integrated attention system supports both parallel and separate operations. As explained by Posner (2012), these networks may not include all possible concepts related to attention, but it is proposed that the model encompasses most or all of the various concepts of attention that have been proffered in the literature.

The networks are associated with specific mental operations that are postulated to carry out real-life functions described in terms of *alerting, orienting*, and *executive attention*. These operations are defined simply as follows:

- *Alerting* refers to achieving and maintaining an alert state of arousal appropriate to the context;
- *Orienting* refers to directing attention to sensory input; and
- *Executive attention* is the voluntary control of cognition, emotion, and behaviour.

Skill building within a neural network model of attention

The neural network model provides a cohesive guide to operationalise the cognitive tasks of attention. Within the MASTER™ Focus Program the general functions of attention have been extrapolated in terms of skill sets that support important learning behaviours. These are outlined below with reference to the operations of *alerting, orienting,* and *executive attention*.

The alerting network

The MASTER™ Focus Program conceptualises *alerting* as achieving and maintaining an alert state for focused and productive work. This requires brain and body energy "in control" or "in check" as appropriate for the learning or social situation. The functions of this network enable a student to:

- Stay alert or energised to complete work (i.e., "*switch on*");
- Stay motivated to complete work especially if this work is difficult or holds no intrinsic appeal (i.e., "*just do it*"); and
- Sustain attention so the task gets completed (i.e., "*keep on keeping on*").

The alerting network lends understanding of the challenges students may experience in regulating an optimal state of alertness for learning and social engagement. When energy levels are inappropriately high, students may display non-relevant motor activity such as tapping and fidgeting (Ruff & Rothbart, 2001), and experience difficulty engaging productively in classroom learning and social situations. When energy levels are inappropriately low, typical behaviours observed may include daydreaming, vacant staring, signs of physical fatigue, slow processing of information, and low motivation for effortful learning.

Although it is acknowledged that students vary in their motivation to learn, some students may experience a developmental difficulty *activating alertness* to engage in work that is arduous or uninteresting. What makes this developmental difficulty especially puzzling for parents and teachers is that mental alertness is more effectively activated and maintained when these students are doing activities that are intrinsically motivating (e.g., playing electronic games or engaging fully in school work that the student likes). This apparent contradiction is underpinned by the operations of the alerting network. A state of mental alertness is more readily activated for personally meaningful activities (Robinson et al., 2012). However, alerting requires proactive control to engage in effortful learning that enables students to undertake arduous or uninteresting work (Rueda et al., 2004). What may be misunderstood as laziness may reflect a developmental weakness in the alerting network (Johnson et al., 2008). Refer to Table 9.1 for a description of the skill sets that are informed by the alerting network.

The orienting network

Selective attention is critically important for learning and performance (Erickson, Thiessen, Godwin, Dickerson, & Fisher, 2015; Posner & Rothbart, 2014). Indeed, effective and efficient learning necessitates selective attention to the most important information in our environment or a given task. The MASTER™ Focus Program conceptualises *orienting* as selectively attending to relevant information whilst inhibiting distraction. In this sense, selective attention is effortful.

TABLE 9.1 Skill building within a neural network model of attention

Skill Common to all Networks

Skill	Description
Self-Talk	*Self-talk* is verbal thought that is directed to oneself. In the MASTER™ Focus Program self-talk is the gate-way skill used in a strategic manner to regulate thinking and behaviour.

Skills Informed by the Alerting Network

Skill	Description
Tune into Your Energy	A settling of physical activity is considered a defining feature of attention and reflective learning (Ruff & Rothbart, 2001). Students learn to intentionally modulate their energy level and movement appropriate to the context. This skill routine encourages students to quieten non-relevant motor activity and/or redirect and refocus mental and physical energy.
Supercharged Thinking	The more formal aspects of education may require students to attend to tasks that do not elicit strong personal interest. The distinction is made between intrinsically appealing activities that compel attention and intrinsically unappealing activities that reduce motivation for effortful learning. *Supercharged thinking* recognises that students require both "will" and "skill" to be successful learners (Pintrich & de Groot, 1990). It encourages motivation to proactively engage in arduous and/or intrinsically uninteresting activities (e.g., homework, household chores).
Brain and Body Breaks	Students learn best when alert and focused. They are encouraged to self-identify signs of mental and physical over- and/or under-activity and to purposefully plan for short structured breaks to support focused and productive work.

Skills Informed by the Orienting Network

Skill	Description
Focused Listening	The act of listening is not necessarily an observable process of attention. Looking however is a reliable index of attention (Ruff & Rothbart, 2001). In *focused listening*, students are directed to focus intentionally on the speaker and the spoken message. It is the ability to inhibit distraction by selectively looking and listening.
Focused Breathing	Daydreaming and mind wandering are distractions of the mind. Attending to distraction whether internal or external can impact negatively on a student's ability to engage in focused and productive work. Students are taught to recognise and self-monitor distraction, and consciously re-orient attention as necessary to meet the demands of the task/situation. *Focused breathing* is a mindfulness activity adapted from the work of Bruno Cayoun (2011). In this activity, students are taught to become aware of both internal and external distraction, and to resist distraction by refocusing attention back to the target of "counting of breaths."

TABLE 9.1 Skill building within a neural network model of attention (*Continued*)

Skills Informed by the Executive Attention Network

Skill	Description
Take a Moment in Time	Impulse control is foundational to learning, and social and emotional functioning, and is integral to self-regulation. *Take a moment in time* is a skill routine of impulse control. In acknowledging that it is easier to replace impulsive behaviour with an appropriate alternative than to stop the impulsive action, *take a moment in time* pairs action and self-talk to encourage intentional rather than impulsive behaviour.
Tune into Thinking	Thoughts can have a critical impact on learning and performance. Challenging tasks require a conscious increase in the reserves of effort, persistence, and motivation. The connections between thinking patterns and learning behaviours are discussed and demonstrated. A key support for effortful learning is to help students develop helpful and productive ways of thinking in reframing unhelpful motivational states.
Planning	Plans have a direct organising influence on behaviour. They support coordination of intentionality, sustained attention, and goal-directed action (Ruff & Rothbart, 2001). Students learn how to use time and resources productively to achieve outcomes.
Goal Setting	A goal is a statement of intention that gives vision and drive to achievement. Students learn how to set goals to focus their learning efforts.

It requires self-monitoring and sustained control of attentional focus. The functions of this network enable a student to:

- Selectively narrow attention to relevant information (i.e., "*notice the speaker, notice the message*"); and
- Filter out distraction, both external and internal (i.e., "*stop, listen, focus on what I should be doing*").

The functions of the orienting network lend further understanding of the challenges students face in everyday learning. When students intentionally narrow focus and sustain control of attentional focus, positive learning behaviours follow that include active listening, on-task behaviour, concentration, and the ability to resist distraction. Conversely, when focus is poorly controlled, learning is compromised with problematic learning behaviours involving passive listening, off-task behaviour, and distractibility. Refer to Table 9.1 for a description of the skill sets that are informed by the orienting network.

The executive attention network

Executive attention is a neurodevelopmental process that undergoes a prolonged period of development. Large developmental shifts occur across development with adolescence acknowledged as a period of notable change (Luna et al., 2015). This finding compels further efforts for proactive self-regulatory skill building during this developmental period. The MASTER™ Focus Program conceptualises executive attention as proactive control of thought, behaviour, and emotion for goal-directed learning. It involves effortful and deliberate action that contrasts with automatic behavioural responses (Chevalier, Martis, Curran, & Munakata, 2015; Posner, 2012). The functions of this network enable a student to:

- Inhibit impulsive responses in the service of goal-directed actions (i.e., *"stop and think before I act"*);
- Activate motivation for effortful learning (i.e., *"get started!"*);
- Set goals, plan, and organise work for timely completion (i.e., *"how do I eat the elephant?"*); and
- Prioritise demands (i.e., to consider both degree of importance and urgency when faced with competing demands).

Effective engagement of the executive attention network supports self-regulated learning. Students plan and organise their work, self-initiate work, time manage, problem solve strategically as difficulties arise, self-monitor performance, and work through to completion. Students with executive attention weakness have notable difficulty project managing their work. They experience problems planning, prioritising, organising, and completing work, and require a good deal of supervision to manage the competing demands of work and life. Table 9.1 provides a description of the skill sets that are informed by the executive attention network.

Metacognitive instructional framework

Since the seminal work of Flavell (1979), metacognition has received widespread attention across the disciplines of education and the psychological sciences. Metacognition is the conscious awareness, monitoring, and control of one's own cognition. As the knowledge or mental activity that serves to regulate thinking (Schneider, 2008), metacognition supports top-down regulatory control that is critical for self-regulated learning (Lyons & Ghetti, 2010; Nelson & Narens, 1994; Shimamura, 2000). Metacognition is a multifaceted construct that is composed of metacognitive knowledge, experience, and skill (Efklides, 2008; Flavell, 1979; Pintrich, 2002; Roebers, 2017) and is outlined as follows:

- Metacognitive *knowledge* is defined as the knowledge of cognition. Put simply, it is "thinking about thinking";
- Metacognitive *experience* involves the feelings and judgments that arise between the individual and the task; and
- Metacognitive *skilfulness* is the strategic application of skills in response to task demands.

The MASTER™ Focus Program was designed to promote students' metacognitive *knowledge* specific to the cognitive domain of attention and executive control (i.e., meta-attention). The program aims to build students' explicit knowledge of strategies to self-monitor, -regulate, and -control attention and broader cognitive control capacities. The program is premised on the understanding that explicit strategy instruction will improve students' metacognitive skilfulness.

As conceptualised in the MASTER™ Focus Program, metacognitive knowledge is composed of *knowledge* of the self, *knowledge* of strategies and *knowledge* of the task. These are defined as follows:

- *Knowledge* of the self – students explore their own abilities (i.e., strengths and weaknesses), strategy use and motivation to self-regulate alertness, attentional orienting, and executive control;
- *Knowledge* of strategies – students learn specific strategies to maintain an alert state, inhibit distraction, and self-regulate behaviour; and
- *Knowledge* of tasks – students build contextual knowledge to guide their understanding of what strategies to use, when to use them, and why to use them.

A metacognitive instructional format is considered developmentally fitting for early adolescence. Structural and functional changes in the adolescent brain enhance mentalising capacity and, in turn, the ability to represent and observe one's own thinking (Dumontheil et al., 2010; Tamnes et al., 2010). These developmental advances in metacognition further the capacity to self-reflect, monitor, and regulate thinking and behaviour (Fernandez-Duque, Baird, & Posner, 2000; Lyons & Ghetti, 2010; Weil et al., 2013). Research to date identifies maturational progression in metacognitive ability throughout adolescence. In particular, age related improvements are demonstrated in the frequency and quality of metacognitive strategy use (Kolic-Vehovec, Zubkovic, & Pahljina-Reinic, 2014; van der Stel & Veenman, 2010), knowledge of task related demands (Kolic-Vehovec et al., 2014; Lockl & Schneider, 2004; Schneider, 2008), and accuracy in self-monitoring learning and performance (Demetriou & Bakracevic, 2009; Paulus, Tsalas, Proust, & Sodian, 2014; Weil et al., 2013). In harnessing the developing capacities and desire for introspection during adolescence, the MASTER™ Focus Program facilitates self-awareness of strengths and weaknesses and engages students in both reflective performance monitoring and strategic adjustment of behaviour.

As developmental advances drive metacognitive sophistication, high school students are ripe for instruction in how to learn effectively and efficiently (Dimmitt & McCormick, 2012). Metacognitive instruction is widely acknowledged for its effectiveness in learning contexts. In a meta-analysis of self-regulatory interventions for the high school context, Dignath and Büttner (2008) demonstrated that cognitive strategy training coupled with a metacognitive theoretical approach had the greatest effect size on academic achievement. Explicit instruction in strategic knowledge increases the likelihood of application (Askell-Williams, Lawson, & Skrzypiec, 2012; Dimmitt & McCormick, 2012), and consequently academic performance (Williams et al., 2002). Across education levels and subject areas, metacognitive skilfulness (i.e., application of appropriate learning strategies) contributes significantly to learning performance, and these gains in performance are independent of student intelligence (van der Stel & Veenman, 2010; Veenman, Kok, & Blöte, 2005; Veenman, Wilhelm, & Beishuizen, 2004).

The metacognitive instructional format of the MASTER™ Focus Program is a developmentally sensitive and efficacious approach to skill building in early adolescence. This format supports proactive and conscious participation in the cognitive processes of attention and cognitive control.

Conclusion

The science of learning underscores an existing gap in the science to practice continuum for the promotion of self-regulatory capacities in young adolescents. Recent research in the fields of developmental neuroscience and cognitive psychology identifies early adolescence as an optimal period for self-regulatory intervention. Nonetheless, educational and clinical efforts in these endeavours have fallen short with few available self-regulatory interventions for this age group. Intended for use in clinical and education settings, the MASTER™ Focus Program provides group-based intervention for young adolescents that promotes metacognitive knowledge specific to the cognitive domains of attention and executive control. Informed by the disciplines of education and cognitive psychology, the program utilises a metacognitive instructional framework that advances knowledge and application of skill sets operationalised from the work of Posner and colleagues (2008; 2007a, 2007b).

In recognition of the opportunity for proactive intervention and skill building mediation in early adolescence, the authors of the MASTER™ Focus Program joined in collaboration with researchers from the Science of Learning Research Centre at The University of Queensland. The aim of the practitioner–researcher collaboration was to investigate the effects of a metacognitive intervention on both neural and functional markers of attention and cognitive control in young adolescents. Of the three multi-disciplinary research themes of the Science of Learning Research Centre (i.e., understanding, measuring, and promoting learning), the MASTER™ Focus Program directly aligns with the Centre's initiative of improving learning outcomes by developing skills and strategies to support learning in functional settings.

References

Ansari, D. & Coch, D. (2006). Bridges over troubled waters: Education and cognitive neuroscience. *Trends in Cognitive Sciences*, *10*(4), 146–151. doi:10.1016/j.tics.2006.02.007.

Askell-Williams, H., Lawson, M. J., & Skrzypiec, G. (2012). Scaffolding cognitive and metacognitive strategy instruction in regular class lessons. *Instructional Science*, *40*(2), 413–443. doi: 10.1007/s11251-011-9182-5.

Ayduk, O., Mendoza-Denton, R., Mischel, W., Downey, G., Peake, P. K., & Rodriguez, M. (2000). Regulating the interpersonal self: Strategic self-regulation for coping with rejection sensitivity. *Journal of Personality and Social Psychology*, *79*(5), 776–792. doi:10.1037/0022-3514.79.5.776.

Benzing, V., Schmidt, M., Jäger, K., Egger, F., Conzelmann, A., & Roebers, C. M. (2018). A classroom intervention to improve executive functions in late primary school children: Too "old" for improvements? *British Journal of Educational Psychology*, 26th June 2018. doi: 10.1111/bjep.12232.

Best, J. R., Miller, P. H., & Naglieri, J. A. (2011). Relations between executive function and academic achievement from ages 5 to 17 in a large, representative national sample. *Learning and Individual Differences*, *21*(4), 327–336. doi: https://doi.org/10.1016/j.lindif.2011.01.007.

Cayoun, B. (2011). *Mindfulness-integrated CBT: Principles and practice*. Chichester, West Sussex, UK: Wiley.

Chevalier, N., Martis, S. B., Curran, T., & Munakata, Y. (2015). Metacognitive processes in executive control development: The case of reactive and proactive control. *Journal of Cognitive Neuroscience*, *27*(6), 1125. doi: 10.1162/jocn_a_00782.

Demetriou, A., & Bakracevic, K. (2009). Reasoning and self-awareness from adolescence to middle age: Organization and development as a function of education. *Learning and Individual Differences*, *19*(2), 181–194. doi: https://doi.org/10.1016/j.lindif.2008.10.007

Diamond, A. (2013). Executive functions. *Annual Review of Psychology*, *64*(1), 135–168. doi: 10.1146/annurev-psych-113011-143750.

Diamond, A., & Ling, D. S. (2016). Conclusions about interventions, programs, and approaches for improving executive functions that appear justified and those that, despite much hype, do not. *Developmental Cognitive Neuroscience*, *18*, 34–48. doi: https://doi.org/10.1016/j.dcn.2015.11.005.

Dignath, C., & Büttner, G. (2008). Components of fostering self-regulated learning among students. *A Meta-Analysis on Intervention Studies at Primary and Secondary School Level*. *Metacognition and Learning*, *3*(3), 231–264. doi: 10.1007/s11409-008-9029-x.

Dimmitt, C., & McCormick, C. B. (2012). Metacognition in education. In G. Harris, M. Urdan, S. Sinatra, & A. P. Association (Eds.), *APA educational psychology handbook* (1st ed.). Washington, DC: American Psychological Association.

Dumontheil, I., Apperly, I. A., & Blakemore, S.-J. (2010). Online usage of theory of mind continues to develop in late adolescence. *Developmental Science*, *13*(2), 331–338. doi: 10.1111/j.1467-7687.2009.00888.x.

Efklides, A. (2008). Metacognition: Defining its facets and levels of functioning in relation to self-regulation and co-regulation. *European Psychologist*, *13*(4), 277–287. doi: 10.1027/1016-9040.13.4.277.

Erickson, L. C., Thiessen, E. D., Godwin, K. E., Dickerson, J. P., & Fisher, A. V. (2015). Endogenously and exogenously driven selective sustained attention: Contributions to learning in kindergarten children. *Journal of Experimental Child Psychology*, *138*, 126–134. doi: https://doi.org/10.1016/j.jecp.2015.04.011.

Fan, J., McCandliss, B. D., Fossella, J., Flombaum, J. I., & Posner, M. I. (2005). The activation of attentional networks. *NeuroImage*, *26*(2), 471–479. doi: 10.1016/j.neuroimage.2005.02.004.

Fernandez-Duque, D., Baird, J. A., & Posner, M. I. (2000). Executive attention and metacognitive regulation. *Consciousness and Cognition*, *9*(2), 288–307. doi: https://doi.org/10.1006/ccog.2000.0447.

Flavell, J. H. (1979). Metacognition and cognitive monitoring: A new area of cognitive-developmental inquiry. *American Psychologist*, *34*(10), 906–911.

Fox, S. E., Levitt, P., & Nelson, C. A. 3rd. (2010). How the timing and quality of early experiences influence the development of brain architecture. *Child Development*, *81*(1), 28–40. doi: 10.1111/j.1467-8624.2009.01380.x.

Fuhrmann, D., Knoll, L. J., & Blakemore, S.-J. (2015). Adolescence as a sensitive period of brain development. *Trends in Cognitive Sciences*, *19*(10), 558–566. doi: https://doi.org/10.1016/j.tics.2015.07.008.

Gogtay, N., Giedd, J. N., Lusk, L., Hayashi, K. M., Greenstein, D., Vaituzis, A. C., … Ungerleider, L. G. (2004). Dynamic mapping of human cortical development during childhood through early adulthood. *Proceedings of the National Academy of Sciences of the United States of America*, *101*(21), 8174–8179. doi: 10.1073/pnas.0402680101.

Grossman, A. W., Churchill, J. D., McKinney, B. C., Kodish, I. M., Otte, S. L., & Greenough, W. T. (2003). Experience effects on brain development: Possible contributions to psychopathology. *Journal of Child Psychology and Psychiatry*, *44*(1), 33–63. doi: 10.1111/1469-7610.t01-1-00102.

Heckman, J. J., & Kautz, T. (2012). Hard evidence on soft skills. *Labour Economics*, *19*(4), 451–464. doi: 10.1016/j.labeco.2012.05.014.

Hwang, K., Velanova, K., & Luna, B. (2010). Strengthening of top-down frontal cognitive control networks underlying the development of inhibitory control: A functional magnetic resonance imaging effective connectivity study. *The Journal of Neuroscience*, *30*(46), 15535–15545. doi: 10.1523/jneurosci.2825-10.2010.

Johnson, K. A., Robertson, I. H., Barry, E., Mulligan, A., Dáibhis, A., Daly, M., … Bellgrove, M. A. (2008). Impaired conflict resolution and alerting in children with ADHD: Evidence from the Attention Network Task (ANT). *Journal of Child Psychology and Psychiatry*, *49*(12), 1339–1347. doi: 10.1111/j.1469-7610.2008.01936.x.

Kistner, S., Rakoczy, K., Otto, B., Dignath-van Ewijk, C., Büttner, G., & Klieme, E. (2010). Promotion of self-regulated learning in classrooms: Investigating frequency, quality, and consequences for student performance. *Metacognition and Learning*, *5*(2), 157–171. doi: 10.1007/s11409-010-9055-3.

Kolic-Vehovec, S., Zubkovic, B. R., & Pahljina-Reinic, R. (2014). Development of metacognitive knowledge of reading strategies and attitudes toward reading in early adolescence: The effect on reading comprehension. *Psychological Topics*, *23*(1), 77–98.

Leutwyler, B. (2009). Metacognitive learning strategies: Differential development patterns in high school. *Metacognition and Learning*, *4*(2), 111–123. doi: 10.1007/s11409-009-9037-5.

Lockl, K., & Schneider, W. (2004). The effects of incentives and instructions on children's allocation of study time. *European Journal of Developmental Psychology*, *1*(2), 153–169. doi: 10.1080/17405620444000085.

Luna, B., Marek, S., Larsen, B., Tervo-Clemmens, B., & Chahal, R. (2015). An integrative model of the maturation of cognitive control. *Annual Review of Neuroscience*, *38*(1), 151–170. doi: 10.1146/annurev-neuro-071714-034054.

Lyons, K. E., & Ghetti, S. (2010). Metacognitive development in early childhood: New questions about old assumptions. In A. Efklides & P. Misailidi (Eds.), *Trends and prospects in metacognition research*. Boston, MA: Springer.

Melby-Lervag, M., & Hulme, C. (2013). Is working memory training effective? A meta-analytic review. *Developmental Psychology*, *49*(2), 270–291.

Meltzer, L., Pollica, L. S., & Barzillai, M. (2007). Executive function in the classroom: Embedding strategy instruction into daily teaching practices. In L. Meltzer (Ed.), *Executive function in education: From theory to practice* (pp. 165–193). New York, NY: Guilford.

Nelson, T. O., & Narens, L. (1994). Why investigate metacognition. In J. Metcalfe & A. P. Shimamura (Eds.), *Metacognition: Knowing about knowing*. Cambridge, MA: MIT Press.

Nota, L., Soresi, S., & Zimmerman, B. J. (2004). Self-regulation and academic achievement and resilience: A longitudinal study. *International Journal of Educational Research, 41*(3), 198–215. doi: https://doi.org/10.1016/j.ijer.2005.07.001.

Ordaz, S. J., Foran, W., Velanova, K., & Luna, B. (2013). Longitudinal growth curves of brain function underlying inhibitory control through adolescence. *The Journal of Neuroscience, 33*(46), 18109–18124. doi: 10.1523/jneurosci.1741-13.2013.

Otero, T. M., Barker, L. A., & Naglieri, J. A. (2014). Executive function treatment and intervention in schools. *Applied Neuropsychology: Child, 3*(3), 205–214. doi: 10.1080/21622965.2014.897903.

Paulus, M., Tsalas, N., Proust, J., & Sodian, B. (2014). Metacognitive monitoring of oneself and others: Developmental changes during childhood and adolescence. *Journal of Experimental Child Psychology, 122*, 153–165. doi: https://doi.org/10.1016/j.jecp.2013.12.011.

Pintrich, P. R. (2002). The role of metacognitive knowledge in learning, teaching, and assessment. *Theory into Practice, 41*(4), 219–225. doi: 10.1207/s15430421tip4104_3.

Pintrich, P. R., & de Groot, E. V. (1990). Motivational and self-regulated learning components of classroom academic performance. *Journal of Educational Psychology, 82*(1), 33–40. doi: 10.1037/0022-0663.82.1.33.

Posner, M. I. (2012). *Attention in a social world* doi: 10.1093/acprof:oso/9780199791217.001.0001.

Posner, M. I., & Fan, J. (2008). Attention as an organ system. In J. R. Pomerantz (Ed.), *Topics in integrative neuroscience: From cells to cognition*. Cambridge, UK: Cambridge University Press.

Posner, M. I., & Rothbart, M. K. (2007a). *Educating the human brain*. Washington, DC: American Psychological Association.

Posner, M. I., & Rothbart, M. K. (2007b). Research on attention networks as a model for the integration of psychological science. *Annual Review Psychology, 58*, 1–23.

Posner, M. I., & Rothbart, M. K. (2014). Attention to learning of school subjects. *Trends in Neuroscience and Education, 3*(1), 14–17. doi: https://doi.org/10.1016/j.tine.2014.02.003.

Redick, T. S., Shipstead, Z., Harrison, T. L., Hicks, K. L., Fried, D. E., Hambrick, D. Z., ... Engle, R. W. (2013). No evidence of intelligence improvement after working memory training: A randomized, placebo-controlled study. *Journal of Experimental Psychology General, 142*(2), 359–379. doi: 10.1037/a0029082.

Redick, T. S., Shipstead, Z., Wiemers, E. A., Melby-Lervåg, M., & Hulme, C. (2015). What's working in working memory training? An educational perspective. *Educational Psychology Review, 27*(4), 617–633. doi: 10.1007/s10648-015-9314-6.

Robinson, L. J., Stevens, L. H., Threapleton, C. J. D., Vainiute, J., McAllister-Williams, R. H., & Gallagher, P. (2012). Effects of intrinsic and extrinsic motivation on attention and memory. *Acta Psychologica, 141*(2), 243–249. doi: https://doi.org/10.1016/j.actpsy.2012.05.012.

Roebers, C. M. (2017). Executive function and metacognition: Towards a unifying framework of cognitive self-regulation. *Developmental Review, 45*, 31–51. doi: https://doi.org/10.1016/j.dr.2017.04.001.

Rueda, M. R., Fan, J., McCandliss, B. D., Halparin, J. D., Gruber, D. B., Lercari, L. P., & Posner, M. I. (2004). Development of attentional networks in childhood. *Neuropsychologia, 42*(8), 1029–1040. doi: 10.1016/j.neuropsychologia.2003.12.012.

Ruff, H., & Rothbart, M. K. (2001). *Attention in early development themes and variations*. New York: Oxford University Press.

Schneider, W. (2008). The development of metacognitive knowledge in children and adolescents: Major trends and implications for education. *Mind, Brain, and Education, 2*(3), 114–121. doi: 10.1111/j.1751-228X.2008.00041.x.

Shimamura, A. P. (2000). Toward a cognitive neuroscience of metacognition. *Consciousness and Cognition, 9*(2), 313–323. doi: https://doi.org/10.1006/ccog.2000.0450.

Shonkoff, J. P. (2000). Science, policy, and practice: Three cultures in search of a shared mission. *Child Development, 71*(1), 181–187. doi: 10.1111/1467-8624.00132.

Steinberg, L. (2014). *Age of opportunity: Lessons from the new science of adolescence.* Boston, New York: Houghton Mifflin Harcourt.

Tamnes, C. K., Østby, Y., Fjell, A. M., Westlye, L. T., Due-Tønnessen, P., & Walhovd, K. B. (2010). Brain maturation in adolescence and young adulthood: Regional age-related changes in cortical thickness and white matter volume and microstructure. *Cerebral Cortex, 20*(2), 534–548. doi: 10.1093/cercor/bhp118.

UNICEF Office of Research – Innocenti. (2017). *The adolescent brain: A second window of opportunity.* Innocenti, Florence: UNICEF Office of Research.

van der Stel, M., & Veenman, M. V. J. (2010). Development of metacognitive skillfulness: A longitudinal study. *Learning and Individual Differences, 20*(3), 220–224. doi: https://doi.org/10.1016/j.lindif.2009.11.005.

Veenman, M. V. J., Kok, R., & Blöte, A. W. (2005). The relation between intellectual and metacognitive skills in early adolescence. *Instructional Science, 33*(3), 193–211. doi: 10.1007/s11251-004-2274-8.

Veenman, M. V. J., Wilhelm, P., & Beishuizen, J. J. (2004). The relation between intellectual and metacognitive skills from a developmental perspective. *Learning and Instruction, 14*(1), 89–109. doi: https://doi.org/10.1016/j.learninstruc.2003.10.004.

Weil, L. G., Fleming, S. M., Dumontheil, I., Kilford, E. J., Weil, R. S., Rees, G., ... Blakemore, S.-J. (2013). The development of metacognitive ability in adolescence. *Consciousness and Cognition, 22*(1), 264–271. doi: https://doi.org/10.1016/j.concog.2013.01.004.

Whitebread, D., & Basilio, M. (2012). The emergence and early development of self-regulation in young children. *Profesorado revista de Curriculum y Formacion del Profesorado, 16*(1). Retrieved 30 June 2018, from http://www.ugr.es/~recfpro/rev161ART2en.pdf

Williams, W. M., Blythe, T., White, N., Li, J., Gardner, H., & Sternberg, R. J. (2002). Practical intelligence for school: Developing metacognitive sources of achievement in adolescence. *Developmental Review, 22*(2), 162–210. doi: https://doi.org/10.1006/drev.2002.0544.

PART III
Technology and learning

We are living in an ever-changing world, where technology can transform the way we function. From the earliest records of history, the concept of technology has been used as a vehicle to support human learning and understanding. Viewing technology through the lens of learning can offer innovative ideas to enhance pedagogy and practice. This burgeoning area of enquiry has formed through a deep history of research into learning, changing policies and shifts in society (Part 1), and a desire to find more innovative approaches with which to apply the science of learning (Part 4). Technology offers an innovative and pragmatic means to tie the understanding and subsequent application of the science of learning in today's global society.

The goal of education is not to simply transmit knowledge to passive recipients, but to structure the learner's engagement with knowledge, in order to make them active participants and internalise that knowledge as their own (Laurillard, 2008). In a time where information is fast-paced, and readily available at the touch of a keyboard, available technologies can assist as a mechanism for imparting learning. Educators can utilise technologies in the classroom and prudently devise conditions for learners to enable them to explore, synthesise, and problem solve using the range of resources available (Maina, Craft, & Mor, 2015).

In Part 3, the role of technology in the science of learning is explored, linking the 'why' of the science of learning to the means with which to address and enhance the transfer of learning. The science of learning takes a deeper look into the cognitive and neurological processes that take place, and then designs learning to maximise such factors. It can be seen as a computational process, which shares many similarities with technology (Meltzoff, Kuhl, Movellan, & Sejnowski, 2009). Technology has the ability to support the design of learning to maximise engagement, motivation and retention of key learning activities.

Law's chapter explores the place of technology in learning and education, as both a curriculum area and medium for use in learning. Technology has an integral role in the holistic nature of contemporary education in the 21st century, with educators tasked with the crucial role of teaching '21st century skills' to learners. Education must 'future proof' itself, to enable individuals to prepare for jobs that do not exist at present. Technology becomes a vital component of such teaching. Law explores the role played by technology in knowledge creation through connecting minds, and offers insights into the role of technology in 21st century education.

Lodge, Kennedy and Lockyer's chapter extends on the previous chapter, by focusing on the relationship between teachers and students through the use of technology and the impact technology can have on learning. In contemporary classrooms, technology is expected, particularly in higher education settings where students are on campus less and less, and remote, flexible learning practices are necessary. Through the science of learning, technologies can be shaped in order to provide the best means with which to support education and cognitive growth.

Through both chapters in this part of the book, the role that technology can play in the science of learning is apparent. From providing a means with which to communicate learning, to measuring real time emotions, to connecting learning across countries, cultures, ages and stages, technology is interconnected throughout learning, and through empirical research, it serves to enhance the way in which education can be delivered to learners.

References

Laurillard, D. (2008). Technology enhanced learning as a tool for pedagogical innovation. *Journal of Philosophy of Education*, 42, 521–533.

Maina, M., Craft, B., & Mor, Y. (Eds.). (2015). *The art & science of learning design*. Sense Publishers, Netherlands.

Meltzoff, A. N., Kuhl, P. K., Movellan, J., & Sejnowski, T. J. (2009). Foundations for a new science of learning. *Science*, *325*(5938), 284–288.

10
DESIGN FOR LEARNING IN AN AGE OF RAPIDLY EVOLVING TECHNOLOGY

Nancy Law

Introduction

People learn through direct and indirect interactions with the world, and reflections on those interactions. The richness and complexity of the interactions and feedback available plays a critical role in determining a person's learning outcomes. Human society, even from its early days, has created technology to communicate knowledge and understanding to others, allowing human learning to be cumulative, across time and space. From cave paintings to writing, paper making, printing, audio-visual technologies, to all forms of digital technology today, an important function of technology is to mediate information and experiences in ever more sophisticated and easily accessible forms (Lin, 2014; Rogers, 1986). The deployment of such technologies to support learning has not only helped to advance human learning, it has also repeatedly demonstrated the naivety of our understanding about learning, as well as spurred new paradigms of learning and learning research. The shifts from the dominance of a behaviourist conceptualisation of human learning, to cognitive, constructivist, and constructionist models in academic and education communities are prompted by the observation that ever more sophisticated ways of information presentation per se would not help people to learn complex knowledge and skills (Harasim, 2012). Simplistic models of the good teacher as an effective presenter and subject matter expert are slowly beginning to be eroded. Explorations on the social dimensions of learning have received increasing attention since the middle of the 20th century. Advent of the internet before the turn of the millennium has spawned the area of research known as computer-supported collaborative learning (CSCL), which encompasses the development of new technologies and methods to study and scaffold socially organised forms of learning (Koschmann, 2012; Cress et al., in press).

Advances in technology and globalisation have also brought about deep socio-economic changes that call for changes in the goals of education. Solid mastery of core knowledge and skills valued in the industrial age is no longer adequate, and schools are now tasked with fostering new competences (often referred to as 21st century skills) such as critical thinking, communication, collaboration, and creativity for knowledge creation (Pellegrino & Hilton, 2013). A core tenet of this chapter is that connecting minds is fundamental to knowledge building and learning, and a primary function of technology for supporting learning is as a conduit for connecting minds. Twenty-first century learning is best facilitated in learning environments whose physical, digital, social, and task features are guided by appropriate design principles grounded on learning sciences research (Law, 2017; Lin & Spector, 2017; West, Ertmer & McKenney, 2020). Such principles should be applied to the learning design for students, teachers, school leaders, and policymakers at and across these multiple levels.

Technology, connectivity, and the social creation of knowledge

It is generally recognised that advances in information and communication technology have been a key driver in catapulting the developed world into a knowledge society. This section explores the role played by technology in knowledge creation through connecting minds, and hence what its roles in education in the 21st century can be.

We begin with a very brief review of the history of philosophical thinking about technology, its nature, and contribution to human society (Reydon, n.d.). Up until the Middle Ages, technology was closely connected with the concept of craftsmanship, which was centred around imitating and improving on nature's designs. As such, technology plays the role of augmenting human performance. When Francis Bacon proposed that nature can be investigated through experiments using man-made technological artefacts (ibid.), it represented a fundamental methodological shift in the investigation of nature, moving from being a philosophical endeavour to an empirical one. At the same time, it also elevated the role of technology to artefacts created by humans that serve as instruments in scientific experimentation. Heidegger (1962, cited in Reydon, n.d.) argued that in this role, technology also serves as a way of knowing about nature. In addition, many of the new technologies developed have allowed us to go beyond what initially appears to be limited by nature. Hence technology is also an approach to manipulating reality, an approach that challenges humans to challenge the limits apparently set by nature, and in the process uncover new knowledge about nature.

The above short description depicts two roles played by technology in the knowledge creation process that are commonly found in the literature: to augment human performance (this includes what is referred to as challenging nature) and as a way of knowing. There is a third and very important catalytic role played by technology in the knowledge creation process that has not been given due attention: that of connecting minds over time and space. These are the inscription or information preservation technologies, and information communication technologies (ICT). The former includes cave paintings, oracle bone scripts, papyrus scrolls, printed books, to audio and video tapes, CD-ROMs to all kinds of digital data storage such as data clouds, which are in some sense, inscription technologies. The earliest cave paintings date back to more than 30,000 years. We would not have been able to know about the lives of these earliest human civilisations without the artefacts they created to communicate their ideas and thoughts. Ideas and thoughts are transient and cannot be passed on through space and time without such inscriptions. The nature of the information stored has extended and advanced from paintings to written texts, to audio and visual images, to video and 3D images. Further, the costs and ease of production and replication of such artefacts have plummeted greatly through time.

Another associated change is in the ease of transporting (i.e., communicating) the information stored in these artefacts in terms of speed and costs. It is much easier to transport books compared to Egyptian clay tablets, and much easier to make woodblock printed copies of books than handwritten copies. The advent of audio and video broadcasting through electromagnetic waves has changed fundamentally the mode of information flow via physical artefacts, which is greatly constrained in terms of scalability and speed, to simultaneous one-to-many broadcasting through space. Digital technology bringing interactivity, especially through the advent of the internet, has further revolutionised simultaneously the preservation, replication, and transmission technology. These characteristics coupled with the powerful servers, search engines, and advances in information science and engineering have provided ordinary citizens opportunities to access and manipulate information that were unimaginable even at the end of the 20th century.

The emergence of Web 2.0 technology changed the read-only web to a read-write web (Aghaei, Nematbakhsh & Farsani, 2012; Faraj & Shimizu, 2018), thereby democratising who can have a voice, i.e., the right and the ability to communicate ideas over the internet. All the technology-mediated communications before Web 2.0, such as newspapers and websites had a steep communication gradient: they are strongly biased towards the rich and powerful, as the access to disseminating information was greatly limited to a small group of individuals and organisations that have the resources and know-how to do so. The Web 2.0 democratised information traffic such that even minority voices can be heard. This democratisation of information communication has brought revolutionary changes to collaboration, social participation, and knowledge creation.

There is a rich literature on knowledge creation as a social process, from work on scientific revolutions (Kuhn, 1962), to discussions of the knowledge creation model in organisations (Nonaka & Nishiguchi, 2001), to theory about systemic innovation (Brown & Duguid, 2001), just to name a few. While the foci, scopes, and perspectives taken on the nature and process of knowledge creation differ in the literature, there is a common theme that runs through, which is the importance of social connectivity and social interactions in the knowledge creation process. Just as Gutenberg's invention of the printing press has contributed much to the changes associated with Renaissance and the Copernican Revolution (Eisenstein, 1980), each major advance in information preservation, replication, and transmission technology has also contributed to acceleration in knowledge production, which is well illustrated by the exponential growth of knowledge since the invention of the internet, web, and social networking technology. These changes as well as the advances in transportation and telecommunication technology have facilitated "face-to-face meetings" to take place much more easily through global travel and various forms of synchronous communication. With these changes, the mode of knowledge production has also changed.

While knowledge creation has always been a process of social co-construction, the nature of the contributions made by the social process and the kinds of social processes involved have changed with the advances in technology. When the mediation of social interactions through information and communication technologies were less efficient and less sophisticated, for mediated social interactions across individuals and events that were not co-located in space and time, the social co-constructions were largely at the level of critique and exploration of ideas as described in Kuhn (1962). There is now an increasing dominance of team production of knowledge which has not been witnessed before (Wuchty, Jones & Uzzi, 2007; Mukherjee et al., 2017). Since the 1980s, there has been an increasing strategic move in research funding agencies to encourage interdisciplinary team science (Ledford, 2015). New forms of collaboration and knowledge creation have also arisen: crowdsourcing, the open source movement (Wittke & Hanekop, 2011), and citizen science (Curtis, 2018).

In the next section, we discuss the implications of these technological and social developments on learning and education.

Education: from learning as accumulation of knowledge to building 21st century capacities

The ability to accumulate and pass on knowledge and skills through millennia across widely separated spaces via social interactions and human-created artefacts is a prime distinguishing feature of the human race, and provides the cornerstone for education. At a simple level, we may conceptualise the accumulation process as knowledge building (or knowledge creation), and the passing on process as teaching and learning. However, for a very long time in human history, the rate of increase in human knowledge globally has been relatively slow. Further, travel and communication among people have been largely limited to close geographic neighbourhoods such that accumulation of knowledge at a personal level has largely been limited to what has been passed on directly from others. Schools as educational institutions started to blossom in the industrial age as a response to the social demands for a workforce that has mastery of specific knowledge and skills. Education has been dominated by an economic discourse, with schools serving as part of the production system and students as the output in the form of human resource (Cheng, 2015).

With advances in technology, particularly in the areas of transportation and communication, and the increasing pace of globalisation, the rate of growth of human knowledge has also escalated exponentially. Mastery of well-defined knowledge and skills is no longer adequate for ensuring competence to cope with changes in everyday life or the workplace. The World Declaration on Education for All launched in 1990 reflects a global consensus that it is a basic human right for everyone to have access to an education that meets basic learning needs required to improve lives and transform societies (UNESCO, 2000), and includes learning to know, to do, to live together, and to be.

With the increasing importance of education, what are considered as the most important learning outcome goals are also changing. Since the turn of the millennium, "21st century skills" have become the focal education goal in education policy documents in many countries. While different countries and consortia may define the skills/abilities somewhat differently (e.g., Partnership for 21st Century Skills, 2009; Singapore Ministry of Education, 2015), there are common themes that are considered to be core capacities for 21st century well-being, such as creativity, critical thinking, communication, collaboration (4Cs), self-directed learning, and lifelong learning. It is evident that these learning outcome goals are not focussing on specific knowledge or skills, but generic capacities that are generative. There is an implicit shift from a model of learning as a process of consumption (i.e., acquiring what has been well defined and developed) to that of capacity building and knowledge creation, and hence the process of learning has to be productive. Thus, in this model, the processes of learning and knowledge creation are similar.

Even though education and learning should not be confined within an economic discourse, there is a clear rationale from the perspective of social and economic well-being that prominence is given to 21st century capacities (or skills, as often referred to). UNESCO (2008) published a very influential *ICT Competency Standards for Teachers: Policy Framework* which put forth the argument that the integration of ICT into the school curriculum should be aligned with the broader education reform context, as well as the state of economic development of the country. This framework is grounded on an economic model that identifies three primary approaches to increase the productivity of a workforce: capital deepening, higher quality labour, and technological innovation. Each of these productivity enhancement approaches needs to be supported by the respective compatible educational approach: technology literacy, knowledge deepening, and knowledge creation, in order to foster the relevant qualities needed for the workforce. The 4Cs, self-directed learning, and lifelong learning are crucial for problem solving and knowledge creation.

Twenty-first century learning: agency, connectivity, and connectedness

With the shifting focus in the goals of education from efficient acquisition of known knowledge and skills to the effective fostering of knowledge creation capacity, the process of learning and teaching also has to change. The practice of organising learning in classrooms where students sit at their own desks, making individual efforts to acquire knowledge and skills, is a "consumption" model suited to the technological advances and needs of the industrial age: the progressively improved technology for replication and broadcasting of information served to meet the goals of mass production of workers, equipping the next generation with the appropriate standard of knowledge and skills for the workplace. This model of learning was itself a social construction, which was not grounded on research or understanding of how people learn. It does not provide the environmental conditions adequate for addressing the social need for education to prepare students for knowledge creation. It is also not an effective model for most kinds of learning.

There are a number of prominent theorists of socially organised learning. Vygotsky's (1980) theory about the zone of proximal development has inspired many in the design and organisation of learning in groups. Lave and Wenger (1991) argued that effective professional learning should be situated in communities of practice through a process of deepening engagement beginning with peripheral participation. With the inclusion of collaboration as one of the key 21st century skills, it is not surprising that social learning pedagogies have been promoted in the curriculum policy documents in many countries. However, collaborative learning per se does not address the educational goal of preparing students for knowledge creation.

Scardamalia and Bereiter (2003) introduced the concept of knowledge building both as a theory of how knowledge is created and a theory of how learning can take place. Knowledge, as defined in this framework, is public knowledge, referred to as conceptual artefacts (Bereiter, 2002) that can be used, modified, and improved by others. The challenge in the knowledge age is for collaborative learning to go beyond gaining new knowledge or skills, and to succeed in inducting and guiding learners onto a developmental trajectory from natural inquisitiveness to disciplined creativity. Learning science research shows that knowledge building does not happen naturally by putting learners to study/work in groups (Scardamalia & Bereiter, 1999). Face-to-face and/or mediated connectivity through classroom organisations and online technologies is necessary but insufficient to ensure learners have the connectedness (i.e., the capacity to make use of connectivity to achieve personal, social, work, or economic goals; OECD, 2012) to engage in knowledge building. To do so requires the application of appropriate design principles to the construction of the learning environment and tasks that would help learners to develop the necessary socio-metacognitive capacity to engage in the generation and continual improvement of ideas, which is fundamental to knowledge creation (Laurillard, 2013).

Pedagogical design principles for 21st century learning

Theoretical advances are fundamental to any discipline or field of research, including education. However, as argued eloquently by Collins (1992), education is not an analytical science such as the natural sciences or psychology, but a design science. "A design science of education, education must determine how different designs of learning environments contribute to learning, cooperation, and motivation." (ibid. p. 15) Within this paradigm of education as a design science, technology plays an important role in providing us with powerful tools to try out different designs based on theoretically grounded design principles (Collins, Joseph & Bielaczyc, 2004).

For collaborative learning to lead to knowledge creation, it requires an intentional cultivation and establishment of the necessary socio-cognitive dynamics among learners to foster a collective cognitive responsibility among the community of learners for knowledge advancement (Scardamalia, 2002). Empirical studies of the development trajectory of students' engagement show a three-stage knowledge building developmental trajectory as a collective (Law, 2005):

1. Evolving a socio-dynamic conducive to open exploration of ideas through encouraging sharing and non-judgmental consideration of diverse ideas as a foundation for developing an understanding;
2. Developing a progressive inquiry orientation through seeking clarification, comparing, connecting, and building on each other's ideas to improve one's own as well as the collective understanding;
3. Developing a socio-metacognitive orientation to generate higher level conceptualisations of the problems and solutions in the process of navigating complexities typically found in authentic inquiry through summarising, evaluating, and reflecting on individual and group learning.

Recent research has shown that to nurture these kinds of learning outcomes requires focussed efforts in designing the appropriate learning environments that bring learners together in appropriate organisational forms and contexts (Istance & Kools, 2013). Key elements of a learning environment include: pedagogical approach, task design, social interaction design, assessment and feedback design, and physical and digital learning environment design (Law & Liang, in press). The design principles that guide each of these key elements are briefly described below:

Pedagogical approach

This is the core design principle that defines the role of the learners in the learning process, and the pedagogy of choice is self-directed learning, as described by Knowles (1975, p. 18):

> In its broadest meaning, "self-directed learning" describes a process by which individuals take the initiative, with or without the assistance of others, in diagnosing their learning needs, formulating learning goals, identifying human and material resources for learning, choosing and implementing appropriate learning strategies, and evaluating learning outcomes.

Self-directed learning focusses on fostering students' ownership of learning, providing opportunities for students to set their own learning goals; plan, manage, and monitor their own learning process; evaluate the outcomes of their own learning; and to reflect on, revise and further extend their own learning.

Task design

The learning task needs to be open-ended to provide scope for learners to make their own decisions in the self-directed learning process. The task context should be relevant and meaningful to motivate learners' engagement.

Social interaction design

Collaboration and team work is a core part of the learning process. Research on teamwork in multidisciplinary projects has identified some crucial organisational strategies and principles for success that has a strong focus on a shared goal, balanced contribution, and engagement of members, provision of a psychologically safe social environment for sharing of ideas and capable of embracing failure and conflict, and build in interdependence among members and teams for critical decisions (Pentland, 2012; Chan, 2012).

Assessment and feedback design

Assessment and feedback needs to be compatible with and supportive of the learning goals and the pedagogical approach adopted. The performance criteria for evaluating the achievement of the targeted learning outcome goals should be made explicit and discussed. Furthermore, group assessment, peer feedback, as well as peer- and self-assessment should be integrated into the learning process (Nicol & Macfarlane-Dick, 2006; Wanner & Palmer, 2018).

Physical and digital learning environment design

Face-to-face meetings are found to be the most valuable form of social interaction for team interactions, and structuring of physical spaces and work routines such as coffee breaks to encourage informal interactions are found to bring about higher energy levels and engagement in social interactions that result in higher levels of team performance (Pentland, 2012). On the other hand, computer-mediated environments are playing significant roles in supporting collaborative knowledge creation in blended and totally online CSCL and computer-supported collaborative work (CSCW). The design of these digital environments needs to provide support for shared resources and activities and for collaborative sense-making, including representational and knowledge management tools suited to the specific knowledge domain, support for group formation, perspective taking among individuals and groups, and the co-construction and negotiation of shared knowledge artefacts (Stahl, 2017).

Sociotechnical designs for multilevel learning

The above design principles focus on the sociotechnical design of the learning environment for learners. However, as Istance and Kools (2013) point out, any consideration of the learning environment needs to go beyond the pedagogic core of learners, teachers, content, and resources to encompass the learning environment for multilevel learning involving teachers, school, and policy level leadership as well as families and the broader community. In addition to principles of learning design at the classroom interaction level, such as collaborative self-directed inquiry and appropriate performance criteria and feedback, technology integration for pedagogical innovation needs to pay attention to critical variables associated with the classroom social structure, which includes cultural beliefs, practices, socio-techno-spatial relations, and interactions with the world outside of the classroom (Bielaczyc, 2006). As classrooms are embedded within schools and the wider community, social and political milieu, there are additional design principles that need to be further explored and developed, such as design principles for leadership learning and building learning partnership with multiple stakeholders for aligned innovation to achieve 21st century learning at multiple levels of the education system (Law, Kampylis & Punie, 2015).

Instructional technology: learning technology or a pervasive medium for knowledge creation, empowerment, and participation?

The roles played by technology in human society do not depend simply on the functional capabilities of the technology, but on the social, legal, economic, and associated policies, organisational and governance infrastructures. The invention of automobiles is only one of many necessary conditions for the horse-drawn carriage to be replaced by cars as the predominant means of transportation in a city (Geels, 2005). The process of appropriating a new technology into the social fabric of life in any specific sector of social activity is a process of sociotechnical co-evolution (Geels & Kemp, 2007) involving reimagining different goals, actors, operations, and processes.

As mentioned at the beginning of this chapter, technology can serve the roles of augmenting human performance, as a way of knowing, and as a conduit to connect minds over time and space. These characteristics of technology are in principle perfect for fostering 21st century capacities in learners, as technology can be used as empowering tools for the learner to create, problem solve, communicate, and collaborate. However, to realise these potentials requires deep changes in classroom practices and the roles of learners and teachers, as the prevalent conception of learning is through instruction, an outdated understanding that was formed when knowledge creation was extremely slow. The field of instructional technology emerged with the invention of audio-visual technologies (Reiser, 2001). Such development took place not simply because the invention of radio and television broadcasting greatly extended the richness and complexity of the information being communicated, as well as in the scale of its reach. Instructional technology prospered also because of an urgent need for masses of people to be instructed on different operations during the wars. The audio-visual technologies were not envisioned as tools for empowering learners, nor for giving learners a voice. As long as the conception of learning is primarily through being taught, then the role of technology will remain within the realm of instructional technology irrespective of the functional characteristics of the technology (Law, 2017).

To realise the potential that current and emerging technologies can bring to how people learn requires deep changes in learning and teaching practices, whether in formal or informal learning contexts. With the ever-faster rates of technological innovation, it is difficult for us to anticipate what might be the new tools available to learners and teachers in ten, or even five years from now. However, one can confidently anticipate that the outcome of technological advancement will bring more powerful augmentation, more powerful ways of learning, and even greater connectivity to people and artefacts across space and time. On the other hand, whether we can leverage technological advances in the service of learning is a sociotechnical design challenge. Teachers need to give design attention to the classroom social infrastructure (Bielaczyc, 2006) for the designed learning interactions and engagement to be realised. Changes in classroom practices necessarily involve attendant changes in organisational routines, resource allocation, as well as policy and strategic priorities, which are inter-related and interdependent (Law et al., 2016). Principals and school leaders need to identify tensions in the existing sociotechnical infrastructure within the school, and between the school and the wider educational and social system, if the intended technology-supported pedagogical innovation is to be realised and sustained. As shown in many case studies on the scalability of learning innovations supported by digital technology (e.g., Kampylis, Law & Punie, 2013; Looi & Teh, 2015), successful change can be realised through multiple pathways for technology, but all of these involve a process of sociotechnical co-evolution involving the interaction and agency of stakeholders at various levels and sectors to achieve alignment across the system.

This chapter has provided a short treatise on the theme of design principles for 21st century learning grounded on a rich interdisciplinary literature from the learning sciences, education, education technology, and business innovation. It is underpinned by a core assumption that the most important learning outcome goal for the 21st century is to foster learners' collaborative knowledge creation capacity. Learning and knowledge creation are both fundamentally social in nature, and technology plays a key role in supporting both processes through connecting minds across space and time. The principles for the design of a sociotechnical system to scaffold 21st century learning as described here summarises the current state of knowledge. These principles need to be further refined and developed at theoretical, methodological, and technological levels to guide policy and practice to support 21st century learning.

References

Aghaei, S., Nematbakhsh, M. A., & Farsani, H. K. (2012). Evolution of the World Wide Web: From WEB 1.0 TO WEB 4.0. *International Journal of Web & Semantic Technology*, 3(1), 1–10.

Bereiter, C. (2002). *Education and mind in the knowledge age*. Mahwah, NJ: Lawrence Erlbaum Associates.

Bielaczyc, K. (2006). Designing social infrastructure: Critical issues in creating learning environments with technology. *The Journal of the Learning Sciences*, 15(3), 301–329.

Brown, J. S. & Duguid, P. (2001). Knowledge and organization: A social-practice perspective. *Organization Science*, 12(2), 198–213.

Chan, A. (2012). *Principles of Social Interaction Design*. pp. 175. Retrieved June 6, 2020 from https://www.academia.edu/download/31402192/SxD_Principles-AdrianChan-2012.pdf

Cheng, K. M. (2015). Learning in a different era: Do our education systems do enough to enable learners to flourish as independent, autonomous and well-balanced individuals? *European Journal of Education*, 50(2), 128–130.

Collins A. (1992). Toward a design science of education. In E. Scanlon & T. O'Shea (Eds.), *New directions in educational technology. NATO ASI Series (Series F: Computer and Systems Sciences)* (Vol. 96, pp. 15–22). Berlin, Heidelberg: Springer.

Collins, A., Joseph, D., & Bielaczyc, K. (2004). Design research: Theoretical and methodological issues. *Journal of the Learning Sciences*, 13(1), 15–42.

Cress, U., Wise, A., Rose, C., & Oshima, J. (Eds.). (in press). *International handbook of computer supported collaborative learning*. Berlin, Heidelberg, Springer.

Curtis, V. (2018). *Online citizen science and the widening of academia: Distributed engagement with research and knowledge production* (pp. 193). Cham, Switzerland: Springer.

Eisenstein, E. L. (1980). *The printing press as an agent of change*. Cambridge: Cambridge University Press.

Faraj, S. & Shimizu, T. (2018). Online communities and knowledge collaborations. In *Oxford Research Encyclopedia of Business and Management*.

Geels, F. W. (2005). The dynamics of transitions in socio-technical systems: A multi-level analysis of the transition pathway from horse-drawn carriages to automobiles (1860–1930). *Technology Analysis & Strategic Management*, 17(4), 445–476.

Geels, F. W. & Kemp, R. (2007). Dynamics in socio-technical systems: Typology of change processes and contrasting case studies. *Technology in Society*, 29(4), 441–455.

Harasim, L. (2012). *Learning theory and online technologies*. New York, NY: Routledge.

Istance, D. & Kools, M. (2013). OECD Work on Technology and Education: Innovative learning environments as an integrating framework. *European Journal of Education*, 48(1), 43–57.

Kampylis, P., Law, N., & Punie, Y. (Eds.). (2013). *ICT-enabled innovation for learning in Europe and Asia: Exploring conditions for sustainability, scalability and impact at system level*. Luxembourg: Publications Office of the European Union.

Knowles, M. S. (1975). Self-directed learning. *A guide for learners and teachers*. Englewood Cliffs, NJ: Cambridge Adult Education.

Koschmann, T. (2012). *CSCL: Theory and practice of an emerging paradigm*. Milton Park, Abingdon, Oxon, Routledge.

Kuhn, T. S. (1962). *The structure of scientific revolutions*. Chicago: The University of Chicago Press.

Laurillard, D. (2013). *Teaching as a design science: Building pedagogical patterns for learning and technology*. NY: Routledge.

Lave, J. & Wenger, E. (1991). *Situated learning: Legitimate peripheral participation*. Cambridge, UK: Cambridge University Press.

Law, N. (2005). Assessing learning outcomes in CSCL settings. In T.-W. Chan, T. Koschmann, & D. Suthers (Eds.), *Proceedings of the Computer Supported Collaborative Learning Conference (CSCL) 2005* (pp. 373–377). Taipei: Lawrence Erlbaum Associates.

Law, N. (2017). Instructional design and learning design. In L. Lin & M. Spector (Eds.), *The sciences of learning and instructional design: Constructive articulation between communities* (pp. 186–201). New York, NY: Routledge.

Law, N., Kampylis, P., & Punie, Y. (2015). Multiple pathways to enhance multilevel learning for scaling up systemic ICT-enabled learning innovations: Lessons from 7 European and Asian Cases. In C. K. Looi & L. W. Teh (Eds.), *Scaling educational innovations* (pp. 197–223). Singapore: Springer.

Law, N. & Liang, L. (in press). A Multilevel Framework and Method for Learning Analytics Integrated Learning Design. *Journal of Learning Analytics*.

Law, N., Niederhauser, D. S., Christensen, R., & Shear, L. (2016). A multilevel system of quality technology-enhanced learning and teaching indicators. *Journal of Educational Technology & Society, 19*(3), 72–83.

Ledford, H. (2015). Team science. *Nature, 525*(7569), 308–311.

Lin, C. A. (2014). Communication technology and social change. *Communication technology and social change* (pp. 17–30). New York, NY: Routledge.

Lin, L. & Spector, M. (Eds.). (2017). *The sciences of learning and instructional design: Constructive articulation between communities*. New York, NY: Routledge.

Looi, C. K. & Teh, L. W. (Eds.). (2015). *Scaling educational innovations*. Singapore: Springer.

Ministry of Education. (2015). 21st century competencies. Retrieved from https://www.moe.gov.sg/education/education-system/21st-century-competencies, accessed 30 June 2018

Mukherjee, S., Romero, D. M., Jones, B., & Uzzi, B. (2017). The nearly universal link between the age of past knowledge and tomorrow's breakthroughs in science and technology: The hotspot. *Science Advances, 3*(4), e1601315.

Nicol, D. J. & Macfarlane-Dick, D. (2006). Formative assessment and self-regulated learning: A model and seven principles of good feedback practice. *Studies in Higher Education, 31*(2), 199–218. doi: 10.1080/03075070600572090

Nonaka, I. & Nishiguchi, T. (2001). *Knowledge emergence: Social, technical, and evolutionary dimensions of knowledge creation*. New York: Oxford University Press.

OECD. (2012). *Connected minds: Technology and today's learners*. Paris: Centre for Educational Research and Innovation, OECD Publishing.

Partnership for 21st Century Skills. (2009). *P21 framework definitions*. Retrieved 30 June 2018, from http://www.p21.org/storage/documents/P21_Framework_Definitions.pdf

Pellegrino, J. W. & Hilton, M. L. (2013). *Education for life and work: Developing transferable knowledge and skills in the 21st century*. Washington, DC: The National Academies Press.

Pentland, A. (2012). The new science of building great teams. *Harvard Business Review, 90*(4), 60–69.

Reiser, R. A. (2001). A history of instructional design and technology: Part I: A history of instructional media. *Educational Technology Research and Development, 49*(1), 53–64.

Reydon, T. A. C. (n.d.). Philosophy of technology. *Internet Encyclopedia of Philosophy*.

Rogers, E. M. (1986). *Communication technology: The new media in society (Series in communication technology and society)*. New York: Free Press; London: Collier Macmillan.

Scardamalia, M. (2002). Collective cognitive responsibility for the advancement of knowledge. In B. Smith (Ed.), *Liberal education in a knowledge society* (pp. 67–98). Chicago: Open Court.

Scardamalia, M. & Bereiter, C. (1999). Schools as knowledge building organizations. In D. H. Keating, C. (Ed.), *Today's children, tomorrow's society: The developmental health and wealth of nations* (pp. 274–289). New York, NY: Guilford.

Scardamalia, M. & Bereiter, C. (2003). Knowledge building. In J. W. Guthrie (Ed.), *Encyclopedia of education* (2nd ed., pp. 1370–1373). New York, NY: Macmillan Reference.

Stahl, G. (2017). Group practices: A new way of viewing CSCL. *International Journal of Computer-Supported Collaborative Learning*, *12*(1), 113–126.

UNESCO. (2000). The Dakar framework for action. *Education for all: Meeting our collective commitments*. Paris: Author.

UNESCO. (2008). ICT competency standards for teachers: Policy framework. Retrieved 30 June 2018, from http://www.unesco.org/new/en/communication-and-information/resources/publications-and-communication-materials/publications/full-list/ict-competency-standards-for-teachers-policy-framework/

Vygotsky, L. (1980). *Mind in society: The development of higher psychological processes*. Cambridge, MA: Harvard University Press.

Wanner, T. & Palmer, E. (2018). Formative self- and peer assessment for improved student learning: The crucial factors of design, teacher participation and feedback. *Assessment & Evaluation in Higher Education*, *43*(7), 1032–1047.

West, R. E., Ertmer, P., & McKenney, S. (2020). The crucial role of theoretical scholarship for learning design and technology. *Educational Technology Research and Development*, *68*, 593–600.

Wittke, V. & Hanekop, H. (2011). *New forms of collaborative innovation and production on the internet-an interdisciplinary perspective*. Göttingen: Universitätsverlag Göttingen.

Wuchty, S., Jones, B. F., & Uzzi, B. (2007). The increasing dominance of teams in production of knowledge. *Science*, *316*(5827), 1036–1039.

11
DIGITAL LEARNING ENVIRONMENTS, THE SCIENCE OF LEARNING, AND THE RELATIONSHIP BETWEEN THE TEACHER AND THE LEARNER

Jason M. Lodge, Gregor Kennedy and Lori Lockyer

Introduction: educational technologies in the 21st century

Educational technologies are increasingly commonplace and expected in formal learning environments. In addition to traditional multimedia like videos and audio, these technologies now allow for students to interact with these environments, providing much richer learning experiences (for an overview, see Freina & Ott, 2015). As these technologies continue to evolve and become more sophisticated, it will have profound implications for formal education environments. One of the most pressing of these implications is what these technologies will mean for the relationship between the student and the teacher. As technology continues to impact on the ways in which students learn, it is also, and will continue to impact on the ways in which teachers and students interact with each other and with content. In this chapter, we provide an overview of the impact of these technologies, particularly on higher education, and discuss the implications of emerging educational technologies for the student–teacher relationship. Specifically, this discussion is aligned with research from the science of learning. The implications of emerging trends and understanding how these technologies can be best deployed to enhance student learning need to be built on a foundation of research on how students learn. We offer suggestions for emerging priorities for science of learning researchers and educators.

There are obvious signs that learning, both within formal education environments and beyond, is increasingly being mediated via technology. Mobile devices now mean that there is potential to access a wealth of information at anytime and anywhere with a network connection. One of the clearest examples of the impact this availability of networked devices has had is the fundamental change in how people go about developing certain kinds of knowledge. In order to see how to bake a pavlova or to erect a fence, many people will now go to online videos as a first option in order to see the process in action. Videos are particularly well-suited to this form of procedural learning (Lee & Lehto, 2013). The availability of networked devices and multimedia allows for easy access to demonstrations of almost any procedural task imaginable. The ease of access to this kind of resource raises questions about how teachers and educational institutions adapt to a world where information and knowledge are available on demand.

The emergence of new technologies has raised questions about what the impact on education will be since the invention of the printing press (see Moodie, 2016). What is perhaps different about the trends emerging in the 2000s and 2010s is that information and knowledge are no longer predominantly the domain of institutions. Even after the Gutenberg's invention made books available to the masses, the majority of these books were still to be found within university, monastery, or library walls. It was also only possible to carry a certain number of books around, as anyone who attended school in the 20th century can attest. The capacity to both access and store vast (practically limitless) information in mobile devices is a change that is fundamentally different to those that have come before. Students in higher education contexts are constantly connected and are interacting with each other and with content using mobile devices (Gikas & Grant, 2013). These trends raise questions about how these devices influence the ways in which students acquire, store, update, and use information and knowledge. Under what conditions do these technology tools lead to the most effective learning experiences? Do they serve as a distraction if not deliberately integrated into learning activities? When these devices are incorporated deliberately into learning activities, how are students using them to make sense of ideas and apply them in practice? There is a significant role for the science of learning in exploring and understanding these trends and unpacking the implications for students and teachers.

While the growing use of educational technologies is evident in all levels of formal education, it is perhaps in higher education that some of the most profound changes are taking place. Students are increasingly engaging in their studies in "blended," "flipped," or online modes with significant proportions of the learning activities they undertake occurring in digital environments (Siemens, Gasevic & Dawson, 2015). In particular, students increasingly engage in acquiring information and developing knowledge online. Some commentators have suggested that the impact of these new practices heralds the end of higher education as we know it (e.g., Christensen & Eyring, 2011). However, as we outline in this chapter, established and emerging research paints a far more complex and nuanced picture than a simplified dichotomous tension between traditional and digitally mediated educational offerings. There are advantages and disadvantages to learning in both physical and virtual settings, with teachers needing to employ different strategies and tactics in diverse environments.

Data, analytics, and their impact on learning and learning environments

The growing use of data, sophisticated algorithmic work, and increasingly accessible and cost-effective adaptive environments are resulting in an evolution in digital and emerging technologies. Data and analytics are being used in ever more sophisticated ways to track students' progress, predict their learning trajectory, and inform interventions. These developments have allowed much more targeted and personalised learning experiences which support the development of learning complex concepts and ideas, not just procedures and declarative facts.

The field of learning analytics, for example, has grown rapidly since the first *Learning Analytics and Knowledge* (LAK) conference in 2011. Learning analytics innovations are focussed on collecting and analysing data generated about, for and from students about various aspects of their learning (Sclater, 2017). This includes audit trail data generated as students interact with digital environments, personal data about who they are, what their preferences might be, and data about their knowledge and abilities generated through assessment. There are significant ethical implications associated with the collection and analysis of these data (Slade & Prinsloo, 2013). There are, at the same time, significant opportunities to better understand how students learn broadly and to gain insight into how individual students learn (Lodge & Corrin, 2017; Siemens et al., 2015). These findings can then be used in order to provide personalised feedback and other interventions.

The initial focus for the field of learning analytics broadly was to find indicators that students in higher education were potentially at risk and failing or withdrawing (e.g., Macfadyen & Dawson, 2010). There were, however, also earlier attempts to draw on audit trail data to gain insight into student learning processes (e.g., Kennedy & Judd, 2004). These studies laid a foundation for exploration of the use of "big data" and analytics to help understand how students are learning in digital environments. In the years since the first LAK conference, there has been increased interest in how these data might contribute to an understanding of student learning. Aligned with this has been a trend towards integrating learning analytics with design (e.g., Lockyer, Heathcote & Dawson, 2013) and with ideas and methods from educational psychology (e.g., Gašević, Dawson & Siemens, 2015). This trend was particularly apparent at the 2018 LAK conference where the most cited articles in the proceedings were from educational psychology literature and not from technical domains that had, up until that point, dominated the discussion about big data and analytics in education.

It is always difficult to predict future trends but there is reason to believe that some recent emerging technologies, such as machine learning (ML) and artificial intelligence (AI) could follow a similar trajectory to that of learning analytics. These technologies are poised to have a significant effect on education in the near future, as in other domains (Jordan & Mitchell, 2015; Luckin, 2018). Luckin (2017), for example, argues that AI systems can and will fundamentally change the way assessment is carried out in education. AI-based systems will allow for continuous assessment and real-time feedback that aligns much more closely with what is understood about quality learning and feedback. There is some conjecture about what counts as AI and what role it will play in education (Roll & Wylie, 2016). What is less controversial, however, is that it is likely that the advanced processing and adaptability provided by AI platforms will contribute, as is learning analytics, to our understanding of how students learn. There are, in parallel, also great possibilities for drawing on the science of learning to provide personalised interventions including through feedback, prompts, and tailored learning pathways in digital environments using these same technologies (e.g., Pardo, 2018). These trends suggest the coming to fruition of the promise of multimedia learning; adaptability in real-time and personalisation built on data mining and predictive algorithms. It is difficult to see how the potential of these technologies will be fulfilled without drawing on the science of learning to provide a foundational knowledge base describing how students learn.

The realisation of the full potential of learning analytics, ML and AI in education may still be a work in progress, however, there have been significant advances to date. There are already advanced, adaptive environments available that are being used for both research and educational purposes. Some of these systems have been in use for some time. For example, there are already sophisticated simulation environments for training pilots (Huet et al., 2011), surgeons (Piromchai et al., 2017), and dentists (Perry, Bridges & Burrow, 2015). What these environments share though is a focus on procedural tasks. It is much more complicated and difficult to develop an environment that can facilitate learning in complex conceptual domains. These domains include biological systems, climate, social and political phenomena as examples. These are all phenomena that require complicated mental structures or schema in order to understand them, which in turn rely on or are inhibited by prior knowledge (Carey, 2009). Understanding these concepts is difficult even without considering the additional complexity that comes with the application of this knowledge, which adds a further set of complexities. Focussing on the acquisition and updating of complex concepts of this kind, Dalgarno, Kennedy and Bennett (2014), for example, found that people adopt a variety of strategies when working through simulations to help them understand complex biological and meteorological concepts. The challenge with facilitating the learning of these more complex ideas is that it requires some understanding or assessment of how each individual makes sense of the concept to begin with. As the vast literature on conceptual change has demonstrated, there are many different reasons why an individual student might misunderstand a concept (Amin & Levrini, 2017). Each student constructs meaning in their own way (as per Bruner, 1962). Therefore, while adaptive systems have taken some forward leaps, there is still some way to go before these environments can cope with the significant diversity in how individual students make sense of complex ideas.

Taken together, developments in ML, AI, and learning analytics point to a situation where it will be possible to acquire even complex conceptual ideas in digital environments. However, adapting these environments on the basis of how each individual constructs meaning and develops mental schema remains a significant challenge. For example, it is relatively easy to see when a student might reach an impasse in a digital environment based on their activity within the environment. It is much more difficult to make a prediction about why (Arguel, Lockyer, Lipp, Lodge & Kennedy, 2017). Chi's (2013) categorisation of misconceptions partly explains what the difficulty is. Depending on how students structure related ideas in their mind, that structure will limit the way in which new information can be incorporated. So, one individual may see a very large dog and assume it is a horse, hence placing the example of the dog into the wrong conceptual schema (horse). Another may see a horse and assume it is a very large dog if they do not have a pre-existing conception of "horse." The problem with providing personalised instruction in a digital environment is therefore not just about what the overall level of prior knowledge is but how that knowledge is structured in students' minds.

Helping students develop their conceptual understanding is therefore a key challenge for developers of adaptive digital learning environments, given the need to be able to predict not just overt behaviour but the ways in which each student is making sense of both the ideas they are being exposed to and developing their capacity to monitor and update their own understanding. The research in the science of learning, examining how students acquire concepts (e.g., Schoor & Bannert, 2011), how they change their conceptual understanding (e.g., Amin & Levrini, 2017), how they make judgements about what they know and think they know (e.g., Lodge, Kennedy & Hattie, 2018), and how they self-regulate their learning (e.g., Broadbent & Poon, 2015) are all critical for informing the development of these technologies. Integrating what is known about how students learn is required here in order to make better predictions about what students are having trouble with and to provide appropriate interventions. Research on these fundamental processes are all critical if digital environments are to be fully responsive to student needs and learning trajectories.

Technologies that are and will continue to impact on education need to be built on a foundation that includes a deep understanding of how students learn. Without this, the kinds of technologies available will struggle with facilitating learning beyond procedural domains or simple adaptations that treat all students as the same on the basis of observable behaviour rather than the underlying cause. It will also be difficult to determine what role the teacher will need to play working alongside these environments. The science of learning will contribute here in two ways. First, the capacity for conducting laboratory-based experiments leads to increased confidence that different kinds of conditions and interventions cause specific outcomes. Second, and perhaps more importantly, if these technologies are to fulfil their potential, the science of learning will help to better understand individual differences. With learning scientists, designers, data scientists, and developers working together with teachers, it is possible that the potential of adaptive educational technologies will finally be realised after what seems like decades of promise (e.g., Wenger, 1987).

Teacher and student relationships in the digital world

With ML and AI evolving rapidly and being used in new domains, it is tempting to think that there will soon be sophisticated programs and platforms that can replace teachers altogether. One of the strongest indicators of how difficult this is likely to be comes from a study conducted by Koedinger, Booth and Klahr (2013). Using a modelling approach, these researchers attempted to map out the total possible number of ways in which instruction can be delivered. This "teacher model" included factors such as how and when feedback should be delivered, how examples are used, and a multitude of other instructional factors. It quickly became apparent that teachers are constantly navigating a decision set that is practically infinite. The researchers abandoned the model building process about half way through coding in all the factors with the number of possible instructional options already well over 200 trillion. The model also did not take into account content, context, or the variability that is brought to educational environments by students and teachers. This exercise shows how complex the task of teaching is. It also suggests that, even when the critical social elements of teacher–student interaction are removed, the number of decisions required to effectively deliver instruction makes the task of teaching extraordinarily complex.

It is unlikely that technologies will be able to replace teachers or teaching in the short term given the complexity teachers deal with in practice. However, the fourth industrial revolution is here and digital technologies are here to stay in our virtual and physical classrooms (Aoun, 2017). The question becomes one of when and how technologies can be most effectively used, for what, and understanding what implications this has for the teacher–student relationship. The science of learning points to vital elements teachers bring to educational environments that are difficult to simulate digitally. Beyond just what students know (epistemology), modelling of knowledge and professional ways of being (ontology) are critically important to quality higher education (Dall'Alba & Barnacle, 2007). To date, it is difficult to simulate this modelling of professional ways of being virtually or digitally (e.g., Cunningham, 2015; Mastel-Smith, Post & Lake, 2015).

The extensive research on the contributions of social cognition to learning across many domains (Blakemore, 2010) is one example of the importance of the interactions between students and teachers. Many of the subtle nuances of applying knowledge in practice in professional contexts, as explained by social cognition, require seeing these processes in action and that means seeing them demonstrated by a teacher. Additionally, when it comes to the direct relationship between students and their teachers, there is also great difficulty in simulating the ability of a teacher to read and respond to student emotions. Although affective technologies are developing rapidly (see Calvo, D'Mello, Gratch & Kappas, 2015), they do not come close to replicating the capacity a teacher has for seeing when a student is confused or frustrated and adequately intervening. For example, our research suggests there is potential in further exploring how confusion can be identified and managed in digital environments (e.g., Arguel et al., 2017). However, it will be some time before these environments can be built to operate at a capacity nearing that of a human teacher in a face-to-face setting. What is critical in the meantime then is to better understand how best to build environments that can respond to students in productive ways.

The changing student–teacher dynamic in higher education

Partly in response to broader trends associated with the ubiquity of technologies, there are already signs of significant change in policy and practice across higher education settings. While debatable, some have argued that the core teaching approach in universities has not changed for centuries (e.g., Lai, 2011). In other words, while there has been some movement away from traditional pedagogical approaches, the relationship between students and their teachers has been predominantly through the lecture or other didactic approaches. Essentially academics have broadcast what is in their minds to students. Mounting evidence over an extended timeframe about the value of active learning (e.g., Bell & Kozlowski, 2008; Freeman & Eddy, 2014), underpinned by constructivist learning theories and instructional frameworks, has put increasing pressure on the lecture as a viable means of teaching students in universities (French & Kennedy, 2017). A substantial proportion of this evidence can be traced back to the science of learning. For example, Bell and Kozlowski (2008), examined how the emotional, cognitive, and motivational aspects of active learning contribute to long-term learning and transfer. They found that a complex mix of factors including goal orientation and capacity for metacognition influence the success of active learning activities. An overview of how research such as this is impacting on education, including in universities, has been provided by Yates and Hattie (2013). Thus, the science of learning has already had significant impact on notions of effective teaching in higher education.

Lecturing as the key pedagogical approach in higher education has also come under scrutiny over several decades due to changes in the availability of information and knowledge, as we have previously outlined (see also Laurillard, 2002). In tandem, there has been pressure placed on universities through increases in student numbers and a diversification of student cohorts, often without commensurate increases in government funding for higher education (Marginson, 2016). There has therefore been an ongoing need to enroll students in large classes of various kinds to accommodate the growth in numbers. A tension emerges here because the continued move from elite to mass higher education globally has meant that, economically at least, lectures have remained a central approach

(French & Kennedy, 2017). Easy availability of high quality learning resources outside the university combined with the greater understanding of the value of active learning has created demand for more meaningful and interactive pedagogical approaches on campus (Boys, 2015). From a student perspective, there is also demand for more flexible learning experiences as students lead increasingly demanding lives and have work, career, and other responsibilities competing with their studies for time and attention (Baik, Naylor & Arkoudis, 2015).

These forces are leading to slow but fundamental change in the ways in which higher education is being delivered. With high quality resources now freely available online and an ability to acquire information anytime, there is a need to refocus on the value of the campus experience (Boys, 2015; French & Kennedy, 2017). In particular, the value of interaction between students and between students and academic teaching staff takes on a new level of importance. Sfard's (1998) two metaphors for learning are important here. The critical argument Sfard makes is that there are two central narratives about what learning is. The first, acquisition, is vital but the second, participation, is even more powerful for learning. Participation means not just accumulating knowledge but using it in meaningful ways in collaboration with others and in varying contexts. As technology currently stands, participation of this kind is still more difficult in a virtual or digital environment than on campus (Kebritchi, Lipschuetz & Santiague, 2017). Accessing opportunities for using knowledge in meaningful ways (i.e., application) has improved through increased use of webinars, wikis, and other collaborative tools. However, the capacity to interact with qualified experts and see them model the processes of applying knowledge is difficult to capture in a video. This modelling is highly valuable and necessary in many instances, for example, when clinical reasoning is carried out in a medical setting (e.g., Eva, 2005). Similarly, watching a video of an experienced nurse go about their practice is not quite the same as seeing this same practice firsthand in a live classroom setting or hospital (Mastel-Smith et al., 2015). In addition to having opportunities to use knowledge in meaningful ways, as in active learning, immersive participation and interaction with experts is not something that can easily be recreated in a virtual or digital setting beyond procedural tasks, yet. Digital simulations, virtual role plays, and virtual reality environments are beginning to bridge this gap. How much these environments can and do emulate the application of knowledge and/or provide access to expert application of knowledge remains an open question.

Within this changing context, it is not straightforward to take findings from experimental studies and apply them to such complex and dynamic conditions (Horvath & Donoghue, 2016) in order to understand how student–teacher interaction will change and can be enhanced. However, there are some key areas in which the science of learning can and is having an impact on informing the future of higher education (Lodge, 2016). Research on the effective design of video resources (e.g., Carpenter, Wilford, Kornell & Mullaney, 2013; Muller, Bewes, Sharma & Reimann, 2007) is one example of a relatively straightforward translation process from laboratory to classroom. The research of Muller and colleagues (2007) demonstrates that it is useful to use dialogue and focus on common misconceptions in instructional videos, which proves effective in the design of effective videos for "flipped" and blended approaches. Along similar lines, Verkade et al. (2017) have highlighted the development of instructional strategies that are focussed on addressing student misconceptions that have a grounding in the extensive literature on conceptual change. Both of these evidence-informed approaches incorporate modifications to the way in which teachers mediate the interaction between students and concepts. There are therefore already numerous examples of how the science of learning may be used in understanding and enhancing student–teacher interaction as technology increasingly impacts on policy and practice. These same approaches will continue to prove useful and informative as the nature of student–teacher relationships continues to evolve.

Key priorities for the science of learning

Within this broader context of rapidly evolving technologies and a rethinking of traditional approaches to education, there are several key areas in which the science of learning is and will continue to contribute. We have already discussed the ways in which the science of learning is providing a foundation for the design and use of cutting-edge technologies such as data-driven adaptive learning environments and how these environments might continue to shape the student–teacher dynamic in education. There are also several other key areas, particularly associated with the evaluation of new technologies, helping students to work with technologies and how these technologies can be best deployed to function alongside teachers. We will touch on these areas below.

Informing the development of and evaluating new technologies

Given it is seemingly inevitable that there will continue to be improvements in the capabilities of digital technologies for facilitating learning, there will be a parallel need for informing these developments and determining their effectiveness. This will not only be needed to better understand how teachers and machines will work together to enhance student learning, but also to determine the effectiveness of these technologies themselves in a comprehensive way. One of the major issues with the development of educational technologies is that the research examining the effectiveness of the tools lags well behind the spread of their use (Lodge & Horvath, 2017). In other words, new technologies are created and enter into widespread use often before the educational implications of the technologies are fully understood. As highlighted by Luckin (2017), there is great potential for continuous forms of assessment and feedback beyond the procedural domains such as dentistry where simulations incorporating continuous assessment and feedback are common. Development of these technologies will inevitably rely on a sound understanding of the learning process and evaluation approaches that are specifically designed to determine the impact on learning.

Alongside the overall need for the science of learning to help underpin the development of new instructional technologies, there is a clear need to draw on principles of quality student learning to determine how best to effectively combine the expertise of teachers and power of machines. As the student–teacher dynamic evolves, it will be important to monitor and obtain rigorous data on the best ways to deploy technologies and to set up activities and curricula designed specifically to maximise the benefits of the tools and the teacher. Simplified dichotomies will not sufficiently capture the complex nature of the three-way interaction of students, teachers, and machines. It would seem that the science of learning is well placed to conduct this ongoing monitoring in concert with teachers and educational designers.

Helping students to work with technologies

Alongside a better understanding of how teachers and machines can work together to help students, there is an ongoing need to help students to work with technologies themselves. As it is likely that more of the acquisition side of learning, as per Sfard's (1998) two metaphors, is carried out by students in digital environments, there will be a need to understand how this is occurring and to help enhance it. Students will increasingly be asked to self-regulate their own learning in these contexts. That is, without the nuanced intervention strategies that teachers employ in a classroom, students will need to be self-directed in their learning, in the short to medium term at least. This includes making sound judgements about how much they know compared to how much they need to know, how they are progressing towards completing quality work, and whether or not they need to shift strategies if the approach to their learning is not as effective as it could be. It is critical to determine how best to support students to do so in the absence of a teacher to help with this. The science of learning will play a key role in both understanding how students learn with and adapt to emerging technologies and determining how best to equip them with the right knowledge and skills to get the most out of these environments until such time as these environments are as sophisticated in their intervention strategies as a live teacher is in a classroom. With teachers seemingly likely to play less of a role in acquisition and more of a role in facilitating participation, it is critical to understand what the implications are for student learning.

Determining how technologies can best facilitate teaching and learning

A further area in which the science of learning will assist in understanding the changing student–teacher dynamic in education is through the implications on broader policy and practice. Much of what we have focussed on in this chapter has been the operational aspects of the teacher–student dynamic. Beyond this, there are implications for schools and universities, as well as policy-making bodies and government, as technology increasingly encroaches on education. The increased use of these technologies in classrooms must be driven by what is known about quality learning and not about financial or political motives. The history of educational technologies is littered with examples of technologies that have been implemented for reasons other than what is best for facilitating learning (Watters, 2014). The science of learning has a critical role to play in providing the evidence base for what works to counter the hype so often accompanying the development and spread in the use of technologies in education (see also Lodge & Horvath, 2017).

Conclusions

Developments in emerging educational technologies are already significantly impacting on education. This is apparent through the changing student–teacher dynamic in all levels of education. While it is most obvious in higher education, it is increasingly clear that teachers will be working alongside sophisticated ML and AI systems to help facilitate student learning. The science of learning has and will continue to play a pivotal role in providing a foundation underpinning these technologies and for determining how best the combination of teachers and machines can be deployed to enhance learning. While it has perhaps not received the attention that other implications of emerging technologies have, we have highlighted what these technologies mean for how students and teachers work together and in combination with machines. The complex, social environment of the physical, and virtual classroom will continue to raise issues and problems that will necessitate investigation. As has become apparent in the field of learning analytics, these investigations cannot rely on technical solutions alone but must be driven through a fundamental understanding about how students learn. So, while teachers seem unlikely to be replaced by robots anytime soon, it seems unlikely that researchers in the science of learning will either.

References

Amin, T. G. & Levrini, O. (Eds.). (2017). *Converging perspectives on conceptual change: Mapping an emerging paradigm in the learning sciences*. Abingdon, UK: Routledge.

Aoun, J. E. (2017). *Robot-proof: Higher education in the age of artificial intelligence*. Cambridge, MA: MIT Press.

Arguel, A., Lockyer, L., Lipp, O., Lodge, J. M., & Kennedy, G. (2017). Inside out: Ways of detecting learners' confusion for successful e-learning. *Journal of Educational Computing Research, 55*(4), 526–551. doi: 10.1177/0735633116674732

Baik, C., Naylor, R., & Arkoudis, S. (2015). *The first year experience in Australian universities: Findings from two decades (1994–2014)*. Melbourne: Melbourne Centre for the Study of Higher Education, University of Melbourne.

Bell, B. S. & Kozlowski, S. W. (2008). Active learning: Effects of core training design elements on self-regulatory processes, learning, and adaptability. *Journal of Applied Psychology, 93*(2), 296.

Blakemore, S. J. (2010). The developing social brain: Implications for education. *Neuron*, *65*(6), 744–747.
Boys, J. (2015). *Building better universities: Strategies, spaces, technologies*. Abingdon, UK: Routledge.
Broadbent, J. & Poon, W. L. (2015). Self-regulated learning strategies & academic achievement in online higher education learning environments: A systematic review. *The Internet and Higher Education*, *27*, 1–13.
Bruner, J. S. (1962). *A study of thinking*. New York, NY: Science Editions, Inc.
Calvo, R., D'Mello, S. K., Gratch, J., & Kappas, A. (Eds.). (2015). *The Oxford handbook of affective computing*. New York, NY: Oxford University Press.
Carey, S. (2009). *The origin of concepts*. Oxford, UK: Oxford University Press.
Carpenter, S. K., Wilford, M. M., Kornell, N., & Mullaney, K. M. (2013). Appearances can be deceiving: Instructor fluency increases perceptions of learning without increasing actual learning. *Psychonomic Bulletin & Review*, *20*(6), 1350–1356.
Chi, M. T. H. (2013). Two kinds and four sub-types of misconceived knowledge, ways to change it, and the learning outcomes. In S. Vosniadou (Ed.), *The international handbook of conceptual change* (2nd ed., pp. 49–70). New York, NY: Routledge.
Christensen, C. & Eyring, H. (2011). *The innovative university: Changing the DNA of higher education from the inside out*. San Francisco: Jossey-Bass.
Cunningham, J. M. (2015). Mechanizing people and pedagogy: Establishing social presence in the online classroom. *Online Learning*, *19*(3), 34–47.
Dalgarno, B., Kennedy, G., & Bennett, S. (2014). The impact of students' exploration strategies on discovery learning using computer-based simulations. *Educational Media International*, *51*(4), 310–329. doi: 10.1080/09523987.2014.977009
Dall'Alba, G. & Barnacle, R. (2007). An ontological turn for higher education. *Studies in Higher Education*, *32*(6), 679–691. http://doi.org/10.1080/03075070701685130
Eva, K. W. (2005). What every teacher needs to know about clinical reasoning. *Medical Education*, *39*(1), 98–106.
Freeman, S. & Eddy, S. L. (2014). Active learning increases student performance in science, engineering, and mathematics. *Proceedings of the National Academy of Sciences*, *111*(23), 1–6. http://doi.org/10.1073/pnas.1319030111
Freina, L. & Ott, M. (2015). A literature review on immersive virtual reality in education: State of the art and perspectives. In *Proceedings of eLearning and Software for Education (eLSE)*, 2015 April (pp. 23–24). Bucharest.
French, S. & Kennedy, G. (2017). Reassessing the value of university lectures. *Teaching in Higher Education*, *22*(6), 639–654. doi: 10.1080/13562517.2016.1273213
Gašević, D., Dawson, S., & Siemens, G. (2015). Let's not forget: Learning analytics are about learning. *TechTrends*, *59*(1), 64–71.
Gikas, J. & Grant, M. M. (2013). Mobile computing devices in higher education: Student perspectives on learning with cellphones, smartphones & social media. *The Internet and Higher Education*, *19*, 18–26.
Horvath, J. C. & Donoghue, G. M. (2016). A bridge too far – revisited: Reframing Bruer's neuroeducation argument for modern science of learning practitioners. *Frontiers in Psychology*, *7*, 377. doi: 10.3389/fpsyg.2016.00377
Huet, M., Jacobs, D. M., Camachon, C., Missenard, O., Gray, R., & Montagne, G. (2011). The education of attention as explanation of variability of practice effects: Learning the final approach phase in a flight simulator. *Journal of Experimental Psychology: Human Perception and Performance*, *37*(6), 1841.
Jordan, M. I. & Mitchell, T. M. (2015). Machine learning: Trends, perspectives, and prospects. *Science*, *349*(6245), 255–260.

Kebritchi, M., Lipschuetz, A., & Santiague, L. (2017). Issues and challenges for teaching successful online courses in higher education: A literature review. *Journal of Educational Technology Systems*, *46*(1), 4–29.

Kennedy, G. E. & Judd, T. S. (2004). Making sense of audit trail data. *Australasian Journal of Educational Technology*, *20*(1), 18–32. doi: 10.14742/ajet.1365

Koedinger, K. R., Booth, J. L., & Klahr, D. (2013). Instructional complexity and the science to constrain it. *Science*, *342*, 935–937.

Lai, K. W. (2011). Digital technology and the culture of teaching and learning in higher education. *Australasian Journal of Educational Technology*, *27*(8).

Laurillard, D. (2002). *Rethinking university teaching* (2nd ed.). Abingdon, UK: RoutledgeFalmer.

Lee, D. Y. & Lehto, M. R. (2013). User acceptance of YouTube for procedural learning: An extension of the technology acceptance model. *Computers & Education*, *61*, 193–208.

Lockyer, L., Heathcote, E., & Dawson, S. (2013). Informing pedagogical action: Aligning learning analytics with learning design. *American Behavioral Scientist*, *57*(10), 1439–1459.

Lodge, J. M. (2016). Do the learning sciences have a place in higher education research? *Higher Education Research & Development*, *35*(3), 634–637. doi: 10.1080/07294360.2015.1094204

Lodge, J. M. & Corrin, L. (2017). What data and analytics can and do say about effective learning. *Nature: npj Science of Learning*, *2*(1), 4–5. doi: 10.1038/s41539-017-0006-5

Lodge, J. M. & Horvath, J. C. (2017). Science of learning and digital learning environments. In J. C. Horvath, J. M. Lodge, & J. A. C. Hattie (Eds.), *From the laboratory to the classroom: Translating learning sciences for teachers*. Abingdon, UK: Routledge.

Lodge, J. M., Kennedy, G., & Hattie, J. A. C. (2018). Understanding, assessing and enhancing student evaluative judgement in digital environments. In D. Boud, R. Ajjawi, P. Dawson, & J. Tai (Eds.), *Developing evaluative judgement in higher education: Assessment for knowing and producing quality work*. Abingdon, UK: Routledge.

Luckin, R. (2017). Towards artificial intelligence-based assessment systems. *Nature Human Behaviour*, *1*(0028). doi: 10.1038/s41562-016-0028

Luckin, R. (2018). *Machine learning and human intelligence*. London: UCL Institute of Education Press.

Macfadyen, L. P. & Dawson, S. (2010). Mining LMS data to develop an "early warning system" for educators: A proof of concept. *Computers & Education*, *54*(2), 588–599.

Marginson, S. (2016). *Higher education and the common good*. Melbourne: Melbourne University Press.

Mastel-Smith, B., Post, J., & Lake, P. (2015). Online teaching: "Are you there, and do you care?". *Journal of Nursing Education*, *54*(3), 145–151.

Moodie, G. (2016). *Universities, disruptive technologies, and continuity in higher education: The impact of information revolutions*. New York, NY: Palgrave Macmillan.

Muller, D. A., Bewes, J., Sharma, M. D., & Reimann, P. (2007). Saying the wrong thing: Improving learning with multimedia by including misconceptions. *Journal of Computer Assisted Learning*, *24*(2), 144–155. doi: 10.1111/j.1365-2729.2007.00248.x

Pardo, A. (2018). A feedback model for data-rich learning experiences. *Assessment & Evaluation in Higher Education*, *43*(3), 428–438.

Perry, S., Bridges, S. M., & Burrow, M. F. (2015). A review of the use of simulation in dental education. *Simulation in Healthcare*, *10*(1), 31–37.

Piromchai, P., Ioannou, I., Wijewickrema, S., Kasemsiri, P., Lodge, J. M., Kennedy, G., & O'Leary, S. (2017). The effects of anatomical variation on trainee performance in a virtual reality temporal bone surgery simulator – A pilot study. *The Journal of Laryngology & Otology*, *131* (S1), S29–S35. doi: 10.1017/S0022215116009233

Roll, I. & Wylie, R. (2016). Evolution and revolution in artificial intelligence in education. *International Journal of Artificial Intelligence in Education*, *26*(2), 582–599.

Schoor, C. & Bannert, M. (2011). Motivation in a computer-supported collaborative learning scenario and its impact on learning activities and knowledge acquisition. *Learning and Instruction, 21*(4), 560–573.

Sclater, N. (2017). *Learning analytics explained*. Abingdon, UK: Routledge.

Sfard, A. (1998). On two metaphors for learning and the dangers of choosing just one. *Educational Researcher, 27*(2), 4–13.

Siemens, G., Gasevic, D., & Dawson, S. (2015). *Preparing for the digital university: A review of the history and current state of distance, blended, and online learning*. Report Commissioned by the Bill & Melinda Gates Foundation. Retrieved on April 15, 2018 from http://linkresearchlab.org/PreparingDigitalUniversity.pdf

Slade, S. & Prinsloo, P. (2013). Learning analytics: Ethical issues and dilemmas. *American Behavioral Scientist, 57*(10), 1510–1529.

Verkade, H., Mulhern, T. D, Lodge, J. M., Elliott, K., Cropper, S., Rubinstein, B., Horton, A., Elliott, C., Espiñosa, A., Dooley, L., Frankland, S., Mulder, R., & Livett, M. (2017). *Misconceptions as a trigger for enhancing student learning in higher education: A handbook for educators*. Melbourne: The University of Melbourne.

Watters, A. (2014). *The monsters of education technology*. Seattle, WA: Amazon.

Wenger, E. (1987). *Artificial intelligence and tutoring systems*. Los Altos, CA: Morgan Kaufmann.

Yates, G. C. & Hattie, J. (2013). *Visible learning and the science of how we learn*. Abingdon, UK: Routledge.

PART IV
Research translation

Representing a diversity of disciplines, science of learning research occurs at various levels of granularity. Parts II and III of this book demonstrate the various lenses through which researchers are analysing learning, and provide insights into the type of questions that can be addressed by fundamental and applied research. However, as eluded to by Hattie and Nugent in the prologue, the relevance of these findings to education has been questioned. It is not sufficient that researchers in the science of learning seek to identify the impact of their research at an individual student, teacher, classroom, or school level. As an emerging field of research, the science of learning community must demonstrate its ability to impact education as a whole.

Science of learning is not dissimilar to other fields of research with regard to the translation of research findings into practice. The scale-up and rollout of most new innovation requires a staged approach. Further research and development is often necessary as production is increased. There are critical checkpoints during the process where quality is checked in order to ensure fidelity and stability of outcome is retained before taking production to the next level. In Chapter 13 Leonard and Westwell eloquently describe 'a reflective pause in work' before expanding a project to the next level.

Chapters 12 (Brooks and Burton) and 13 (Leonard and Westwell) provide examples of science of learning research findings being translated to the classroom. Both projects have been rolled out in multiple classrooms across numerous sites, one in the context of primary school literacy and the other middle school mathematics. Underpinned by evidence from the science of learning, the former study has feedback as the core focus, whilst the latter study relates to approaches for developing critical thinking in learners. At different time-points along the journey, the authors share learnings from their reflective pauses. Although the projects vary greatly in context and science of learning principle being adopted, the two projects are united in the key elements they identify as essential for successful translation. A strong message emerging from both projects is how critical the partnership with teachers and school leaders is to achieving sustainable and scalable translation. These key elements are also reflected in the "bespoke" translation model developed by MacMahon et al. in Chapter 14.

All seeking to achieve scalable and sustainable translation of research findings from the science of learning to the classroom, each of the projects described in this part of the book utilises a different model of research translation. Acknowledging the science of learning has tended to adopt an explanatory stance, in Chapter 13 Westwell admits to adopting an educational design research approach grounded in the learning sciences. However, the approach to professional learning is also informed by the science of learning, and practices the "stop and think" mantra of the project. In contrast, Brooks et al. adopt an instructional coaching approach, based on the instructional coaching framework of Knight (2007).

Moving away from the one-way dissemination of information, each of these projects refers to collaboration – between researchers, educators, policymakers, and school leaders. With the co-design of interventions, both researchers and educators contribute to the co-creation of new knowledge, learning from each other. All three projects encapture boundary crossing, teachers crossing the boundary into research and back again. Putting fidelity of principle ahead of fidelity of practice, researchers are gaining a fuller understanding of the complexity of the classroom and the difficulty in isolating causal factors within such a complex environment.

Reference

Knight, J. (2007). *Instructional coaching: A partnership approach to improving instruction.* Thousand Oaks, CA: Corwin Press.

12
RESEARCH TO REALITY: FEEDBACK FOR LEARNING: BUILDING CAPABILITY TO IMPROVE OUTCOMES

Cameron Brooks and Rochelle Burton

Introduction

This chapter outlines the planning, impact, and challenges of a three-year Australian Research Council funded intervention study aimed at building teacher capability, school leader instructional practices, and effective student learning behaviours. To achieve this aim, a feedback model (Hattie & Timperley, 2007) underpinned by evidence-informed practices of clarifying success criteria, comparing student performance to said criteria and developing strategies to close the learning gap, is utilised within the present research. The present study builds off previous pilot work (Brooks, Carroll, Gillies & Hattie, 2017).

Rationale

Learning outcomes for Australian students are at best stagnating and at worst declining. While National Assessment Program Literacy and Numeracy (NAPLAN) data since 2008 has shown isolated improvements, achievement levels of Australian students for the most part have stalled. Data from the 2018 Programme for International Student Assessment (PISA) demonstrates that Australian students are falling behind in reading, mathematical, and scientific literacy (Thomson, De Bortoli, Underwood & Schmid, 2019). Perhaps most concerning is that longitudinal PISA data demonstrates a significant fall in all literacy performance for Australian students since 2000 (Schleicher, 2019). This malaise of student achievement is occurring despite continued increases in educational funding. The key question then becomes, what is required to improve learning outcomes? Australian Council of Educational Research (ACER) Chief Executive, Geoff Masters (2016), states that improving student performance requires changes in teacher practice. He emphasises teachers must be knowledgeable of content, skilled in diagnosing learning needs, and capable of implementing highly effective teaching strategies (Masters, 2016). Such claims correspond with findings that student learning outcomes are greatly influenced by the quality of teaching (Hattie, 2009). After analysing over 800 meta-analyses relating to achievement, it was deducted that the use of feedback is one of the most powerful influences on achievement available to the teacher.

Feedback is typically viewed as information given to the student that is designed to cause modification of actions and result in learning (Shute, 2008). Recently, this cause and effect notion of feedback has been challenged as the provision of feedback is no guarantee of learning (Brookhart, 2017; Sadler, 2010). Using the metaphor of a feedback loop, feedback can be considered to be information about past performance that is used by learners to modify future performance (Boud & Molloy, 2012).

Feedback can serve many different purposes such as to provide: a grade, a justification of a grade, a qualitative description of the work, praise, encouragement, identification of errors, suggestions on how to fix errors and guidance on how to improve the work standard (Sadler, 2010). Wiliam (2013) states that feedback should be either directive and tell students where they went wrong or facilitative and provide guidance on how to improve. Shute, Hansen, and Almond (2007) found that feedback that includes elaborations about how to improve led to improvements in learning efficiency and student achievement. Improvement-based feedback that includes guidance is more effective than statements about whether work is right or wrong as it takes into consideration how feedback is received by learners (Shute, 2008). Literature on student perceptions of feedback includes findings that students become frustrated with feedback that is too general or tells them where they went wrong but does not provide guidance on how to improve (Gamlem & Smith, 2013). Brookhart (2017) proposes that teachers use descriptive, improvement-based feedback rather than evaluative statements or feedback directed to the self.

Effective feedback tells students how they are going in relation to goals and criteria and then provides guidance and opportunities for improvement (Hattie & Timperley, 2007). Seminal research by Locke and Latham (1990) highlights the benefits of increased motivation and higher quality of work outputs when goals are learning- rather than performance-focussed and set with appropriate challenge. Sadler (1989) states that feedback is most effective when it directs students' attention to the feedback standard gap between current performance and goals or standards. Furthermore, Wiliam (2011) advocates that feedback should explicitly connect student performance with key indicators of learning goals or criteria for success. He suggests that teachers use focussed feedback by matching it to the goals and that in terms of quantity, less can often be better than more feedback. Hattie (2009) claims that much of the feedback that is given by teachers is directed to the self, rather than to specific learning elements of tasks. Research directed to the self, commonly given as praise, has been found to have negative impacts upon learning (Dweck, 2007; Skipper & Douglas, 2012).

Van den Bergh, Ros, and Beijaard (2013) conducted research into writing tasks in primary schools and found that only 5% of feedback given was matched to a learning goal. During post-observation interviews, the researchers also found that most teachers could not report the specific learning goals for their lesson. Brookhart (2017) advocates for teachers to consider the comparison point for feedback and states that feedback is more effective when directed to criteria rather than norm-referenced to peers or the self.

The present study: *improving student outcomes: coaching teachers in the power of feedback 2017–2019*

The aim of this study was to address the research problem of declining national literacy results, in particular, a fall in writing results reported by our partner schools. We build upon our previous work, and that of others, by designing a study at scale that investigated how student literacy outcomes in writing can be augmented through a feedback-based, teacher professional learning (PL) intervention. Specifically, we aimed to:

1. *Develop* long-term partnerships between universities, education departments, and school partners to address the problem of declining levels of student achievement;
2. *Investigate* the effects of a "feedback for learning" intervention upon teacher and school leader practice and perceptions of pedagogical change;
3. *Examine* the effects of a "feedback for learning" intervention upon student perceptions of feedback helpfulness;
4. *Measure* the effects of the "feedback for learning" intervention upon student achievement;
5. *Propose* a scalable model to schools of a school-based teacher PL intervention that builds teacher capability and augments student learning outcomes.

Within the Science of Learning Research Centre (SLRC), we prioritise the translation of our research to end users. As such, we developed partnerships with the Queensland Department of Education and individual schools. These partnerships allowed us to collaborate with policymakers, school leaders, teachers, and students for the benefit of all partners. End users, including teachers and school leaders received evidence-informed professional development of which students were the beneficiaries through rich and differentiated learning experiences. Universities also benefitted through the provision of authentic and meaningful contexts with which to develop their research. We believe this project strengthened and consolidated partnerships between universities and schools.

Research design

The study used an embedded mixed methods design (Creswell & Clark, 2011), with both qualitative and quantitative data collection methods. Using a wait-list

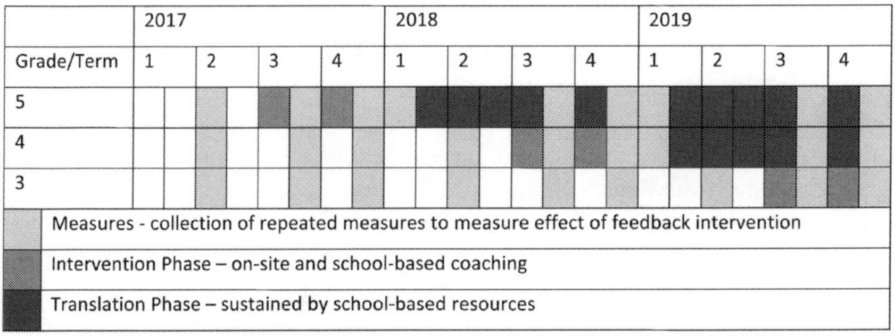

	2017				2018				2019			
Grade/Term	1	2	3	4	1	2	3	4	1	2	3	4
5												
4												
3												

Measures - collection of repeated measures to measure effect of feedback intervention

Intervention Phase – on-site and school-based coaching

Translation Phase – sustained by school-based resources

FIGURE 12.1 Intervention design

control approach, the intervention was administered sequentially to targeted participant groups across the time of the study. As seen in Figure 12.1, the intervention commenced with Year 5 teachers and students, progressed in 2018 to Year 4 teachers and students and concluded with Year 3 teachers and students in 2019.

Participants

The overall study involved approximately 150 classroom teachers (50 Year 5 teachers, 2017; 50 Year 4 teachers, 2018; and 50 Year 3 teachers, 2019), 20 school leaders (Principals and Deputy Principals), 30 instructional coaches (Heads of Curriculum and/or Master Teachers), and 2700 students (from Year 3 to Year 5). Student participant ages ranged between 7.5 and 10.5 years of age. A large student participant sample was purposefully selected to help mediate the effect of missing data due to participant withdrawal. Likewise, the study recruited multiple school and instructional leaders from each school to help account for participant loss during the term of the study.

The intervention

The intervention was based upon Hattie and Timperley's (2007) conceptual model of feedback which posits three feedback questions from the learner's point of view: where am I going? (Feeding up); How am I going? (Feeding back); and, Where to next? (Feeding forward). The notion here is that for feedback to be effective, each of these questions must be answered for or by the learner. Through the addition of feedback levels, this model facilitates the targeting of differentiated, specific feedback to individual learners, depending on their learning needs. Each question works at four feedback levels: task, process, self-regulation, and the self-level. Task level feedback is focussed upon the learning intent and the specific requirements of the task, whilst process level feedback is aimed at the processes, skills, strategies, and thinking required by the learner to complete the task. Self-regulatory level feedback requires the student to use deep learning principles such as relational thinking and self-monitoring to compare and adjust their work in relation to the required standards, criteria, or intent. Feedback to the self-level, most commonly associated with praise, is best avoided due to evidence that it has a detrimental impact on learning (Dweck, 2007; Hattie, 2009; Kluger & DeNisi, 1996).

During the intervention phase of this study, the translation of the conceptual model of feedback was framed by a model of PL that included elements of instructional coaching. "Instructional coaching provides intensive, differentiated support to teachers so that they are able to implement proven practices" (Knight, 2009, p. 29). Similar to other PL methods, instructional coaching creates a shared and valued context for learning (Teemant, 2013). The point of difference, however, is that instructional leaders focus on the implementation of evidence-informed practices (Knight & van Nieuwerburgh, 2012); in this case, feedback processes. Knight's (2007) Instructional Coaching model uses the partnership approach as a theoretical framework to guide its design and implementation. The partnership approach features seven principles: equality; choice; voice; dialogue; reflection; praxis; and reciprocity. This study was guided by these principles to facilitate effective implementation.

The feedback intervention occurred through both formal and informal PL sessions differentiated to align with school and teacher needs. Formal sessions were advantageous as teachers were given withdrawal time to engage with the research practices separate from the responsibilities they had to their students. During the formal sessions, year level teachers from each school were withdrawn from class for professional learning. The intervention primarily consisted of eight, half-day sessions conducted across two school terms. The grouping of teachers allowed for collaboration and the sharing of effective pedagogical practices. An overview of the formal PL sessions are as follows: (1) Engagement – sharing of context, building value propositions, clarifying aims, and objectives and introduction to feedback conceptual model; (2) Collaboration and Planning – teachers and instructional coaches and school leaders working together to plan a writing unit of work that is underpinned by the feedback conceptual model; (3) Formative Assessment Design – teachers and coaches work together to design questions to best elicit student learning in relation to success criteria; (4–7) Feedback sessions – teachers bring student evidence of learning for collaborative discussion about the next steps for improvement; and (8) Reflection – participants reflect upon the PL process and review how the teaching and learning process could be improved.

It was also vital to consider how teachers translate learning from the formal PL sessions into classroom pedagogical practices; hence this research design also incorporated support through differentiation. Using a "coaching the coaches" methodology, the instructional coaches from the research team coached the school and instructional leaders to support the classroom teachers in enacting the feedback intervention. Drawing upon PL frameworks such as the framework of Knight (2007), the following framework guided these sessions: (1) Identification – teachers and coaches choose elements of the feedback intervention as a focus area of practice; (2) Modelling – teachers and coaches view and critique examples of pedagogical practice in the classroom; (3) Collaboration – coaches and teachers jointly frame guidelines and criteria for improving practice from the feedback intervention; and (4) Feedback and Support – teachers receive ongoing feedback and support dependent upon individual needs. The coach from the research team monitored participant learning with the aim of devolving autonomy to the school-based coach and subsequently to the teachers themselves.

Following the intervention phase, teachers moved into the translation phase of the study. The translation phase was designed to test the sustainability of the feedback intervention as teachers were supported by the school resources only and not resources specific to the study. The translation phase began with a meeting between researchers and all school-based instructional leaders (Head of Curriculum and Master Teachers) and school leaders (Principal and Deputy Principal). The aim of this meeting was to tailor the feedback, formative assessment, and instructional practices to the needs of the school. Content in this session was underpinned by partnership approach theory (Knight, 2007), with connections made between the instructional leaders and school leaders context and the purpose of the intervention. In the translation phase, the school leaders and school-based instructional coaches implemented processes to continue to support teachers in enacting the intervention. During the translation phase, it was expected that the school instructional leaders continued to collaborate, model, provide feedback, and support teachers. This occurred through practices such as year level formative assessment meetings in staff non-contact time or during alternate week staff meeting sessions. To gradually build capability in the instructional leaders the translation phase load was built incrementally across the time of the study. It was clear that in-group champions emerged throughout the intervention and could be utilised to support other teachers to enact the intervention.

Measures

Baseline measures were collected from participants prior to the commencement of the PL sessions to measure the effect of the feedback intervention. First, school generated data were collected, including NAPLAN results, reading data and A–E grading against the Australian Curriculum. Second, students were asked to provide a writing sample under standardised conditions. Third, a student feedback perception questionnaire (SFPQ) was administered to gain insight into the types and levels of feedback that students found helpful to learning. Fourth, qualitative interviews were conducted with teachers, school leaders, instructional coaches, and student focus groups, to gain understanding of their perceptions of how differing types, levels, and purposes of feedback affected learning. To measure the effect of the feedback intervention, these measures were repeated pre- and post-intervention and pre- and post- the translation phase of the study.

Impact: preliminary findings

At the time of writing, data from the study are being collated and analysed. Whilst it is too early to report overall findings, we instead share reflections from participants. Teachers, school leaders, and students, have clearly shown the impact of the intervention through the sharing of their perceptions. Over the three years, interview data captured the story of how pedagogy underpinned by effective feedback impacted schools and classrooms.

The first year of the study saw teachers shifting their perceptions on the role of the student in effective feedback. The intervention required teachers to reflect on who was active and who was passive in the feedback process. A large percentage of teacher participants reported that prior to the intervention, they were the ones who were doing all the thinking; writing feedback, telling students information, editing their work; fixing the work for them! For example,

> Well, at the beginning, I guess I thought that feedback was teacher-based; so it would be that I am the person to give the feedback. Previously, I have been spending a lot of time writing out notes and those sort of things. I guess feedback in that way has changed, too. It's kind of student-centred ... they are a bit more active in that process; and sort of work with each other, as well as me. So it's kind of like a group effort, the process of giving feedback.

This shift in learning behaviours was observed by school leaders who reported less unidirectional feedback processes occurring and more instances where they believed teachers were creating opportunities for students to be involved in generating feedback for themselves and peers.

> I think the key thing is their view of the role they can take ... but, also, ways that they can get students to give feedback to each other.
>
> Teachers are much more explicit about where kids are heading; a lot more clarity in both teachers and kids; a lot more opportunities for kids to be active in monitoring their own progress.

Students themselves clearly discussed taking ownership of their learning and the steps they needed to take to improve their work. The use of a variety of resources such as models and success criteria enabled students to develop an understanding of what success looked like and how to get there. These resources, when used together, were a key process of clarifying success, an integral part of the effective feedback, and a focus of the intervention. Schools named the marrying of these resources, "bump it up walls, improvement walls (IW), and step up walls."

> I found it helpful when I had to make a persuasive paragraph; because it [IW] told me that I needed to do better on well-structured paragraphs; so I could look over and see what I needed to improve on and try and get that into my writing.

In 2018, Year 5 teachers and students were in the translation phase of the study and Year 4 teachers and students were the focus of the active intervention. Building upon preliminary findings from 2017, we continued to focus on strategies that promoted active learning, integral to building student self-regulation. The introduction of students critiquing differing quality samples of work developed clarity for the teacher and for the student and promoted students thinking. This involved students being placed in small groups and being given models or examples with the "right" thinking and models that contained deliberate misconceptions. The teacher, acting as a facilitator of feedback, asked the student groups probing questions such as, which model is more effective? Why? What makes it better? What could we call that feature? How does your work compare to this?

> I think that [the IW] has helped the students because there is a model to go to. I think using non-examples ... is now part of everything that I am teaching. And I guess the idea of "are the kids being active with this concept for a lesson?" So introducing something on cohesion, "Are they being active in that lesson?" I think that's what I have thought about.

A strength to the research design was that our school leaders remained relatively consistent over the intervention time frame and were therefore able to continue to work with teachers throughout their schools in effective feedback processes. Whilst many schools saw the value of making learning visible for their students, of great importance was the emphasis on creating resources as a process of learning and not a product to be placed on the wall by the teacher.

> It's [the intervention] probably refined my understanding of the feedback process and the importance of student agency in unpacking the marking guides and the importance of the step up wall in that process. And at every stage, the students being involved and active ... I guess before, it was important that I put the beautiful step up wall there, but I didn't unpack it. I just made it clear that, "This is what a C, a B and an A looked like; and this is what we're running with." My practice, once I started working in feedback, was that I gave samples to the students and they did all of the unpacking; and they looked at what the strengths/weaknesses were of each of those documents before they hit the wall.

Our Year 4 students, whilst younger, were still able to articulate the benefits of active learning and the use of resources to improve, in particular, comparing of their work to examples and non-examples.

> Well, looking at the not so good one helps me because I can see what this person's done and if I have done a better job of that; and seeing if I am improving from my last text. When I finish my draft, I go up and look in the bump it up wall and see where mine fits and see how I can make it better.

In 2019, our teachers and students were drawn from the Year 3 cohort. Again, building on successful implementation of strategies from the previous year, a focus was on further developing a culture of learning, where students could comfortably critique their own and critique others' work in a productive way. For many teachers, this shaped classroom practice and the use of technology was pivotal to engaging students in learning.

> My previous practice has always been to spend a week modelling. We have always given a pre-test, but I would then spend quite some time modelling what I expected … whereas this time I tried to use that model and get them to have a go first, every single day. So rather than feed them what I wanted to see, they had a go first; and then we refined it and looked at it. I would often take samples – get the children to comment on each other's work; and then get them to volunteer each other's work and put it under the visualiser.

School leaders were able to observe processes that were beginning to develop and evolve throughout the school, and the embedding of effective feedback for learning in classrooms.

> So teachers, particularly this year I have seen all the teachers using the "three-step approach," where they will give a clear example and non-example and allow students the opportunity to identify which is the most effective piece; and then clarify "why"; and then search for that evidence within their own work; on top of using the "Bump it Up wall"; they will use that also to back up their evidence.

A recurring theme across the years was that activating students early in the feedback or learning process by co-constructing success appears to be a crucial mediator of successful learning outcomes. This was actualised in the classroom with students critiquing a range of work samples including those with deliberate misconceptions to develop what Sadler (2010) would refer to as a nose for quality.

Researcher reflections: drivers and barriers

During the course of this study many drivers and barriers specific to the implementation of the intervention were identified, which require further discussion.

Collaboration was a key factor of success pertaining to the intervention. Collaboration was first required at a macro level between universities, Queensland Department of Education, and schools. Second, collaboration was also required at a micro level within and between research teams, school leadership teams, and teaching teams. As noted by Kelly and Cherkowski (2015), meaningful collaboration requires trust, shared values, and a common purpose. At the feedback PL sessions, researchers anecdotally noted increased levels of trust as new relationships formed and strengthened. Increased efficacy was also reported due to observable improvements in student self-regulation and learning outcomes. Observations of cases of reluctant teacher participation and low usage of the feedback intervention, however, also showed that meaningful collaboration may be a more distant goal for some. A key challenge was to work with these teachers and leadership teams to understand how best to engage them in the process.

The role of the Queensland Department of Education teacher in residence was pivotal to the delivery of the feedback PL intervention. Of particular note was the capability of the teacher in residence to clarify understanding of the Australian Curriculum for teachers and her skill in using coaching strategies to build pedagogical capability in teachers and school leaders. The teacher in residence sits in a unique position as she holds currency of practice in schools, yet is also informed by the latest evidence-informed research. This balanced skillset was pivotal in engendering teacher and school leader participation and collaboration in the project.

Leadership within the school was both a driver and a barrier to the implementation of the intervention. The feedback intervention prompted teachers to clarify the learning intent with their students and to consistently use formative assessment strategies to guide the next steps in learning for every student. For many teachers, this required a change in practice. As facilitators of the intervention, we found that whilst we were working with teachers to foster improvement, the engagement and subsequent follow through from the leadership team influenced the take up of the intervention. For example, many of the schools adopted team feedback coaching processes into their regular teacher PL practices. This served to further build upon collaboration among teachers and further embedded the feedback intervention. It is likely that such decisions were advantageous in building teacher capability and student outcomes in these schools.

Teacher capability in the *what* (curriculum content knowledge) and the *how* (pedagogical skills) of teaching was an important variable of the study. With a teacher sample of over 150 teachers, there was a high degree of variability in teaching knowledge. The feedback intervention was contextualised within the English strand of the Australian Curriculum. The Achievement Standards of the Australian Curriculum require students to demonstrate both surface and deep understanding. Teachers are therefore required to clarify, teach, assess, and feedback to students on uni- and multi-structural skills such as defining and locating, along with relational skills such as evaluating and justifying. This requires, at the very least, for teachers to be able to: (i) interpret what the Achievement Standards are asking of students; (ii) formatively assess current student understanding; (iii) consider how they might best close the gap between where students are and where they need to be; and (iv) reflect and assess impact. An expectation within the feedback sessions was that teachers would collect formative assessment evidence for discussion as to when and how to move students from surface to deep learning. This was a fundamental step for effective teaching and thus the feedback intervention needed to be responsive to variability in teacher capability in this area and differentiate accordingly.

Contributions to research and practice

This recent study provides education departments, universities, private industry, and schools with a scalable and sustainable model for implementation. The research design affords consideration to the needs of end users to facilitate later adoption. The design and intervention methods may be replicated in other schools and across a range of year levels. For instance, the research is based upon evidence-informed practices to build teacher pedagogical capability. Enactment of the feedback model is achievable for schools as the intervention may be gradually scaled up within a school from the intervention through to translation phases. Sustainability of the intervention is prioritised with a gradual release of responsibility and resourcing across the time of the study. Attrition of participants was also considered with a range of participants (principals, deputy principals, instructional leaders, and teachers) being coached in the intervention so as to best ensure future continuation. Furthermore, feedback and formative assessment are recognised as highly cost effective practices to improve teaching quality and student achievement (Higgins et al., 2016). Intervention methods, such as coaching and effective feedback, from this study, will provide schools and policymakers with a clear and rigorous model for future enactment.

The research tests a unique methodology in teacher professional learning. The intervention synthesised three high leverage pedagogical practices of feedback, formative assessment, and instructional leadership and coaching. This was a unique approach as there have been no studies to date that combine these practices in an intervention-based model. Formative assessment has been identified as a key driver for improving student achievement (Wiliam, 2011) and this research used a formative assessment cycle to provide feedback to both teachers and their students about current progress and pathways for improvement. Acknowledging principles of effective translation, the study considered both the product (feedback) and processes (professional learning) for transformation.

The study advances knowledge about teaching by focussing upon highly effective teaching and learning strategies. Too often schooling is a passive experience for students where they are only invited to test themselves against the learning objectives at the end of the learning period. Learning can become a one-time shot, where feedback arrives too late and is terminal with no opportunity for implementation. Effective learning models see learners as active agents in their own learning (Zimmerman & Schunk, 2012). The feedback for learning model provides teachers with a model of teaching that is designed to seek and address the learning needs of their students. The study provides rich data for policymakers and schools regarding both the use and effect of high yield teaching and learning strategies such as feedback and formative assessment.

The study supports long-term strategic alliances between universities, government departments, and schools. The translation of research from universities to end users is a key pillar of this study. It is imperative that Australian teachers are knowledgeable and skilled in using highly effective, evidence-informed teaching strategies. In turn, students become the beneficiaries of highly effective teaching practices. Through our research within the SLRC, we have developed partnerships with government departments, including the Queensland Department of Education. This partnership has produced tangible outcomes with a Department teacher in residence who joined our research team, building her knowledge and capability in undertaking evidence-based research. Concurrently, we have forged new partnerships with Department schools and have undertaken research in authentic contexts for the benefit of end users. Direct and positive links between partners provides for a bi-directional flow of information. This means that schools are not just the recipients of research-based interventions. Rather through a positive partnership, they have an active voice and can provide feedback to universities to shape further research for the benefit of future end users. Framing the research as a partnership allowed ownership by teachers of the project without loss of fidelity. In knowledge mobilisation, partnerships transcend individuals in identifying key principles and procedures for in-practice deployment. By working closely with industry and end users, we aimed to shape our research towards addressing current problems of practice and provide schools and policymakers with a sound evidence-base to make future decisions.

This research was directly aligned with the Queensland Department of Education research priority of pedagogy, curriculum, and assessment. The feedback intervention model required teachers to make active and explicit links between pedagogy, curriculum, and assessment. One of the challenges the Department faces, is in the implementation of evidence-informed research into the classroom on a large scale, without compromising the integrity of the initial research findings. Through the engagement with project officers from the Department's School Improvement Division, Evidence Hub, and Research Office, this project has provided a robust model for application and transfer of research knowledge to the classroom. Recognising the importance of this project, the Department has provided in-kind support over the duration of this project. Leadership support from each partner school was crucial to the success of the research project. Members of the school leadership team from each school were actively engaged with the research programme. This aligned with the Queensland State Schools Strategy 2016–2020 – Every Student Succeeding – aiming to raise the performance of each state school student and teacher. Teachers and school leaders in each partner school collaborated with and learnt from researchers and one another in the project, about effective feedback practice.

References

Boud, D. & Molloy, E. (2012). Changing conceptions of feedback. In D. Boud &E. Molloy, *Feedback in higher and professional education understanding it and doing it well* (pp. 21–43). Abingdon, Oxon; New York, NY: Routledge.

Brookhart, S. M. (2017). *How to give effective feedback to your students*. Alexandria, VA: Association for Supervision and Curriculum Development.

Brooks, C., Carroll, A., Gillies, R. M., & Hattie, J. (2019). A matrix of feedback for learning. *Australian Journal of Teacher Education, 44*(4). http://dx.doi.org/10.14221/ajte.2018v44n4.2

Creswell, J. W. & Clark, P. V. L. (2011). *Designing and conducting mixed methods research* (2nd ed.). Thousand Oaks: Sage Publications.

Dweck, C. S. (2007). The secret to raising smart kids. *Scientific American Mind, 18*(6), 36–43. https://doi.org/10.1038/scientificamericanmind1207-36

Gamlem, S. M. & Smith, K. (2013). Student perceptions of classroom feedback. *Assessment in Education: Principles, Policy & Practice, 20*(2), 150–169. https://doi.org/10.1080/0969594X.2012.749212

Hattie, J. A. (2009). *Visible learning: A synthesis of 800+ meta-analyses on achievement*. Abingdon: Routledge.

Hattie, J. & Timperley, H. (2007). The power of feedback. *Review of Educational Research, 77*(1), 81–112. https://doi.org/10.3102/003465430298487

Higgins, S., Katsipataki, M., Villanueva-Aguilera, A. B., Coleman, R., Henderson, P., Major, L. E., & Mason, D. (2016). *The Sutton Trust-Education Endowment Foundation Teaching and Learning Toolkit*. London: Education Endowment Foundation.

Kelly, J., & Cherkowski, S. (2015). Collaboration, collegiality, and collective reflection: A case study of professional development for teachers. *Canadian Journal of Educational Administration and Policy, 169*, 1–27.

Kluger, A. N. & DeNisi, A. (1996). The effects of feedback interventions on performance: A historical review, a meta-analysis, and a preliminary feedback intervention theory. *Psychological Bulletin, 119*(2), 254–284. doi: 10.1037/0033-2909.119.2.254

Knight, J. (2007). *Instructional coaching: A partnership approach to improving instruction*. Thousand Oaks, CA: Corwin Press.

Knight, J. (2009). *Coaching: Approaches and perspectives*. Thousand Oaks, CA: Corwin Press.

Knight, J. & van Nieuwerburgh, C. (2012). Instructional coaching: A focus on practice. *Coaching: An International Journal of Theory, Research and Practice, 5*(2), 100–112. https://doi.org/10.1080/17521882.2012.707668

Locke, E. A. & Latham, G. P. (1990). *A theory of goal setting and task performance*. NJ, Englewood Cliffs: Prentice Hall.

Masters, G. N. (2016). *Policy insights issue 5: Five challenges in Australian school education*. Camberwell, Victoria: ACER.

Sadler, D. R. (1989). Formative assessment and the design of instructional systems. *Instructional science, 18*(2), 119–144. https://doi.org/10.1007/BF00117714

Sadler, D. R. (2010). Beyond feedback: Developing student capability in complex appraisal. *Assessment & Evaluation in Higher Education, 35*(5), 535–550. https://doi.org/10.1080/02602930903541015

Schleicher, A. (2019), *PISA 2018 insights and interpretations*. Retrieved June 20, 2019 from https://www.oecd.org/pisa/PISA%202018%20Insights%20and%20Interpretations%20FINAL%20PDF.pdf.

Shute, V. J. (2008). Focus on formative feedback. *Review of Educational Research, 78*(1), 153–189. https://doi.org/10.3102/0034654307313795

Shute, V. J., Hansen, E. G., & Almond, R. G. (2007). Evaluating ACED: The impact of feedback and adaptivity on learning. *Frontiers in Artificial Intelligence and Applications, 158*, 230.

Skipper, Y. & Douglas, K. (2012). Is no praise good praise? Effects of positive feedback on children's and university students' responses to subsequent failures. *The British Journal of Educational Psychology, 82*(Pt 2), 327–339.

Teemant, A. (2013). A mixed-methods investigation of instructional coaching for teachers of diverse learners. *Urban Education, 49*(5), 574–604.

Thomson, S., De Bortoli, L., Underwood, C., & Schmid, M. (2019). PISA 2018: Reporting Australia's Results. *Volume I Student Performance*. Australian Council for Educational Research (ACER). Retrieved June 20, 2019 from https://research.acer.edu.au/ozpisa/35.

Van den Bergh, L., Ros, A., & Beijaard, D. (2013). Teacher feedback during active learning: Current practices in primary schools. *British Journal of Educational Psychology, 83*(2), 341–362.

Wiliam, D. (2011). *Embedded formative assessment*. Bloomington, IN: Solution Tree Press.

Wiliam, D. (2013). Feedback and instructional correctives. *SAGE handbook of research on classroom assessment, 1*, 197–214.

Zimmerman, B. J., & Schunk, D. H. (Eds.). (2012). *Self-regulated learning and academic achievement: Theory, research, and practice*. New York, NY: Springer Science & Business Media.

13

TRANSLATING THE SCIENCE OF LEARNING THROUGH CO-DESIGN: WORKING WITH TEACHERS TO PRIORITISE EXECUTIVE FUNCTIONING SKILLS IN MATHEMATICS EDUCATION

Simon N. Leonard and Martin S. Westwell

Introduction

The Empowering Local Learners (ELL) project involves a collaboration between a partnership of local schools (a high school and its feeder primary and pre-schools) in the regional South Australian towns of Port Augusta and Quorn, and the Flinders Centre for Science Education in the 21st Century (Science21). It is a project that has taken place at the translational end of the research work of the Science of Learning Research Centre, and this chapter marks the end of its five-year pilot phase.

The ELL project has taken place in a professional and practice context of educational challenge with numerous factors from the low socio-economic status of the community to high levels of staff turnover contributing to a history of poor academic performance at the schools. Mindful of the challenges of the setting, ELL was designed with an explicit ambition to disrupt current assumptions about mathematics teaching and learning. The educational design task was approached via a rejection of the assumption that "more of the same, but better" was a sufficient strategy. Setting out to both significantly improve student performance in standardised testing such as Australia's National Assessment Program Literacy and Numeracy (NAPLAN), and also to empower students as competent lifelong learners in this place with a history of educational challenge, the project has sought not simply to improve teaching practice, but to change practice in a sustainable way. The change sought has been to ensure that the teaching and learning occurring in mathematics moved away from being content-driven and to instead provide greater support for the development of cognitive executive functions (Diamond, 2013).

The project pilot has been successful. While causal factors are difficult to isolate within such a complex environment – and further research beyond this five-year pilot is warranted – the ELL pilot appears to have had a remarkable impact. To take just one indicator of this success, the number of Year 9 students reaching the minimum benchmark in NAPLAN testing has risen each year of the pilot. Prior to the pilot this measure showed just 67% of students achieving this standard, which is a very low outcome by national standards. Five years later, however, it had risen to 98%. This is a remarkable improvement. Perhaps more remarkable still is the teacher analysis of test performance that has found that the improvement has been in questions requiring higher-level problem-solving skills rather than simple recall or fluency. This suggests the improvement has largely been in the capacity of students to apply their mathematics learning.

Perhaps the more pleasing success of ELL for the teachers involved, however, has been the observed improvements in student disposition, with a growing view across the partnership that is summarised in one student's statement that *"maths is hard, but now we like hard."* Another example of this dispositional change in action was a student "mutiny" in which the class refused to start their physical education (PE) lesson, usually a favourite, because they wanted to continue doing mathematics.

Translating the science of learning

Understanding how translational projects such as ELL have success across multiple school sites and year-on-year is an important task for educational research and policy as this type of success has proven elusive (Fishman, Penuel, Hegedus, & Roschelle, 2011; Stanford et al., 2017). The angst over the so-called gap between theory and practice is long standing in education, but has been renewed by the emergence of an interest in learning from new scientific fields such as those typically grouped under the science of learning banner. This has led to a proliferation of literature on the gaps between the science of learning and educational practice. To take just neuroscience as an example, N. Beauchamp and C. Beauchamp (2012) reviewed no fewer than 86 articles on the apparent gap between neuroscience and educational practice, and there have been many more since. In doing so they identified a range of factors holding the gap open, including a misapplication of research findings, the engagement of multiple disciplines in the space, conflicting value sets and different uses of language. The responses to such challenges have varied, from the call to valorise the emerging field of educational neuroscience as the dominant discipline informing educational practice (Morris & Sah, 2016; Pincham et al., 2014), to alternative calls for a transdisciplinary approach that contextually accords equal and differential weight to a range of knowledge inputs from education studies, neuroscience, and other academic and practitioner spheres (Knox, 2016).

The ELL project is one in keeping with the calls for trans-disciplinarity, and the primary purpose of this chapter is to report on how such a complex task has been achieved. The chapter is written at a significant point in the project cycle, as it is set to expand into additional school partnerships in different locations. The chapter itself is an artefact of the iterative method of the overall project and represents a reflective pause in the work before it expands. The reportage here is based on the engagement between the project team and the lead author, who has acted as a critical friend late in the pilot phase. The result is essentially a discussion connecting the experiences of the pilot with some key ideas in the wider literature on the translation of the science of learning in real-world settings. The discussion is by no means exhaustive, but it provides a basis for the design of future practice and research as the ELL project moves into a new phase and will inform similar projects elsewhere.

The chapter begins with an orientation to the project. This is followed by a discussion of some key ideas for undertaking translational research that emerge from the discussions about this project. These ideas include: the understanding and valuing of multiple value propositions; working with the multi-direction pressures within a practice setting; the advantages of project officers being vulnerable participants; and the benefits of putting fidelity of principle ahead of fidelity of action. The chapter will conclude by highlighting some key elements of the project design and thinking about the costs of expansion.

Empowering local learners

The ELL project is essentially an ongoing teacher professional learning (PL) process that has emerged from analysis of learning data at the participating school Partnership. The teacher coordinating the project for the Partnership, Shane Loader (SL) described the genesis of the project this way:

SL: *[The need] identified through analysis of the NAPLAN data was that – we knew our kids were struggling with their numeracy capacity and we kind of assumed that it was in those lower level skills – but when we looked at NAPLAN, and we compared it to the national levels of achievement [what] was really lacking was looking at those more complex non-routine questions that come up in the later part of the NAPLAN test, so that is where we started.*

When we looked at classrooms, what we noticed was that there were probably very few of those types of questions occurring within the learning. That the teaching was very much based around either text books or worksheets or fairly low level procedural work. So for the teachers, we identified the need to probably rethink some of the task design.

While not unheard of (see for example Beveridge, Groundwater-Smith, Kemmis, & Watson, 2005), it is unusual for such a bottom-up analysis of data to lead to a sustained response across multiple school sites. It is also unusual for schools and teachers to have a major role in the ongoing design of multi-school PL, which is more commonly delivered in a top-down manner. The model that has evolved in ELL is explicitly one of co-design that sought to develop a PL community in which teachers were not simply passive recipients of a pre-designed program (Mockler, 2011; Nehring & Fitzsimons, 2011), but in which the project officers as external agents also took an important role (Wright, 2016). The external agents in the ELL have been two teachers seconded from classroom practice.

Co-design within ELL is organised around meetings that occur at one of the school sites twice a term, or about once every five school weeks. The classroom teacher involvement is for two years, although many have stayed engaged with the overall project in subsequent years as "champions" for the approach within their schools. In the first year the typical pattern is for the project officers to model the design of a lesson that facilitates the development of executive functions while learning mathematics content. The project officer then teaches the class of one of the participating teachers while the entire group of teachers are in the room observing. The afternoon is then spent conducting an evaluation of what occurred, with a particular focus on the types of questions that can be asked around a task to promote executive function. In the second year the teachers from the Partnership take a greater role in the development and delivery of tasks to be undertaken, and there is greater emphasis for the project officers in developing teacher knowledge about executive function.

The choice to focus on building executive function has a substantial and growing evidence base. The core executive functions include: response inhibition – the suppression of actions that are inappropriate; interference control – the capacity for selective attention; working memory – the cognitive system that holds information available for processing; and cognitive flexibility – the capacity to see things from different perspectives (Diamond, 2013). The first two of these functions are often referred to together in ELL through the heuristic mantra "stop and think." Surfacing in ideas such as self-directed learning and temperament (Bridgett, Oddi, Laake, Murdock, & Bachmann, 2013; Rothbart, Evans, & Ahadi, 2000), the idea that improving executive function is important for learning and learners is not new or controversial (Cantin, Gnaedinger, Gallaway, Hesson-McInnis, & Hund, 2016; D'Mello & Graesser, 2014; Dux et al., 2009; Kyndt, Cascallar, & Dochy, 2012; McClelland & Wanless, 2012). Nevertheless, executive skill training has remained on the periphery of school practice and is often implemented as additional study skills rather than as a central component of learning design. The efficacy of this peripheral treatment is doubtful, with research continuing to find that the home and not the school is the source of most executive function development (Effeney, Carroll, & Bahr, 2013).

The ELL project sought to change the positioning of executive function (EF) in learning design as the project officers Kristin Vonney (KV) and Deb Lasscock (DL) describe:

KV: *Basically slowing kid's thinking down, and in so doing developing the three core executive functions: impulse control, cognitive flexibility, and supporting working memory. By doing those three things ... we help them become better problem solvers and reasoners. So that is the premise. The way I think about it when I am designing a lesson,*

> *I keep the executive functions over here, and the teacher will say "so this is the content I want to teach." I then try and design activities that will allow the development of those executive functions and think of the questions I will ask the students, or try and get the students to ask of themselves.*
>
> DL: *It is digging deeper. Mathematics is our vehicle … but it is "how can we think about this in another way that will be more effective and how can we use it for solving problems."*

Two key components of the approach have been that the project officers explicitly model their design thinking, and that they require the participating teachers to engage with students in order to understand the student thinking during the demonstration lessons. As Shane Loader explained:

> SL: *[The project officers] deliver model lessons. They [the teachers] sit in and watch … and they sit with the kids and listen to them as well, so they can listen to how kids are engaging with those sorts of problems. And that's a really important first step for the teachers that we are working with.*

A "worked example"

An example of the kind of learning activity that emerges with this focus on executive function is a simple card game for working with fractions. In the game students lay the cards, each bearing a fraction, face down. They then turn over a card each with the person holding the card with the highest value keeping the set of cards, and the person with the most sets being the winner. While traditional approaches to teaching fractions tend to focus on the application of process (simplify, multiply numerators, etc.), this game creates the situation where students need to prove they have the highest value card. Even for adults, this requires some degree of stop and think skills, as this critical friend (CF) found in playing the game when the first set of cards turned over revealed 2/4, 4/4 and 10/10:

> CF: *Now obviously 10/10 "feels" like it is the largest fraction.*
>
> DL: *And so in the classroom you would have those conversations – prove it to me.*
>
> KV: *So a lot of kids will say, "well mine's bigger." So we'll say, "ok, can you show me your thinking, can you say it another way, can you draw us a diagram?"*

Activities such as this require enough impulse control to negate the cognitive bias (Kahneman, 2011) that 10/10 is larger than 4/4. The activity also requires cognitive flexibility as the student may choose a number of ways to represent her or his thinking. Discussing this further:

> DL: *I don't know that we can over-emphasise the representation, and I don't know that we do it very well in primary schools and preschools, to get the kids to think about it in a non-symbolic way and then move to symbolic.*
>
> KV: *We ask them "why have you chosen to describe it verbally, or why have you decided to draw a picture?" … A lot of kids could do things like that procedurally but then when*

they actually have to either give a real-life example, or describe it verbally, then very quickly they [the teachers] realise that they [the children] actually have no real idea what is going on and [can't] think about it flexibly.

DL: *I think even diagrammatically they would struggle, as kids just don't understand that they can show their thinking as a diagram in mathematics as opposed to, it's just this stuff to find an answer to.*

Also discussing cognitive flexibility, Shane Loader observed that through the project teachers were trying to:

SL: *Get kids to engage with challenge, to look at unfamiliar situations, and to realise that, yeah, at that point of time, they've got it in them to make a start on that. They can look at the information that they've got available, they can slow down how they think about it, then really plan a way that they might tackle it. And realise that even if they don't quite get to the resolution at that point, that they've got some more information, that they've now got to be able to think about the question in a different way. And to realise that it is not them alone that has to be doing that. I think, in the past, maths classrooms are places where individual work was a predominant practice, but now ..., to be able to work with others, to hear different perspectives, to be able to bounce ideas off each other, and be able to debate the accuracy or effectiveness of those ideas, has really given kids a way into looking at these [more complex] tasks that they maybe didn't have before. Because it was all based on their current understanding and being able to draw whatever they could from what the teacher gave them.*

Just as the use of executive function in learning is not contentious, the activity in this worked example is not revolutionary. Research in the science of learning, and in other forms of mathematics learning research that have gone before it have provided many examples of highly effective teaching and learning activities. The most salient feature of the ELL project is not the activities it is producing. Rather it is the way such activities have been widely adopted as common practice across a number of school sites in a seemingly sustainable way. How this has occurred is worthy of further research, and an expansion of the project beyond the pilot phase will provide significant opportunities for such research. The task of this chapter is to begin the design of that research.

Learning from ELL

The translational research of the ELL project has taken the form of Educational Design Research (EDR, Kelly, Baek, & Lesh, 2008; McKenney & Reeves, 2012), which is also known as Design Based Research (DBR). EDR is an approach to translational educational research that has emerged largely in a field known as the learning sciences, a field distinct from those who identify as being involved in the science of learning. While the sciences of learning, such as educational neuroscience, have tended to adopt an explanatory stance, the learning sciences field has increasingly positioned itself as a design science, with an explicit focus on improving the functional performance of learning designs in real-world settings. The distinction is similar to that between research in, say, physics and engineering. The learnings from the project are presented here as a set of design principles, many of which require testing in future research.

A clear and simple "value proposition" may assist in implementation across multiple sites

Value proposition is an idea from the world of marketing that highlights, usually in clear and simple terms, why a customer might pay for a product or service. Educational researchers are not, by and large, known for their marketing skills, but the selling of a value proposition by the project leader, Martin Westwell (MW) seems to have been an essential part of the success of ELL:

MW: So the approach is always about being useful. So, having an impact.

... as researchers we might think "this research and this idea – the executive functions in our case – has got value," but you've also got to think about the value proposition for people. And one of the things we know is that when you look across the socio-economic status the lower SES kids tend to have lower levels of executive functions: impulse inhibition, working memory, cognitive flexibility.

So we're going into the schools and we're talking to the leaders about what's stopping their kids being effective learners in mathematics. So, yes the performance, but back to them being effective learners. And we show them some ideas about executive functions. [We say with] kids with low working memory – you tend to see "this" – and it is not really a behavioural issue, it's an expression of a developmental need. And if they've not got the "stop and think" skills and you present them with a maths problem that looks like "this" – then you're likely to see this behaviour. And they'll go "Yeah! That's it! That's our kids, you're describing our kids!"

So, what we're doing here is, we are establishing a common set of values. This isn't a project that we're doing "to" teachers or leaders that's been decided on by some manager or someone in the upper echelons – "you are going to do this" – this is them signing up to it and saying "yes, we recognise this is a thing and we're in it" ... clearly thinking about the value proposition for the teachers, the leaders the kids, was the initial approach.

This awareness of the different value propositions for all involved seems to be a key element of the successful translation of the science of learning into educational practice, but it is not clear how such awareness is best achieved. In this case the project leader has a background in research science, but has been immersed in education and public policy for many years. He is also highly charismatic and well known in South Australia. The presence of such a person to act as a pivot between the science of learning and educational practice fields cannot be relied upon.

In future research an awareness and testing of relevant social theory will be useful. Abbott's (2005) linked ecologies model, for example, suggests that when actors from one social ecology are seeking to make changes in another social ecology, it will be more successful when actors in both ecosystems stand to benefit from the change. Mutual benefit may be what Westwell is describing here. Others have argued, however, that projects such as ELL might be best understood as complex networks (Jacobson, Kapur & Reimann, 2016; Scott, Woolcott, Keast, & Chamberlain 2017), and be best sustained by the construction of boundary-crossing sub-systems (Akkerman & Bakker, 2011). If this is so then the boundary crossing of the project officers that will be explored in the next section may have been more influential on success of ELL than the establishment of a common set of values.

Boundary crossing may provide ways of working with multi-directional pressures

Research is increasingly demonstrating that learning is influenced by dozens, if not hundreds of variables (Musso, Kyndt, Cascallar, & Dochy, 2012) and that these variables interact in complex ways (Jacobson et al., 2016). It is therefore not unreasonable to suggest that approaches to shifting educational practice may need to be complex and nuanced. The nature of research practice, however, is that research scientists often join the educational discussion without a full appreciation for these complexities and interactions. This means that instructional leaders and instructional designers – including classroom teachers – can experience an apparent deluge of incomplete advice. ELL seems to have effectively handled this by using boundary crossing teachers as the project officers. The project has not had researchers talking at teachers, rather it has invited teachers, as project officers, to cross the boundary into research, and back again.

KV: *Schools are weird little microcosms of weirdness. So I tread carefully [when discussing pedagogical change] ... I think Principals are under such a lot of pressure, so they grab anything they can to help develop student cognition ... so what we've got better at over the years ... is very deliberately to say, "so all of the programs you are [already] doing, [our work] is all going to support that" ... if you can improve student executive function skills, it's going to help them do everything else, all the other things that you're doing ... and even when the teachers have said to us "your approach is the complete opposite of the John Fleming Model" [a model of direct instruction used by a number of schools in the Partnership], so we've got clever at [showing] how our ideas, thinking and principles can help you do the John Fleming stuff. And so we've had to acknowledge it, but, our ideas, thinking, and principles will help teachers do that. So we've been a little bit more strategic.*

DL: *That's one of the complexities, because it is "what can you do" [in a complex classroom] ... so if it's our kids aren't very good at behaviour, I think what many of the teachers are seeing is that you can change your attitude to behaviour if you're thinking about executive functions. So, if it is, "oh, look at that, that was really naughty," that's one attitude; but if it is "oh, if you were thinking about your stop and think skills" ... and then the kids see themselves as learners and not that kid in the classroom who can get out of here quickly.*

The project leader is also clearly aware of the importance of boundary crossing mechanisms in this type of project.

MW: *More often than not, the neuroscience ends up backing up what the educators already knew. If you look at, you know, the research on wait time from the 1970s for example, neuroscience is just catching up now on what is actually going on when you look at that and that activity in the brain and those kinds of things – we're starting to see a kind of neuro-chemical rationale for some of the things we've known about in cognitive science and psychology ... so the science of learning, it's not about saying "what has neuroscience ever given to education" or "what has education ever given to neuroscience" it's much more of that interplay [of different perspectives on the same problem]. Disciplinary people say naïve things about each other's disciplines, but we need to have people at the pivots.*

Translating this principle into the ELL context, Westwell noted that for teachers:

MW: *Expertise isn't enough. Teachers' practice isn't influenced by expertise, it is influenced by other teachers. So that's why we have got teachers [the project officers] involved in the project.*

The human factors in play here are an important part of translational research. Teaching practice, like all professional practice, should be directed by the best evidence. Researchers into professional practice such as Mahon, Kemmis, Francisco, and Lloyd (2016), however, have argued that practice has features beyond knowledge, because it is formed and conducted in social settings, shaped by discourses, and it is dramaturgical. Dramaturgy is a sociological concept that suggests that the ways in which a person presents themselves to others is responsive to the cultural values, norms, and beliefs of the setting (Kemmis, 2005). With this richer view of practice, it becomes evident that changing practice requires more than changing practitioners, but also changing such things as the discourses in which practices are constructed, and shifting the values, norms, and beliefs to which practitioners respond. At least two responses to human factors are evident in the ELL project, vulnerability, and fidelity of principle. They are discussed in the following sections.

Vulnerability may be more important than expertise

A common theme in the discussions of the ELL project from all the actors was that it was a "project" and not a "program" – it was not something being done to the teachers, it was something being done with them. This discourse seemed much more important than a description of the design process that had been chosen. It resonated with many comments that teachers are constantly asked to respond to new directions from their department or their political masters.

An important background to this discourse is the move in most anglophile countries, and certainly in Australia, to a performative approach to teacher governance (Ball, 2003; Leonard & Roberts, 2016). Through mechanisms such as the need to annually demonstrate at least competence against a set of standards, the dramaturgical nature of teaching practice has been reinforced and it has become dangerous to be seen to fail. As the standards are essentially peer assessed, or assessed by a school leader who has been a classroom teacher, the safe course of action is to replicate existing practice and to perform like everyone else. From the outset, however, the ELL project had rejected current practice as a design solution. As such, it was asking teachers to step into unsafe space. A critical response to this seems to have been the capacity of the project officers to themselves be vulnerable, or unsafe, when working with the teachers.

KV: *I'm secondary trained, so primary is just another world to me. So I said to these teachers, "I don't know if this is going to work. This could be just a complete stuff up. I don't have time to trial, it, I don't have access to classrooms to trial it." And this teacher looked at me and she said, "That's great, because you're giving me permission to go away and fail." And in that instant … the teachers realised that I was putting myself out there … PL doesn't often happen like that [where the presenter can fail].*

DL: *People see you as someone who relates to a classroom, as opposed to someone who is giving you stuff that will change their lives.*

The conditions in which those delivering PL are able to or allowed to be vulnerable is unclear and requires further investigation. Those delivering PL typically need to develop a high level of credibility to be taken seriously, and a consistent pattern of failure can quickly move the impression of that person from that of risk taking to that of incompetence. On the other hand, risk taking within a community of practice seems to be an essential element of the co-design model that has been adopted in this project. The use of the project officer intermediaries may be an effective means of achieving this, in that the professional capital of the researchers in the project is protected.

Fidelity of principle over complexity of action may be a useful way to engage complexity

Schools are complex places that can defy attempts to maintain fidelity of action when implementing an educational innovation. ELL responded to the reality of teacher practice by trying to achieve fidelity of principle rather than fidelity of action, as the project leader describes:

MW: *Let me do the heuristic, and then perhaps unpack it a little. So the heuristic is fidelity of principle and not fidelity of action. Because you can get fidelity of action and lose the principle, there's loads of good examples of that where thinking that you're doing it the right way you take your eye off what you're trying to achieve or the principle that you're trying to put in place in order to do it the "right" way.*

We think that's important if you think about schooling as a complex system. So in a complex system there is no such thing as best practice. Best practice only exists in simple systems — and when people do things like RCTs [randomised control trials] what they'll often do is they'll deal with the complexity of schooling by making it as simple as they can. They'll control the crap out of everything — trying to keep everything else the same. And of course you've got big numbers so you can randomise some of that stuff out but you try to keep everything else the same and get everyone to do the same thing in the same way. And that is probably a hangover from RCTs coming from medicine ...

But of course in education — or maybe it is not an "of course" — but if you think about education being much more of a complex system then that fidelity of action is, and I'm going to say, inappropriate. Now the principle, being enacted, but being enacted in different ways, making sure that what you're doing is research that recognises the varying expertise of the teachers, is important ... so you're dealing with the complexity by dealing with the complexity and keeping it complex rather than trying to pretend it's simple. ... in the RCTs you pretend that it's simple, then you take away all the constraints and say "carry on doing that" — and it just doesn't work!

So you've got to differentiate for your teachers. You can't just say "do this," you've got to think about the differentiation of the teachers ...

The fidelity of principle heuristic adopted in the ELL project is notably out of step with the current performative assumptions of teacher governance (Leonard, 2015). Often citing the gold standard of medical research (see for example Productivity Commission, 2016) fidelity of action has become the dominant approach, with systems designed to ensure that teachers replicate a standardised best practice wherever possible. Even in medicine, however, the limitations of so-called best practice and the gold standard of the RCT when applied to individual patients in the real world have long been established (Feinstein & Horwitz, 1997). Among the most pressing of these limitations of the controlled nature of medical research is that real patients tend to have illnesses that disqualify them from the research studies.

Beyond the policy world, the preference for fidelity of principle or fidelity of action has been the subject of strident debate within the learning sciences. Some in the field clearly support the need to develop strong principles (Bereiter, 2014), while others maintain that teachers need a much higher level of engineering-style support to move from principle to practice (Janssen, Westbroek, & Doyle, 2015). It seems that ELL may have actually taken a third way here, by supporting the implementation of principle through co-design with well-trained project officers. It is consistent with longstanding research showing that reform type approaches to teacher professional development are most effective at supporting changes to practice (Garet, Porter, Desimone, Birman, & Yoon, 2001; Hargreaves & Fullan, 2012; Lowrie, Leonard, & Fitzgerald, 2018). Reform approaches are typified by the provision of structures for teachers to work collaboratively and to engage with real problems of practice.

Teacher professional learning should also be informed by an understanding of executive function

In applying the fidelity of principle approach, ELL has taken an approach to PL that is also informed by the science of learning and has practiced its own "stop and think" mantra. As the Partnership coordinator explains it:

SL: *This isn't a program that has had Flinders University come in and make a presentation once a year or twice a year. The nature of them coming in twice a term, and then having homework to do between sessions as well, has meant that the teachers that have been involved in this work have continuously had the ideas at the front of their mind. It means that they haven't had to make huge changes to their practice immediately. What they've been able to do is make a small change, to be able to reflect on that, and to be able to think about how they might be able to push that learning forward ... with these quick cycles of improvement, those small changes add up to quite big changes over two years.*

The approach highlights slow and gradual change of practice:

SL: *And we really only get them to focus on questioning in the first year, because to jump in at the point of task design is kind of too big a leap, sometimes ... to change every task they're doing. Whereas, I guess, jumping in at the level of questioning they can still do the tasks that they're currently doing but they can add to the sophistication and the thinking of that task by putting a layer of questioning over the top of that.*

... What they don't get as much in the first year is the deep understanding of the theory of what's occurring in the class. They do get some of it ... but in the second and subsequent years they spend a lot more time unpacking the implications of the research ... and that's the point where we can start addressing task design, when they can understand the principle of what lays behind those lessons that they saw in the first year, they can start thinking about how they start applying that to how they design learning in their own spaces.

Clearly what is occurring here in translating the research of the science of learning to practice is much more than presenting a set of research findings. Even though the executive functioning ideas appear quite simple – control impulse, reduce load on working memory – the implications for practice are quite complex and significant learning is required on the part of the practitioner. What should be clear from the successes of ELL is that processing knowledge from the science is only part of the task. Applying the science to the changing of practice requires many more steps, and these steps will probably be quite slow. This project, however, suggests that there may be significant advantages to ensuring those steps are taken regularly and over a sustained period of time. Just how regularly and over what period the intervention is required for sustained and scalable change is an important matter for future research.

Another structural element that appears important in the PL within ELL is the ongoing intentionality of the program. There has essentially been an application of the fidelity of principle heuristic to the PL as well as the classroom learning. This is also explained by the Partnership coordinator:

SL: *The way we work with the teachers, it's kind of how we aim for the teachers to work with the kids. We want to look at where the kids are at the moment and aim to move their learning forward from there, and it is kind of the same thing with the teachers. I guess each batch of teachers that comes into this project comes from their own teaching experience, so it is figuring out where they are and what they need at that point of time, and thinking collectively as a group what's going to move that learning forward ... So the professional development program develops after each session. Seeing how the teachers engage with the tasks, the activities, the ideas that are presented in that session, and going, "Well, where to next? Do we need to spend more time on that? Do they have it? Do we need to develop a more sophisticated idea around this? Do we need to shift completely and head in a different direction?" So, I guess it makes it really hard to write down what the professional development looks like, because it evolves as the teachers evolve.*

Future design and research

ELL has shown emphatically that it is possible to build successful mathematics learning programs around a focus on executive function. As the project moves to its next phase, however, it must make more specific contributions to design and theoretical knowledge if this success is to be sustained and replicated elsewhere. The discussion in this chapter has pointed to many possibly fruitful avenues for future inquiry. The importance of a common value proposition, for example, seems worthy of further investigation. Such an investigation might have a particular focus on how common value propositions might be established other than through the advocacy of a significantly influential person within the system, which seems an approach unlikely to scale to thousands of schools.

Some other issues for further research that have been raised in this chapter include: the nature of effective boundary crossing within systems such as ELL; the possible need for those influencing change to be vulnerable, or at least peers; the use of co-design as an approach to reform teacher PL; and the most appropriate timing of co-design within the school year. We will conclude the chapter with some thoughts on how a project which investigates such questions might be scaled and sustained.

While slow (professional) learning seems consistent with the research from the science of learning, it seems likely to be costly. These costs will be apparent both for delivery of a project such as ELL, and for the ongoing changes teachers make to their practice. This is evident in the reflections of one of the champion teachers, who was aware of the time cost:

TW: *It was quite new, it was different to what kids were used to, and it takes time. It's about your planning and your intentionality. I've had some bad lessons because I haven't been prepared. I've gone in and had a good idea and I've asked them a question and they haven't been able to share their thinking, and I've had nowhere to go from there ... Now, when I'm doing my lessons, I plan ahead. So what are the responses the kids are going to give me? What questions can I ask — so if they get stuck, what questions can I ask to pull out their thinking. How can I adjust it to get them into that task?*

Such time costs are one of the reasons that some within the learning sciences advocate for a higher level of educational engineering support (Janssen et al., 2015), arguing that it is impractical for teachers to devote the time needed to reform their practice as new findings emerge from the science of learning and other educational research. Or, more particularly, they argue that teachers need to perceive a reasonable return on investment if they are to spend the time, which in a sense returns the discussion to the idea of the value proposition.

The fact that the value proposition of the ELL project was sold by a well-known and charismatic educational leader was discussed above, and is important here in considering the costs of scalability. Just as this model creates a significant cost in teacher time, it also creates a significant cost in developing a common set of values and it is unlikely that the investment of symbolic and social capital required from the project leader to sustain this pilot over five years can be replicated in a sustainable and scalable way. In discussing the cost of the project, the project leader acknowledged as much:

MW: *This project was [expensive], definitely. We were doing lots of travelling. There was lots of me, in the beginning — but it is designed not to be [laughs].*

It was his belief, however, that the cost could be overcome:

> *... Once you've got those two or three key teachers, they can work across a Partnership and have an enormous influence across that partnership. And then of course what you're doing is, over time, you have got your two or three key influencers working with the partnership and in the first year you find your "good to greats" — who are also your influencers — and you bring them on as the influencers for the second year, so these guys can step back a bit, and you build a self-sustaining process. From time to time, you might need some input from external expertise, from a university or elsewhere, for them to be testing their thinking, to make sure they're not going down a wrong track.*

This is optimistic, but even with optimism, the way ahead is intentional but slow. What is evident through the experience of the ELL project, and this is perhaps the key issue for future implementation research, is the need to ensure that teachers who are able to make effective use the science of learning are able to influence the discourses, cultures, values, and beliefs of teacher practice. As the project leader observed:

MW: *There's a funny thing that's going on, where the people who are perhaps the "good to greats" and the potential influencers. Schools don't know how to deal with them. There's a bunch of people across the state, who are in schools, doing great things in science and maths in primary schools, but they're not having an influence beyond their classroom, in their school, partnership, across the state. And often what they do is they'll pop out of the school, and they'll win a prize, and they'll go abroad and get something and try and bring it back, or they'll – through the science teachers association or in some non-standard or some ad hoc way, they'll try and help and influence the practice of others. So they're there, and they've got those characteristics that we're looking for … but it is a short list, so if you wanted to scale it quickly, that would be a challenge.*

References

Abbott, A. (2005). Linked ecologies: States and universities as environments for professions. *Sociological Theory, 23*(3), 245–274.

Akkerman, S. F., & Bakker, A. (2011). Boundary crossing and boundary objects. *Review of Educational Research, 81*(2), 132–169.

Ball, S. J. (2003). The teacher's soul and the terrors of performativity. *Journal of Education Policy, 18*(2), 215–228.

Beauchamp, N., & Beauchamp, C. (2012). Understanding the neuroscience and education connection: Themes emerging from a review of the literature. In S. D. Sala and M. Anderson *(Eds.), Neuroscience in education* (Chapter 2). Oxford: Oxford University Press.

Bereiter, C. (2014). Principled practical knowledge: Not a bridge but a ladder. *Journal of the Learning Sciences, 23*(1), 4–17.

Beveridge, S., Groundwater-Smith, S., Kemmis, S., & Watson, D. (2005). Professional learning that makes a difference: Successful strategies implemented by priority action schools in New South Wales. *Journal of In-Service Education, 31*(4), 697–710.

Bridgett, D. J., Oddi, K. B., Laake, L. M., Murdock, K. W., & Bachmann, M. N. (2013). Integrating and differentiating aspects of self-regulation: Effortful control, executive functioning, and links to negative affectivity. *Emotion, 13*(1), 47–63.

Cantin, R. H., Gnaedinger, E. K., Gallaway, K. C., Hesson-McInnis, M. S., & Hund, A. M. (2016). Executive functioning predicts reading, mathematics, and theory of mind during the elementary years. *Journal of Experimental Child Psychology, 146*, 66–78.

D'Mello, S. & Graesser, A. (2014). Confusion and its dynamics during device comprehension with breakdown scenarios. *Acta Psychologica, 151*, 106–116.

Diamond, A. (2013). Executive functions. *Annual Review of Psychology, 64*(1), 135–168.

Dux, P. E., Tombu, M. N., Harrison, S., Rogers, B. P., Tong, F., & Marois, R. (2009). Training improves multitasking performance by increasing the speed of information processing in human prefrontal cortex. *Neuron, 63*(1), 127–138.

Effeney, G., Carroll, A., & Bahr, N. (2013). Self-regulated learning: Key strategies and their sources in a sample of adolescent males. *Australian Journal of Educational and Developmental Psychology, 13,* 58–74.

Feinstein, A. & Horwitz, R. (1997). Problems in the "evidence" of "evidence-based medicine." *The American Journal of Medicine, 103*(6), 529–535.

Fishman, B. J., Penuel, W. R., Hegedus, S., & Roschelle, J. (2011). What happens when the research ends? Factors related to the sustainability of a technology-infused mathematics curriculum. *Journal of Computers in Mathematics and Science Teaching, 30*(4), 329–353.

Garet, M. S., Porter, A. C., Desimone, L., Birman, B. F., & Yoon, K. S. (2001). What makes professional development effective? Results from a National Sample of Teachers. *American Educational Research Journal, 38*(4), 915–945.

Hargreaves, A. & Fullan, M. (2012). *Professional capital: Transforming teaching in every school.* New York, NY: Teachers College Press.

Jacobson, M. J., Kapur, M., & Reimann, P. (2016). Conceptualizing debates in learning and educational research: Toward a complex systems conceptual framework of learning. *Educational Psychologist, 51*(2), 210–218.

Janssen, F., Westbroek, H., & Doyle, W. (2015). Practicality studies: How to move from what works in principle to what works in practice. *Journal of the Learning Sciences, 24*(1), 176–186.

Kahneman, D. (2011). *Thinking, fast and slow.* London: Allen Lane.

Kelly, A. E., Baek, J. Y., & Lesh, R. A. (2008). *Handbook of design research methods in education: Innovations in science, technology, engineering, and mathematics.* New York, NY: Routledge.

Kemmis, S. (2005). Knowing practice: Searching for saliences. *Pedagogy, Culture & Society, 13*(3), 391–426.

Knox, R. (2016). Mind, brain, and education: A transdisciplinary field. *Mind, Brain, and Education, 10*(1), 4–9.

Kyndt, E., Cascallar, E., & Dochy, F. (2012). Individual differences in working memory capacity and attention, and their relationship with students' approaches to learning. *Higher Education, 64*(3), 285–297.

Leonard, S. N. (2015). Stepping outside: Collaborative inquiry-based teacher professional learning in a performative policy environment. *Professional Development in Education, 41*(1).

Leonard, S. N. & Roberts, P. (2016). No time to think: the impact of the logics of new public management on teacher pre-professional learning. *Journal of Education Policy, 31*(2), 142–160.

Lowrie, T., Leonard, S. N., & Fitzgerald, R. (2018). STEM Practices: A translational framework for large-scale stem education design. *EDeR. Educational Design Research, 2*(1).

Mahon, K., Kemmis, S., Francisco, S., & Lloyd, A. (2016). Introduction: Practice theory and the theory of practice architectures. In K. Mahon, S. Francisco, & S. Kemmis (Eds.), *Exploring education and professional practice: Through the lens of practice architectures* (pp. 1–30). Singapore: Springer Singapore.

McClelland, M. M., & Wanless, S. B. (2012). Growing up with assets and risks: The importance of self-regulation for academic achievement. *Research in Human Development, 9*(4), 278–297.

McKenney, S. & Reeves, T. C. (2012). *Conducting educational design research.* New York, NY: Routledge.

Mockler, N. (2011). Beyond "what works": Understanding teacher identity as a practical and political tool. *Teachers & Teaching, 17*(5), 517–528.

Morris, J. & Sah, P. (2016). Neuroscience and education: Mind the gap. *Australian Journal of Education, 60*(2), 146–156.

Musso, M., Kyndt, E., Cascallar, E., & Dochy, F. (2012). Predicting mathematical performance: The effect of cognitive processes and self-regulation factors. *Education Research International*, *2012*, 1–13.

Nehring, J. & Fitzsimons, G. (2011). The professional learning community as subversive activity: Countering the culture of conventional schooling. *Professional Development in Education*, *37*(4), 513–535.

Pincham, H. L., Matejko, A. A., Obersteiner, A., Killikelly, C., Abrahao, K. P., Benavides-Varela, S., ... Vuillier, L. (2014). Forging a new path for Educational Neuroscience: An international young-researcher perspective on combining neuroscience and educational practices. *Trends in Neuroscience and Education*, *3*(1), 28–31.

Productivity Commission. (2016). *National education evidence base*. In Report no. 80 Retrieved from 30 June 2018, http://www.pc.gov.au/inquiries/completed/education-evidence/report/education-evidence.pdf

Rothbart, M. K., Evans, D. E., & Ahadi, S. A. (2000). Temperament and personality: Origins and outcomes. *Journal of Personality and Social Psychology*, *78*(1), 122–135.

Scott, A., Woolcott, G., Keast, R., & Chamberlain, D. (2017). Sustainability of collaborative networks in higher education research projects: Why complexity? Why now? *Public Management Review*, *20*(7), 1068–1087.

Stanford, C., Cole, R., Froyd, J., Henderson, C., Friedrichsen, D., & Khatri, R. (2017). Analysis of propagation plans in nsf-funded education development projects. *Journal of Science Education and Technology*, *26*(4), 418–437.

Wright, N. (2016). Developing professionally: Examining the value of an external agent to the professional growth of teachers experimenting with mobile digital technologies. *Educational Action Research*, *25*(2), 223–238.

# 14

DEVELOPING A MODEL FOR THE TRANSLATION OF SCIENCE OF LEARNING RESEARCH TO THE CLASSROOM

Stephanie MacMahon, Annita Nugent and Annemaree Carroll

Introduction

In Australia, there have been increasing calls for the development of a systematic approach to the translation of evidence-based findings into schools in order to improve student outcomes. Compared to other Organisation for Economic Co-operation and Development (OECD) countries, Australian students continue to demonstrate widespread academic decline (Department of Education and Training, 2018). In order to stem this decline, a key recommendation in the Commonwealth Department of Education and Training (DET) 2018 review of school education is for a systematic approach to developing, sharing, and implementing evidence-informed innovations and best practice in a broader and timelier manner than currently exists (Department of Education and Training, 2018). This emphasis on evidence-informed practice is in line with a similar growing expectation internationally (Cooper, Levin, & Campbell, 2009). Furthermore, the Australian Professional Standards for Teachers articulates that all teachers should demonstrate capacity to engage with research about how students learn and how to teach, and that more accomplished teachers develop and lead evidence-informed practices in the classroom (AITSL, 2017). However, concerns around how evidence is translated into practice, the impact of related complexities, and the undervaluing of professional experience and knowledge as evidence have led to criticism of evidence-based reform (Cooper et al., 2009; Palinkas, He, Choy-Brown, & Locklear Hertel, 2017). Therefore, to advance effective pedagogical engagement with evidence-informed practice, a systematic approach to research translation that addresses these concerns is needed.

The multi-disciplinary field of the science of learning is vested in this discussion, seeking to translate research findings by developing and engaging with specific tools, methodologies, and translational models that can generate evidence-based claims about learning (Barab & Squire, 2004). While there are a range of research translation models developed, applied, and evaluated in fields such as medicine and social work, there are contextual and content differences that place limitations on using these models in education settings. There are some models for the translation of research to educational contexts, however, most of these models have not been empirically developed or validated (Levin, 2011; Lysenko, Abrami, Bernard, Dagenais, & Janosz, 2014). This chapter outlines the challenges faced in research translation across education, confirming the case for developing a process model. Through an examination of existing models and a synthesis of the literature, six principles for effective research translation are proposed. These principles have guided the development of the Science of Learning Research Centre (SLRC) Triadic Model of Research Translation, which are presented and discussed. Processes for implementing and evaluating this model are outlined to conclude the chapter, along with considerations for future applications.

Background

Research translation is the process that supports the efficacy, dissemination, and implementation of research into practice, and involves the design and evaluation of translation strategies, as well as the production of knowledge and evidence around the translation process itself (Palinkas & Soydan, 2011). The term "translation" is one of many terms applied to all or part of the processes involved in actioning research findings: other terms include knowledge transfer, research utilisation, diffusion, dissemination, knowledge exchange, knowledge mobilisation, knowledge-to-action, and implementation (Graham et al., 2006). For the purpose of this chapter, "translation" will be used as the umbrella term to describe the processes underpinning the integration of research into educational practice.

The process of translating research findings into practical educational contexts is complex and challenging, particularly if findings originate in a highly controlled laboratory setting or are synthesised across disciplines (Daniel, 2012; Glasgow, 2009). Educational contexts – such as within schools and universities – are highly dynamic, frequently unpredictable, and are shaped by the individual and collective beliefs, attitudes, values, knowledge, and skills of those within it, both teachers and students (Guskey, 2002). Furthermore, these attributes along with the organisational structures of educational environments have considerable influence upon a practitioner's engagement with research and evidence-informed practice (Lysenko et al., 2014). These complexities must be considered if research translation is to be efficacious (Daniel, 2012). Therefore, new paradigms and new approaches to frame research translation must be considered (Choudhury & Slaby, 2012; Howard-Jones et al., 2016; Immordino-Yang, 2016; Master, Meltzoff, & Lent, 2016).

Knowing about something is simply not enough – it must be explored and applied in practice for it to be fully realised. The burgeoning multi-disciplinary field of the science of learning promises great advances in our understanding *about* learning: the underlying processes, how it can be measured, and promoted, and furthermore, what this means for effective teaching and ultimately student outcomes. However, the applications of these findings to practice creates difficulties due to multiple factors including conflicting philosophical and methodological "cultures" (Palinkas & Soydan, 2012), and a range of contextual and professional complexities (Daniel, 2012; Glasgow, 2009; Lysenko, et al., 2014). The need to develop evidence-informed approaches to research translation in educational contexts – particularly multi-disciplinary research – is urgent, as educational institutions and policies globally increase their expectations around evidence-based and evidence-informed practice (Burns & Schuler, 2007; Cooper et al., 2009).

The research–practice gap

With the increasing national and international emphasis on evidence-informed practice, the need for effective actionable, sustainable, and scalable translation of research findings is imperative (Cooper et al., 2009; Department of Education and Training, 2018; Master et al., 2016). However, the path from research to educational practice is challenging and slow (Daniel, 2012; Glasgow, 2009), largely due to the long-standing and multi-faceted research–practice gap (See Figure 14.1).

The gap between research and practice across a range of fields including education is well acknowledged (Begun, Berger, Otto-Salaj, & Rose, 2010; Green, Ottoson, Garcia, & Hiatt, 2009; Z. P. Neal, J. W. Neal, Lawlor, & Mills, 2015). Neal et al. (2015) define the research–practice gap as an absence, distortion, or break in the exchange of information between research and practice or as the lack of translation of evidence-based strategies into practice or policy. This disruption can be the result of philosophical, methodological, or contextual differences between research and practice, and has been the basis of strong criticism directed at evidence-based reform.

Palinkas and Soydan (2012) propose that effective translation can be philosophically challenging if there are competing paradigms involved: the laboratory

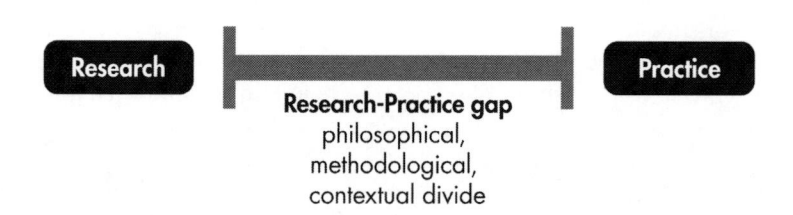

FIGURE 14.1 Research–practice gap

is highly controlled and clinical, existing within a positivist paradigm, whilst the classroom operates within a social constructivist context. These philosophical differences can also mean methodological challenges: laboratory-based findings may not allow for the complexities of the classroom and school contexts. Consequently, criticism exists around the way in which evidence is defined and implemented, often including an undervaluing of the importance of professional knowledge and experience as evidence (Cooper et al., 2009; Palinkas et al., 2017). While scientific methods such as randomised controlled trials are perceived by some – namely those working in laboratory-based research – as the "gold standard" in terms of evidential rigour, others – predominantly practitioners – argue that this definition of evidence devalues other forms of evidence, particularly the "craft wisdom" (McKenney & Reeves, 2013, p. 11) gained through practical, real-world experience (Palinkas et al., 2017).

In addition to these philosophical and methodological challenges, contextual differences – professional, geographical, social, and personal – contribute to trials in communication and collaboration between researchers and practitioners and highlight differences in professional and personal goals (Begun et al., 2010; Green et al., 2009; Neal et al., 2015). The gap between research and practice can highlight the contextual differences between the places of knowledge development and of knowledge application (Green et al., 2009). It can also be problematic for practitioners as it limits information about and access to evidence-based practice, while for researchers it is problematic because it restricts their understanding of context and therefore reduces their ability to engage in practice-based research (Wandersman, 2003). Schools are limited in their capacity (and time) to source, interpret, and apply research, and these restrictions consequently diminish the priority of engaging with research (Lysenko et al., 2014), while academics effectively share their research, but are reluctant and often unsure about how to make recommendations on the application of findings to practice (Cooper et al., 2009; Wandersman, 2003). These challenges add to existing criticism around the nature of evidence and how it is used to inform practice.

The recognition of these challenges, along with the increased expectation for engagement with evidence-informed practices, further propels the momentum behind calls for more rigourous scholarship around and systematic approaches to research translation (Cooper et al., 2009; Green et al., 2009; Shonkoff & Bales, 2011). In order to develop a rigourous and effective approach to research translation into school contexts, the theoretical foundations of existing models of translation across other fields should be considered.

Theoretical frameworks of research translation

A review of the literature reveals a breadth of terms and constructs that sit under the umbrella of research translation, and the terms draw on a range of theoretical frameworks to shape current models, including diffusion, dissemination, implementation, and ecological systems theories (Green et al., 2009; Neal et al., 2015).

Diffusion: natural unintentional spread of ideas

FIGURE 14.2 Diffusion of research findings to practice

Diffusion theory explores the natural, unintentional spread of ideas and actions within a particular social system (Green et al., 2009; Neal et al., 2015). The process of research diffusion is linear: taken from research and communicated unintentionally to practice (see Figure 14.2). This theory can help explain the, sometimes mindless, adoption of ideas or practices that appear to be fashionable or whose evidence is taken for granted (Green et al., 2009). These sometimes misleading or misconstrued ideas and practices can spread via conduits such as word of mouth and various forms of media (Neal et al., 2015). Within the science of learning, common examples of the potential dangers of diffusion include the impact on pedagogical practice of particular neuromyths – widespread false beliefs about neuroscience and its application to learning – such as learning styles or hemispheric dominance (Howard-Jones, 2014; Master et al., 2016). The unintentional manner that underpins the diffusion approach means that implementation is less systematic and integrated than other models, and this presents challenges to authenticity, rigour, and validity.

Dissemination theory incorporates the more intentional, conscious sharing of new ideas and research findings to target audiences and the wider public but maintains the linear stream of knowledge and communication (see Figure 14.3). Dissemination occurs through forums such as publishing, workshops, social media, professional learning, and conferences (Green et al., 2009; Neal et al., 2015). This approach is the *modus operandi* of university researchers, and is therefore familiar and often perceived as the end-point of their role in research translation. Attending conferences and reading informative texts or posts may be interesting and even empowering for practitioners. However, this dissemination model is ineffective in facilitating deep understanding or sustained implementation of research findings into practice as there is limited or no engagement with the practical context (Stafford-Brizard, Cantor, & Rose, 2017). Whilst opportunities for research dissemination have increased – particularly through various online forums – due to inadequate measurements there is very little current evidence of how these opportunities inform practice and enhance outcomes for learners (Cooper et al., 2009; Currie et al., 2005).

Dissemination: intentional sharing of knowledge and ideas

FIGURE 14.3 Dissemination of research to practice

Implementation theory provides some explanations for the mechanisms by which implementation of research findings are most likely to succeed (Nilsen, 2015). Implementation as a process within research translation refers to the adoption of research findings into practice (Graham et al., 2006). Implementation theory has guided the development of models and frameworks designed to investigate the effectiveness of implementation. In relation to research translation, implementation theory has been drawn upon as it has been found that even when information reaches practitioners (perhaps through diffusion or dissemination), and they intend to adopt it, information can still be misconstrued or implementation wanes (Green et al., 2009).

Diffusion, dissemination, and implementation are all parts of the research translation continuum aimed at applying new research knowledge and need to be considered intentionally and systematically (Nilsen, 2015). Synthesising these various components of the translation continuum, *knowledge utilisation* is a broad theoretical frame applied in a range of fields including health and education that includes knowledge transfer, application, and implementation (Green et al., 2009). This theoretical frame aims to use knowledge to solve social problems through research intervention and policy (Green et al., 2009). In medical literature, successfully translating research into practice is usually undertaken through the provision of medical practice guidelines, and this process is often conceptualised as moving through three phases: from awareness, through acceptance, to adoption (Green & Seifert, 2005). In this model, practitioners engage knowledge with increasing proficiency over time across these phases, building upon their current skill set and applying processes in relevant, one-on-one contexts (Green & Seifert, 2005). However, a range of social, political, and cultural forces influences the success of the adoption and acceptance of new knowledge. Acknowledging and integrating the various socio-cultural and personal forces that exist within the context is therefore essential for effective translation of research into highly complex environments, such as schools. Many models that sit within these above theoretical frameworks are uni-directional and linear in their focus: transferring knowledge from research to practice, therefore not capturing the diversity and complexity of the classroom and school environment. Furthermore, they are unable to integrate research knowledge with the unique contextual and professional needs found in the real-world school setting (Guskey, 2002; Stafford-Brizard et al., 2017). Ecological systems theory provides a theoretical framework that can achieve this contextual integration.

Recognition of professional contexts is essential for effective research translation. Systems-based, integrated models of research translation based on *ecological systems theory* are able to effectively engage with the contextual needs and limitations of both practitioners and researchers more so than the linear, uni-directional theories and models discussed earlier. A distinguishing feature of ecological systems-based bi-directional or multi-directional models is that they explore the integration or mobilisation of knowledge in authentic settings (Cooper et al., 2009), promoting a partnership between researchers and practitioners through which the research agenda is collaboratively developed (Green et al., 2009). Translational models built on an ecological systems approach acknowledge contextual variances including political, social, and personal systems and factors that may impede or enhance acceptance and adoption of research findings (Graham et al., 2006). These various contextual complexities must be carefully considered when designing systematic approaches to research translation, and underpin several of the principles established to inform the design of the SLRC Triadic Partnership Model of Research Translation.

Principles of effective research–practice translation

Bridging the research–practice divide takes time, effort, planning, commitment, understanding, and strong interpersonal relationships between partners: qualities often overlooked in the rush to apply research to practice (Begun et al., 2010; Neal et al., 2015). In order for learner outcomes to be positively impacted by research findings, the research–practice gap must be bridged, teacher capacity developed, and research findings explored in authentic contexts. Through a review of the literature and existing models, the characteristics of effective research–practice collaborations and translation have been synthesised into six proposed principles: these are presented below along with discussion of how they have been applied to the SLRC Triadic Partnership Model.

An ecological systems model of research translation best supports the inherent complexities and interactions that exist within and between research and practice contexts

Effective research translation needs to be sensitive to both the research and school contexts, recognising the inherent variability, needs, limitations, and possibilities that exist within the relevant and interrelated complex systems (Stafford-Brizard et al., 2017). These dynamic contextual complexities are best served through an ecological systems model design. An appreciation of the systems influencing each partner enables better understanding of the motivations for being involved in a project of research translation. Effective research collaborations are built on a strong understanding of the motivations, organisational systems, and cultures of the various participants (Begun et al., 2010). Teacher pedagogical decisions in the classroom are shaped by both external and internal influences: by the pedagogical frameworks and practices of their school communities and by their individual professional identities – their professional skills, knowledge, beliefs, attitudes, and values (Bahr & Mellow, 2016; Beijaard, Meijer, & Verloop, 2013; Pillen, Den Brok, & Beijaard, 2013). Therefore, they are more likely to engage in educational innovations and pedagogical practices – including research and evidence-informed practice – if they perceive it to be of contextual and professional value (Bahr & Mellow, 2016; Beijaard et al., 2013). Similarly, researchers are more likely to engage with practitioners when they can see the value in the application of their work to authentic contexts. These opportunities also provide for researchers valuable insight into the challenges and opportunities for further research that can impact classroom practice.

Knowing *why* each participant in a translational partnership wants to collaborate is important to understanding *how* they may contribute. Likewise, understanding and respecting the organisational expectations, cultures, policies, procedures, limitations, and constraints is important in determining participant behaviour and engagement, including the level of time commitment. Respecting these organisational and professional parameters builds trust within the partnership, and making these explicit can facilitate the articulation of shared goals. Furthermore, building a shared understanding of the professional needs of all collaborating partners can also assist in the development of a common language around the projects and the research (Begun et al., 2010).

An awareness of the complexities and interconnectedness of effective research translation is evident in the process of *knowledge mobilisation*, the translational term preferred by Cooper et al. (2009). Knowledge mobilisation captures not just the intellectual components but also the intent, direction, and effort evident in socio-cultural and multi-directional aspects of effective research–practice engagements. Knowledge is a key construct in the knowledge mobilisation process, and exists at various levels: knowledge about the research and knowledge about how to use it (Cooper et al., 2009). Furthermore, interpersonal knowledge – knowing about each other in the research–practice partnership – is also essential (Begun et al., 2010). This knowledge involves knowing and valuing the context, motivations, expectations, limitations, and constraints of one another, and working together collaboratively to accommodate these (Begun et al., 2010). Furthermore, knowledge of one's own practice and willingness to explore change is also essential for successful implementation of research evidence (Lysenko et al., 2014). However, the ability to access and develop these essential forms of knowledge are often undermined by the social, cultural, philosophical, and geographical differences between university and school contexts, factors that contribute considerably to the research–practice gap, and can interfere with the successful dissemination and implementation of research findings (Begun et al., 2010; Neal et al., 2015). The Knowledge-to-Action (KTA) process model of Graham et al. (2006) is an example of a knowledge exchange model used extensively in the translation of health-related research. Similarly, *cultural adaptation* models explore individual contextual needs in order to systematically consider and adapt research findings to individual contexts (Cabassa & Baumann, 2013). Research partnerships based on cultural adaptation models recommend: equal collaboration between partners, drawing on their relevant expertise; developing an understanding of practitioner needs and problems; modifying and documenting the process of implementation and adaptation, monitoring through iterative evaluation; and ensuring practitioner context is central (Cabassa & Baumann, 2013).

Systems-based models can allow for the various research and practice complexities, and foster a bi-directional or multi-directional engagement between the various interacting parties and their contexts. More linear models of research translation are largely driven by the agenda of the researchers, with the expectation of change and knowledge growth lying with the practitioner. A truly collaborative research translation partnership should see a change and growth in knowledge, beliefs, values, and practice of both practitioners and researchers over time through multi-directional interactions. These developments should subsequently be shared with the professional contexts of both parties in order to inform, not just future educational practice, but future research agendas, pre-service teacher education, research translation, and policy. Models that can support the interconnectedness of the various forms of knowledge and the range of contexts have been shown to be more effective in translating research into practice.

The professional contexts and motivations of partners are acknowledged in the SLRC Triadic Partnership Model of Research Translation through the inclusion of their contextual systems of influence and impact. Teachers and school leaders exist within systems of learners, pedagogy, curriculum, community, and policy, all of which bring with them unique and complex needs and influences (Brown, 1992). Likewise, researchers exist within complex systems of learners, academics, research and development, funding priorities, and policy. Community expectations and policy influence both sets of systems in varying ways. The needs, parameters, limitations, and opportunities of these systems are acknowledged within the SLRC Model through scaffolding opportunities for partners to share contextual influences and expertise, valuing input from all parties, and exploring findings in context.

The highly integrated network of stakeholders that exist within both school and university contexts is further complicated by the influence of individual and collective beliefs, knowledge, perceptions, and practices (Guskey, 2002; Lysenko et al., 2014). For translation and implementation of research findings to be successful, consideration needs to be given to the various complexities and challenges faced by schools and university contexts, including scaling of research findings, finances, time, infrastructure, context, current knowledge, and practice, and most significantly, access to information (Cooper et al., 2009; Green et al., 2009; Lysenko et al., 2014; Neal et al., 2015). Therefore, for research translation in education to be effective, there needs to be the capacity to foster sustained effective links between research and schools, building beyond the dissemination of research to fostering continued interaction and collaboration (Begun et al., 2010; Cooper et al., 2009; Neal et al., 2015; Palinkas & Soydan, 2012; Stafford-Brizard et al., 2017). Over the course of the SLRC Partner Schools Project partnership, these various personal, professional, and contextual factors are explored.

Effective collaborations require time, effort, and strong interpersonal relationships to ensure success

Research collaborations need to adopt a longitudinal perspective in order to build the interpersonal and professional relationships so essential to their success (Begun et al., 2010). In effective research translation partnerships, the unique contributions of all partners are respected through bi-directional and/or multi-directional interactions (Begun et al., 2010). These multi-directional interactions facilitate understanding of both the scientific and educational contexts, a process essential for the accurate representation of research into practice (Howard-Jones et al., 2016). Therefore, interpersonal communication and interaction between all partners is key to effective research collaboration and transformation (Neal et al., 2015; Palinkas & Soydan, 2012).

Knowledge exchange emphasises collaboration between researchers and practitioners along the entire translation continuum, resulting in mutual learning through all phases from the planning of the research problem through to the evaluation of the implementation (Graham et al., 2006). This process ensures the research and its findings are relevant and meaningful for both practitioners and researchers. At the core of the KTA Model (Graham et al., 2006) is the construction of tailored knowledge around the identification of a contextually relevant problem. Commencing with knowledge inquiry and synthesis, new knowledge is created using an action research cycle that enables the development of knowledge tools and products that are tailored to the context. This KTA model ensures that the process has relevance and meaning for both researchers and professionals at all stages of the translation continuum.

Cultural exchange supports the transformation of knowledge from a positivist to a social constructivist context, similar to that experienced when translating research from a laboratory-based setting to the social context of the school and classroom (Palinkas & Soydan, 2012). It acknowledges the differing cognitive (knowledge) and affective (motivational) elements for each partner, and draws on these differences in design. Therefore its success relies heavily on the opportunity for effective interpersonal interactions between researchers and practitioners (Palinkas & Soydan, 2012). The term "culture," as it is used in this context, includes the dynamic development of shared identity, beliefs, values, thoughts, and behaviours, which are transmitted and shaped through social interactions, observations, and actions within an identified context (Cabassa & Baumann, 2013). Cultural exchange involves the transaction of culturally (or professionally) diverse knowledge, attitudes, and practices in a bi-directional process that encourages debate and compromise, and through which all participants are transformed (Brekke, Ell, & Palinkas, 2007; Palinkas & Soydan, 2012). Cultural exchange integrates and accommodates the shared understandings and values (cultural systems) of interacting partners such as researchers, practitioners, and policymakers, and acknowledges the social processes and contextual considerations involved in translation (Cabassa & Baumann, 2013).

These interactions and resulting relationships are most effectively built via "small world networks": networks of practitioners systematically connected to networks of researchers (Neal et al., 2015). Small networks of teachers or schools who interact on common issues have been shown to effectively impact on teacher practice (Cooper et al., 2009). In the SLRC Triadic Partnership Model, a team of up to five staff members – including members of the school leadership team – represents school communities. These teams are regularly clustered with other school teams to network and share ideas. These clusters are provided with ongoing interaction with small groups of researchers whose work aligns with the identified research focus of the teams and cluster. Keeping these teams small enables the development of ongoing interpersonal relationships between practitioners and researchers, allowing for the development of mutual understanding and respect for various personal and professional needs. This process is most effectively facilitated by a research broker.

Collaborations between practitioners and researchers are more effective when facilitated by a research broker: an individual knowledgeable in both research and education

As has been discussed, the opportunity to develop relationships and productive collaborations is essential for the formation of the various forms of knowledge required by all partners, and is fundamental to effective partnerships (Begun et al., 2010; Cooper et al., 2009; Neal et al., 2015). To assist with this, several successful models of effective research translation propose the inclusion of a research broker or facilitator: individuals or organisations who support the process of translation across the continuum (Cabassa & Baumann, 2013; Cooper et al., 2009; Neal et al., 2015).

The role of the research broker is to facilitate the establishment of appropriate collaborations and the exchange of knowledge between research partners, and to assist in the translation of research findings into a contextually relevant format (Palinkas et al., 2017). This role may include assisting the practitioner to develop the knowledge and skills to be able to select, adapt, implement, evaluate, and disseminate the application of evidence-based practices (Cabassa & Baumann, 2013). They may also assist practitioners through locating or summarising research findings that address particular real-world problems, or assist researchers in developing and exploring real-world research questions. (Neal et al., 2015).

In a multi-disciplinary field such as the science of learning, there are multiple stakeholders and audiences. The contextual and professional needs and expertise of these diverse audiences need to be considered, particularly in relation to the development of relevant research questions and the translation of findings. Effective research brokers need to be familiar with the target audiences and knowledgeable about both education and research (Cabassa & Baumann, 2013). As stated earlier, researchers – aware of their limited knowledge of the realities of classroom practice – are often reluctant to suggest classroom implications for their findings, whilst practitioners may be too reductive or liberal in their translation of findings to practice, unaware of the limitations or parameters of findings. Therefore, the research broker plays a fundamental role in bridging the gap between research and practice. They may also play a role in communicating research to extended partners, such as students, parents, other teachers, policymakers, and other researchers. Consequently, the key personnel in the SLRC Triadic Partnership Model are practitioners, researchers, and brokers.

Through engaging in iterative collaborative partnerships between practitioners, researchers, and brokers, emphasis is placed on co-learning as partners collaboratively define the research agenda (Green et al., 2009), and this has shown to increase engagement with evidence-informed practice (Begun et al., 2010; Bilsker & Goldner, 2000; Fraser, 2003; Gass, 2005). This collaborative approach to the identification of the research agenda and the subsequent exploration and intervention are supported by the systematic approach of design-based research (DBR) methodology. This methodology provides a framework for research to be systematically explored in authentic contexts.

The translation of research findings around learning and teaching needs to be systematically explored in context

A fundamental premise of the exploration of "learning" within the science of learning is that learning, cognition, knowing, and context are interconnected and interdependent. Exploring constructs surrounding learning outside of the learning environment provides an incomplete understanding of learning and the learning process. Likewise, exploring learning only in applied settings can undermine the impact of other variables that cannot be controlled in that environment (Barab & Squire, 2004). Therefore, rather than the linear, uni-directional nature of research dissemination or previous translational processes, effective translational processes involve a collaborative approach to the exploration of contextually relevant issues through the establishment of an iterative dialogue between researchers and practitioners. Through drawing on the relevant expertise brought to the collaboration by the various partners, researchers can develop a greater understanding of the real-world contexts of their research, whilst practitioners can enhance their understanding of the methodological and philosophical considerations, assisting in developing research questions that frame real-world practice (Begun et al., 2010; Currie et al., 2005; Green et al., 2009).

Complicating this process further, the science of learning draws upon basic and applied research findings relating to a range of learning constructs explored in diverse disciplines and contexts. In order to generate meaningful evidence-based claims about learning, specific tools and methodologies need to be developed and utilised that can investigate these claims in relevant contexts, namely the classroom (Barab & Squire, 2004). DBR is one such methodology that was developed specifically for the purpose of research having an impact in the classroom (Anderson & Shattuck, 2012; Brown, 1992). DBR has been identified as an effective "best practice" methodology useful for complex learning environments such as schools, as it involves both evaluation and empirical analysis (Anderson & Shattuck, 2012). Quality DBR is defined by: being situated in authentic educational contexts; ongoing collaborative partnership between researchers and practitioners; the collaborative development of a research problem; the collaborative design and testing of an intervention; and the development of design principles that can inform learning theory (Anderson & Shattuck, 2012). The collaborative identification of a research focus, development of an intervention, collection and analysis of data, and discussion of implications within the SLRC Triadic Partnership Model of Research Translation utilises a DBR approach. This iterative approach supports the building of capacity in partners whilst contributing further to the broader understanding of learning, teaching, and translation and positively impacting upon learner outcomes.

Building capacity in partners fosters professional self-efficacy

Teachers' reluctance to engage with research and evidence-based practice has been found to be largely due to a lack of awareness of the research and its implications, and low self-efficacy in terms of how to access, understand, and apply findings to their practice (Lysenko et al., 2014). To address these concerns, research findings, and implications need to be relevant to the teaching and learning context of individuals, and resonate with practitioners' professional beliefs, attitudes, knowledge, skills, and values (Lysenko et al., 2014). Teachers develop within the context of the professional environment in which they work. For teachers to become more discerning of research and independent in their engagement with research processes and practice, they need to be provided with the environmental and professional support to develop positive dispositions towards and capability in research (Lysenko et al., 2014). Given that the implementation of research findings potentially involves the changing of practice and the shifting or grafting of prior knowledge, practitioners need to believe that this process will have a positive impact upon learner outcomes (Guskey, 2002; Huberman, 2002). Furthermore, opportunities need to be provided for practitioners to build their knowledge and awareness of research through direct involvement in research activities. This has been shown to assist in promoting positive attitudes towards research and increase self-efficacy around engagement (Lysenko et al., 2014). Developing professional expertise in research involves not just the application of findings to practice, but proficiency in accessing, reading, understanding, and assessing the quality of research (Lysenko et al., 2014). Effective models of research translation, therefore, need to provide the opportunity for practitioners to build competence in sourcing and appraising research, and in translating that research validly into their own contexts with increasing independence and confidence (Lysenko et al., 2014).

Likewise, a research partnership can support the development of researcher knowledge and awareness around the implications of findings for practice, and build capacity and self-efficacy in making recommendations for translation and for further contextually relevant research. This knowledge and capacity can then inform further research directions, be the impetus for collegial discourse, and be embedded into university teacher preparation programs. Over time, and with appropriate guidance and support, practitioners can become increasingly autonomous in their engagement with and critical assessment of evidence-based and

Developing a model for the translation **215**

evidence-informed practice, whilst researchers can become more attuned to the contextual needs and implications of research for educational practice, and for the development of pre-service teacher training. A truly collaborative research translation partnership should see a change and growth in knowledge, beliefs, values, and practice of both practitioners and researchers. These developments should subsequently be shared with the professional contexts of both parties in order to inform not just future educational practice, but future implications for pre-service teacher education, research translation, research agendas, and policy.

Supportive leadership and professional contexts manifest in greater partner engagement

The identification and implementation of professional learning requires the involvement and support of school leadership if it is to be successful (Hunzicker, 2011; Knight, 2011). Organisational structures that support engagement with evidence-informed practice have been shown to be essential to developing positive teacher attitudes to research and to implementing and reflecting upon evidence-informed practice (Lysenko et al., 2014). Effective professional learning requires practitioners to have time to engage in knowledge development, discussion, praxis, and reflection (Knight, 2011). In the SLRC Triadic Partnership Model, it is recommended that the school teams involve members of the school leadership in order to facilitate the required time and support needed for a longitudinal project of change practice.

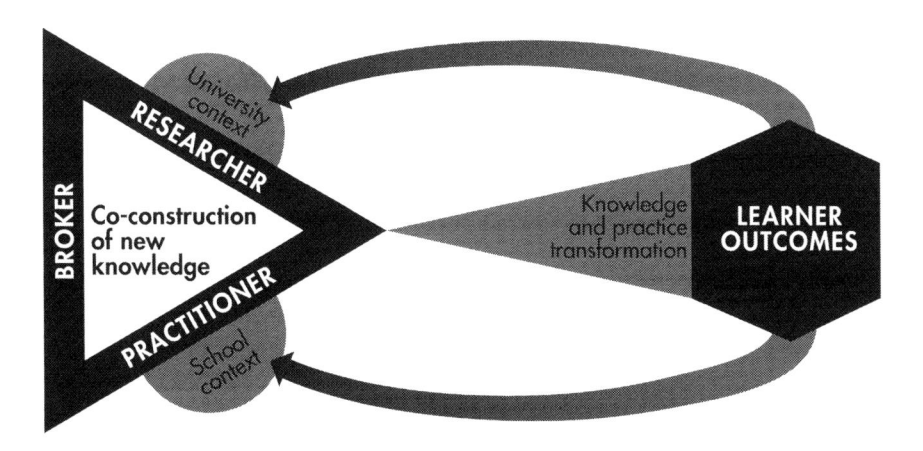

SLRC Triadic Partnership Model of Research Translation

Each of the above evidence-informed principles of effective research translation have been captured in the SLRC Triadic Partnership Model (see Figure 14.4). The SLRC Triadic Partnership Model is currently being trialled and evaluated

FIGURE 14.4 SLRC triadic partnership model of research translation

through a unique university–school partnership program in Queensland and Victoria. The Partner School Program was established as a collaborative partnership between the University of Queensland, University of Melbourne, and a range of Queensland and Victorian schools, with the support of the respective state departments of education and independent education sectors.

The model is characterised by the partnership between researchers and educators, facilitated by research brokers, to collaboratively address educator-led priorities. In addition to the generation of new knowledge relating to school-identified focus areas, the model provides training and awareness in research methodology and processes to educators, and affords researchers an insight into the context in which their research will be applied. The SLRC Partner Schools Program aims to establish a network of research–practice partnerships through which the science of learning can find a meaningful, authentic space in which to explore contextually relevant research findings. At the same time, it endevours to develop awareness, skill, knowledge, and critical enquiry in partners to drive a more rigourous, increasingly autonomous engagement with research-informed practice in schools, and to promote a relevant research agenda in universities. It is anticipated that by engaging in this more systematic, contextualised, partnership approach to exploring and translating research into practice, evidence-informed actionable outcomes can be achieved. The partnership is designed to retain greater fidelity to the research on which the outcomes are grounded, and therefore be more sustainable and have greater potential for scalability. The emerging, authentic, contextualised findings will then be able to further inform future research agendas, teacher training programs, and pedagogical practice.

Conclusion

The opening section of this chapter outlined why there is a need for a systematic approach to science of learning research translation. The expectation of governments and policymakers that educational institutions and practitioners engage more with evidence-based and evidence-informed practice has been frequently met with frustration by schools as access to research, and the capacity to interpret, implement, and evaluate findings has been difficult. Furthermore, the research is often conducted in a removed context making it less relevant and valuable to individual schools and practitioners. The model presented in this chapter aims to address many of the barriers currently limiting the engagement of effective evidence-based practice in educational contexts. Establishing direct, ongoing partnerships between practitioners and researchers can facilitate collaboration on contextually relevant projects. The establishment of ongoing relationships enables practitioners to communicate their needs, ideas, and questions. It also provides them with essential support to develop their capacity to access, engage with, understand, interpret, and conduct research with increasing confidence and independence. These skills can be further transferred to other aspects of their own or colleagues practice, developing a critical and discerning approach to professional growth and development. This partnership provides important capacity and knowledge building opportunities for researchers, experiencing first-hand how the research is being applied to practice in an authentic setting, and analysing the potential challenges and opportunities this presents. Having the opportunity to work alongside practitioners and witness potential application could assist researchers to progress a more relevant research agenda.

Hattie (2012) challenges teachers to "know thy impact": to understand how what they do impacts upon learner outcomes. This same mantra could equally be applied to the research community – challenging them to take an active role in observing and responding to the impact of their research on authentic teaching and learning in the classroom. As stated in the introduction, knowing *about* something is simply not enough – it must be explored and applied in practice in order to be fully realised. It is hoped that by developing an evidence-informed, systematic approach to science of learning research translation, the impact of quality teaching, learning, and research can be experienced more readily and broadly.

References

Anderson, T. & Shattuck, J. (2012). Design-based research: A decade of progress in education research? *Educational Researcher*, 41(1), 16–25.

AITSL Australian Institute for Teaching and School Leadership (2017). Australian Professional Standards for Teachers. Retrieved January 1, 2018 from http://www.aitsl.edu.au/australian-professional-standards-for-teachers/standards/list

Bahr, N. & Mellow, S. (2016). *Building quality in teaching and teacher education*. Camberwell, Victoria: ACER.

Barab, S. & Squire, K. (2004). Design-based research: Putting a stake in the ground. *Journal of the Learning Sciences*, 13(1), 1–14.

Begun, A. L., Berger, L. K., Otto-Salaj, L. L., & Rose, S. J. (2010). Developing effective social work university–community research collaborations. *Social Work*, 55(1), 54–62.

Beijaard, D. C., Meijer, P. C., & Verloop, N. (2013). The emergence of research on teachers' professional identity: A review of literature from 1988 to 2000. *Advances in Research on Teaching*, 19, 205–222. https://doi.org/10.1108/S1479-3687(2013)0000019013

Bilsker, D. & Goldner, E. M. (2000). Teaching evidence-based practice in mental health. *Research on Social Work Practice*, 10, 664–669.

Brekke, J. S., Ell, K., & Palinkas, L. A. (2007). Translational science at the National Institute of Mental Health: Can social work take its rightful place? *Research on Social Work Practice*, 17, 123–133. doi: 10.1177/1049731506293693

Brown, A. L. (1992). Design experiments: Theoretical and methodological challenges in creating complex interventions in classroom settings. *The Journal of the Learning Sciences*, 2(2), 141–178. Retrieved June 1, 2017 from http://www.jstor.org/stable/1466837

Burns, T. & Schuler, T. (2007). The evidence agenda. In OECD (Ed.), *Evidence in education: Linking research and policy* (pp. 15–32). Paris: OECD. Retrieved July 1, 2018 from http://www.oecd.org/edu/ceri

Cabassa, L. J. & Baumann, A. A. (2013). A two-way street: Bridging implementation science and cultural adaptations of mental health treatments. *Implementation Science*, 8(90), 1–14.

Choudhury, S. & Slaby, J. (2012). *Critical neuroscience: A handbook of the social and cultural contexts of neuroscience*. West Sussex, UK: Wiley-Blackwell.

Cooper, A., Levin, B., & Campbell, C. (2009). The growing (but still limited) importance of evidence in education policy and practice. *Journal of Educational Change, 10*, 159–171.

Currie, M., King, G., Rosenbaum, P., Law, M., Kertoy, M., & Specht, J. (2005). A model of impacts of research partnerships in health and social services. *Evaluation and Program Planning, 28*, 400–412.

Daniel, D. B. (2012). Promising principles: Translating the science of learning to educational practice. *Journal of Applied Research in Memory and Cognition, 1*, 251–253.

Department of Education and Training. (2018). *Through growth to achievement: The report of the review to achieve educational excellence in Australian schools*. Canberra: Department of Education and Training.

Fraser, M. W. (2003). Intervention research in social work: A basis for evidence-based practice and practice guidelines. In A. Rosen & E. K. Proctor (Eds.), *Developing practice guidelines for social work intervention: Issues, methods, and research agenda* (pp. 17–35). New York: Columbia University Press.

Gass, E. (2005). The path to partnership: A new model for understanding university–community partnerships. *Professional Development: The International Journal of Continuing Social Work Education, 8*(2/3), 12–23.

Glasgow, R. E. (2009). Critical measurement issues in translational research. *Research on Social Work Practice, 19*(5), 560–568.

Graham, I., Logan, J., Harrison, M., Straus, S., Tetroe, W., Caswell, N., & Robinson. (2006). Lost in knowledge translation: Time for a map? *The Journal of Continuing Education in the Health Professions, 26*(1), 13–24.

Green, L. W., Ottoson, J. M., Garcia, C., & Hiatt, R. A. (2009). Diffusion theory and knowledge dissemination, utilization and integration in public health. *Annual Review of Public Health, 30*(1), 51–74.

Green, L. A. & Seifert, C. M. (2005). Translation of research into practice: Why we can't "just do it." *Journal of the American Board of Family Practice, 18*(6), 541–545.

Guskey, T. R. (2002). Professional development and teacher change. *Teachers and Teaching, 8*(3), 381–391, doi: 10.1080/135406002100000512

Hattie, J. (2012). Know thy impact. *Educational Leadership: Feedback for learning, 70*(1), 18–23.

Howard-Jones, P. (2014). Neuroscience and education: Myths and messages. *Nature Reviews Neuroscience, 15*, 817–824.

Howard-Jones, P. A., Ansari, D., De Smedt, B., Laurillard, D., Varma, S., Butterworth, B., Goswami, U., & Thomas, M. S. C. (2016). The principles and practices of educational neuroscience: A comment on Bowers (2016). *Psychological Review, 123*(5), 620–627.

Huberman, A. (2002). Moving towards the inevitable: The sharing of research in education. *Teachers and Teaching, 8*(3), 257–268.

Hunzicker, J. (2011). Effective professional development for teachers: A checklist. *Professional Development in Education, 37*(2), 177–179, doi: 10.1080/19415257.2010.523955

Immordino-Yang, M. H. (2016). *Emotions, learning, and the brain: exploring the educational implications of affective neuroscience*. New York, NY: WW Norton & Co.

Knight, J. (2011). *Unmistakable impact: A partnership approach for dramatically improving instruction*. Thousand Oaks, CA: Corwin.

Levin, B. (2011). Mobilising research knowledge in education. *London Review of Education, 9*, 15–26. doi: 10.1080/14748460.2011.550431

Lysenko, L. V., Abrami, P. C., Bernard, R. M., Dagenais, C., & Janosz, M. (2014). Educational research in educational practice: Predictors of use. *Canadian Journal of Education, 37*(2), 1–26.

Master, A., Meltzoff, A. N., & Lent, R. (2016). Neuroscience, psychology, and society: Translating research to improve learning. *Prospects, 46*, 191–198.

McKenney, S. & Reeves, T. (2013). Educational design research. In M. Spector, D. Merrill, J. Elen, & M. J. Bishop (Eds.). *Handbook of research on educational communications and technology* (pp. 131–140). London: Springer.

Neal, Z. P., Neal, J. W., Lawlor, J. A., & Mills, K. J. (2015). Small worlds or world apart? Using network theory to understand the research-practice gap. *Psychosocial Intervention, 24*, 177–184.

Nilsen, P. (2015). Making sense of implementation theories, models and frameworks. *Implementation Science, 10*(53), 53.

Palinkas, L. A. & Soydan, H. (2011). *Translation and implementation of evidence-based practice (Building social work research capacity)*. New York, NY: Oxford University Press.

Palinkas, L. A. & Soydan, H. (2012). New horizons of translational research and research translation in social work. *Research on Social Work Practice, 22*(1), 85–92.

Palinkas, L. A., He, A. S, Choy-Brown, M., & Locklear Hertel, A. (2017). Operationalizing social work science through research–practice partnerships: Lessons from implementation science. *Research on Social Work Practice, 27*(2), 181–188.

Pillen, M. T., Den Brok, P. J., & Beijaard, D. (2013). Profiles and change in beginning teachers' professional identity tensions. *Teaching and Teacher Education, 34*, 86–97.

Shonkoff, J. P. & Bales, S. N. (2011). Science does not speak for itself: Translating child development research for the public and its policymakers. *Child Development, 82*, 17.

Stafford-Brizard, K. B., Cantor, P., & Rose, L. T. (2017). Building the bridge between science and practice: Essential characteristics of a translational framework. *Mind, Brain and Education, 11*(4), 155–165.

Wandersman, A. (2003). Community science: Bridging the gap between science and practice with community-centred models. *American Journal of Community Psychology, 31*(3/4), 227–242.

DISCUSSANT

Charting New Waters in the Science of Learning: Reflections on the Emergence of the Science of Learning in Australia and Its Place on the International Landscape by an Outside Insider

Sean H. K. Kang

Introduction

The *science of learning* is a relatively new label referring to an exciting field that studies learning from a multi-disciplinary perspective, chiefly drawing from neuroscience, psychology, and education (each of which are established disciplines in their own right). The field has made strong headway, particularly in Australia with the establishment of a Science of Learning Research Centre (SLRC) funded by the Australian Research Council, to which the editors of this book belong. I am honoured to have been invited the opportunity to offer my views on recent developments in the field of the science of learning in this concluding chapter.

As a cognitive psychologist who studies learning and memory and is interested in the educational implications of my research, I identify strongly with the science of learning field and am proud to belong to it. During my post-doctoral training at the University of California, San Diego some years ago, I was affiliated with the Temporal Dynamics of Learning Center (a US National Science Foundation-funded Science of Learning Center) and gained valuable experience learning from and working with people from different disciplines (e.g., computer science) and professions (e.g., teachers). In fact, one of the co-principal investigators affiliated with that center was a professor from The University of Queensland specialising in computational cognitive science and artificial intelligence, and so there was an Australian connection to the science of learning even back then (~15 years ago).

The preceding chapters in the book do not merely document developments of the science of learning field in most recent years. They were written by diverse authors with wide-ranging expertise, and I enjoyed reading, thinking about, and learning from the various perspectives. It was gratifying to see a coming together of a seemingly eclectic mix – a demonstration of the science of learning in all its diversity, yet unified in its overarching goal of furthering our understanding of the learning process so as to facilitate it. A number of major themes emerged from the chapters including the influence of social and emotional factors on learning, the impact of technology on education, and bridging the gap between research and practice in order to achieve lasting impact. In the following sections I will discuss each of these.

Who we are, how we got here

Human beings are capable of social imitative learning that is qualitatively different from the learning exhibited by even our closest primate relatives (e.g., Herrmann, Call, Hernández-Lloreda, Hare, & Tomasello, 2007). This kind of learning allows for the development of culture and its associated artefacts (e.g., physical tools, language, number system; Tomasello, 2000), and deliberate instruction is a universal characteristic found across all human groups (Cole, 2010). In other words, the way we learn separates us from other animal species, and learning is at the heart of what makes us human. If that alone were not sufficient justification for the importance of studying learning, there are obvious practical reasons for wanting to deepen our understanding of the complex learning process in order to find ways to improve education delivery and student learning.

Since *science of learning* is a fairly recent term, it is important to define what it means. In the prologue Hattie and Nugent provide a nice historical perspective of how other related interdisciplinary fields involving education (e.g., educational psychology, educational neuroscience, learning sciences) came to be, and how the science of learning might be distinguished from them. As implied by the label, in the science of learning the scientific approach is paramount: testable hypotheses are proposed, empirical studies are designed, data are collected, and the results are used to update our knowledge or theories. The specific methods may differ (depending on the discipline and the research question), but the common denominator is that scientific evidence should drive decision-making and improvements in education. The field of education has been criticised for being influenced more by ideology than evidence (Carnine, 2000). This deficiency has come to the attention of policymakers and funding agencies. There is now a growing effort to ground educational policy and practice on rigorous scientific evidence. In Chapter 1 of this book McGaw discusses the influential role that international intergovernmental organisations such as the OECD and UNESCO have played in driving evidence-informed learning policy. The science of learning, with its combination of researchers from psychology, education, and neuroscience, is well positioned to contribute to the transformation of modern education.

To illustrate the development of the field, Nugent, Lim, and Lent (Chapter 2) describe the efforts in three countries to organise and invest in science of learning research, starting with the US National Science Foundation's (NSF) creation of six large-scale Science of Learning Centers, which subsequently inspired similar initiatives in Australia and Brazil. Aside from the NSF, the US Department of Education's Institute of Education Sciences (established in 2002) is another major source of funding for such research in the United States. It is heartening to see how the field is gradually gaining traction in more countries. For instance, Singapore's National Research Foundation started an initiative to fund science of learning research in 2015.

A hallmark of the science of learning approach is multi-disciplinarity. In order to have a fuller understanding of the learning process and tackle the problems faced in education, it is critical to draw expertise from across multiple disciplines. The simple reality is that a single discipline on its own does not possess all the knowledge and methods to address the multifaceted challenges in the classroom. Unfortunately, academics are accustomed to staying within their own disciplinary silos, and there needs to be sufficient infrastructure, opportunities, and incentives for interacting and collaborating across disciplines. Having formal structures such as the SLRC or research funding programs that require cross-disciplinary collaboration are definitely helpful, but the issue of people from different disciplines not sharing a common language still remains (see Nugent, Carroll, Hattie, & Dulleck, Chapter 3, for a candid account of the challenges encountered by the SLRC).

In my view, it is crucial for researchers from different disciplines to recognise that there can be multiple levels of analysis or investigation, and that understanding at each level is necessary in order to have a complete understanding. In cognitive science, for instance, Marr (1982) differentiated three levels of explanations: computational (the goal of the program, what problems it solves), algorithmic (the specific algorithms or processes that carry out the goal), and implementational (the physical hardware). The levels are distinct yet complementary, and, importantly, each one is vital to a full understanding of the functioning of the system. Viewed this way, the various disciplines each have their role and place, and one is not "better" than another. The research reviewed by Lent, Ribeiro, and Sato (Chapter 4) exemplify the utility of different levels of investigation. Of course, if the goal of the research is translation or application to the classroom, then it is likely that the levels of analysis that lend themselves to feasible interventions will likely be more relevant (e.g., investigations of instructional strategies are more likely to yield specific actionable recommendations for the classroom than research on long-term potentiation in neurons), but probably few would claim that the brain mechanisms underlying memory formation are immaterial to deepening our understanding of how we learn (see Hattie & Nugent, Prologue, on the debate surrounding the contributions of neuroscience to education). Also, Weekes (Chapter 5) describes how neuroscientific methods (brain imaging, measures of skin conductance, and cortisol) have advanced theoretical understanding of the role of anxiety in foreign language use, which may lead to future interventions targeted at reducing anxiety in language learners.

Social–emotional learning

We often think of learning as primarily involving the mind (i.e., learning is a mental process). The discipline that is focussed on the study of the mind is cognitive psychology, and so it should be (and is) very pertinent to the science of learning. Learning and education, however, occur within particular sociocultural contexts (e.g., Lee, 2008; Luke, 2011), and they are influenced by affective and motivational variables (e.g., Elliot & Church, 1997; Hembree, 1988). Therefore, a science of learning that excludes social or emotional factors would be inadequate.

Indeed, there is a wealth of evidence that factors such as self-regulation, social skills, perseverance, academic mindsets, and motivation play a large role in academic success (see Farrington et al., 2012, for a review), and they are usually subsumed under the broad label of "non-cognitive factors" (you will not find these topics mentioned in a cognitive psychology textbook; you are more likely to find them in a social or personality psychology textbook). The cognitive/non-cognitive distinction is perhaps reflective of the disciplinary walls that we tend to erect. An example of how the dichotomy can sometimes be artificial is the concept of stereotype threat (i.e., performance can be impaired when a negative stereotype about one's group is made salient; Steele & Aronson, 1995). Stereotypes are considered a *social* psychological phenomenon, but there is strong evidence that stereotype threat operates by reducing working memory capacity, which is a *cognitive* construct (Schmader & Johns, 2003).

As mentioned in the previous section, the kind of learning that sets humans beings apart from other animals comprises an essential social quality. It is encouraging that the SLRC has given prominence to social–emotional factors in its research foci. For instance, Cunnington, MacMahon, Sherwell, and Gillies (Chapter 8) emphasise the importance of social connectedness in facilitating school learning, and how various neural and physiological measures might be able to shed light on the level of cohesiveness in the classroom. Also, Buckley et al. (Chapter 6) are working on a training program aimed at decreasing mathematics anxiety in teachers by increasing awareness of the issue and its effects, coupled with stress reduction strategies featuring relaxation techniques and cognitive reappraisal. By focussing on teachers, their work recognises the important influence teachers have as mediators of their students' learning and that teachers (not just students) can be useful targets of intervention. In the same vein, Carroll and Bower (Chapter 7) describe a number of evidence-based programs that have been designed to promote emotion regulation and stress reduction, with some of the interventions targeting teachers and others targeting students with teachers as facilitators. Importantly, new technologies such as wristbands that measure electrodermal activity and mobile apps are being used in some of the research to obtain fine-grain real-time data of individuals' emotional functioning over a period of time.

The impact of technology on education

Technology and education have always been intricately linked from the beginning. In the Bronze and Iron Ages, the use of bronze (and later iron) to construct tools revolutionised agriculture, leading to a surge in agricultural productivity that made possible the division of labour. As society became more complex, there was a need for record keeping (using cuneiform, the first writing system), and selected young men were brought together to be trained to become scribes, and those places served as the earliest formal schools (Schmandt-Besserat, 1975, 1996). If we fast forward several thousand years (to the present time), a major issue educators grapple with is how technology should be used in education, especially given the ubiquity of digital devices today. For instance, a 2018 Pew Research Center survey of US teens aged 13 to 17 revealed that 95% have or have access to smartphones (Anderson & Jiang, 2018). Technology can be a double-edged sword. On the one hand, with digital tools students can now access information and communicate with others much more quickly and easily (e.g., Google, text messaging, Skype), potentially shifting the focus of education from knowledge acquisition to collaborative knowledge creation (Chapter 10); on the other hand, there is ample evidence that digital devices can be a distraction – even if one is not using a device, nearby peers using their devices in class can impair one's learning (Sana, Weston, & Cepeda, 2013)!

With advances in computational power and artificial intelligence, it is now possible for instruction to be personalised to each particular student (previously not feasible, unless the student had a personal tutor). Often referred to as *adaptive learning systems* or *intelligent tutoring systems*, the program uses a student's performance on an assessment (quiz) to decide what content is presented next, what kind of hints or feedback to provide, or when the material should be reviewed. Such systems hold much promise, with evidence that algorithms that take into consideration the student's performance when spacing out the review of the material improve learning (e.g., Lindsey, Shroyer, Pashler, & Mozer, 2014; Tabibian et al., 2019). A key advantage of such systems is that they can make decisions at a granularity (e.g., at the level of an individual item) that teachers typically cannot monitor or individualise, and while the students are using the personalised system, the teacher is freed up to interact with smaller groups of students who may need extra attention or guidance (Mozer, Wiseheart, & Novikoff, 2019).

EdTech is a rapidly growing multi-billion-dollar industry (Shulman, 2018). Lodge, Kennedy, and Lockyer (Chapter 11) provide a great overview of how educational technologies have transformed the educational landscape in recent years. They make a cogent argument for why technologies are unlikely to replace teachers (at least not in the foreseeable future), but acknowledge that the teacher–student interaction is altered when education is mediated by modern technology.

Importantly, rigorous research to determine the efficacy of EdTech products is lacking, and to the extent that EdTech companies do research, they typically focus on usability (e.g., how frequently users use a particular feature or product) and user experience (e.g., satisfaction with the product). Another problem is that the decision-makers for product adoption (e.g., school administrators, educators) often do not understand the need for research demonstrating product efficacy.[1]

The science of learning can play a leading role in addressing these deficiencies in the EdTech industry. The two most obvious areas are informing product development and evaluating efficacy. EdTech developers may not have anyone on staff that has expertise in the science of learning, and so it would be useful if relevant research principles and findings are distilled and made accessible to them (e.g., Digital Promise, an independent non-profit organisation authorised by the US Congress to promote technological innovation in education, has created a research map for developers and educators; see https://researchmap.digitalpromise.org/). Once products are developed they need to be properly tested and evaluated for their efficacy, and again, science of learning researchers can help in designing rigorous studies with appropriate measures and control groups. It is also important to consider whether teachers are adequately trained to use or integrate technology in their classrooms (Enyedy, 2014). For instance, certain educational technologies may collect large amounts of student data, but do teachers have the skills that would allow them to access and make sense of the data?

Aside from the use of technology in the instructional process, we should not overlook another big way in which technology has affected education: research. Technological advancements have yielded new research methodologies (e.g., fMRI allows researchers to examine brain activity in vivo, phone apps allow momentary time sampling of emotions, skin conductance can be measured by portable wristbands), providing for novel or multiple converging measures that can shed new light on learning. Many science of learning research projects have employed these advanced research techniques and have yielded a more holistic understanding of the learning process at multiple levels of analysis.

In addition to thinking of technology in terms of physical artefacts (e.g., telephones, computers), we might also include mental artefacts (e.g., literacy, mathematics, scientific reasoning; Hunt, 2012). Just as our physical tools have become more advanced over time, so have our ways of thinking. Advances in statistical analysis (coupled with improvements in computing power) allow for better interpretation of research data (especially when the research design is complex, which is often the case when dealing with large-scale school-based studies; e.g., Schunn et al., 2018). There has also been progress in scientific research practices that have implications for the science of learning. Many fields – including psychology

---

1 For readers interested in the current state of efficacy research in the development and adoption of education technology, I recommend the website http://symposium.curry.virginia.edu/ where you can read more about the findings presented at an academic symposium in 2017 on the topic.

(Open Science Collaboration, 2015), medicine (Begley, 2013), and education (Makel & Plucker, 2014) – have been embroiled in a replicability crisis (i.e., the results of published scientific studies are hard to reproduce) over the past few years, and this has led to increased attention on questionable research practices (Simmons, Nelson, & Simonsohn, 2011) and the need for replication studies.[2] If we want our science to have a beneficial impact on society, we will need to ensure the integrity of the research that forms the evidence base.

Bridging the research–practice gap

Part of the reason for studying the learning process is so that we can optimise it. The practical application of research findings is a major goal of the science of learning, and it underpins the importance of the interdisciplinary collaboration that is at the heart of the field. Cognitive psychologists and neuroscientists are experts at conducting well-controlled experiments in the laboratory that are suited for isolating the mechanisms underlying particular mental phenomena. But there are two main obstacles standing in the way of such research having a meaningful impact on educational practice: (i) it may not be obvious how principles derived from the research can or should be implemented in complex real-world school settings (Daniel, 2012), and (ii) communicating the information effectively to educators. It is therefore crucial to partner with professionals in education (researchers as well as practitioners), who are experts in the classroom.

In my view, what distinguishes the SLRC from other initiatives in the science of learning is its strong emphasis on the translation of research findings into practice. As Nugent, Carroll, Hattie, and Dulleck (Chapter 3) recount, research translation is a foremost priority for the SLRC, and there was an intentional strategy of engaging with various education stakeholders (e.g., policymakers from the state department of education, school leaders, teachers) from the beginning. Although there were initial bumps in the road, effective partnerships have now been established. What we are seeing is not just interdisciplinary collaboration (which is challenging enough) but also interprofessional collaboration. In other words, the efforts go beyond bringing people from different disciplines (but the same profession) together (e.g., psychological scientists, neuroscientists); in the case of the SLRC, people from different disciplines *and* professions now work together, which compounds the difficulty because the goals and priorities differ across professions (e.g., teachers have to ensure that their students pass important exams; policymakers might be concerned about allocating resources and balancing budgets; scientists want to publish their research and secure grant funding).

2 The National Science Foundation and Institute of Education Sciences jointly issued a document in 2018 on the importance of replication and reproducibility in education research and the steps researchers can take to promote corroboration. The document can be retrieved from https://ies.ed.gov/pdf/CompanionGuidelinesReplicationReproducibility.pdf

Interprofessional collaboration is, of course, not unique to the science of learning. For instance, it is common in the healthcare sector (e.g., a hospital patient might be cared for by a team consisting of doctors from various medical disciplines, a nurse, a pharmacist, and a social worker), where there is a growing realisation of the need for interprofessional education (i.e., providing opportunities for medical, nursing, pharmacy, and allied healthcare students to interact and work together during training; Buring et al., 2009). While it may not be feasible for interprofessional education to be part of teacher preparation programs or doctoral research programs, it would probably be helpful for the different professions within the science of learning to have greater interprofessional exposure and interaction.

If we want to be serious about the application of research findings in the classroom (not just a vague or empty promise of something that will be tackled "in the future"), the science of learning projects offer exemplary models for how to get it done. The range and scale of projects undertaken under the auspices of the SLRC that underscore the partnership between researchers and practitioners are quite remarkable. For example, Leonard and Westwell (Chapter 13) describe how teachers helped shape and design a research program on executive functioning and mathematics learning; crucially, a number of teachers (on secondment from the department of education) worked full-time on the research as program officers and were effective intermediaries between the research leaders and the practitioners. Also, Sherlock and Mulvihill (Chapter 9) describe a different kind of research–practitioner partnership – between researchers and clinicians – aimed at examining the efficacy of an attention training intervention. The project could serve as a template for future research-industry collaborations (e.g., in assessing EdTech efficacy, as discussed earlier). In addition to producing actionable recommendations, research also needs to address the issue of scalability. A project by Brooks and Burton (Chapter 12), building on an earlier pilot study, examines in ~150 teachers the effects of a coaching intervention on how they provide feedback to their students. Finally, incorporated into many of the research projects (e.g., Buckley et al., Chapter 6) are professional development opportunities for teachers (e.g., workshops) that disseminate useful findings from the science of learning.

There have been previous efforts to apply the science of learning at scale (e.g., Schunn et al., 2018, examined the impact of incorporating certain cognitive science principles on middle school science learning in over 160 schools), as well as previous research–practitioner partnerships that were very fruitful (e.g., see Agarwal, Bain, & Chamberlain, 2012, for reflections by a teacher, a principal, and a scientist on a 5-year school-based research project). The SLRC stands out, however, in terms of the deliberate thought and consideration that was put into making the research–practitioner relationship more equal and bidirectional (MacMahon, Nugent, & Carroll, Chapter 14). It is probably far more common in other research projects for researchers to call the shots and educators expected to follow along (educators usually do get to offer feedback, but it is still up to the researchers to make the key decisions). The SLRC's research accomplishments are very impressive, and I suspect that the productivity is in part due to the strong relationships that have been formed. The findings from the various research projects will undoubtedly have an impact on the field (and on student learning). However, I think the largest contribution of the SLRC will be in terms of its experience and guidance in forging effective partnerships among scientists, educators, and other stakeholders (chronicled in this book). The NSF Science of Learning Centers in the US may have helped inspire the creation of the SLRC. In just a few short years, the SLRC now serves as a model worth emulating.

Final thoughts

The Australian SLRC has set the cornerstone Down Under for the science of learning as a distinct field of study that is worthy of attention and full of promise. But the work is not finished. Science is a cumulative endeavour – future research will build on past efforts in a continual process that will lead to new insights and refinement of knowledge. The field of the science of learning provides a roadmap for how interdisciplinary and interprofessional partnerships can be achieved to carry out the difficult task of research translation, and it is my fervent hope that researchers, educators, school administrators, policymakers, and funding agencies will capitalise on the foundation that has been laid and continue to invest in the science of learning. The unique learning capacities of human beings, in part, define who we are as a species. Efforts to better understand and promote learning will reinforce our common humanity and should be our obligation towards future generations.

References

Agarwal, P. K., Bain, P. M., & Chamberlain, R. W. (2012). The value of applied research: Retrieval practice improves classroom learning and recommendations from a teacher, a principal, and a scientist. *Educational Psychology Review*, 24(3), 437–448.

Anderson, M. & Jiang, J. (2018). *Teens, social media & technology 2018*. Retrieved March 1, 2019 from http://www.pewinternet.org/wp-content/uploads/sites/9/2018/05/PI_2018.05.31_TeensTech_FINAL.pdf

Begley, C. G. (2013). Reproducibility: Six red flags for suspect work. *Nature*, 497(7450), 433–434.

Buring, S. M., Bhushan, A., Broeseker, A., Conway, S., Duncan-Hewitt, W., Hansen, L., & Westberg, S. (2009). Interprofessional education: Definitions, student competencies, and guidelines for implementation. *American Journal of Pharmaceutical Education*, 73(4), 59.

Carnine, D. (2000). *Why education experts resist effective practices (and what it would take to make education more like medicine)*. Washington, DC: Thomas B Fordham Foundation.

Cole, M. (2010). What's culture got to do with it? Educational research as a necessarily interdisciplinary enterprise. *Educational Researcher*, 39(6), 461–470.

Daniel, D. B. (2012). Promising principles: Translating the science of learning to educational practice. *Journal of Applied Research in Memory and Cognition*, 1(4), 251–253.

Elliot, A. J. & Church, M. A. (1997). A hierarchical model of approach and avoidance achievement motivation. *Journal of Personality and Social Psychology*, 72(1), 218–232.

Enyedy, N. (2014). *Personalized instruction: New interest, old rhetoric, limited results, and the need for a new direction for computer-mediated learning*. Boulder, CO: National Education Policy Center. Retrieved March 1, 2019 from https://nepc.colorado.edu/publication/personalized-instruction

Farrington, C. A., Roderick, M., Allensworth, E., Nagaoka, J., Keyes, T. S., Johnson, D. W., & Beechum, N. O. (2012). Teaching adolescents to become learners. *The role of noncognitive factors in shaping school performance: A critical literature review.* Chicago: University of Chicago Consortium on Chicago School Research. Retrieved March 1, 2019 from https://files.eric.ed.gov/fulltext/ED542543.pdf

Hembree, R. (1988). Correlates, causes, effects, and treatment of test anxiety. *Review of Educational Research, 58*(1), 47–77.

Herrmann, E., Call, J., Hernández-Lloreda, M.V., Hare, B., & Tomasello, M. (2007). Humans have evolved specialized skills of social cognition: The cultural intelligence hypothesis. *Science, 317*(5843), 1360–1366.

Hunt, E. (2012). What makes nations intelligent? *Perspectives on Psychological Science, 7*(3), 284–306.

Lee, C. D. (2008). The centrality of culture to the scientific study of learning and development: How an ecological framework in education research facilitates civic responsibility. *Educational Researcher, 37*(5), 267–279.

Lindsey, R.V., Shroyer, J. D., Pashler, H., & Mozer, M. C. (2014). Improving students' long-term knowledge retention through personalized review. *Psychological Science, 25*(3), 639–647.

Luke, A. (2011). Generalizing across borders: Policy and the limits of educational science. *Educational Researcher, 40*(8), 367–377.

Makel, M. C. & Plucker, J. A. (2014). Facts are more important than novelty: Replication in the education sciences. *Educational Researcher, 43*(6), 304–316.

Marr, D. (1982). *Vision.* San Francisco: WH Freeman and Co.

Mozer, M. C., Wiseheart, M., & Novikoff, T. P. (2019). Artificial intelligence to support human instruction. *Proceedings of the National Academy of Sciences, 116*(10), 3953–3955.

Open Science Collaboration. (2015). Estimating the reproducibility of psychological science. *Science, 349*(6251), aac4716.

Sana, F., Weston, T., & Cepeda, N. J. (2013). Laptop multitasking hinders classroom learning for both users and nearby peers. *Computers & Education, 62,* 24–31.

Schmader, T. & Johns, M. (2003). Converging evidence that stereotype threat reduces working memory capacity. *Journal of Personality and Social Psychology, 85*(3), 440–452.

Schmandt-Besserat, D. (1975). *First civilization: The legacy of Sumer.* Austin, TX: Blanton Museum of Art, University of Texas.

Schmandt-Besserat, D. (1996). *How writing came about.* Austin, TX: University of Texas Press.

Schunn, C. D., Newcombe, N. S., Alfieri, L., Cromley, J. G., Massey, C., & Merlino, J. F. (2018). Using principles of cognitive science to improve science learning in middle school: What works when and for whom? *Applied Cognitive Psychology, 32*(2), 225–240.

Shulman, R. D. (2018, January 26). EdTech investments rise to a historical $9.5 billion: What your startup needs to know. Retrieved March 1, 2019 from https://www.forbes.com/sites/robynshulman/2018/01/26/edtech-investments-rise-to-a-historical-9-5-billion-what-your-startup-needs-to-know/

Simmons, J. P., Nelson, L. D., & Simonsohn, U. (2011). False-positive psychology: Undisclosed flexibility in data collection and analysis allows presenting anything as significant. *Psychological Science, 22*(11), 1359–1366.

Steele, C. M. & Aronson, J. (1995). Stereotype threat and the intellectual test performance of African Americans. *Journal of Personality and Social Psychology, 69*(5), 797–811.

Tabibian, B., Upadhyay, U., De, A., Zarezade, A., Schölkopf, B., & Gomez-Rodriguez, M. (2019). Enhancing human learning via spaced repetition optimization. *Proceedings of the National Academy of Sciences, 116*(10), 3988–3993.

Tomasello, M. (2000). Culture and cognitive development. *Current Directions in Psychological Science, 9*(2), 37–40.

INDEX

Italicized and **bold** pages refer to figures and tables respectively, and page numbers followed by "n" refer notes.

academic performance, emotion regulation 95–96
ACER *see* Australian Council of Education Research (ACER)
AcqKnowledge 4.1 software 73
adolescence: emotion regulation 96; self-regulated learning capacities 126
agency 145–146
alerting, defined 128
alerting network, MASTER™ Focus Program 129, **130–131**
ANS *see* autonomic nervous system (ANS)
anxiety ix, 45–46; defined 64–65 *see also* foreign language anxiety; mathematics anxiety (MA)
ARC *see* Australian Research Council (ARC)
artificial intelligence (AI) 64, 156–158
assessment and feedback design, learning 148
attention, neural network model of, skill building within 128, **130–131** *see also* MASTER™ Focus Program
Australia 8; National Assessment Program: Literacy and Numeracy 9; PMSEIC report 23–24; science of learning in 23–25
Australian Council of Education Research (ACER) 23, 24, 32, 171

Australian Research Council (ARC) viii, 8, 24, 87, 171, 220; Funding Rules 31; intervention study 171–183; objectives 31; Special Research Initiative 31, 38 *see also* Science of Learning Research Centre (SLRC)
autonomic nervous system (ANS) 64, 65, 69

Bacon, Francis 142
Bartlett, Perry 23
Bengtsson, Jarl 10
bias, social connectedness 114–116
biometric measurement 118–120
biometric wristbands 118–119
Bower, Julie, Dr ix
brain: hyperscanning during learning 55–59, *57*; language areas 2; learning and, associations between 2; mind brain education 2, 3; mirror neurons 113; mirror processes 113; neuron 2; study of 3
"Brain Glossary" 11
"Brain Maps" 11
Brain Mechanisms and Learning in Ageing project 11
Brain Mechanisms and Youth Learning project 11
"Brain Primers" 11
brain research: OECD's work on 10–11; UNESCO-IBE's work on 12–13; UNICEF's work on 13–14; World Bank's work on 14–15

Index

Brain Research through Advancing Innovative Neurotechnologies (BRAIN) initiative, NSF 22
Brazil 8; science of learning, emergence of 25–28
Brazilian Ministry of Education 28
Brazilian Network of Science for Education 25–28, 45
Broca, Paul 2
Brooks, Cameron x
Buckley, Sarah ix
Burton, Rochelle x

Cajal, Ramon y 2
callosal dysgenesis 53
cAMP response element-binding protein (CREB) 49
Carroll, Annemaree ix, x, 8, 36
Center for Educational Research and Innovation (CERI) 10
chameleon effect 113
class avoidance 69
classroom: cohesion in, promoting 116–117; connections in, measurements 117–120; learning, neuroscience and 4–5 *see also* education; learning
classroom, emotion regulation in 93–106; academic performance and 95–96; adolescence 96; *KooLKIDS* program 100–101; of learning ix; MBSR and HEP study with science of learning 105–106; *Mindfields High School Junior (MHSJ)* 103; *Mindfields High School Junior (MHSJ) Gamified* 103–104; *Mindfields High School Senior (MHSS)* program 104; *Mindfields Intensive* program 102, *102*; *Mindful practice for teachers (MPT)* 106; norms and values 114; research methodologies 96–99; social classroom environment 114; student interventions 99–100; teacher interventions 99, 104–105; well-being and 95–96 *see also* self-regulation
cognitive control 125–126
cognitive development 3
cognitive psychology 1; MA and 81–82 *see also* science of learning
cognitive training programs 126
cohesion, in classroom, promoting 116–117
collaborations/collaborative learning 147; knowledge exchange 211; research translation 210–213
collaborative networks, science of learning (US NSF) 21–23

Collaborative of Academic, Social and Emotional Learning (CASEL) 99
communication and translation framework *39*, 39–42; community groups, media, social media 42; education departments 42; educators 40–41; government and policymakers 41–42; policy advocacy groups 41; researchers 40; school leaders 41
community engagement 31
community groups 42
computational modelling 64
computerised axial tomography (CAT) scans 3
connectedness 145–146 *see also* social connectedness
connection(s)/connectivity 145–146; biometric measurement 118–120; in classroom, measurements 117–120; computational methods 118; real-time metrics 118; technology and 142–144, 145–146; wearable technology devices 117–120 *see also* social connectedness
connectome 52–55, *54*
conscience 48
CORTB 73
CORT-E 71–72, 74
cortisol (CORT), FLA and 70–71
CORTS 73
CpE Network 26, 26n3, 28
cultural adaptation models 209
Cunnington, Ross ix, x

data and analytics, digital learning environments 156–159
dictation, foreign language anxiety and 65, *66*
diffusion tensor imaging (DTI) 63
diffusion theory 206, *206*
digital learning environments 154–164; changing student–teacher dynamic in higher education 160–162; data, analytics, and their impact on 156–159; educational technologies in 21st century 154–155; key priorities for science of learning 162–164; teacher and student relationships 159–160 *see also* technology(ies)
dissemination theory 206, *206*
DTI *see* diffusion tensor imaging (DTI)
Dulleck, Uwe ix, 8

#EarlyMomentsMatter 14
Earth 47
#EatPlayLove 14

ecological systems theory 207–208
education 1, 2, 7, 144–145; impact of viii; international organisations' work on assessment 9–10; mind brain education 2, 3; neuroscience and 4–5; technology and 224–226 *see also* classroom; learning; learning, design for; science of learning
educational neuropsychologist 3
educational neuroscience 3, 4
Educational Neuroscience Classroom 32, 33, *33*
educational neuroscientist 3
educational technologies, in 21st century 154–155
education departments 42; communication and translation framework *39*, 39–40
Education Working Paper Series (OECD) 12
educators 40–41 *see also* teacher(s)
EEG *see* electroencephalography (EEG)
electrodermal activity, measurement 97–99; wearable technology devices for 97–98, 117–118
electroencephalogram (EEG) 2, 33; portable systems 118
electroencephalography (EEG) 55, 56; hyperscanning of brain and body during learning 55–59, *57*
ELL *see* Empowering Local Learners (ELL) project
embodied experience of emotion 93–94 *see also* emotion(s)
emotional factors viii, 46
emotionality, mathematics anxiety and 82–83
emotion regulation, in classroom 93–106; academic performance and 95–96; *KooLKIDS* program 100–101; of learning ix; MBSR and HEP study with science of learning 105–106; *Mindfields High School Junior (MHSJ)* 103; *Mindfields High School Junior (MHSJ) Gamified* 103–104; *Mindfields High School Senior (MHSS)* program 104; *Mindfields Intensive* program 102, *102*; *Mindful practice for teachers (MPT)* 106; research methodologies 96–99; student interventions 99–100; teacher interventions 99, 104–105; well-being and 95–96 *see also* self-regulation
emotion(s): appraisal approaches 93; basic approaches 93; challenges of measuring, research methodologies 96–99;

embodied experience of 93–94 *see also* social emotions
Empatica E4 wristbands 97
Empowering Local Learners (ELL) project: co-design within 188; complexity of action 194–196; executive function 196–197; future design and research 197–199; learning from 190–199; multi-directional pressures 192–193; overview 185–186; science of learning, translating 186–187; value proposition 191–192; vulnerability 193–194; worked example 189–190
executive attention, defined 128
executive attention network, MASTER™ Focus Program **131**, 131–132
executive function/executive functioning 45; ELL project 196–197
experience, metacognitive 132
experimental classrooms 2

face-to-face meetings 144, 146, 148
feedback 172; effective 172; intervention study 173; model of 174–175 *see also* intervention study, ARC
FLA *see* foreign language anxiety (FLA)
FLCAS *see* Foreign Language Classroom Anxiety Scale (FLCAS)
*f*NIRS *see* functional near-infrared spectroscopy (*f*NIRS)
foreign language anxiety (FLA) 45–46, 63–74; cognitive neuroscience of 64; cortisol (CORT) 70–71; current studies 68; defined 64–65; dictation and, correlation between 65, *66*; early studies of 68; electrodermal activity and self-ratings of 70–71; HPA axis and 71–74, *74*; literature review 65–66; models of 65–68, *67*; MoI and 64, 66–67; neurobiological model 73–74; neurobiological modelling of (next steps) 71–73; overview 63–64; and science of learning 68–70; theoretical models *67*, 67–68 *see also* language learning; mathematics anxiety (MA); second language anxiety (SLA)
Foreign Language Classroom Anxiety Scale (FLCAS) 69–70
functional magnetic resonance imaging (*f*MRI) 2, 105
functional near-infrared spectroscopy (*f*NIRS) 55–58, *57*, 69–70; hyperscanning of brain and body during learning 55–59, *57*

gamma-aminobutyric acid (GABA) 64
gender stereotypes, mathematics anxiety 85
globalisation 142
Global Science of Learning Education Network (GSoLEN) 29
GMV *see* gray matter volume (GMV)
government 41–42; role of ix
gray matter volume (GMV) 63
group behaviour 114–116; conscious and unconscious factors 117; group bias 115 *see also* social connectedness
group bias 115

Hattie, John viii, ix, 1, 8, 36
Health Enhancement Program (HEP) 105–106
Hebb, Donald 2
HEP (Health Enhancement Program) 105–106
higher education ix
higher education, changing student–teacher dynamic in 160–162
holists 48
HPA axis *see* hypothalamic-pituitary-adrenal (HPA) axis
human society, role of technology in 141, 149–150
hyperscanning: of brain and body during learning 55–59, *57*; overview 56; realistic settings 57
hypothalamic-pituitary-adrenal (HPA) axis 71; and FLA 71–74, *74*

IBE Speaks (blog) 13
ICT Competency Standards for Teachers: Policy Framework 145
imitation, social connectedness and 112–114 *see also* social connectedness
immediate-early genes (IEGs) 49
Immordino-Yang, M. H. 93–94
implementation theory 207
information communication technologies (ICT) 143
information processing 64
in-group associations 114, 115
instructional technology 149–151
Interdisciplinary research partnerships x
interdisciplinary science of learning, US NSF on 18–23, 18n1; collaborative networks (Phase 2) 21–23; science of learning centers (phase 1) 19–21, **20**; standing research program, science of learning as (phase 3) 23
International Association for the Evaluation of Educational Achievement (IEA) 9

International Brain Research Organization (IBRO) 12
international organisations, work on assessment 9–10
International Society of the Learning Sciences (ISLS) 3
intervention study, ARC 171–183; collaboration 180; contributions 181–183; drivers and barriers 180–181; feedback-based (2017-2019) 173; feedback model 174–176; measures 176–177; participants 174; preliminary findings (impact) 177–179; rationale 171–173; research design 173–174, *174*; student outcomes, improving 173
interviews 96–97
ISLS *see* International Society of the Learning Sciences (ISLS)

Japanese Ministry of Education, Culture, Sports, Science and Technology 11

Kang, Sean, Dr viii
Kennedy, Gregor ix
knowledge: exchange 211; metacognitive 132, 133; mobilisation 209; pervasive medium for creation 149–151; of the self 133; social creation of 142–144; of strategies 133; of tasks 133; transfer of 31; utilisation 207
knowledge-to-Action (KTA) process 209, 211
KooLKIDS Intensive program 101
KooLKIDS program 100–101
KooLKIDs Whole of Class program 101
The Lancet (journal) 13

language areas, brain 2
language learning ix, 63; neurochemistry and, interaction between 64 *see also* foreign language anxiety (FLA)
Lattes CV Platform 28, 28n4
Law, Nancy ix
leadership, research translation and 215
learner engagement 112
learning 3–4; brain and, associations between 2; brain and body hyperscanning during 55–59, *57*; collaborative 147; emotional regulation ix; factors 1; mathematics anxiety impact on 81–82, 84–86; mind brain education 2, 3; pedagogical approach 147–148; research findings, implementation ix–x; self-directed 147–148; self-regulation of 45–46; technology and 139–140 *see also* classroom; education; science of learning

learning, design for 141–151; as accumulation of knowledge (21st century capacities) 144–145; assessment and feedback design 148; instructional technology 149–151; overview 141–142; pedagogical design principles for 21st century learning 146–148; physical and digital learning environment design 148; social interaction design 148; sociotechnical designs for multilevel learning 149; task design 148; technology, connectivity, and social creation of knowledge 142–144; twenty-first century learning 145–146 *see also* technology
learning analytics 156–159
Learning Analytics and Knowledge (LAK) conference 156
Learning Interaction Classroom 32, 33, *33*
learning science(s) 3–4; OECD's work on 10–11; UNESCO-IBE's work on 12–13; UNICEF's work on 13–14; World Bank's work on 14–15 *see also* mind brain education; science of learning
Learning Sciences and Brain Research project (OECD) 11–12
Lent, Roberto ix
Leonard, Simon x
linguistics 64
Lipp, Ottmar 24
Lockyer, Lori ix
Lodge, Jason ix
long-term potentiation (LTP) 70, 71

MA *see* mathematics anxiety (MA)
machine learning (ML) 156–158
MacMahon, Stephanie x
macro-scale level, neuroplasticity 55–59, *57*
magnetic resonance imaging (MRI) 3, 4
Marope, M. 12
MASTER™ Focus Program 125–134; alerting network 129, **130–131**; description *127*, 127–128; executive attention network **131**, 131–132; metacognitive instructional framework 132–134; orienting network 129–131, **130**; overview 125–126, *127*; rationale 127; skill building within neural network model of attention 128; theoretical foundations 128
Masters, Geoff 23, 171
mathematics anxiety (MA) 78–88; deep breathing 83; emotionality and 82–83; gender stereotypes 85; multidisciplinary research framework 80–87;

overview 78–79; physiological component 82–83; PISA 85–86; psychological approach 79–80; research 87–88; state MA 80, 82–84; strategies 82–84; teaching and learning, impact on 81–82, 84–86; trait MA 80, 84–87; working memory 82; worry components 82, 83 *see also* foreign language anxiety (FLA)
mathematics education x
MBSR (Mindfulness Based Stress Reduction) 105–106
McGaw, Barry viii, 1, 7
media 42
medium of instruction (MoI), FLA and 64, 66–67
memory(ies), sleep-dependent mechanisms of 49–52, *50*, *51*
meso-scale level, neuroplasticity 52–55, *54*
metacognition, role of ix
metacognitive instructional framework, MASTER™ Focus Program 132–134
micro-scale level, neuroplasticity 49–52, *50*, *51*
mind brain education 2, 3
Mindfields High School Junior (MHSJ) 103
Mindfields High School Junior (MHSJ) Gamified 103–104
Mindfields High School Senior (MHSS) program 104
Mindfields Intensive program 100, 102, *102*
Mindfulness Based Stress Reduction (MBSR) 105–106
Mindful practice for teachers (MPT) 106
minimal group paradigm 115
mirroring/mirror processes 113; automatic 113; functional role 113; social connectedness and 112–114 *see also* social connectedness
mirror neurons 113
multilevel learning, sociotechnical designs for 149
Mulvihill, Aisling, Dr ix

National Assessment Program Literacy and Numeracy (NAPLAN) data 9, 171, 176, 185–187, 186, 187
National Science Foundation (NSF), United States 18–23, *19*; BRAIN initiative 22; on interdisciplinary science of learning 18–23, 18n1; science of learning centers (phase 1) 19–21, **20**; science of learning collaborative networks (Phase 2) 21–23; standing research program, science of learning as (phase 3) 23; vision 18–23

neural network model of attention, skill building within 128, **130–131** *see also* MASTER™ Focus Program
neurochemistry, and language learning 64
neuron 2
neuropathology 64
neuroplasticity 2; cells and persons, building bridges between 59; defined 48; macro-scale level 55–59, *57*; meso-scale level 52–55, *54*; micro-scale level 49–52, *50, 51*; multiple levels 47–59; sleep-dependent mechanisms of memory 49–52, *50, 51*
neuropsychology 64
neuroscience 1, 2, 7; advances in 3; classroom learning 4–5; MA and 81–82; mind brain education 2, 3; technological advances 4 *see also* science of learning
N-methyl-D-aspartate (NMDA) 49
Nugent, Annita viii, ix, x, xi, 8

OECD *see* Organisation for Economic Co-operation and Development (OECD)
OECD-CERI 11
Organisation for Economic Co-operation and Development (OECD) viii, 7, 10, 41, 202; Center for Educational Research and Innovation (CERI) 10; Education Working Paper Series 12; *Learning Sciences and Brain Research* project 11–12; online collection 11; PISA 1, 10; *Putting Student Learning at the Centre* (education policy outlook (2018)) 1; work on brain research and learning science 10–11
orienting, defined 128
orienting network, MASTER™ Focus Program 129–131, **130**
out-group associations 15, 114

Pasteur's quadrant 26
PEN (Psychology, Education and Neuroscience) Principles, SLRC 36
personal device assistant (PDA) 97
phrenology 2
physical and digital learning environment design, learning 148
Piaget, Jean 2
PISA *see* Programme for International Assessment (PISA)
policy: magnifying impact on 15; science of learning 7–8
policymakers 41–42

positron emission tomography (PET) scans 3
preoccupation 69
Prime Minister's Science, Engineering, and Innovation Council (PMSEIC) report 4, 23–24
professional self-efficacy 214–215
Programme for International Assessment (PISA) 1, 10, 85–86, 171
Progress in International Reading Literacy Skills (PIRLS) 1
Prospects (publication) 12
psychology 2, 7; mathematics anxiety (MA) 79–80 *see also* science of learning
Psychology, Education and Neuroscience (PEN) Principles, SLRC 36
Putting Student Learning at the Centre (education policy outlook (2018)), OECD 1

quality education 1 *see also* education
Queensland Brain Institute (Australia) 23
Queensland Department of Education 173, 180, 182

rapid-eye movements (REM) sleep 49, *50*
reductionists 48
research broker, role of 212
researchers 40
research institutions, role of ix
research methodologies: emotion regulation 96–99 *see also specific techniques*
research–practice gap *204*, 204–205, 226–228
research translation 169–170; activities, SLRC 35–36, **37–38**; background 203–204; collaborations 210–213; cultural exchange 211; diffusion theory 206, *206*; dissemination theory 206, *206*; ecological systems model 208–210; ecological systems theory 207–208; implementation theory 207; interpersonal relationships 210–212; knowledge mobilisation 209; knowledge utilisation 207; leadership 215; model for 202–216; overview 202–203; principles of 208–215; professional self-efficacy 214–215; research broker, role of 212; of research findings 213–214; research–practice gap *204*, 204–205; SLRC Triadic Partnership Model *215*, 215–216; theoretical frameworks 205–208, *206*
RIKEN-Brain Science Institute (Japan) 11
Rose, Steven 47–48

S★ 98
S★² 98
S★³ 98–99
school leaders 41
science of learning 4, 220; background 2; developments of 220–222; FLA and 68–70; intergovernmental organisations viii–ix; international perspectives ix; intersection of disciplines in 18, *19*; MBSR and HEP study with 105–106; multi-disciplinarity 222; overview 1–2; PMSEIC report 4; policy perspective 7–8; translating 186–187 *see also* interdisciplinary science of learning; learning
science of learning (international perspective) 9–15; international organisations' work on assessment 9–10; OECD's work 10–12; policy and practice, magnifying impact on 15; UNESCO-IBE's work 12–13; UNICEF's work 13–14; World Bank's work 14–15
science of learning (national efforts) 18–29; Australia 23–25; Brazil 25–28; United States National Science Foundation (NSF) 18–23, *19*; US establishment of interdisciplinary science of learning program 18–23, *19*
Science of Learning and Augmented Intelligence (SL) Program 23
Science of Learning Centers Program 19–21, **20**; goals of 19; strategies 19–21
Science of Learning Research Centre (SLRC) viii, ix, x, 8, 24, 25, 87, 173, 220, 226; Annual Report (2013) 31–32; communication and translation framework *39*, 39–42; developing avenues for research translation 35–36, **37–38**; early challenges 34–35; Educational Neuroscience Classroom 33, *33*; establishment 32–36; funding 32–33; learning outcomes, improvement 34–35; outreach and translation activities 38–42, *39*; performance indicators 32; programs of research 34, *34*; Psychology, Education and Neuroscience (PEN) Principles 36; research infrastructure 33; research translation activities 35–36, **37–38**; SLRC Partner Schools Program 35; translation, thinking about 42–43; Translation Team 36 *see also* Australian Research Council (ARC)

SCL *see* skin conductance level (SCL)
SCR *see* skin conductance response (SCR)
second language anxiety (SLA): defined 65 *see also* foreign language anxiety (FLA)
self-concept 97
self-directed learning 147–148
self-efficacy 214–215
self-regulation ix, 96; defined 45; of learning 45–46; processes 45 *see also* emotion regulation
self-report measures 96–97
sharp wave–ripples (SWRs) 49
Sherlock, Deberea, Dr ix
skilfulness, metacognitive 132
skill building, within neural network model of attention 128, **130–131** *see also* MASTER™ Focus Program
skin conductance 68–69
skin conductance level (SCL) 65, 68, 69, 73
skin conductance response (SCR) 68, 74
sleep-dependent mechanisms, of memory 49–52, *50*, *51*
slow wave sleep (SWS) 49, *50*
SLRC Partner Schools Program 35, 41, 43, x
SLRC Triadic Partnership Model 210, 213, *215*, 215–216
small-group cooperation 116
SNS *see* sympathetic nervous system (SNS)
social and emotional functioning 45
social connectedness: classroom, connections measurements in 117–120; cohesion in classroom, promoting 116–117; group behaviour and bias 114–116; imitation and 112–114; mirroring and 112–114; secure learning environment building through 112–120
social coordination 113
social creation, of knowledge 142–144
social–emotional learning 223–224
social emotions 94–95 *see also* emotion(s)
social factors viii, 46
social identity theory 114–115; in-group associations 114, 115; out-group associations 114, 115
social interaction design, learning 148
social media 42
social physiological compliance 119
sociometric badges 97

sociotechnical designs, for multilevel learning 149
Special Research Initiative viii
state MA 80; physiological component 82–83; worry components 82, 83 *see also* mathematics anxiety (MA)
student feedback perception questionnaire (SFPQ) 176
student interventions: emotion regulation 99–100 *see also* teacher and student relationships
supported collaborative work (CSCW) 148
support for collaborative learning community (CSCL) 3
sympathetic nervous system (SNS) 69
systems-based models 209–210

t* app 97
task design, learning 148
teacher and student relationships: changing dynamic in higher education 160–162; digital learning environments 159–160
teacher efficacy 40
teacher model 159
teacher(s): interventions, emotion regulation 99, 104–105; *Mindful practice for teachers (MPT)* 106 *see also* educators
teaching: mathematics anxiety impact on 81–82, 84–86; technologies in 163–164
technology(ies) 3–4; advancements 4–5, 63; advances in 142; connectivity and 142–144; current and emerging 150; developmental history 141–142; and education 224–226; helping students to work with 163; impact of viii; instructional 149–151; and learning 139–140; learning sciences 3–4; new, development and evaluation 162–163; place of 140; role of ix, 139; social creation of knowledge and 142–144; in teaching 163–164; wearable devices 117–120 *see also* digital learning environments; learning, design for
trait MA 80, 84–87; learning and teaching, impact on 84–86; strategies 86–87 *see also* mathematics anxiety (MA)
transcranial magnetic stimulation (TMS) 3
transfer, of knowledge 31

translation 31; SLRC research translation activities 35–36, **37**–**38**; thinking about 42–43 *see also* communication and translation framework; research translation
transpersonal neuroplasticity ix
Trends in International Mathematics and Science Study (TiMSS) 1
Turing test 5
21st century learning 145–146; as accumulation of knowledge 144–145; educational technologies 154–155; pedagogical design principles for 146–148
'21st century skills' 140

UK Lifelong Learning Foundation 11
United Nations Children's Emergency Fund (UNICEF) 7; work on brain research and learning science 13–14
United Nations Educational, Scientific and Cultural Organization International Bureau of Education (UNESCO-IBE) 7, 41; work on brain research and learning science 12–13
United States 8; interdisciplinary science of learning program 18–23, 18n1, *19*; science of learning centers (phase 1) 19–21, **20**; science of learning collaborative networks (Phase 2) 21–23; standing research program, science of learning as (phase 3) 23
University of Hong Kong 66, 68, 69, 70, 72
University of Melbourne 40; Learning Interaction Classroom 32, *33*
University of Queensland 40; Educational Neuroscience Classroom 32, *33*
unobtrusive recording device 118–119
US National Assessment of Educational Progress 9
US National Science Foundation 11

wearable technology 117
wearable technology devices: biometric wristbands 118–119; electrodermal activity measurement 97; relatively naturalistic measurement 117; unobtrusive recording device 118–119
Web 2.0 technology 143
Weekes, Brendan ix
well-being, emotion regulation 95–96
Wernike, Carl 2
Westwell, Martin x

WHO *see* World Health
 Organization (WHO)
working memory 82
World Bank 7; work on brain research
 and learning science 14–15; *World
 Development Report (2018)* 14–15

World Development Report (2018) 14–15
World Health Organization (WHO) 13
worry components, mathematics anxiety
 82, 83

Yates, G. 1